Architecture Transformed

Architecture

A History of the Photography of Buildings from 1839 to the Present

TRANSFORMED

Cervin Robinson

Joel Herschman

The Architectural League of New York
New York, New York

The MIT Press
Cambridge, Massachusetts
London, England

Second printing, 1988

This book was set in Garamond by DEKR CORPORATION and printed and bound by TOPPAN PRINTING COMPANY in Japan.

Library of Congress Cataloging-in-Publication Data

Robinson, Cervin.
Architecture transformed.

Bibliography: p
Includes index.
1. Photography, Architectural—History, I.
Herschman, Joel, 1936– . II. Title.
TR659.R624 1986 778.9'4'09 86-20883
ISBN 0-262-18121-5

To Sam and Moses

Contents

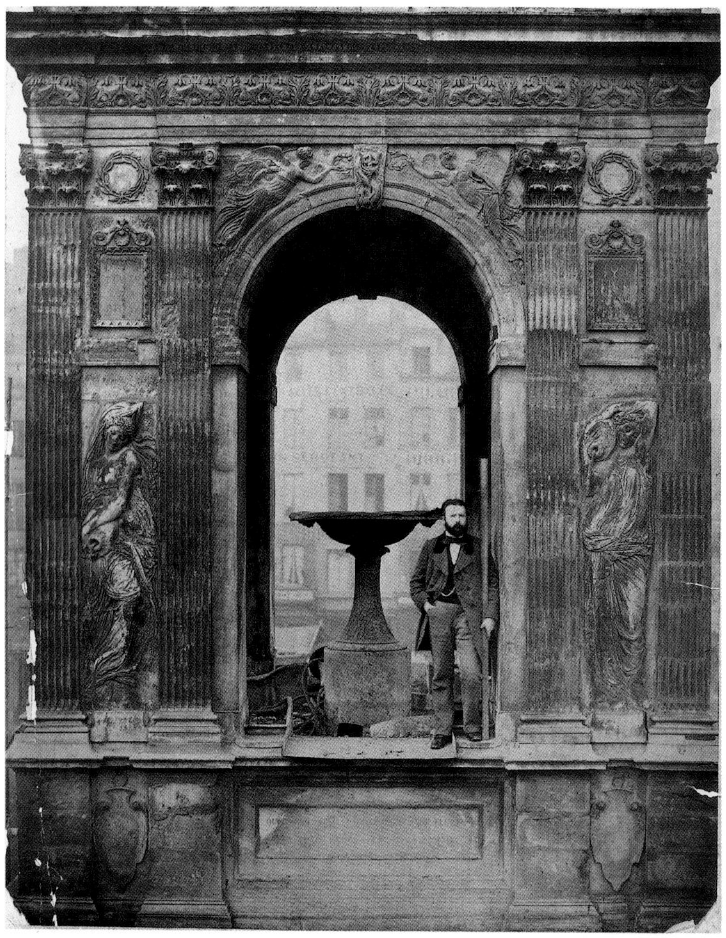

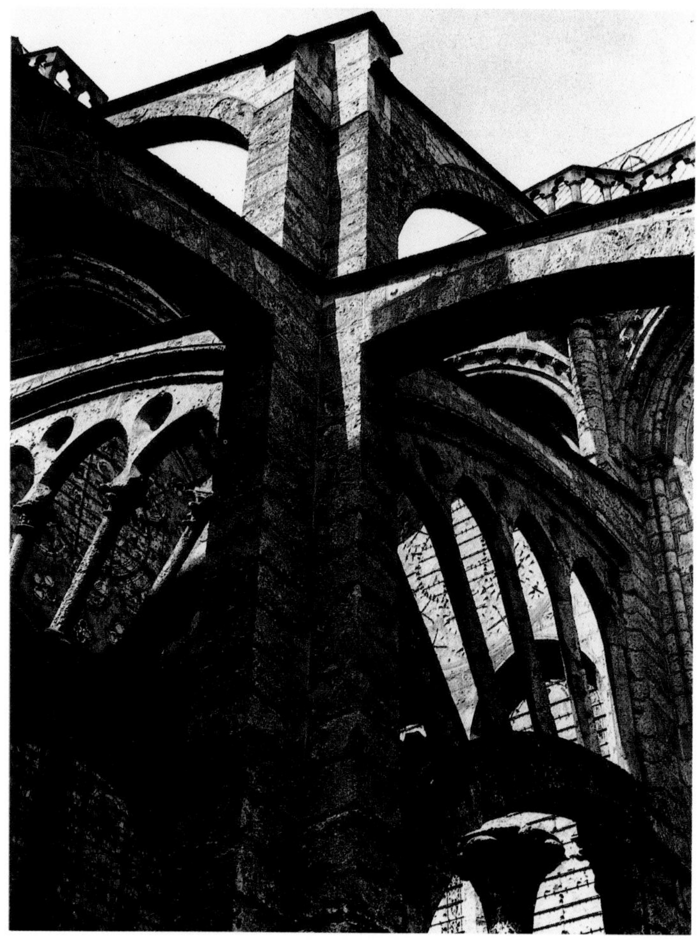

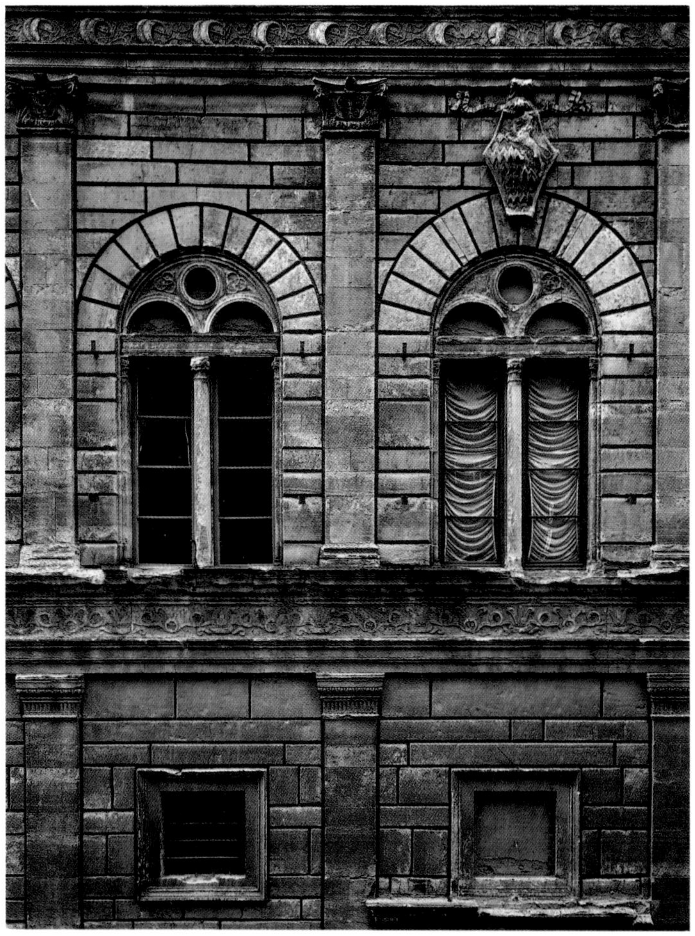

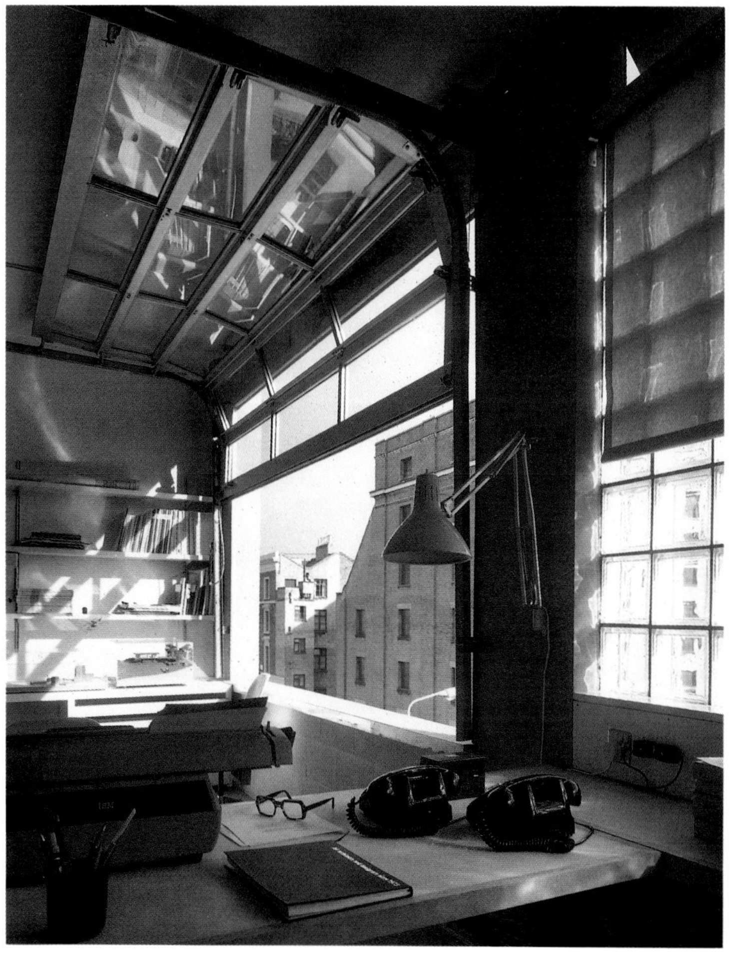

Acknowledgments

It is appropriate that this book should have been written under the auspices of the Architectural League of New York. Its message is that for almost a century and a half photographers have made expressive statements through their pictures, and for two thirds of that time photography has been the league's silent partner in its exhibitions and publications.

The book was made possible by funds from the New York State Council on the Arts and the National Endowment for the Arts. It was set in motion through the energies and support of, respectively, Deborah Nevins and Robert A. M. Stern, who was the league's president when the project was undertaken. At that time we were fortunate in having an advisory committee made up of Reyner Banham, Patricia Hills, William H. Jordy, James F. O'Gorman, and Robert A. Sobieszek, to all of whom we express our appreciation. We have also depended on the long-term support and encouragement of the league's former executive director, Marita O'Hare, and the continued support and encouragement of her successor Rosalie Genevro. Our thanks are due Elizabeth Feeley, who has handled much of the job of assembling photographs, especially those of the period after 1880.

We are indebted to many institutions and their staff members, especially Shirley Hind of the Architectural Press, London; Herbert Mitchell, Janet Parks, and other members of the staff of the Avery Architectural Library at Columbia University; Sabine Hartmann of the Bauhaus-Archiv; Françoise Frey of the Bibliothèque de la Chaux-de-Fonds, Switzerland; Evelyne Tréhin of the Fondation Le Corbusier; Marie Spina of Haines Lundberg Waehler; Anita Anderson of the Gallatin Library of IIT; Barbara Galasso of the International Museum of Photography at George Eastman House; C. Ford Peatross, Mary Isen, and Evelyn Nave of the Library of Congress; Thomas D. Grischkowsky of the Museum of Modern Art; Peter Gottlieb of the Historical Collections and Labor Archives of the Pennsylvania State University Libraries; Marika Schnitker of the Nederlands Documentiecentrum voor de Bouwkunst; Carolyn A. Davis of the George Arents Research Library of Syracuse University; and Dieter Radicke of the library at the Technische Universität Berlin. We would also like to acknowledge our debt to the staffs of The National Monuments Record; the Print and Photograph Collection, Victoria and Albert Museum; the Photothèque of the Caisse Nationale des Monuments Historiques; the Photothèque of the Musée Carnavalet; the Photographic Collection, Historisches Museum Stadt Wien; and the J. Paul Getty Museum; as well as to the Science Museum Photographic Collection, London.

Our appreciation for help of many different kinds goes to Douglas Brenner, Laura Bridgman, Mosette Broderick, Cass Canfield, Jr., Richard W. Cheek, William Clark, Nicholas Cooper, Robert Damora, Mark Haworth-Booth, Peter Galassi, John T. Hill, Lucy Hodgson, André Jammes, Katherine Kreilkamp, Jean-Claude Lemagny, Bernard Marbot, Joseph W. Molitor, Philippe Néagu, Francesco Passanti, Françoise Reynaud, Gustina Scaglia, D. B. Thomas, and Drexel Turner.

Finally we thank Judith Herschman for extraordinary editorial and biographical assistance.

Cervin Robinson
Joel Herschman

Introduction

This book is a history of style in photography, and its purpose is to demonstrate that from the beginning photographers have used their pictures to make critical and expressive statements. The extraordinary photographs in the book, some of them well known and others never publicly shown, were taken by photographers from countries that produced major architectural monuments in the nineteenth and twentieth centuries. They illustrate how these men and women, both those who worked on commission and those who photographed for themselves, succeeded in showing the man-made world with clarity and a point of view.

The book advances two ideas. First, alternative manners of depicting buildings were apparent from the earliest days of photography and continue to this day; one formula stresses the factual component of pictures, and the other, their emotional content, both expressive devices. Second, photographers consciously capitalized on the significant interrelationship between any pair of subjects isolated in a picture in order to make critical statements.

Style is best illustrated by pictures of one subject, for differences then are revealed by the manner of picture taking. As a full-time architectural photographer and part-time architectural historian and critic myself, I find buildings the most absorbing subject for pictures. Even if I were not so engaged, I would find architecture especially suitable for this study because it forms one of the classic subjects of photography. From the invention of the medium in the 1830s up to the present, architecture has been a major genre of commercial work, and it now attracts the energies of photographers who are not committed to architectural professionally but can choose any subject they find rich in potential.

More than the other two classic subjects, portraiture and landscape, architecture sets the approach to picture taking in relief: the subject is clearly something given, and what photographers elect to do with it is their accomplishment and reflects their style. Moreover we can perceive that the architectural community has made demands of photographers and can recognize—as we are unlikely to in fashion and landscape—where they have succeeded in fulfilling them and where not, however handsome their pictures. And there are instances in which succeeding generations have done the same building, one that we ourselves may know at firsthand, allowing us to understand the problems they all faced and to see how each solved them.

The essence of picture taking has always been selection, but we can interpret this act in different ways. Now we tend to see it as emphasizing *how* one photographs rather than *what* one photographs. However, this is a recent phenomenon. In the 1930s photographers were identified by what they showed in their pictures, and innovators saw themselves as capturing what had never been taken before. If they had evident predecessors in this subject matter, they accepted them as naïfs who offered no real competition, much as their contemporaries, the International Style architects, condescended to acknowledge nineteenth-century engineers as their unsophisticated precursors. By the 1950s anyone who had made a reputation in the 1930s believed that the opportunities facing younger photographers were considerably diminished and unpromising because so much had already been recorded.

In the view of the late 1940s and 1950s technological progress represented the thrust of history as a whole, style was reflected in a generation's approach to technique and a photographer's choice of camera, and an artist's success came from a perceptive choice of subjects. A historical survey from 1839 to 1949 focused on the progression from calotype or daguerreotype to modern color reproduction by way of the conquest of motion by faster emulsions, smaller cameras, and flashbulbs, each step of this progress opening up new possibilities for pictures. During this 110-year span attitudes toward technique shifted several times: one generation manipulated its negatives and prints to create artistic pictures, and the next responded by promoting "straight" prints. Meanwhile the reputations of individual photographers became indissolubly linked with their cameras, as Henri Cartier-Bresson's was with his Leica and Edward Weston's was with his eight-by-ten view camera. A photographer had possibilities opened to him by technological progress, and his career could be summarized by describing what subjects had attracted him, what camera he used, and what kind of print he favored.

This historical attitude was applicable to the thirties for various reasons that kept it acceptable even into the early 1960s. Red-sensitive emulsions, which rendered blue skies a dark gray, came into general use in the 1930s, superannuating earlier white-skied pictures in the same way sound films had made silent ones old fashioned. Skies now became a part of pictures, no longer simply their pale backgrounds.

Several innovative cameras, the twin-lens Rolleiflex, the Speed Graphic with synchronized flash, and the Contax or Leica, seemed liberating: they made possible precise action pictures that had been inconceivable before and produced a style all their own. But the smallest of these, the Contax and Leica, made negatives so small that they could not be successfully cropped in the enlargement they required. The large, older cameras that were the alternative to the new ones produced negatives that were contact printed to make pictures that could only be diminished by trimming. In either case a feeling arose against using only parts of images and became a moral issue: prints should not be cropped. Sharp prints on glossy commercial papers made distinction easy between serious work and that of latter-day pictorialists on textured papers, just as the flat roofs of proper International Style buildings set them in gratifying contrast to the work of architects who had not yet seen the light of modernism. So significant were matters of equipment and technique that editors of photographic publications, including those of the Museum of Modern Art's *Photography: A Short Critical History,* of 1937, felt a compulsion to identify camera, choice of film, and exposure, as well as details of development and printing, for each image.

Above all, the community of serious photographers was surprisingly small, allowing each to have one or sometimes several subjects as his own particular domain—Ansel Adams his National Parks, Edward Weston his nudes and sand dunes, and Walker Evans his vernacular American architecture. Devotees were few enough in the 1940s that when, as a teenager, I was encouraged to make an impromptu visit to Alfred Stieglitz, to drop in for Sunday dinner at Edward Weston's, and to ask Berenice Abbott to show me Atget prints, each seemed to welcome a visit from a stanger. Stieglitz complained that he had discarded too many of his own pictures; Abbott showed me her Atget collection; Weston brought out the eight-by-ten transparencies that were his last work. Each was less competitive and more generous than comparable figures would be now. It was a smaller world.

History written about 1950 also reflected the long-standing belief that commercial pictures, and therefore contemporary architectural photographs, could not be art. There was also a renewed conviction that people alone were the only proper subject of picture taking. Buildings were an eccentric choice of subject, and taking pictures of architecture for money rather than "for yourself" seemed not only eccentric but crass.

The belief that people were central arose from the 1950s answer to a question that had been important to the 1930s, which was whether one could record one's experience or only learn how things looked in photographs. Could a photographer show people unaffected by the camera (candidly) or at best simply line them up for their pictures? After World War II the work of Henri Cartier-Bresson seemed to demonstrate that it was possible to record people in the midst of their daily activities without affecting their actions by the presence of the camera. If one could do this, then people could be the subjects of our pictures. "Henri Cartier-Bresson will tell you, if you press him," wrote Beaumont Newhall in *Popular Photography* in January 1947, "that photography is for him a kind of sketchbook, journal, or diary. . . ." The evidence that one could capture experience came from Cartier-Bresson's exhibition at the Museum of Modern Art in 1947 and from his book *The Decisive Moment,* published in 1952. Popular acceptance of the view was marked by the success of the exhibition and book *The Family of Man* in 1955.

Fundamental changes have occurred in photography in the last quarter century. The number of photographers is vastly increased today, and every genre is shared by a great many rivals. Whereas a few innovative cameras once produced distinctive pictures, now a large camera on a tripod is often used to make pictures in the style of a small, hand-held instrument, or vice versa, and format size is made apparent in prints principally by the inclusion of black negative edges. If technical shibboleths were the rule then, the situation now is close to a free-for-all. Once an art market developed for photographs, hostility to commercial work became muted, for not only were parallels between the commercial and art markets apparent but galleries found themselves searching the commercial past for merchandise.

Moreover it became increasingly obvious that people in photographs had reacted to the camera. The suspicion that pictures provided a distorted portrait of experience was confirmed by the plates in *Diane Arbus,* published in 1972, in which subjects, some said goaded by the photographer, were seen head on, looking at the camera, and often lit by the most atificial of lights, on-camera flash. If one could not record experience undistorted, then a picture of a family's living room, say, might be more revealing than an image of their guarded faces. A change in the content of serious photography had been signaled the year before by the retrospective exhibition of Walker Evans's work at the Museum of Modern Art, in which buildings and other artifacts predominated. Thereafter no portrait of America was possible without its share of pictures that could best be described as architectural.

What form of history is appropriate for a study of these architectural photographs that are now essential to our view of ourselves? Some historians have described interplay between the camera and the traditional arts of painting and drawing. But photographers' methods are so different from those of traditional artists that pointing out resemblances often obscures understanding. The form of analysis common in the history of painting, which traces back chains of formal influence, is not useful here, for replication is not fundamental to photography as it is to the traditional, two-dimensional arts. Intrinsic to them are calligraphic strokes that are part cultural sign and part personal symbol, which can make the must rudimentary drawing of great interest.

The comparable fundamental act in photography is quite different; it is the effort to remove all doubt on the part of the viewer that pictures, though made by a machine, are wholly intended and therefore an individual's creation. A photographer accomplishes this by the pointed way he places objects in his pictures, by the significant relationships he establishes between these objects, and by his evident craftsmanship. His useful models are not the much-repeated figures that an art historian can trace but may instead be the general character and meaning of some earlier prints or photographs that can impart a corresponding meaning to his picture of a quite different subject.

From the 1930s to the 1950s pictures were described as simply found. "To pivot the camera slowly around watching the image change on the ground glass is a revelation," wrote Edward Weston in *Camera Crafts* in 1930. "One becomes a discoverer, seeing a new world through the lens. And finally the complete idea is there, and completely revealed." In contrast I find myself and others constructing pictures in ways that seem to me to form the very basis of expression in architectural photographs present or past. I am drawn to two perspectives that are analogous to the two kinds of portraits, those that record people in their daily activities and those that are of people lined up for their pictures. The first is an oblique view that brings textured surfaces close to the camera and draws the viewer into the experience of a building; the second is a head-on one that resembles an architectural elevation and offers an objective, factual point of view. Many, perhaps most photographs, do not fall wholly into either category, but those that do are especially effective. Many photographers have used both approaches. But views that present oblique, textured surfaces close to the camera are particularly characteristic of pictorialist work of the first years of the century, and head-on views are similarly characteristic of 1930s documentary work. The oblique view is that of photojournalism; the head-on view appears repeatedly in portraits by Richard Avedon and Diane Arbus; many of Jerry Uelsmann's pictures combine an upper, head-on image with a lower oblique one reaching toward the viewer. These two ways of showing a subject allow photographers to inflect their statements in alternative ways, and either way can become an index of the style of an individual or of a generation.

If perspective tells us whether a photographer wishes to present the point of view of a disinterested observer or of a partisan, the secondary subjects in his pictures tell us what he means to say about his main subject. Some architectural photographers have used foliage, machines, or the human figure to tell us that new buildings are organic, functional, or humanistic—and therefore good. Others have juxtaposed banal structures ironically to eminent buildings to distance themselves from their subjects. Such appositions are a clear, recurrent stylistic device in all genres of photography. In architecture the full range of juxtapositions has certainly been present since the 1920s and probably from the beginning.

The factors that seemed fundamental a generation ago, the impact of technological development, choice of equipment and printing medium, and choice of subject still exist, but their character has changed. We put up with technological development rather than welcome it. A radically new product that inexorably supplants an older one is like the superhighway we regret but use because it is more convenient than an older road we would have preferred to continue driving on. The impetus for the turn to the pervasive use of color film in the late 1970s came from developments in offset reproduction and from the demands by advertisers for color on the editorial pages of magazines, not from a desire by photographers and magazine editors to pass beyond black-and-white technology. The change solved no problems that architectural photographers had been interested in, such as how to include people in pictures; it only distracted them from those questions and presented them with new and, as it happened, less interesting ones, such as how to reconcile fluorescent light sources with incandescent ones.

Cameras bear an ambiguous relationship to pictures. For most photographers the artistic medium is their camera and film. For most collectors "medium" means printing paper, generally with a hard eye to its relative permanence. Some cameras are indispensible to particular jobs, as anyone will know who is accustomed to using the movement called "perspective control" and finds himself using equipment without that capacity. In practice photographers adopt equipment and techniques that are up-to-date when they start their careers and remain constant to them, equipment and techniques that younger photographers, unless attempting to be archaic, will no longer choose. Nevertheless, work is not characteristically limited by choice of camera; for example, much of the work of the 1930s that shows the influence of the hand camera was in fact taken with large ones on tripods.

New subjects now seem the result of the uncovering by intellect and wit, of small, still-untouched areas of ore in mostly mined-out veins, accomplishments that are primarily conceptual, whereas in the thirties the claiming of a new subject was a major artistic act. Now the most stimulating work seems done either on the general model of an earlier body of work, as pictures of America in the Depression years might be made on the model of ones of the American Civil War, or as the antithesis of a commercial genre, as has happened with special clarity in fashion photography, where skills learned on the young and beautiful have been applied to pictures of the old and ugly in order to provide us with the rheumy eyes, deformities, and offal of the nonfashion work of Richard Avedon, Diane Arbus, and Irving Penn. Comparable work in architecture has been interpreted, perhaps misinterpreted, as more benign and nostalgic but has also offered a needed antidote to the most sterile orthodoxies of new architecture in photographs.

So a key to style lies in the particular approach photographers make to their subjects and in the context within which they show them. And their work is energized by a sense of its connection to earlier or opposite bodies of work.

Even the most recent past, as my coauthor reminds me, is as irrevocably a part of history as are the first years of photography in the last century. This past can all too easily appear merely strange and stylized, something whose superficial characteristics, its printing techniques for instance, are to be knowingly mimicked. Our purpose in this study is to uncover, to the extent we can, the means and intentions behind almost 140 years of achievement in architectural photography and thereby to illuminate the present and guide the immediate future.

Stylistic changes occurred in photography around 1880, 1930, and 1970. We have correspondingly divided this history and its writing into four periods. Joel Herschman has negotiated the scholarly minefield of the first (1839 to 1880), and I have written the remainder (1880 to 1930, 1930 to 1970, and 1970 to the present).

Cervin Robinson

Part I

1839 to 1880

The publication of J. L. M. Daguerre and William Henry Fox Talbot's photographic processes in 1839 opened up unprecedented possibilities for making images. Photography, with its ability to produce pictures with wholly accurate proportions and precise representation of details, was ideally suited to the rendering of architecture. Architecture was, in turn, an ideal subject. Buildings, unlike most other likely subjects, "sat" patiently for the long exposures required by early emulsions. At this time, furthermore, a great variety of buildings were being brought within range of the photographers' lenses by the transportation revolution of the first half of the nineteenth century: by the railroad, the steamship, the suspension bridge. It comes as no surprise that a considerable proportion of the photographs of the first two decades are of architecture. From the effort made by photographers between 1839 and 1880, there would evolve a photographic language that would express architectural forms with the vividness and precision of the older forms of architectural representation based on drawing.

The first phase of photography's history, from 1839 to 1851, tended to emphasize technical and artistic experimentation. A shift took place around 1851 when conditions arose that permitted the beginnings of a new profession. The 1850s saw the appearance of a remarkable group of men, many originally trained as painters or illustrators, who greatly expanded the early limits of photography. Hippolyte Bayard, Gustave Le Gray, Henri Le Secq, Charles Nègre, and Roger Fenton were among those who developed new kinds of photographic vision that were to have considerable impact on the architectural photography of their own and succeeding generations. The Prix de Rome architect Alfred Normand, who photographed in Italy between 1851 and 1854, and the painter Auguste Salzmann, whose photographs of the architecture of Jerusalem were intended to document the theories of the archeologist Félix de Saulcy, were unusual in the period in using the camera with the same directness they might have used on a sketch pad.

Around 1860 several technological improvements occurred, especially to the light-sensitive emulsions. From the sixties on, the increasing ability to arrest movement resulting from these improvements attracted some of the more adventurous spirits of photography to a newly accessible range of subject matter. The growth of professionalization at this time, encouraged by the increasing dependability and ease of utilization of photographic materials, also may have driven away some of the medium's more artistic personalities. Conventional historiography tends to treat the 1860s and seventies as dull decades, dominated, with a few exceptions, by unimaginative artisans. For the photography of architecture this view may be too simple. Some of its leading figures survived the fifties to work creatively in the succeeding years. Edouard Baldus, Charles Marville, and Francis Frith were among them. They were joined by a large number of serious and dedicated professionals. These newcomers, based in both the capitals and provincial centers of Europe, responded to architectural issues in ways that reflected their awareness of the concerns of the period's architects and theorists. They continued and enlarged on the work of the pioneers of the forties and fifties in creating a photographic language richly capable of conveying architectural ideas. Their artistic debt to the generation of the fifties was considerable, but their achievement was the expansion of the scope of architectural photography and the establishment of a new profession.

If 1839 is an inevitable starting point, our terminus, 1880, also reflects the realities of the era. Throughout the period a concerted effort was made to mass-produce photographic images so as to make them available to the widest possible audience. This desire was reflected in attempts both to industrialize the production of the photographic print itself and to develop mechanical means of reproducing photographs. Despite considerable achievements in the latter area, especially in photolithography, mechanical methods of reproduction continued to be too costly to supplant the photographic print, which remained the typical means of distributing architectural photographs. In 1880 the halftone process of reproduction began to be economically viable. In conjunction with other forms of reproduction it would soon shift the balance to mechanically reproduced images. As with the invention of photography, some years passed before the new technology could be fully exploited, but by the 1890s it was beginning to effect a radical change in the way people were able to see photographs of architecture.

The approach of photographers to architectural subjects began to emerge around 1851, and the succeeding years did not see radical shifts in style. The most critical technical problem in photographing architecture, that of image resolution, was already beginning to be solved by 1851. It has been often noted that the soft, sketchlike quality of the early calotype was prized by photographers with a taste for the romantic. The paper fibers of the negative that produced this effect, however, interfered with the crisp resolution of detail in the print needed for architectural photography, which the daguerreotype had established as one of the best features of the new medium. By 1851 Gustave Le Gray's waxed-paper version of the calotype negative was in use in

France. The wax suppressed the fibers so that they were not apparent in the prints. In the same year Frederick Scott Archer's wet-collodion process, which used a glass plate as an emulsion support, laid the resolution problem to rest. It was widely adopted in the British Isles, and during the fifties became the dominant photographic medium there.[1]

By 1851, then, the most inhibiting technical impediment to photographing architecture had essentially been solved. The considerable advances in emulsion sensitivity ("film speed") and convenience of utilization that were to characterize the technical developments of the following three decades were not of a kind to effect profound stylistic changes. The ability to stop motion, which resulted from these advances, was not crucial to photographing architecture. Only in the past few years has film speed evolved enough to make it possible to photograph unposed pedestrians without blurring them, given the small apertures usually used in architectural work. The main changes were the increased facility of photographing under low light levels, which made building interiors more accessible to the camera, and the progressive advance in print resolution due to improvements in emulsion and lens design.

Essentially 1851 was the year in which architectural photography came of age, twelve years after the appearance of the processes of Daguerre and Talbot. Not only were the means available to make crisp, high-resolution prints but other factors emerged that made architectural photography a viable profession rather than an experimental art form. These factors belonged to a world larger than that of the technology of photographic emulsions.

An example is the great London Exhibition of 1851. It provided the framework for the first massive publication of architectural photographs, Phillipe Delamotte's *Reports to the Juries,* an extensive survey of the exhibits and of the Crystal Palace which housed the exhibition and which was the era's most controversial work of architecture. These volumes were consecrated in the public eye by their presentation to the exhibition's royal sponsor, the Prince Consort.[2] In the year 1851 the French Historical Monuments Commission sent five of that nation's leading photographers out to the corners of France on a Mission Héliographique to record, also on a massive scale, its endangered architectural heritage.[3] Of greater importance for the future, by 1851 the first fruits of the French publisher Blanquart-Evrard's efforts to industrialize the publication of the photographic print—the *Album photographique*—had appeared. Blanquart-Evrard's factory at Lille, which could mass-produce prints on his new albumen paper, was short-lived, but it was the first in a long series of attempts to reproduce photographs in large quantity. In the same year an *Imprimérie Photographique* (a photographic printing establishment) was opened in Paris, soon to be imitated in seveal French cities.[4]

The year also saw signs of an increasing awareness among architects of the usefulness of photography in documenting architecture. Baron Isidore Taylor, in a somewhat ambiguous set of remarks, had suggested this to the French Historical Monuments Commission as early as 1839.[5] In 1851 the Parisian architect César Daly offered to absorb the costs of including photographs in his popular architectural magazine in order to promote the medium.[6] France's photographic establishment took a major step with the founding in Paris of the Société Héliographique, the ancestor of the French Photographic Society and the appearance of its journal, *La Lumière.* This was the first viable periodical to treat photographic subjects, both technical and aesthetic, in a serious way.[7] The first organization designed to promote architectural photography per se, the Architectural Photography Association, was not to be founded until 1857 in London.[8]

An attempt by Fox Talbot between 1844 and 1846 to commercialize the photography of art and architecture at his Reading Printing Establishment had proved premature, but by 1851 the essentials seemed to be there: the ability to produce durable, high-resolution prints in sufficient numbers to moderate the price and the institutional framework and recognition needed to ensure distribution on a scale that could provide a living for photographers.

The unprecedently large group of photographers who began to work around 1851 entered a market that was promising, if competitive. The large, educated middle class of the period numbered architecture among its enthusiasms, and architecture was experiencing a ferment that was to provide rich opportunities for photographers. The modern profession of architecture began to emerge in the second quarter of the nineteenth century and with it a number of supporting institutions. The first public museum to house architectural drawings and projects was founded in London by Sir John Soane in 1833. The following year, the first professional organization for architects since the medieval guilds, the Royal Institute of British Architects, was established in London, with a library of books on architecture and drawing. The century's most substantial architectural magazine, *The Builder,* was founded in 1842. It was profusely illustrated with engravings and served a wider audience than the architectural profession itself.

The appearance of A. W. Pugin's *Contrasts* in 1841 has been credited by John Wilton-Ely with creating "a common ground for debate between the articulate profession and an informed public." John Ruskin's *Seven Lamps of Architecture* (1849) and *Stones of Venice* (1851–53) significantly broadened the base of this public in England.[9] The continent saw a parallel excitement. Victor Hugo's best-selling *Notre-Dame de Paris,* first published in 1831, had a historical building as its protagonist. The rise of the restoration movement and the controversy that swirled around it, "to restore or not to restore," was the subject of lively public debate. The study of medieval architecture was given an institutional framework by the foundation in 1834 of the Société Française d'Archéologie and of the Historical Monuments Commission under Prosper Mérimée.[10] Baron Taylor, a member, was already deeply engaged in introducing medieval architecture to the public with his long collaboration, beginning in 1820, in the *Voyages pittoresques et romantiques dans l'ancienne France.*[11]

This activity not only provided considerable impetus to the growth of architectural photography but defined its main subject matter. The architecture of the nineteenth century was largely dominated by a historical revivalism whose chief touchstone was fidelity to its sources. Pugin had put it most strongly: "The only hope of reviving the perfect style is by strictly adhering to ancient authorities."[12] Photographers were in a superb position to provide the data needed to fulfill this program. If accurate reproduction of the forms of the past was essential to the authenticity of revival architecture, an indispensable tool was the largest possible corpus of accurate images of historical architecture. Accuracy was photography's strong suit, the great advantage it had over older forms of architectural representation. That it became available just as the polemic over styles (medieval vs. classical) was gaining momentum was an unusually happy instance of the invention arising to meet the need. The predominance of historical subject matter in the architectural photography of the period is largely due to this situation.

While the architectural ferment of the first half of the nineteenth century opened up a ready market for photographers and played a major role in defining their subject matter, developments in the architectural profession itself saw to it that this market was highly competitive and also provided the iconographic framework in which the photographers worked. For architects the fact that drawing would continue to be their basic tool of design ensured that forms of architectural rendering based on it would retain a powerful hold on the profession throughout the period. In fact the years from 1840 to 1880 are felt by many to be the heyday of architectural drawing. The late eighteenth and early nineteenth centuries had seen a revolution in the ancient traditions of architectural draftsmanship, the main thrust of which was to make images of architecture understandable and more appealing to a wider public. A shift in patronage had occurred away from knowledgeable aristocrats who could read a plan or elevation to a less sophisticated middle class that was beginning to dominate competition committees and was more likely to be influenced by drawings that used perspective, shading, and even color to convey the finished appearance of a project.

The eighteenth century had seen the rise in popularity of the *per angolo,* or two-point perspective, construction. This supplemented the traditional one-point variety, which placed a single vanishing point on the central axis. It was constructed on diagonals, with the two vanishing points at the sides of, or even off, the page. The three-dimensional illusion created by the two-point technique could be greatly enhanced by dramatic lighting of the type used by Piranesi. This brought to architectural rendering an excitement and verisimilitude lacking in the plan and elevation. The gouache paintings of "Athenian" Stuart and the convincingly modeled, populated, and atmospheric perspectives of designers in the circles of Claude-Nicholas Ledoux and Étienne-Louis Boullée carried these developments to remarkable heights. By the dawn of the photographic era atmospheric perspectives were such a necessary part of architectural presentations that leading British offices hired specialists, including watercolorists, to prepare such images for clients or competition committees.[13]

By 1839, then, when photographers first began to turn their lenses on architectural subjects, the manual tradition of architectural rendering was at one of its most dynamic moments. The photographers of the time were themselves often trained in draftsmanship and, sharing a common public with the draftsmen, frequently shared a common approach. The area in which the photographers could outdo the graphic artists was in the accuracy of proportions and the precise delineation of details, or what the age referred to as "truth." The photographers lost no opportunity in pointing this out.

In this period both the elevation and perspective were used to render buildings or projects (1, 2). The elevation was two-dimensional, showing one facade of a structure. Its viewpoint was strictly frontal, and its vanishing point was centered on that facade. The drawing style was most typically linear, although the French Beaux-Arts school of drawing introduced ink washes to model the surfaces, yielding a moderate three-dimensionality. Indications of context were

1 *Joseph Hansom (?)*

Design for the proposed Sussex Memorial, perspective view. Engraving from *The Builder* (September 23, 1843).

2 *Joseph Hansom (?)*

Design for the proposed Sussex Memorial, geometrical elevation. Engraving from *The Builder* (September 23, 1843).

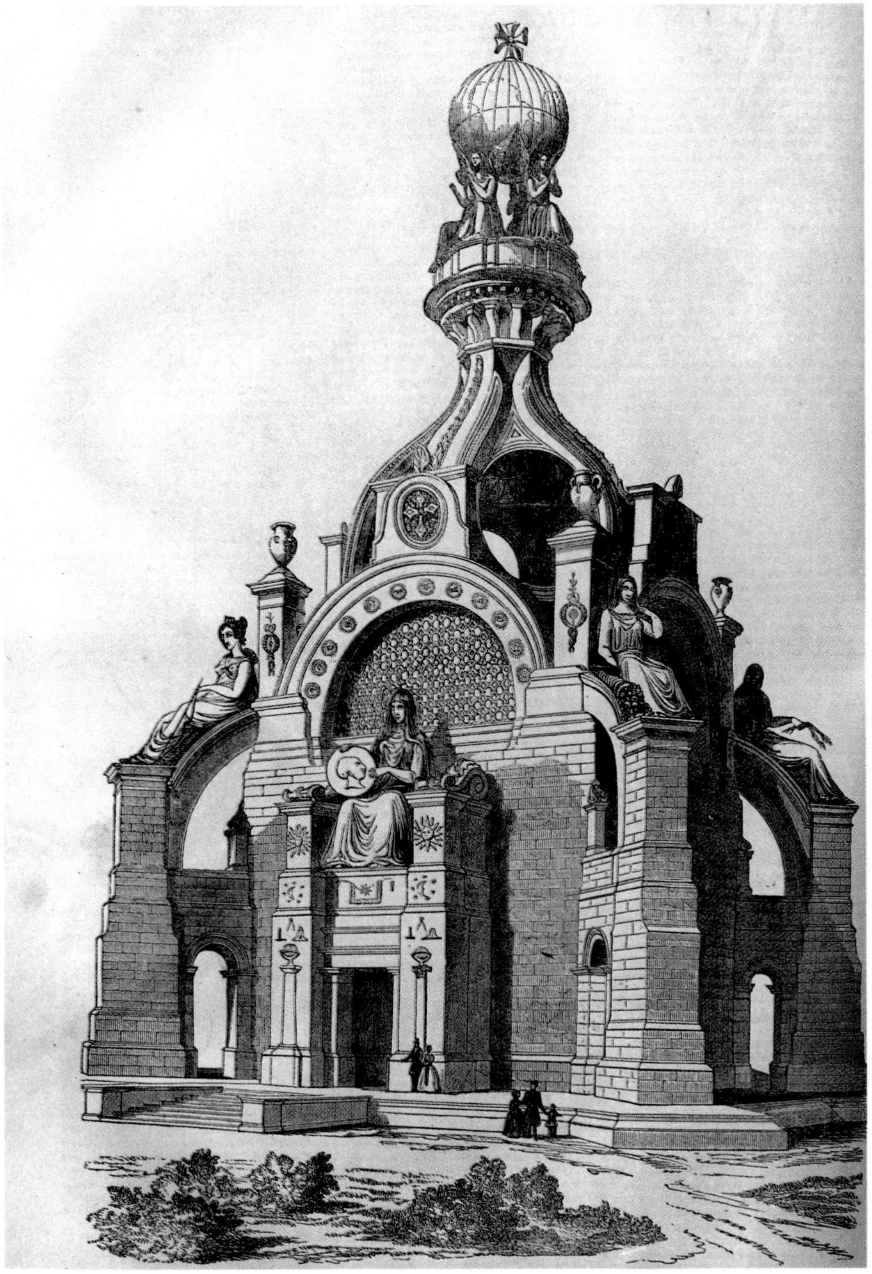

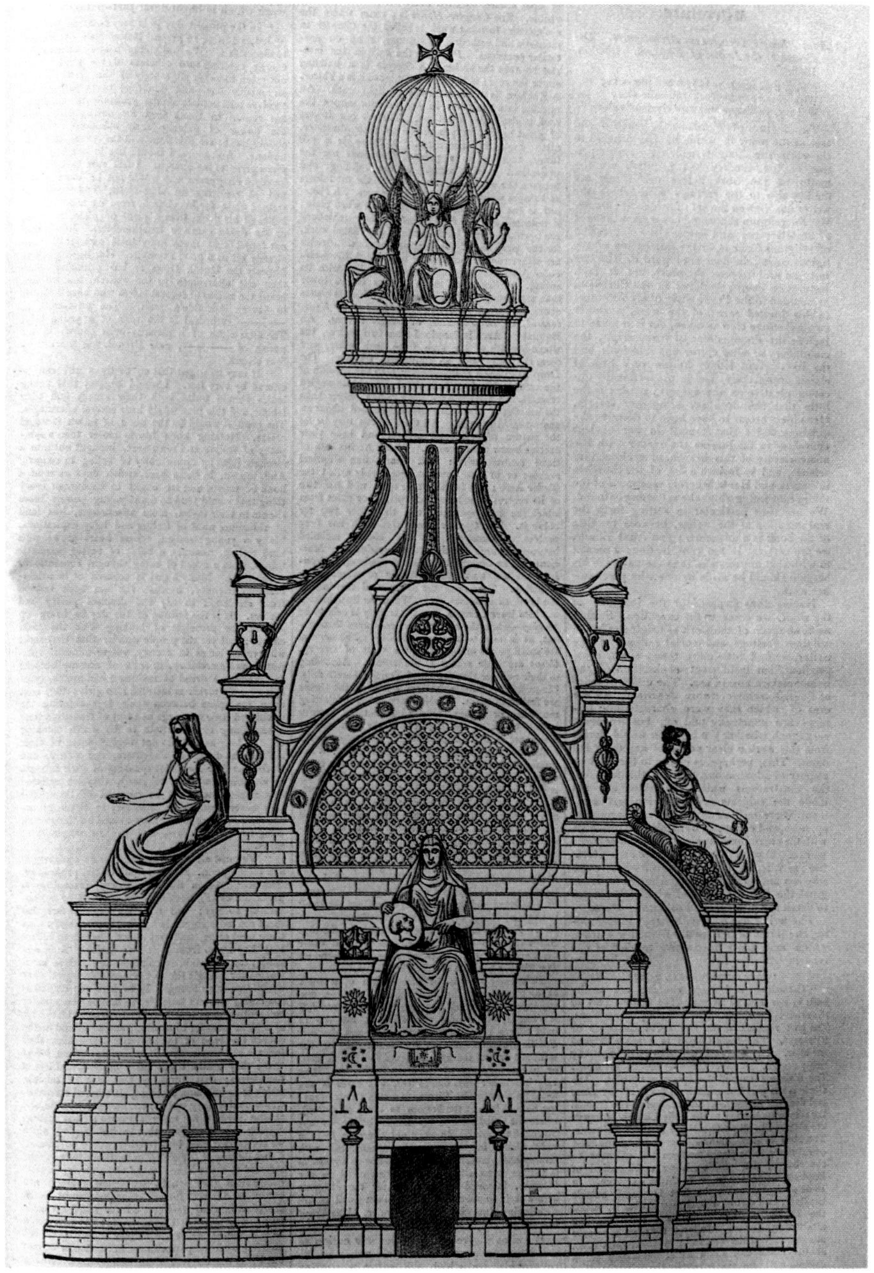

avoided, the facade being isolated on the page. On the other hand, the perspective placed the building diagonally in space. Its diagonal orthogonals created an illusion of three-dimensionality. This illusion was usually enhanced by directional lighting, which gave depth and texture to the surfaces and separated one facade from another. Contextual indicators played an important role. Clouds, trees, shrubbery, vehicles, and especially people were used to set the scene, often with strong foreground elements to locate the viewer in the space. While the elevation served as a diagrammatic representation that transmitted the essential data about a facade, objective and above all proportionally accurate, the perspective tried to convey the actual experience of seeing a building or project in its real or intended context.

The two approaches were quickly adopted by photographers and became increasingly evident in the 1850s with the entry into the profession of numbers of practitioners whose training was in painting or illustration, that is, who were trained draftsmen. Two photographs from the fifties of a famous Paris monument, Jacques-François Blondel's Porte Saint-Denis, demonstrate the process of adaptation (3, 4). The first was taken by Edouard Baldus before 1856, when it was placed in the Bibliothèque Nationale. It was part of a numbered series to be offered for sale. The other, by a photographer whose name is not given, was published in Blanquart-Evrard's *Paris photographique* between 1851 and 1853. Both used the same technique: a waxed-paper calotype negative printed on albumen paper.

The differences between the two photographs result from deliberate choices. Baldus chose to reproduce the effect of an elevation drawing. He climbed to an upper window to place the photographic equivalent of the vanishing point as close as possible to the midpoint of the structure. This did away with the perspective distortion which, given the limited camera movements of the time, would have been produced by tilting the camera. By this he ensured that the arch's proportions would be accurately reproduced in the photograph. His viewpoint had the effect of "flattening-out" the arch so that only the barest hint of depth can be seen. The lighting was chosen to enhance the effect of flattening. The sun's position reduces the shadows, except for that of the cornice, to a network of fine lines like those drawn with a pen. Even the rounded forms of the relief sculpture take on a linear quality. The highlights show no detail, and their contrast with the deep shadows is sharp. Although the surrounding buildings have not been painted out of the negative, a common practice of the time, they have little impact on the composition. The streets are almost empty due to the time of day and the long exposure, which has turned the foreground wagon into a ghost. Baldus has done what he could within the limits of the photographic process to reproduce the two-dimensional, linear, contextless quality of the elevation drawing.

In the view published by Blanquart-Evrard, the photographer has also followed the standard practice of climbing to an upper story. He took a position to the side of the Porte, however, and aimed his camera at its corner, imitating a *per angolo* view with its diagonal, two-point perspective. The corner view brings out the three-dimensional form of the arch, and this three-dimensional effect is enhanced by the lighting. The sun's angle brings up the texture of the stone and creates shadows suggesting the depth of both the architectural carving and the relief sculpture. The light also models the inner curve of the arch so as to convey the possibility of passing through it. Baldus had worked to minimize the surroundings, but here they are emphasized. A strong diagonal of fence defines the foreground and is underlined by the wagon parked next to it. The distance from the fence to the arch seems measurable. The diagonal perspective lines lead the eye along the boulevard and tie the facades of the surrounding buildings into the composition. It is a working day. Vintner's carts and an omnibus are noticeable, and two vendors have spread out their wares in front of the arch.

The two photographs repeat the polarity inherent in the two types of architectural drawing: the clarity unencumbered by context, flatness, linearity, and above all accurate rendering of proportions of the elevation as against the perspective, which reproduces the experience of actually seeing the monument as a three-dimensional structure in its real setting. Each photographer has selected a way of seeing the arch that drawings had made familiar to generations of professionals and amateurs of architecture.

The elevation photograph is probably the one most familiar to connoisseurs of nineteenth-century photography. It could be treated with considerable latitude, according to the photographer's intent and the working conditions, but its essential features remain recognizable. As a compositional device, it reached its peak in the hands of a group of photographers who used Le Gray's waxed-paper negative. Many of their photographs were published by Blanquart-Evrard, who showed a fondness for this type.

Certain buildings seem naturally to have called for the elevation, or head-on, treatment. A long series of photographs of the facade of Notre-Dame in Paris were taken from the same window on the *Parvis* (5, 6, 7). When this

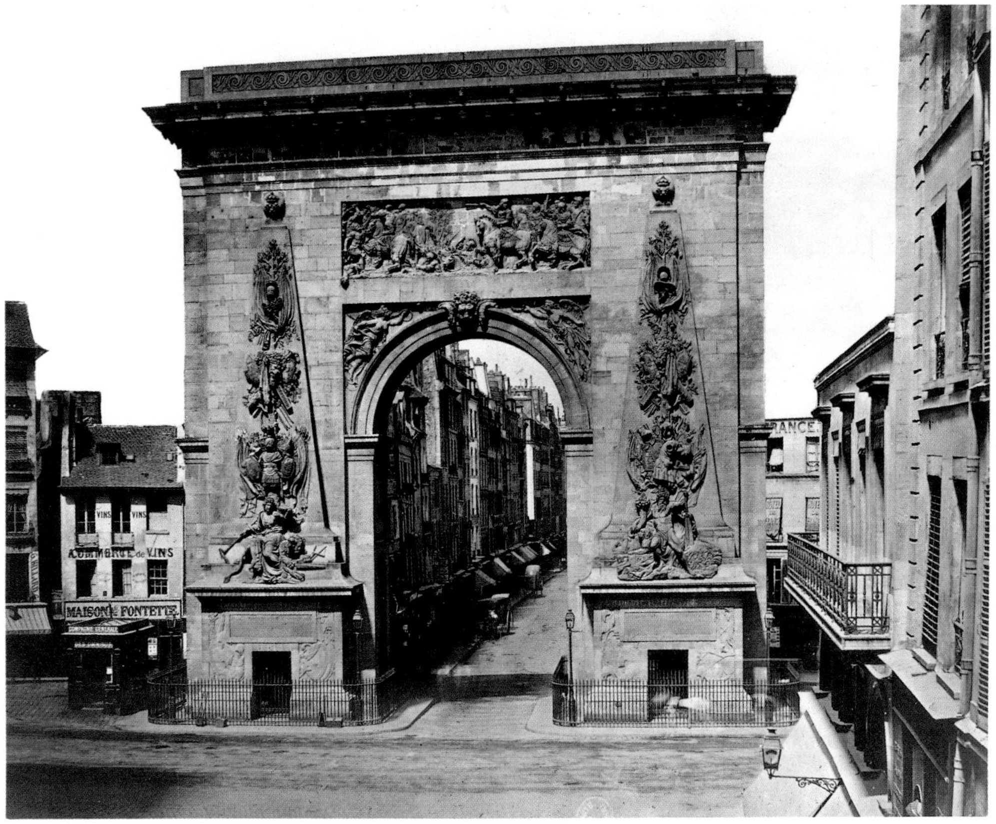

3 *Edouard-Denis Baldus*

Paris, Porte Saint-Denis, ca. 1856.
Albumen silver print.
Collections of the Bibliothèque Nationale.

4 *Photographer unknown*

Paris, Porte Saint-Denis.
From *Paris Photographique* (1851–1853).
Albumen silver print.
Collections of the Bibliothèque Nationale.

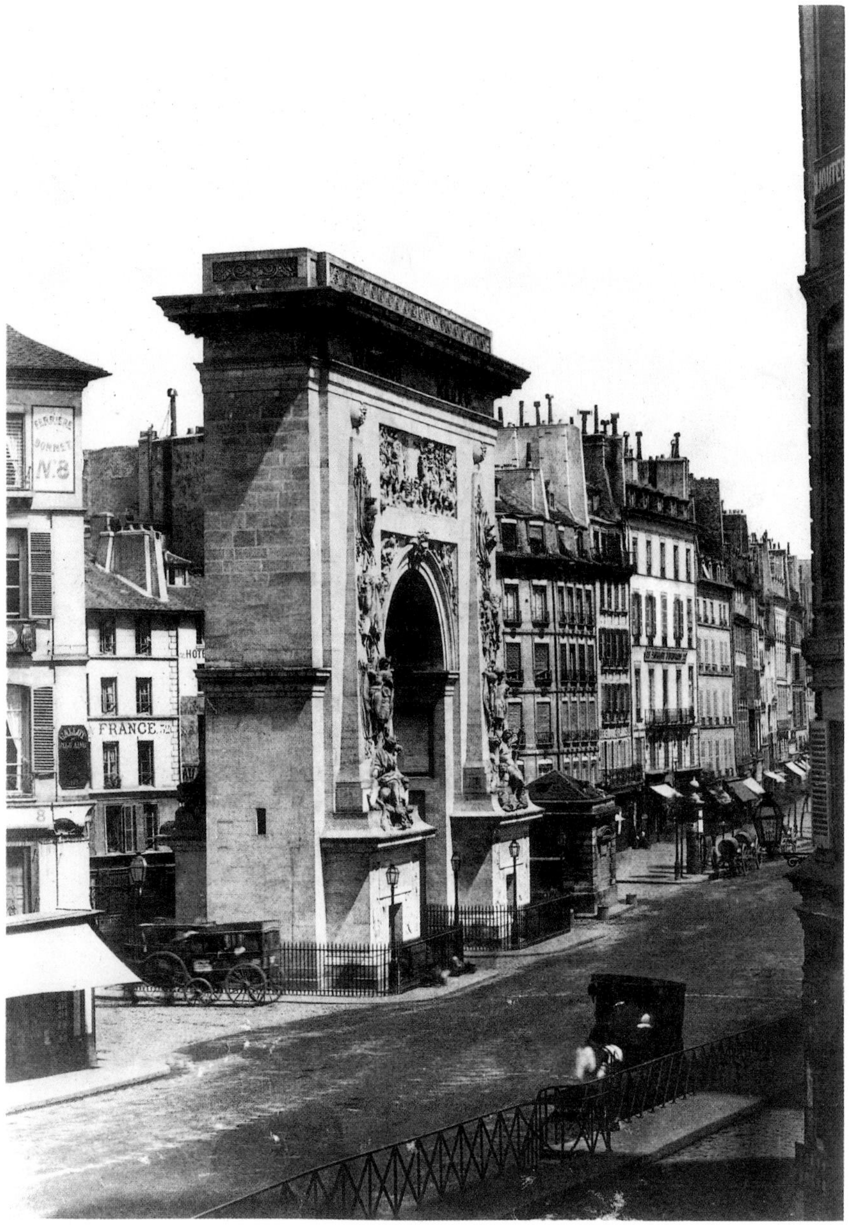

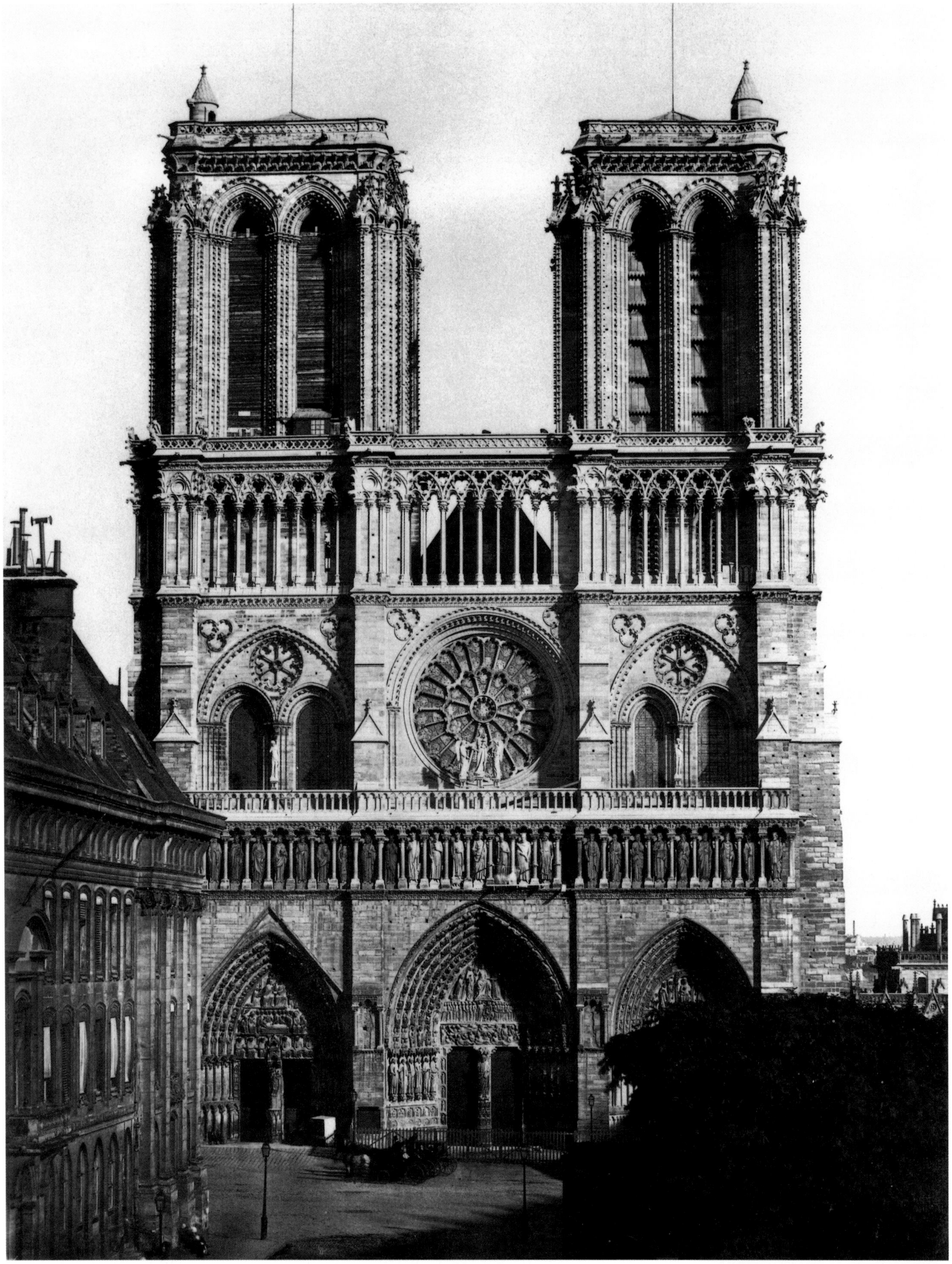

5 *Edouard-Denis Baldus*

Paris, facade of Notre-Dame, ca. 1860.
Albumen silver print.
The J. Paul Getty Museum.

6 *Photographer Unknown*

Paris, facade of Notre-Dame, ca. 1865.
Albumen silver print.
Courtesy of the Frances Loeb Library, Graduate School of Design, Harvard University.

7 *A. Richebourg*

Paris, Notre-Dame, excavations for the Police Prefecture, ca. 1864–1865.
Albumen silver print.
Musée Carnavalet, Paris.

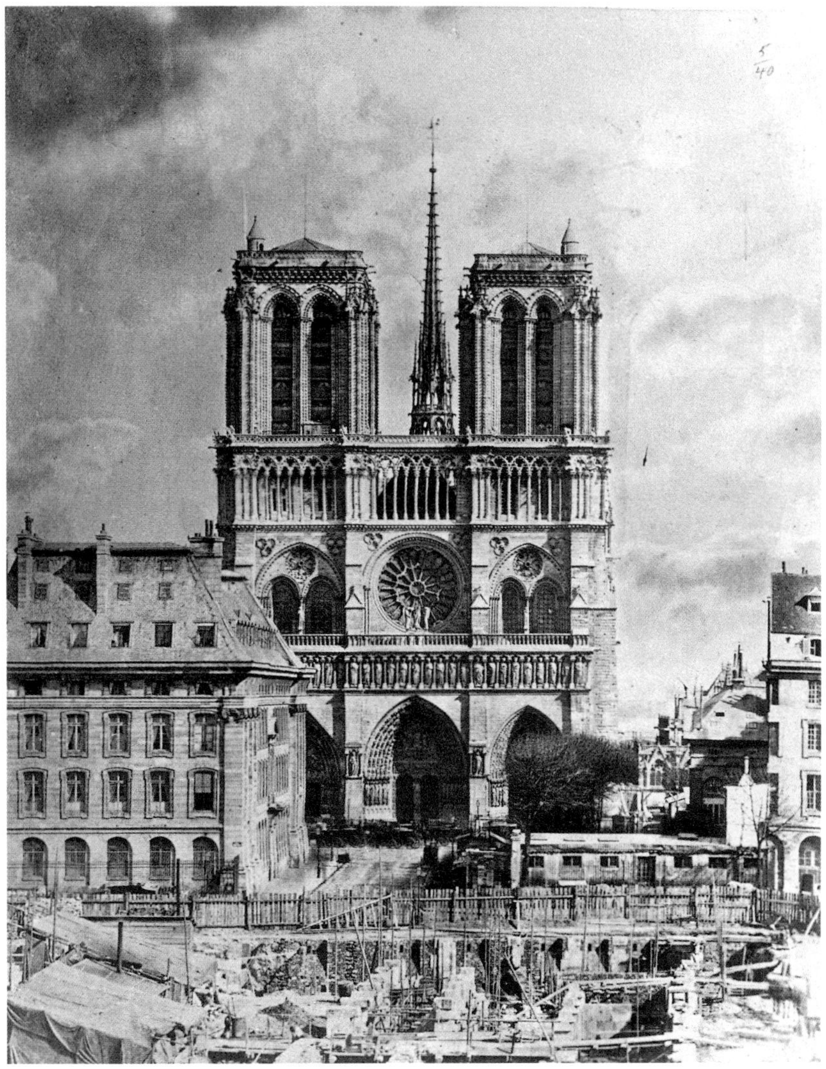

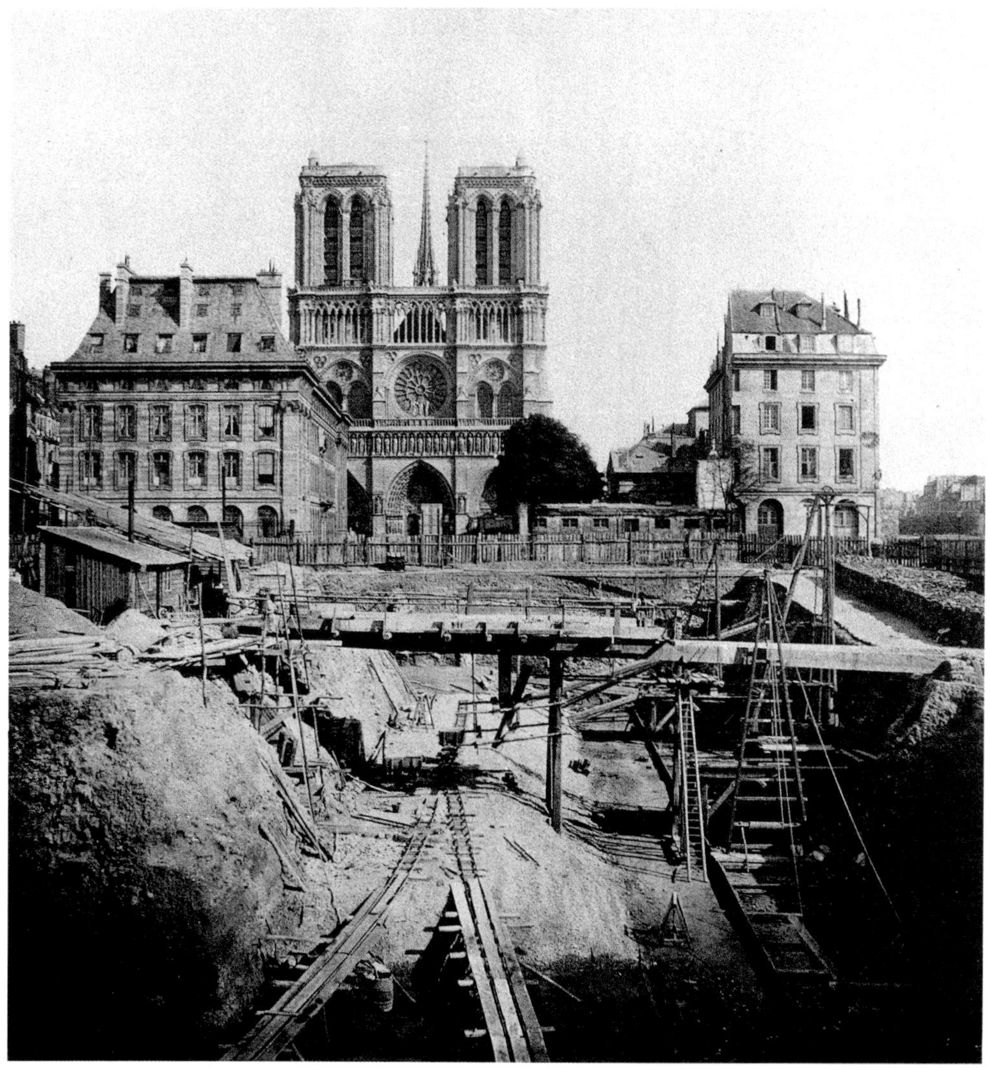

building was demolished in the sixties to make room for the new police barracks, the photographers moved back to a window that offered the same angle of view or to a street-level position on the identical axis.

Le Gray himself showed particular skill in the use of the elevation in photographs taken during the 1851 Mission Héliographique, although he also used the perspective well. A classic use of the elevation is found in his photograph of the early fifties showing Soufflot's Panthéon in Paris (8). An upper window on the rue Soufflot placed him at the midpoint of the facade, ensuring undistorted proportions at the expense of providing a view alien to the experience of the average Paris pedestrian. Again, this viewpoint flattened the building. Throughout his career Le Gray showed exceptional sensitivity to light, and he used it here to intensify the effect of flattening. The direction of the light is almost parallel to the facade. Rather than model the surfaces, it separates them into planes. The pediment sculpture is linearized, and texture is largely eliminated. The brilliantly lit columns of the portico stand before deep shadows that make the depth of the portico unreadable. Similar shadows were achieved with ink wash in Beaux-Arts elevation drawings of the era. The centered camera position and the skillfully chosen lighting conspire to reduce one of Paris's most three-dimensional buildings to the flatness of an elevation drawing.

Edouard Baldus was a master of this technique and applied it more rigorously than his contemporaries. His version of the canonical view of Notre-Dame is notable for an elegant linear effect of light that reduces surface texture and depth (5). His view of the entrance pavilion of the Imperial Library of the new Louvre (1850s), taken between 1855 and 1857 (9), is close to the elevations in Second Empire project drawings. A high, centered camera position avoids perspectival distortion. Extremely tight framing, achieved by using a long focal-length lens or by drastic cropping of the print, works to flatten the facade and eliminate context. The cart, an atypical inclusion, serves to indicate scale. The soft, luminous shadows created by raking light gently model the surface, resembling the shadow effects created by thinned washes of ink in elevation drawings of the period.[14]

At times, the over-rigorous application of the elevation approach can yield a misleading view of a building. A well-known photograph by Henri Le Secq, published unattributed by Blanquart-Evrard in his *Paris photographique* of 1851–1853, shows Vignon's Church of the Madeleine (1807–45) (10). The head-on, upper window camera position obscures the building's blocky, Greek-temple shape. Photographers like Robert MacPherson and James Robertson approached genuine Greek temples from an angle, reproducing the corner viewpoint envisaged by the ancient architects that emphasizes the solid block of the building. Here we are shown a flattened facade. Even the projection of the portico is diminished by the contrasty light. Might Le Secq be commenting on the building as a stage-set version of a Greek temple?

The elevation flourished throughout our period, especially in France. A particularly fine example was taken by Adolphe Braun in 1875, as part of his album on the Paris Opéra (1875). Braun worked from a third-floor balcony overlooking the place de l'Opéra (11). The flat lighting, tight framing, and flattening effect of the viewpoint make this a classic elevation. The facade's proportions are undistorted, and the cupola and the tower housing the stage machinery are totally visible, as they are not when the Opéra is seen from street level. This type of photograph, however, was over thirty years old at this time, and Braun may have felt it lacked something. The next picture in this album was taken a bit earlier in the same day from the identical position (12). The only difference is that he used a shorter focal-length lens. This had the effect of broadening the view to include a large segment of the surrounding urban landscape, especially the place de l'Opéra, which had been conceived as an essential element in the facade's impact. The lens change yields a very different photograph, whose subject is not the facade of the opera house alone, but the interaction between the building and its urban setting. Braun thus responds to the underlying intent of the whole project, which was to create a grandiose, unified urban environment. It might be expected that having come to Paris during Baron Georges Haussmann's transformation of the city, Braun would be sensitive to the interaction of building facade and street, which was one of the great themes of Haussmann's work. Beginning in the fifties and continuing throughout our period, this interaction would be a major topic for photographers on both sides of the channel.

In Vienna the Ringstrasse project, which occupied most of the second half of the century, showed the same concern for the interaction of building and street to create a unified urban environment. A photograph published as a lithograph in the series *Wiener Monumentalbauten* shows Gottfried Semper's Burgtheater (1878) from a balcony of the Rathaus opposite from it (13). Judging from the state of the construction, it must date from around 1878. As the Ring project developed, the associated complex of parks and recreational areas as well as the sweep of the great street itself constituted as much a part of the

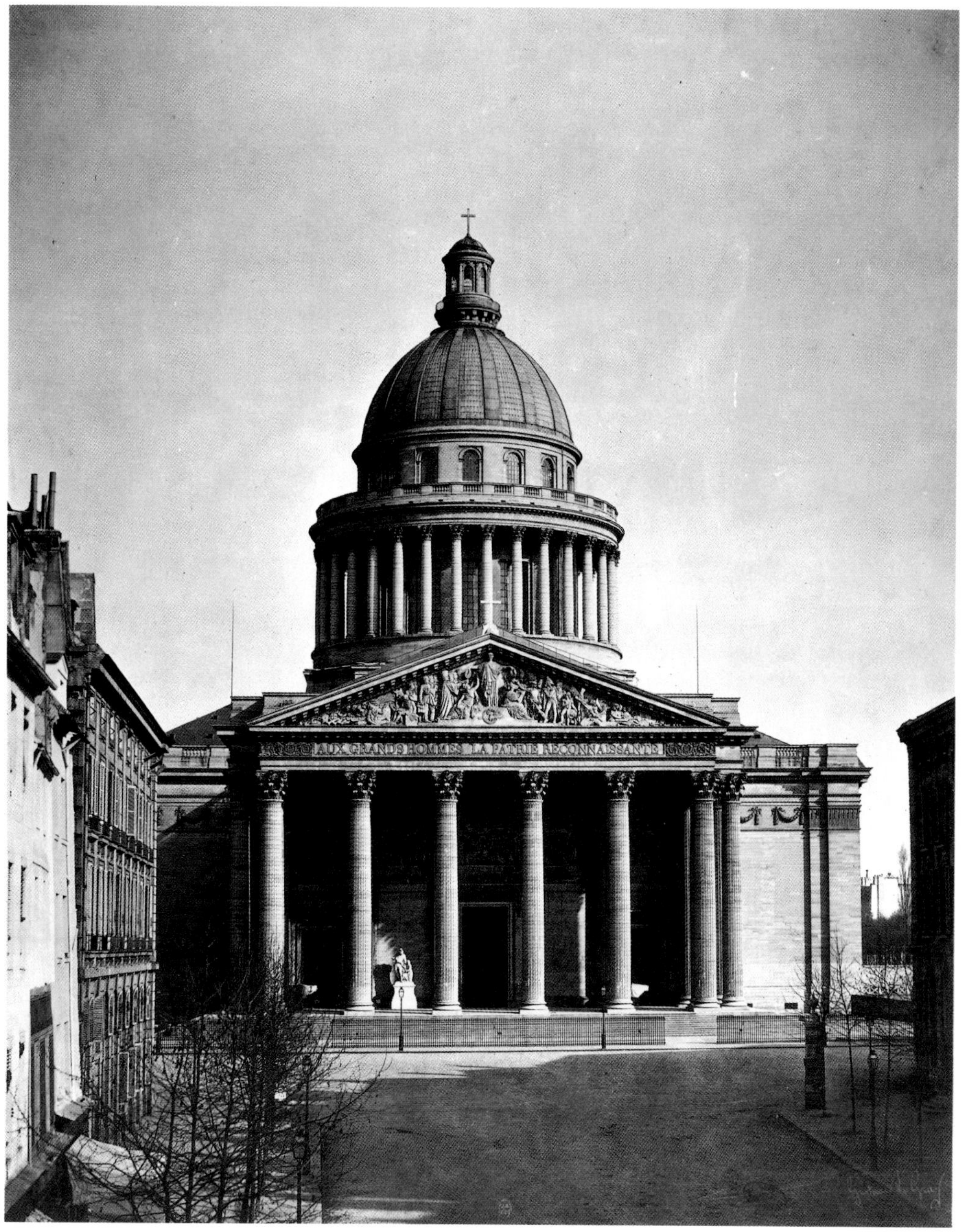

8 *Gustave Le Gray*

Paris, Panthéon, ca. 1849–1856.
Albumen silver print.
Collections of the Bibliothèque Nationale.

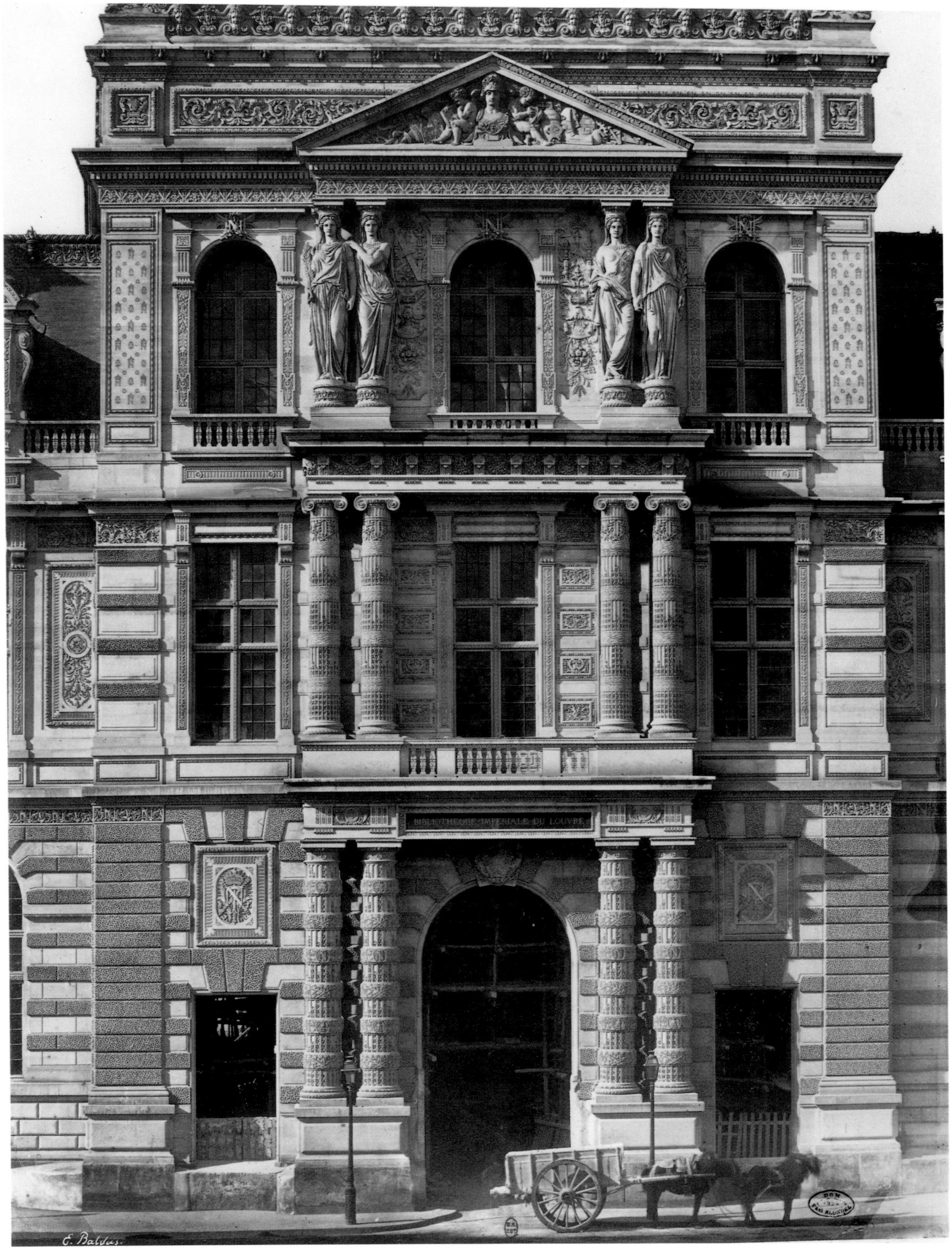
BIBLIOTHEQUE IMPERIALE DU LOUVRE
E. Baldus.

9 *Edouard-Denis Baldus*

Paris, the new Louvre, entry pavilion of the Imperial Library, ca. 1855–1857. Collections of the Bibliothèque Nationale.

10 *Henri Le Secq*

Paris, Church of the Madeleine. From *Paris Photographique* (1851–1853). Albumen silver print. Collections of the Bibliothèque Nationale.

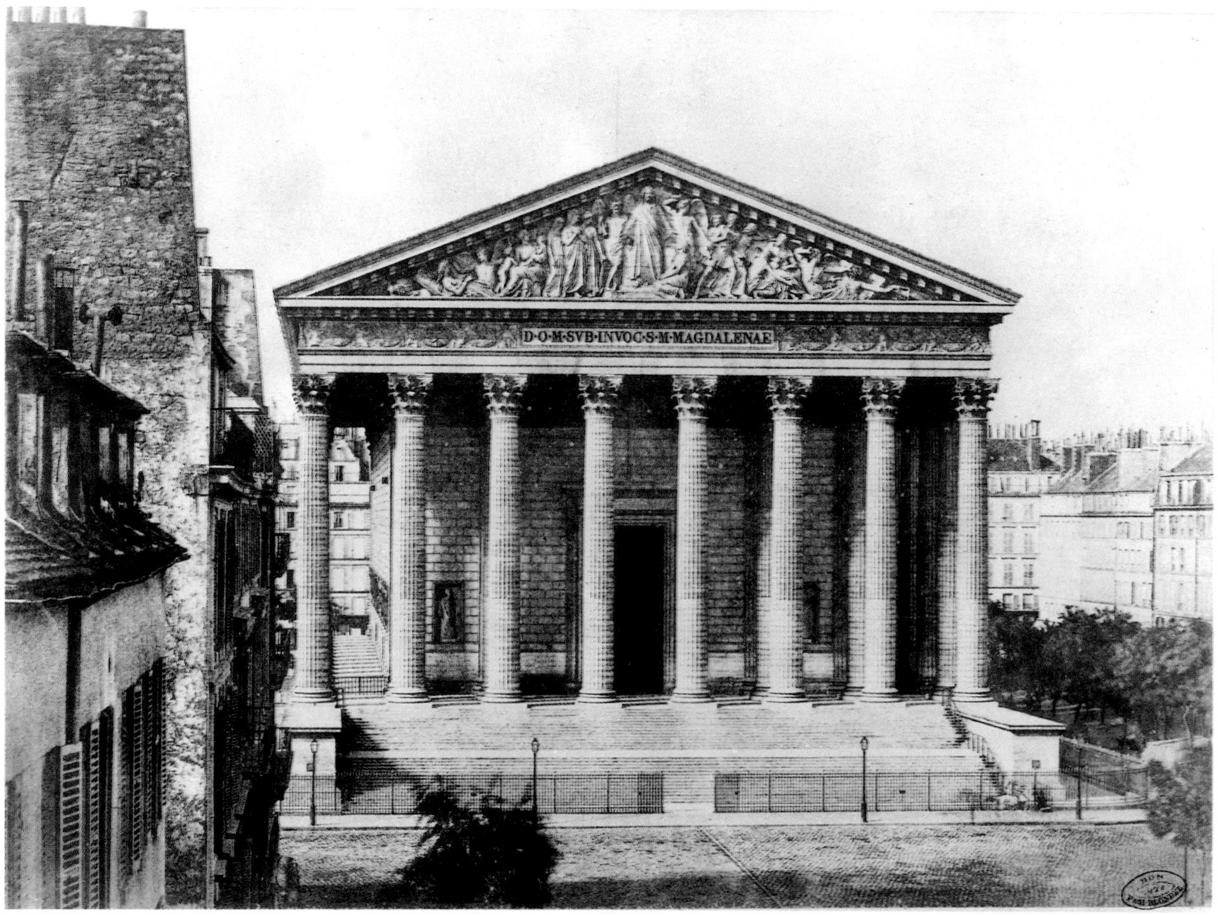

11 *Adolphe Braun*

Paris Opéra, facade.
From *Le Nouvel Opéra* (1875).
Carbon print.
Collections of the Bibliothèque Nationale.

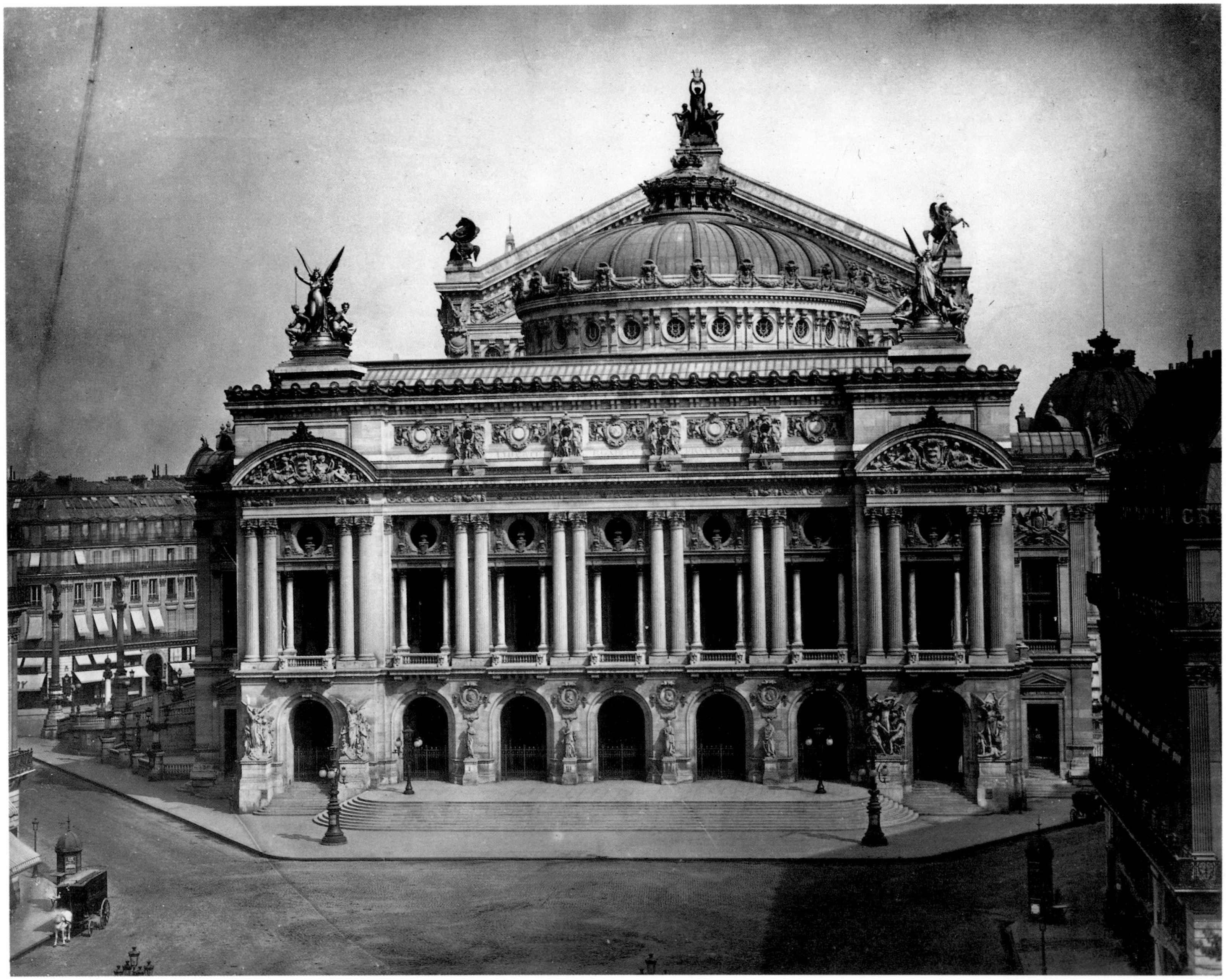

12 *Adolphe Braun*

Paris Opéra, facade.
From *Le Nouvel Opéra* (1875).
Carbon print.
Collections of the Bibliothèque Nationale.

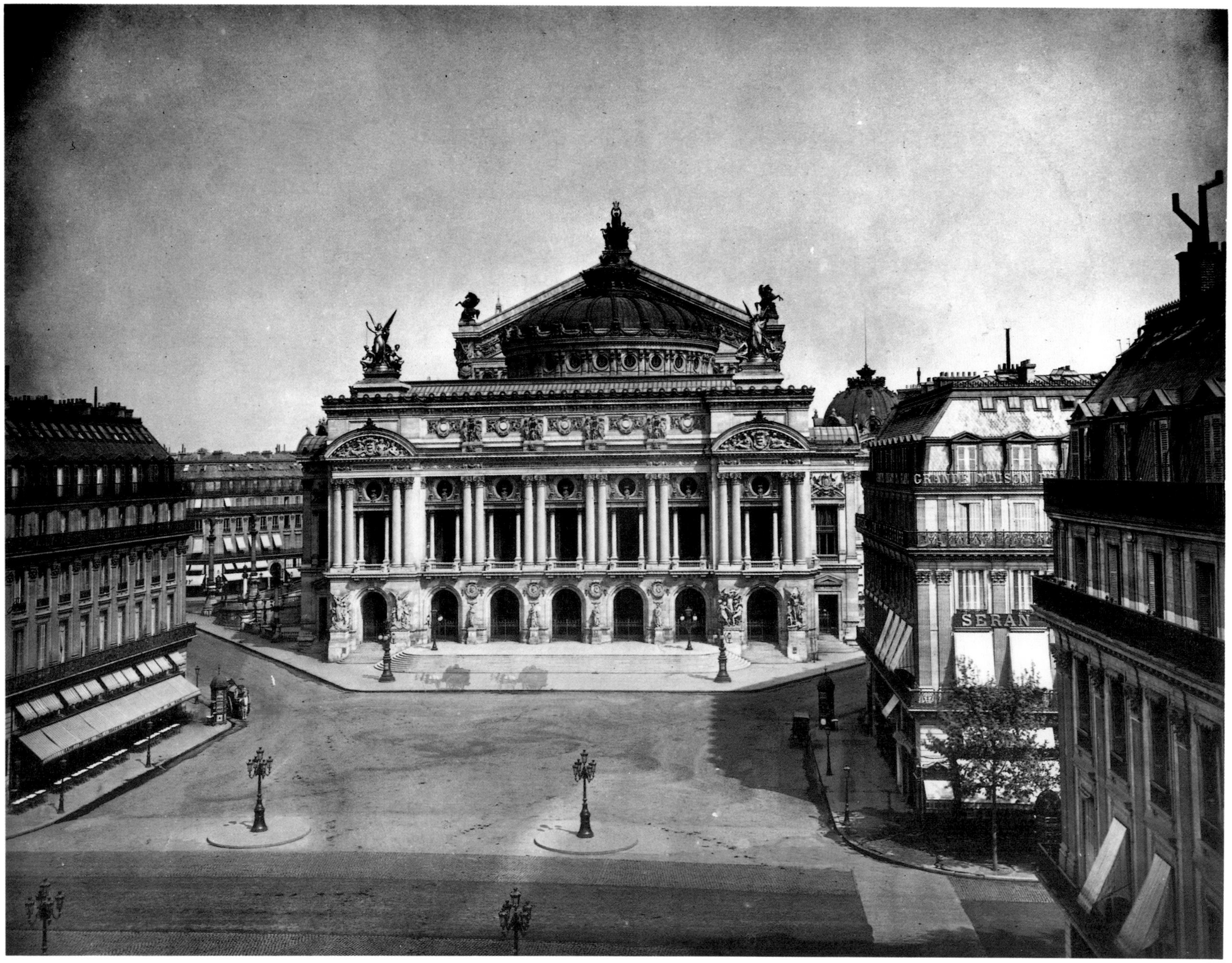

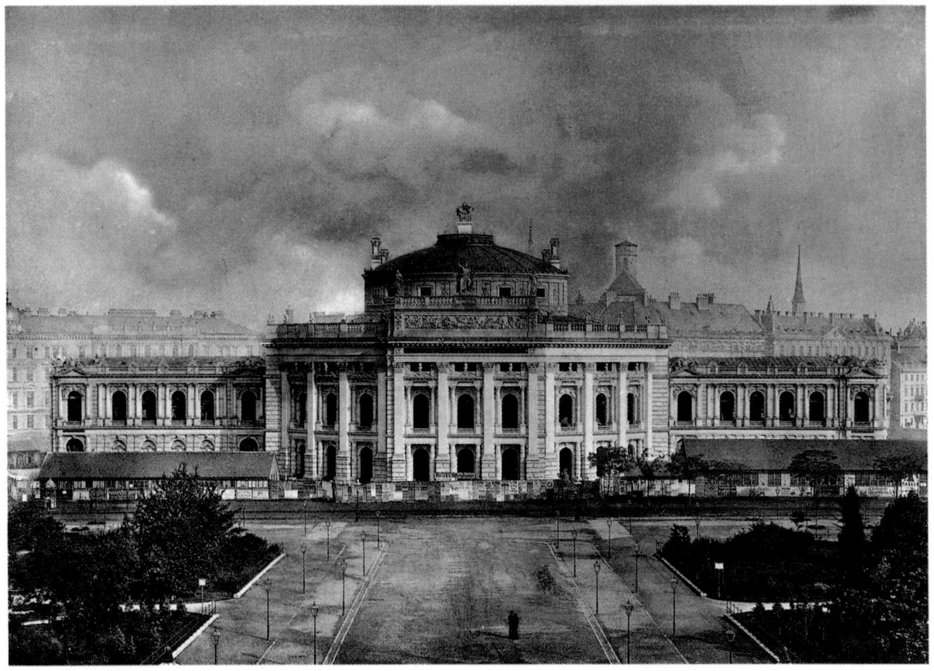

design as any given building and was the subject of many photographs. In this view the choice of camera position and short focal length of the lens reveals an awareness of the urban fabric as the interaction of building and spaces, as evidenced by the inclusion in the foreground of a considerable area of park and boulevard.

The perspective, by its nature, is not so rigorous and formal an approach as the elevation and accordingly is harder to define and identify. Although a natural way to photograph many buildings, a body of photographs can be isolated that shows a definite intent to produce photographic equivalents of the drawn or painted architectural perspective that was throughout the period the most popular way of presenting projects and buildings to the broader public. Intent is the key to understanding this type. The elevation tries to present an objective, undistorted, informative view of a facade, whereas the perspective attempts to recreate the actual experience of visiting the building.

The perspective appeared in the early days of photography. In the daguerrean heyday of the forties it was well utilized by an American, John Plumbe. Around 1846 he produced a series of daguerreotypes of architectural monuments in Washington, D.C., and vicinity, which he intended to convert into salable lithographs.[15] Plumbe utilized both perspective and elevation views. His famous picture of the Capitol is one of the latter. His photograph of the White House is unique in the series in not using a prism to return the direct positive image to a normal left-to-right position (14). Although Plumbe photographed both facades evenly lit, the other features of the perspective are evident, especially the corner, or *per angolo,* view. The absence of nearby buildings necessitated a pedestrian-level viewpoint, which helps to place the viewer on a large expanse of lawn in the foreground. Another of Plumbe's daguerreotype perspectives shows Baltimore's monument to the Battle of North Point (15). The three-dimensional effect of the diagonal placement of the monument is reinforced by strong light and shadow effects which emphasize the cubic mass of the base. The camera angle brings in the old houses around the square, providing a sense of the urban context.

As we have commented, the cubic form of the Greek temple naturally suggests the perspective treatment. James Robertson's photograph of the Hephaistaion in Athens follows this set of conventions closely (16). The three-dimensionality of the corner view is enhanced by the lighting, which leaves the short facade in shadow and underlines the separation of the columns from the cella wall. The eye-level camera position recreates the viewpoint of a visitor to

13 *PHOTOGRAPHER UNKNOWN*
Vienna, Burgtheater.
From *Wiener Monumentalbauten* (1880).
Photolithograph.
Collection of the Historisches Museum, Vienna.

14 *JOHN PLUMBE*
Washington, D.C., White House, ca. 1846.
Daguerreotype.
Collections of the Library of Congress.

15 *JOHN PLUMBE*
Baltimore, monument to the Battle of North Point, ca. 1846.
Daguerreotype.
Collections of the Library of Congress.

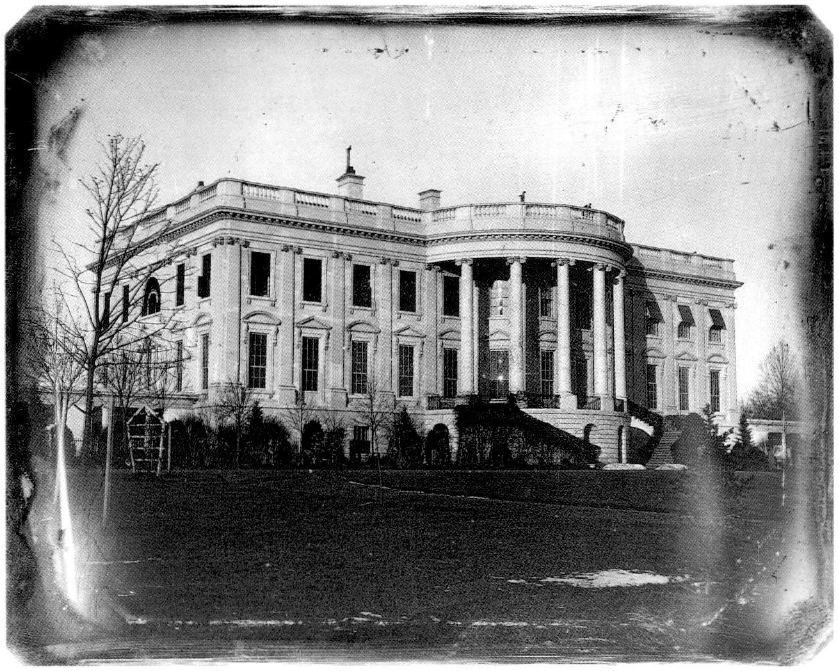

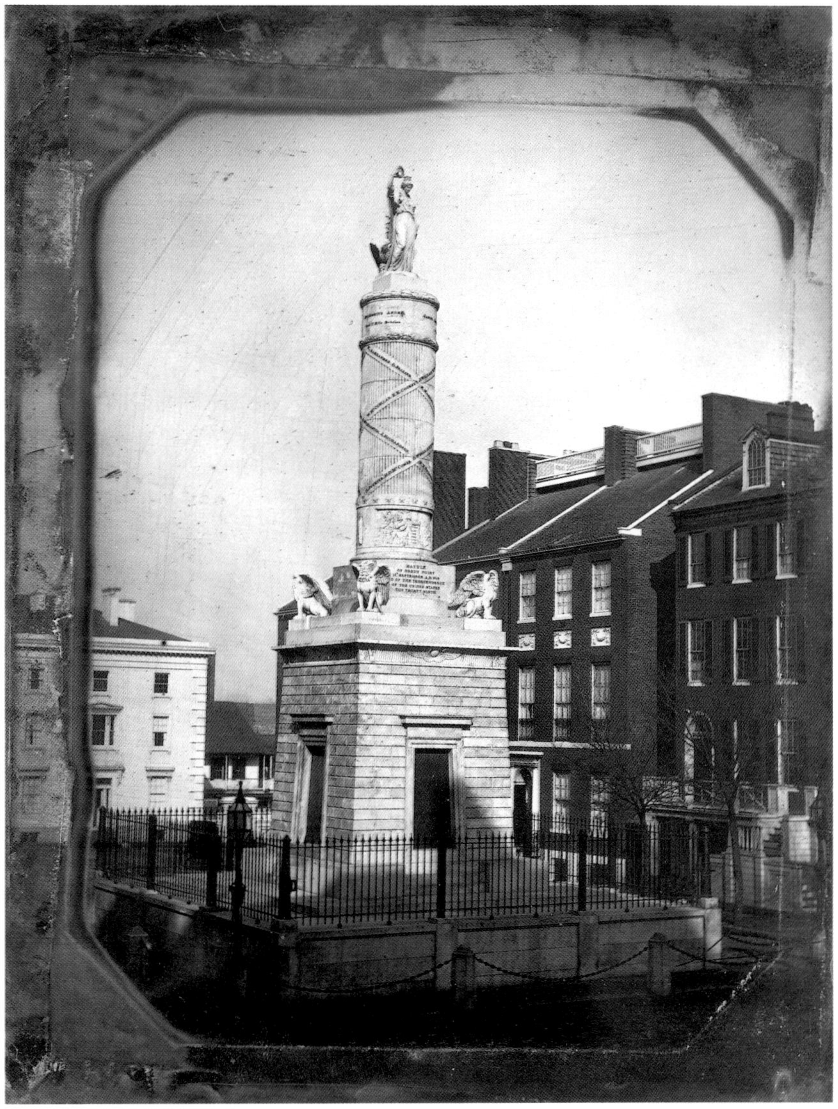

16 *James Robertson*

Athens, Hephaistaion, ca. 1860s.
Albumen silver print.
Collection of the RIBA.

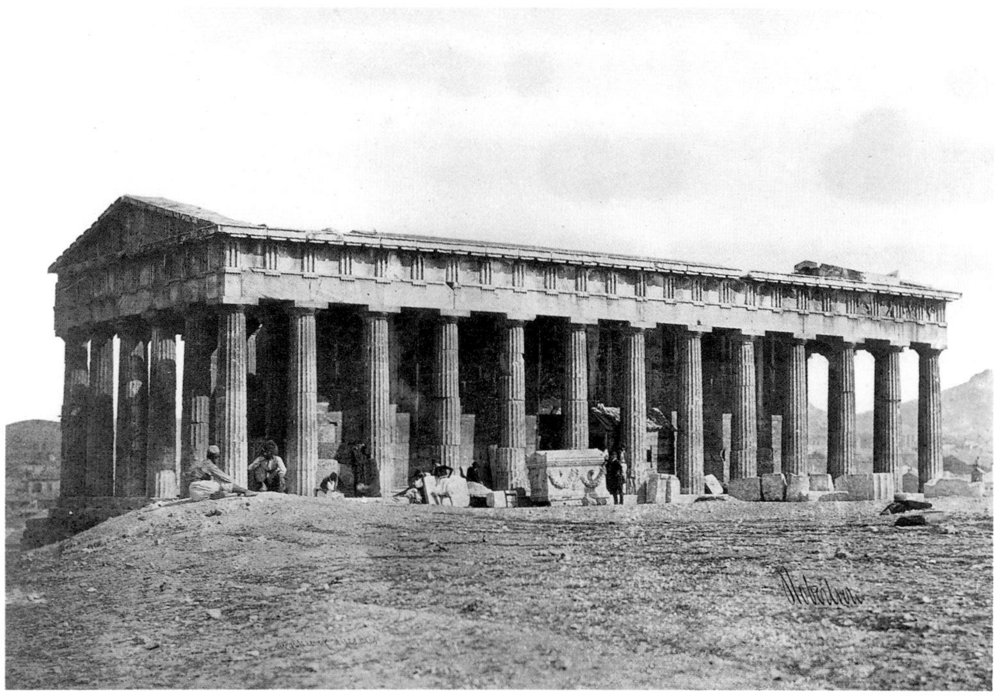

the site, and the people scattered in the temple's shadow add local color in a way reminiscent of the people in Stuart's lithographs in *Athenian Antiquities*. A similar effect is achieved by the Venetian Carlo Ponti in his photograph of the Arch of Septimius Severus in the Roman Forum (17). The view from the road leading down from behind the Capitoline Hill reproduces the experience of a typical tourist. Intense sidelighting strongly models the orders and relief sculpture. Although "pedestrian's-eye" viewpoints are not an inevitable part of the perspective, they contribute to its greatest appeal, the illusion of "being there." In our period the elevation usually used the upper window view.

Perspectives of medieval churches reveal the effectiveness of the perspective's approach in photographing buildings of that period. One, part of Francis Frith's long-lived *Series,* shows the abbey church of Saint Alban's before its notorious restoration begun in 1877, making this a valuable document (18). The diagonal viewpoint is used, with strong foreground elements that link the viewer to the building. This latter is more than a compositional convention, as it serves to establish our position on the site. Frith was at ground level, close to the building, and made dramatic use of the rising front. This was possible because of the greater flexibility of the bellows cameras in general use by the seventies. The powerful bulk of the "Norman" church is made to loom over us with an impressive presence. The corner view exaggerates the "picturesque," irregular massing of the church, bringing to mind John Ruskin's stress on irregularity as a criterion of the "true Gothic."

Although the strict elevation was effective in representing formal architectural compositions, it was less successful in dealing with more modest structures, and departures from the canon became necessary. A case in point is Juan Laurent's photograph of the house of Doña Maria la Brava in Salamanca (19). It was taken before 1882, when this print was purchased by H. H. Richardson, who undoubtedly was drawn to the eminently "Richardsonian" arch of the Romanesque portal.[16] The simple geometric forms of the facade were best rendered by a head-on view, but the texture of the weathered stone and the later sculptural additions needed more modeling to make them visible. By combining a viewpoint of the elevation type with side-lighting borrowed from the perspective, Laurent made a richer image, more evocative of the antiquity of the house, than strict adherence to the elevation or perspective would have achieved. That combinations such as this were found in photographs of the period should not obscure the fact that deliberate choices between one type or the other generally were made.

The perspective was a natural response to vernacular structures with their irregular massing and lack of formal surface articulation. While following Sherman's Civil War campaign through Georgia, George Barnard used it to photograph a farmhouse reduced to near-ruinous state by the vicissitudes of war (20). The low viewpoint reveals lopped trees and a litter of kindling in the foreground, reinforcing the general sense of breakdown. The dramatic potential of the perspective was recognized by the photographers of the 1851 Mission of the French Historical Monuments Commission, as a device to show the dilapidated state of some of the nation's most famous works of architecture and their need of restoration. O. Méstral, in his view of the ramparts of Carcassonne, chose intense side-lighting to bring out the cylindrical forms of the towers and the rough texture of the wall caused by erosion of mortar from the masonry joints (21). The raking light coming toward the lens evokes an image of romantic ruins while simultaneously making a strong case for repointing.

Buildings composed of cylindrical or polygonal forms require the perspective. It was inevitable in a view of a New York state mansion appropriately entitled Font Hill Castle (22). The photograph was published as a lithograph in A. A. Turner's *Villas on the Hudson* of 1860, a pioneering American volume of photographs of country houses. The irregular plan and "picturesque" silhouette of the castle excluded a head-on view, but the photographer chose a raking light, similar to if less dramatic than Méstral's, to bring out the solidity and bulk of its turrets. As far as interiors were concerned, where technical conditions permitted, both elevation and perspective views were taken. In his 1875 photograph of the grand staircase of the Paris Opéra (23), Braun used the diagonal view to emphasize the sweeping movement of the stairs. By making the space seem to envelop the viewer, this viewpoint recreates the spatial experience of this most dynamic of interiors. Frontal views of these same stairs, in which the film plane is parallel to one of the walls, fail to capture this spatial dynamism.

Photographers responded to the intensified awareness of the urban landscape that was linked to Baron Haussmann's reorganization of the Paris street system. As early as the forties the urban fabric itself had become a photographic subject. Although some of Daguerre's earliest experiments might qualify as urban landscapes, and urban views played an important role from N.-M. P. Lerebours' *Excursions Daguérriennes* on, Fox Talbot, while visiting Paris, may have been the first to explore this subject in a serious way (24). Talbot, however, didn't fully exploit the possibilities of the approach. His work character-

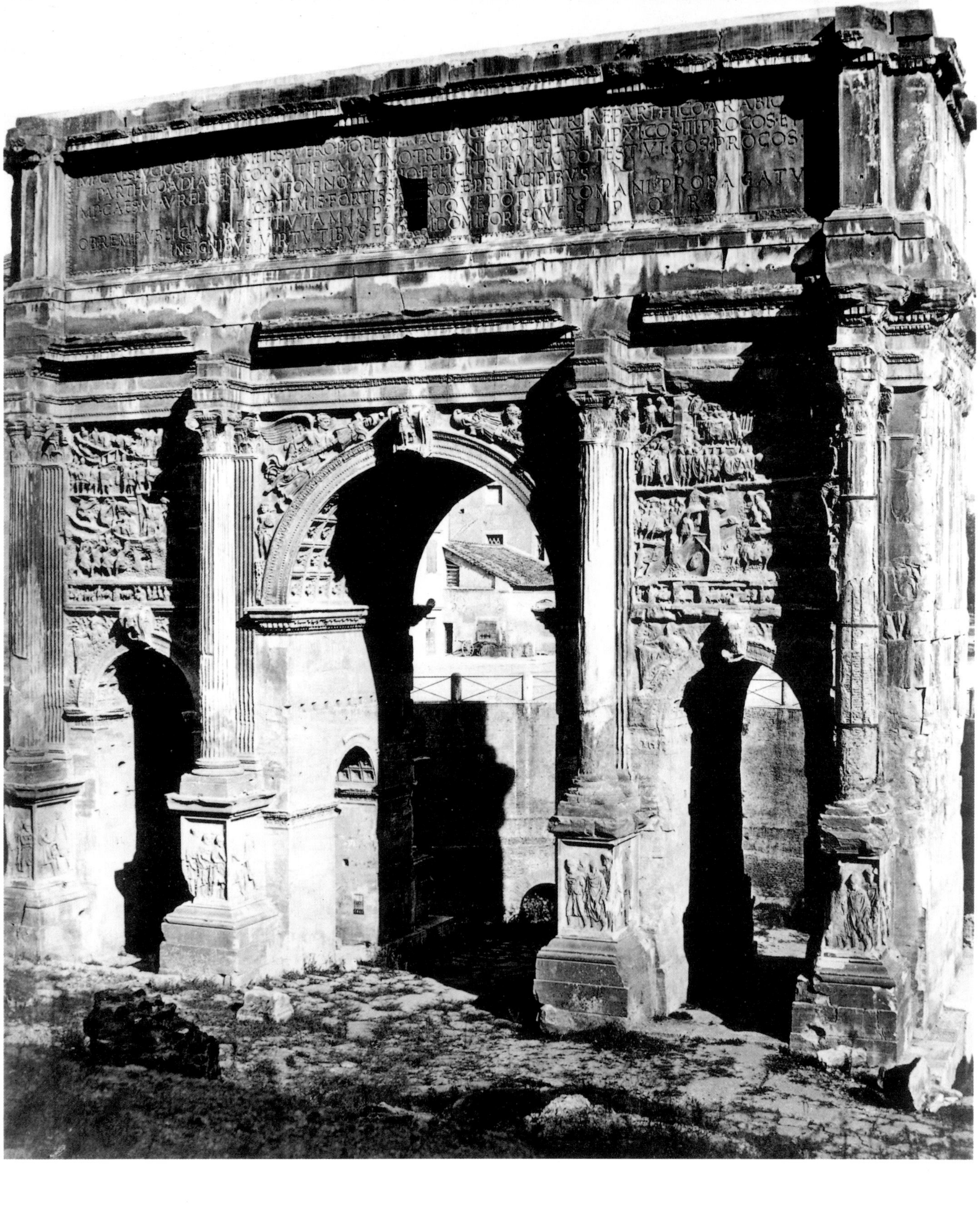

17 *Carlo Ponti*

Rome, Arch of Septimius Severus, ca. 1870.
Albumen silver print.
Collections of the Library of Congress.

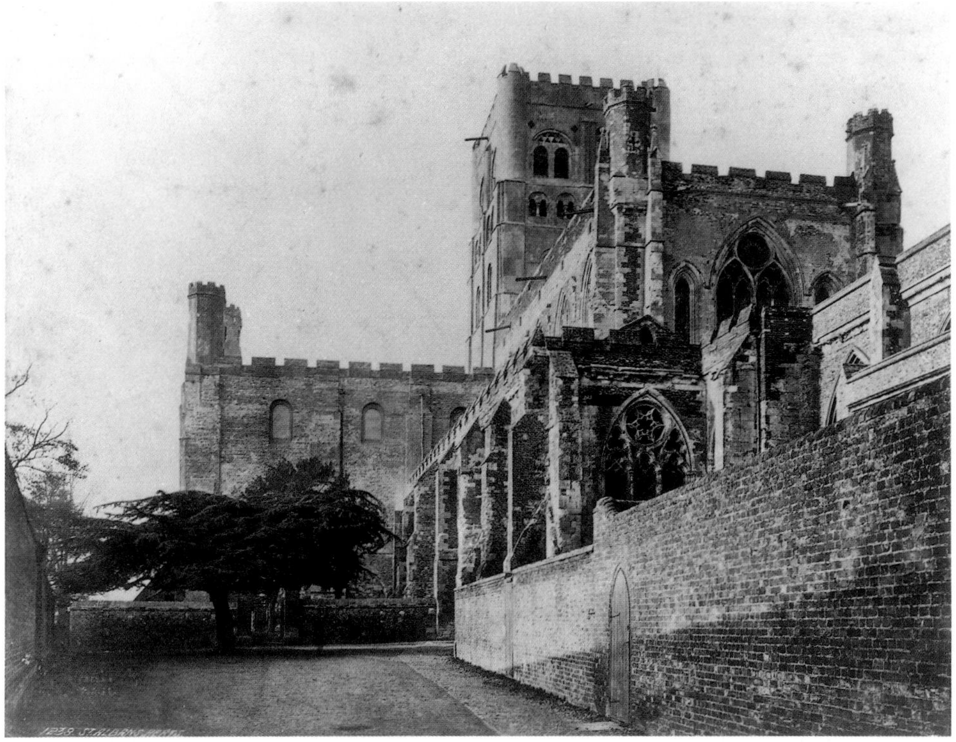

18 *Francis Frith*

Abbey church of St. Alban's, before 1877.
From "Frith's Series."
Albumen silver print.
Royal Commission on the Historical Monuments of England.

19 *Juan Laurent*

Salamanca, house of Doña Maria la Brava, before 1882.
Albumen silver print.
Courtesy of the Frances Loeb Library, Graduate School of Design, Harvard University.

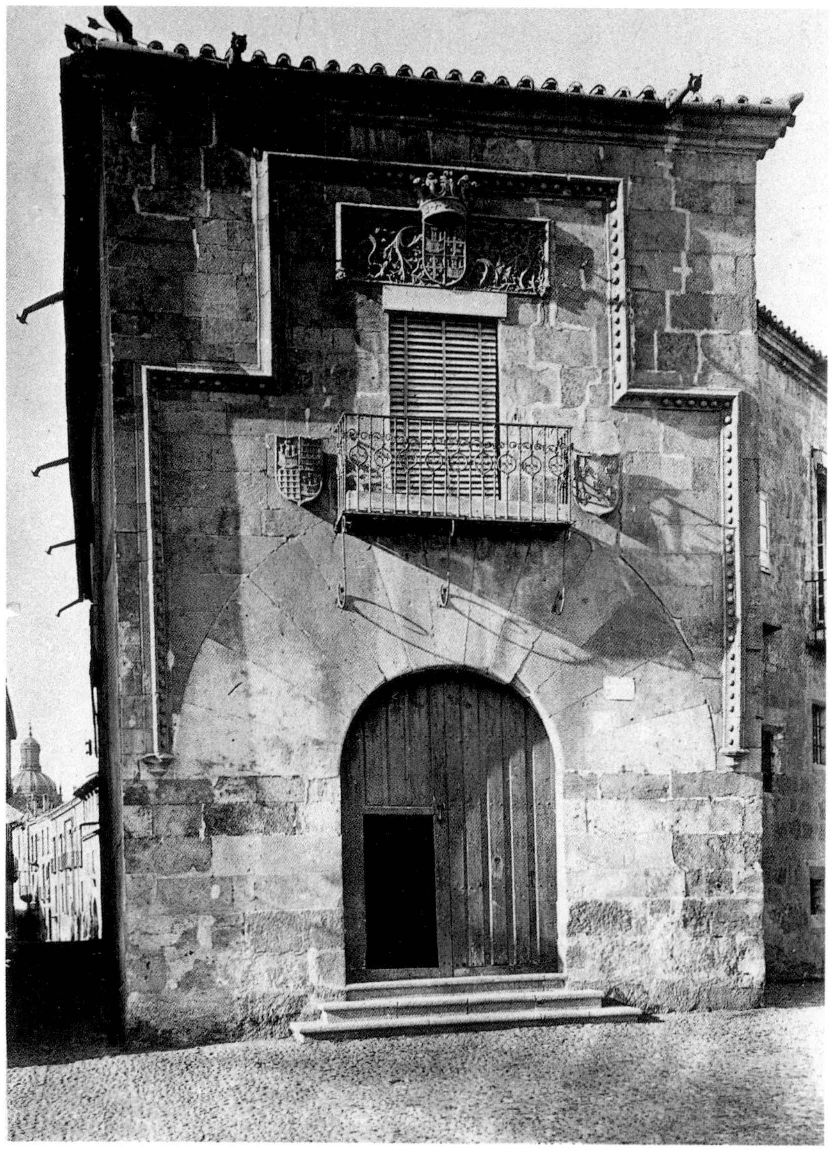

20 *George Barnard*

The John Ross House, Rossville, Ga., 1864.
From *Photographic Views of Sherman's Campaigns* (1866).
Albumen silver print.
Collections of the Library of Congress.

21 *O. Méstral*

Ramparts of Carcassonne.
From Heliographic Mission of 1851.
Modern print from waxed calotype negative of 1851.
Archives Photographiques, Paris.
SPADEM/VAGA, New York, 1986.

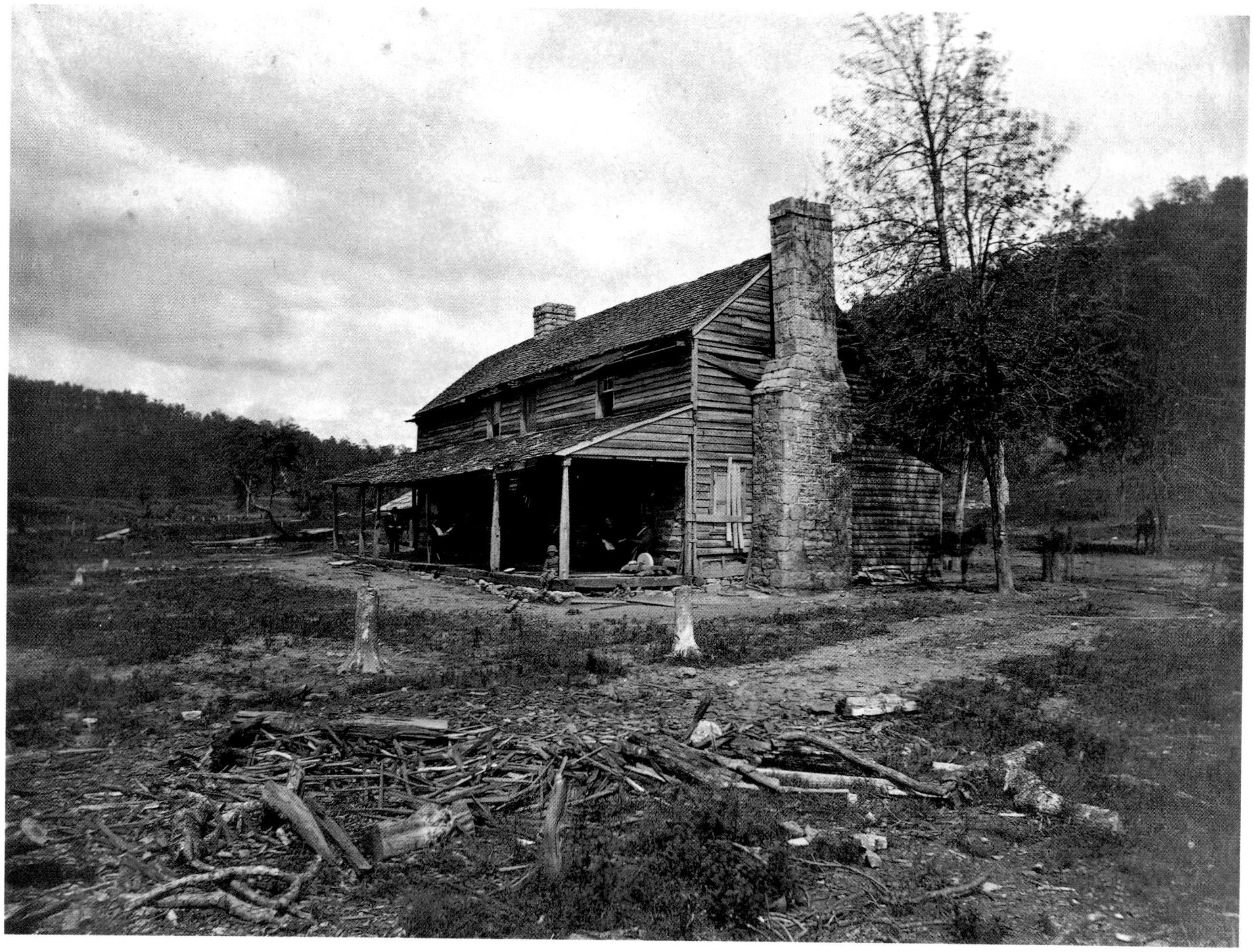

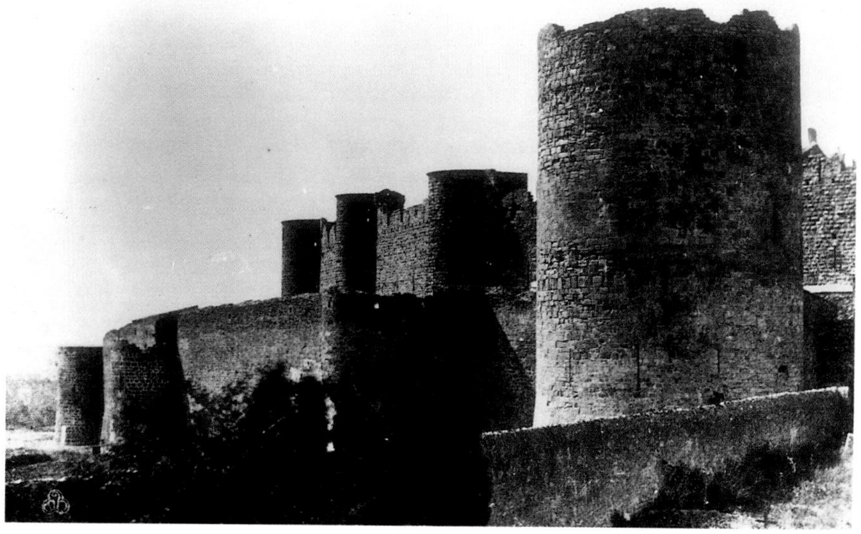

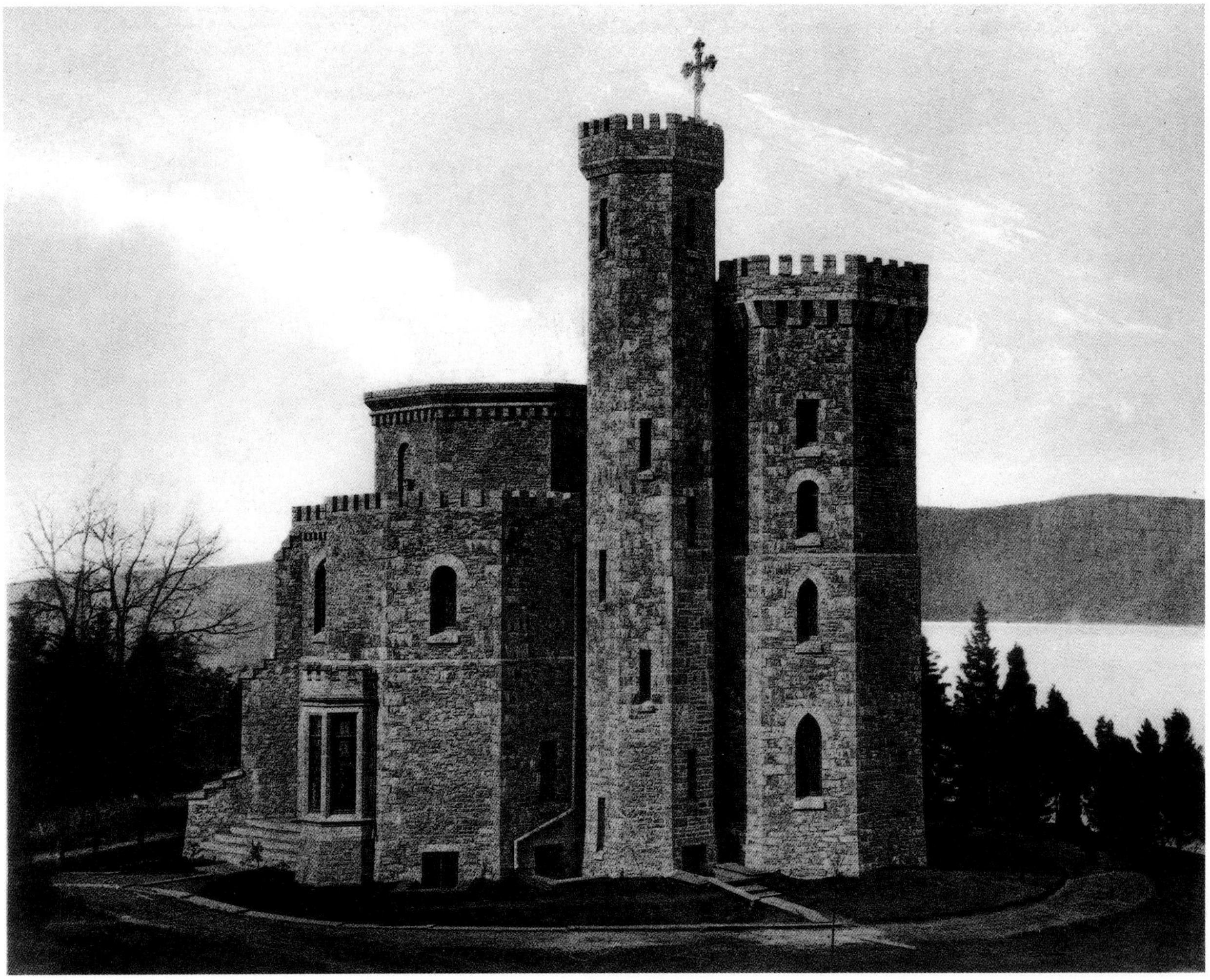

22 *A. A. Turner*

Font Hill Castle.
From *Villas on the Hudson* (1860).
Hand-tinted photolithograph.
Collections of the Library of Congress.

23 *Adolphe Braun*

Paris Opéra, grand staircase.
From *Le Nouvel Opéra* (1875).
Carbon print.
Collections of the Bibliothèque Nationale.

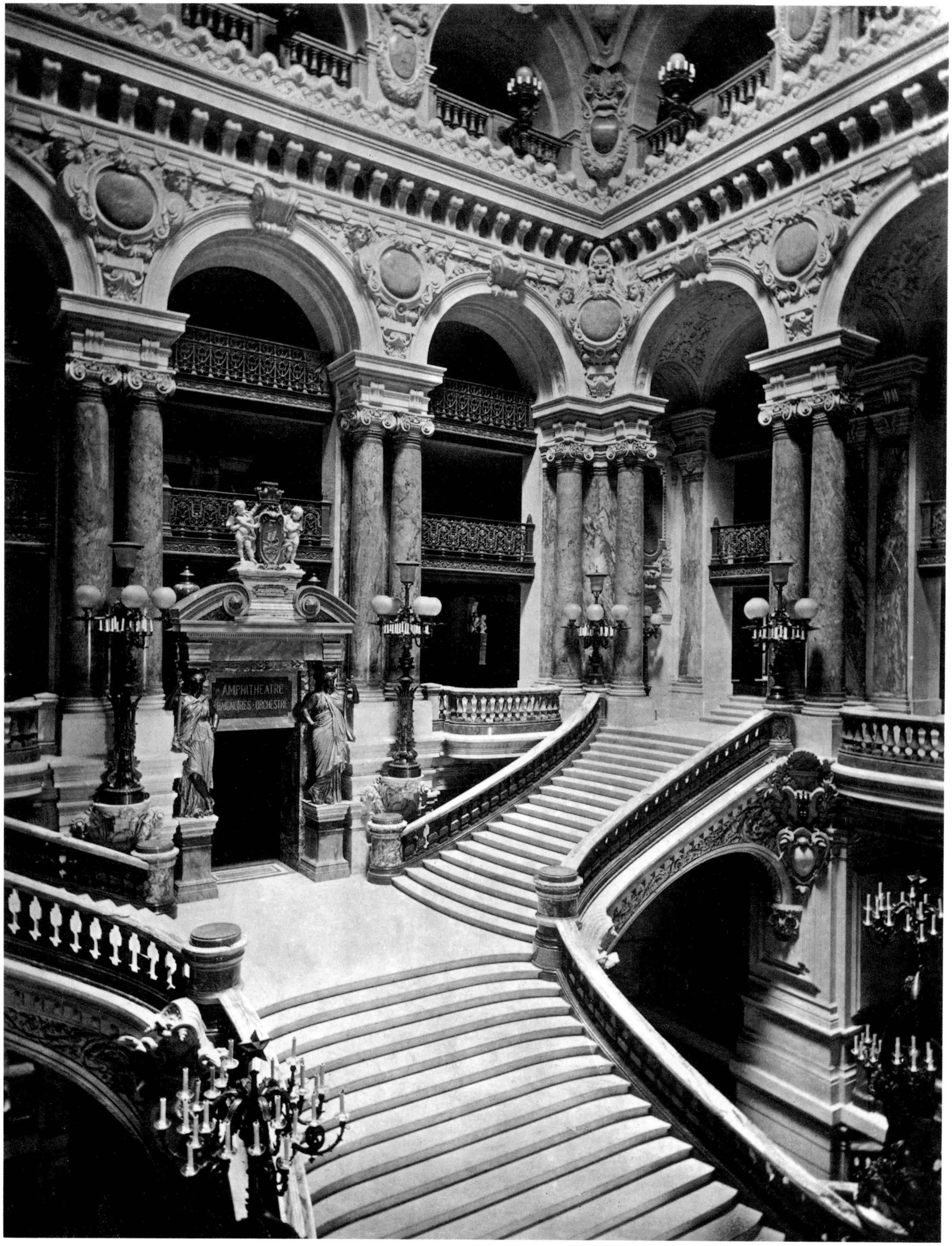
AMPHITHEATRE

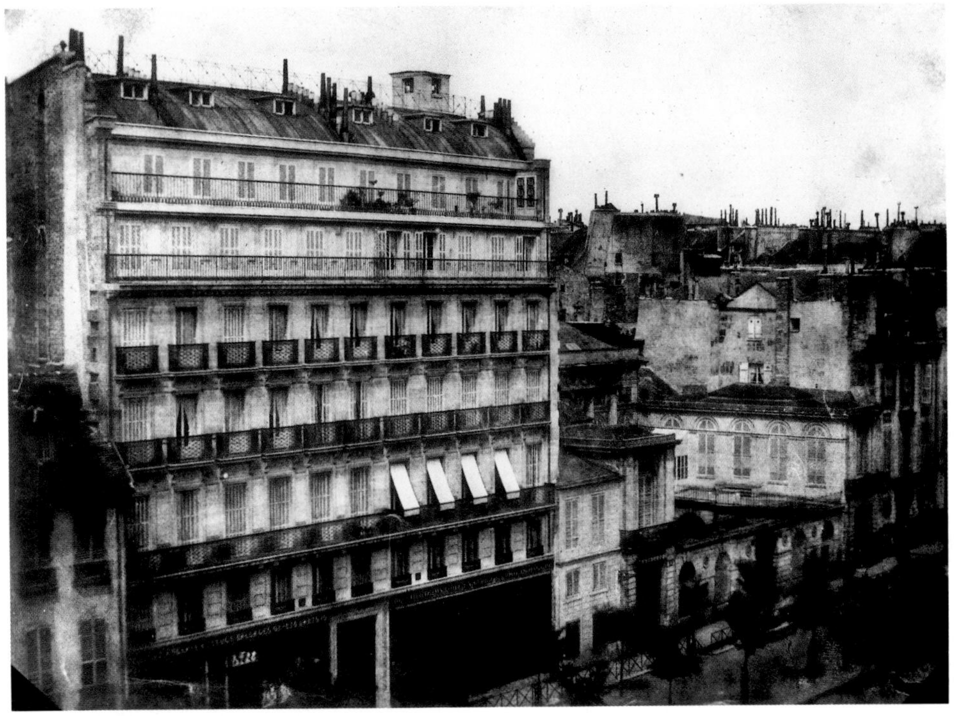

24 *William Henry Fox Talbot*
Paris, apartment block, ca. 1846.
Calotype.
Science Museum, London.

25 *Charles Marville*
Paris, École des Beaux-Arts, courtyard, 1851.
Albumen silver print.
Collections of the Bibliothèque Nationale.

istically shows a reserve and formality, an unwillingness to immerse himself in the life of the street. His urban photographs most often were taken out of windows that were well above the eye level of the pedestrian. The first photographer systematically to immerse himself in the urban fabric appears to have been the Parisian Charles Marville. His early career as an engraver and illustrator may have played a role in this. An awareness of the importance of the street itself in the urban landscape characterized the work of such graphic artists working in Paris from the early years of the century on as the Englishmen Thomas Girtin, Samuel Prout (both father and son), Richard Parkes Bonington, and Thomas Shotter Boys. French artists like Le Secq's friend Charles Méryon and Maxime Lalanne were active in this genre during the period when Marville was photographing, making the streets of Paris their main interest.[17] Marville's photographs of these streets, taken from 1855 on, echo the approach of the artists. The camera is placed at the eye level of the pedestrian and looks into the street itself so that the viewer is enveloped by its space. Marie de Thézy has commented, "What he wants to show is the line of the street, the place where it begins and where it ends."[18] The facades of the buildings at the same time are of interest in themselves and serve to define the space of the street as an architectural entity.

For graphic artists this approach goes back further than the 1820s, but Marville's application of it to photography may date from 1851, in a series of views he took of the courtyards of the École des Beaux-Arts (1839) (25). They were published by Blanquart-Evrard between 1851 and 1853. The image illustrated was deposited by Marville in the Bibliothèque Nationale in 1851. Other photographers had shown these famous courtyards, the heart of French official artistic education, but following Talbot's pattern of the forties had viewed them as separate facades seen from elevated camera positions rather than as spaces surrounded by facades. Marville may be the first photographer to treat a courtyard as a space and to place his tripod directly on the paving to reproduce a pedestrian's viewpoint, so that it appears that the viewer is enveloped by the space. The photograph thus recreates the actual experience of being in the courtyard.

Marville's approach, an innovation in photography although familiar to graphic artists, was used, perhaps independently, by Scottish photographers such as Thomas Keith and Thomas Annan, but his was the most impressive achievement in the genre. As "Photographer of the City of Paris," Marville undertook an exhaustive survey of the city's streets, especially those threatened

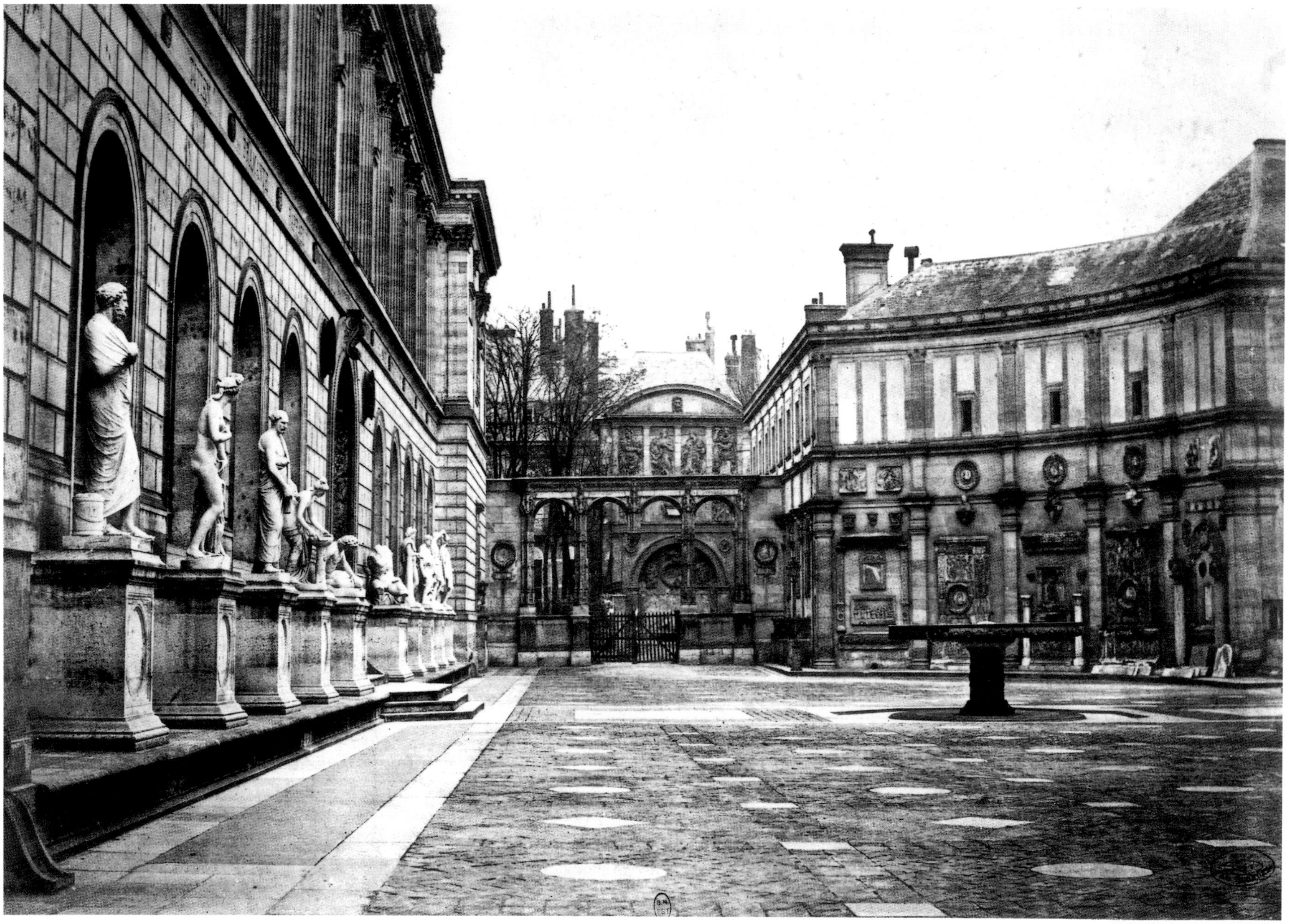

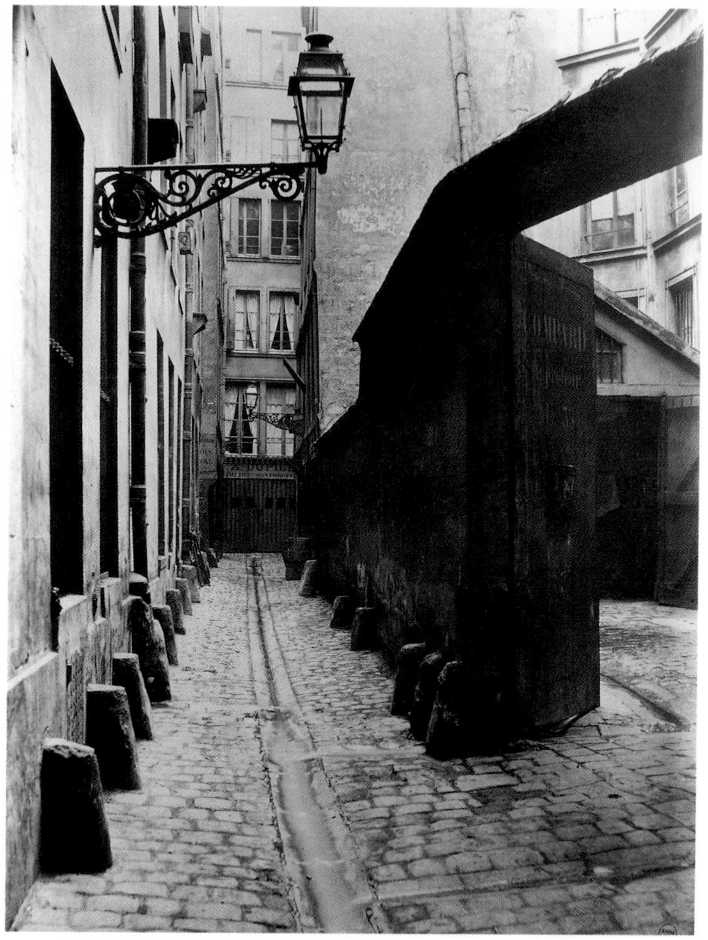

with demolition by Haussmann (26, 27, 28). The streets themselves were his subjects. It has been remarked that he was especially interested in the medieval streets near the Seine that were to disappear, but he also included prosperous newer *quartiers* that were not so different in appearance from Haussmann's boulevards. Annan had shown the old streets of Glasgow with the goal of urban renewal, but Marville can display a genuine sympathy for his old streets. Although frequently in dilapidated and insalubrious states, they are shown as active, functioning environments. The synthesis of building facade and street space by which he conveys the weave of the urban fabric is often enriched by accidental elements that imply vitality and activity: wagons and carts, merchandise for sale, tools momentarily left behind by workmen who will shortly return to take them up, and above all, an amazing efflorescence of advertising signs on the old buildings, which proclaim a flourishing if seedy commercial activity in even the most battered neighborhoods. In this respect Marville may be closer to the English limners of the Paris streets than to Frenchmen such as Méryon who stress the sinister side of the old *quartiers*, although his photographs' somber tonalities can also evoke their tenebrous world.[19]

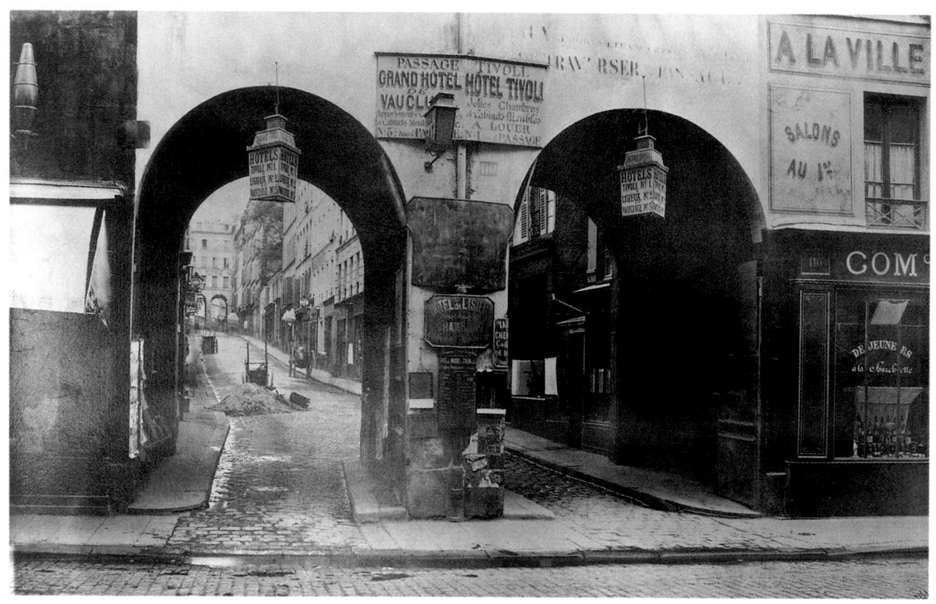

In 1867 the Society for Photographing the Relics of Old London requested the photographers A. and J. Bool to begin a neighborhood-by-neighborhood survey of those of London's historic buildings that were threatened by demolition or in ruinous condition. The first volume of this long series was published by Henry Dixon in 1867 in the form of 120 mounted carbon prints. The Bools's sympathy for the old streets and buildings is more overt than Marville's, although this may in part be due to the nature of the commission. When the Bool name disappears from the series after 1879 and Dixon's remains alone, the images become more conservative in subject matter and style. This may reflect Dixon's taste, or the fact that respectable districts such as Whitehall are being treated. One of the last series done by the Bools includes a view of the medieval church of Saint Bartholomew's, and the Cloth Fair, in one of London's oldest districts (29). Their approach reminds us of that of Marville in photographing the medieval alleys of Paris. We are again at ground level, surrounded and overhung by irregular masses of ancient masonry. The rough textures and somber tones are also reminiscent of Marville. Despite the tuberculogenic darkness of the alley, the Bools evidently saw it as a place of promise. A prominent sign reads "Boys' School," and a nattily dressed young man, alumnus or teacher?, guides our eye into the space, suggesting a hopeful future for the boys who go to school in this dark alley. The Bools's photographs have

26 *Charles Marville*

Alley at rue Montorgueil, ca. 1856–1865.
Albumen silver print.
Musée Carnavalet, Paris.
Photo Lauros-Giraudon.

27 *Charles Marville*

Tivoli arcade, ca. 1865.
Albumen silver print.
Musée Carnavalet, Paris.
Photo Lauros-Giraudon.

28 *Charles Marville*

Paris Opéra, gallery, ca. 1856–1865.
Albumen silver print.
Musée Carnavalet, Paris.
Photo Lauros-Giraudon.

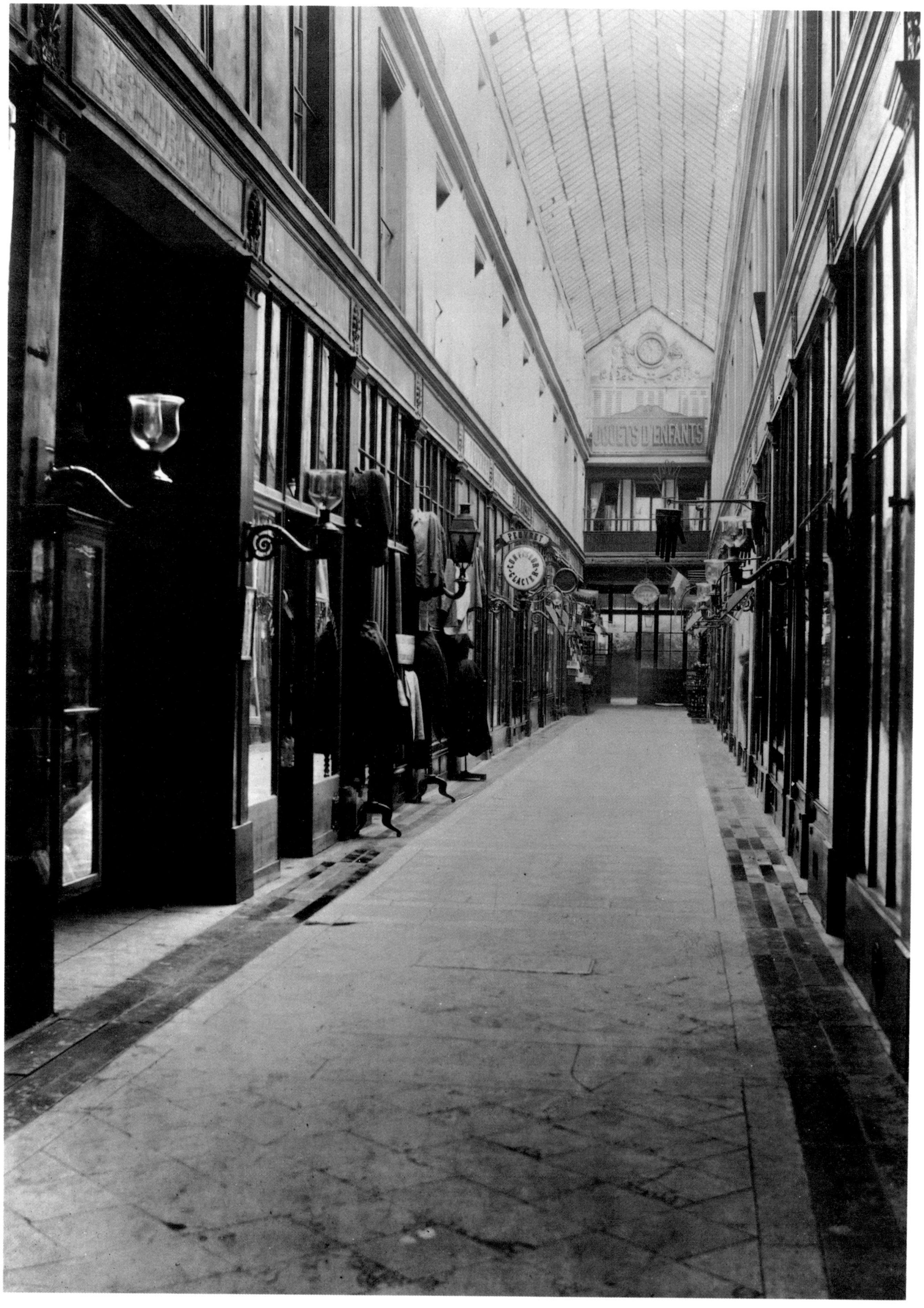

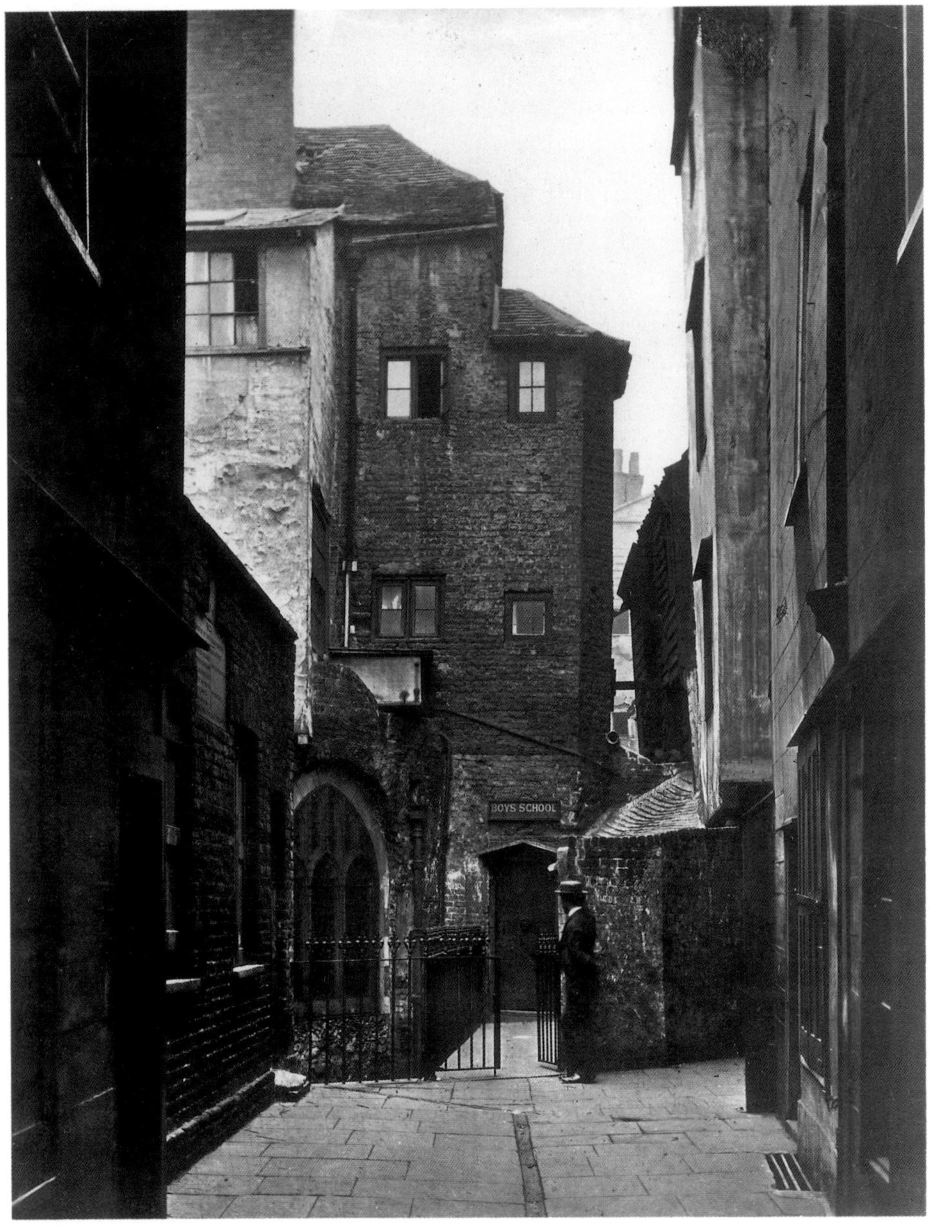

a Puginian quality, not only in the dark tonalities used by Pugin to evoke the richness of medieval architecture as opposed to the pallid face of the neoclasical but even more significantly in the welcoming and humane quality they impart to old buildings.

Essential to the depiction of old cities like London is the sense of an ongoing life. Dixon conveys this feeling in a photograph published in 1883. He attributes the featured building, 73 Cheapside, to Christopher Wren (1632–1723) (30). Despite its antiquity the evolving life of the city has caught it up, so that it has become part of the modern commercial world. This is attested by the multitude of shop and window signs it has sprouted, which reflect the concerns of Victorian society, from consumerism to do-gooding. To underline this adaptation to modern life, Dixon, always meticulous in his compositions, included even more declamatory buildings in the composition. Especially striking is Mr. Wood's next-door optical establishment with the assortment of outsized eyeglass frames that proclaim his métier. This extravaganza receives almost equal billing with the ostensible subject of the photograph. The image is eloquent of the possibilities in adapting old buildings to new uses, a traditional preservationist theme.

The American photographer John Hillers, the hero of many expeditions to the Southwest from 1871 on, applied this approach to photographing old streets to an American Indian pueblo (31). His camera peered down this long, streetlike court so that the buildings surround us, their complex geometry and irregular masonry accentuated by intense contrasts of light and shadow. Hillers presents the pueblo to us as an urban environment. That it is a living city and not a ruin is made clear by the wealth of drying fruit in the foreground, on the platform used by Hillers as a vantage point.

These photographs, with their goal of conveying the urban experience by immersing us in the city's fabric, may be the ancestors of this century's townscape photographs. Another photographic tradition of the period deserves mention in this context. This is the aerial, or bird's-eye view, one of the era's most popular ways of depicting the urban scene. As it has been widely illustrated, two examples might suffice to define its qualities.

The first, dating from after 1876, was taken from the cupola of Soufflot's Panthéon in Paris (32). It shows a large segment of the Left Bank, looking down the newly extended and regularized rue Soufflot toward the Luxembourg Palace and Garden. Beyond we can see Saint-Sulpice and the Invalides. This is not, however, a catalog of famous monuments. The subject of the photograph

29 *A. & J. Bool*

London, St. Bartholomew's and the Cloth Fair, 1877.
From *SPROL* (1877).
Carbon print.
Royal Commission on the Historical Monuments of England.

30 *Henry Dixon*

London, 73 Cheapside, 1883.
From *SPROL* (1883).
Carbon print.
Royal Commission on the Historical Monuments of England.

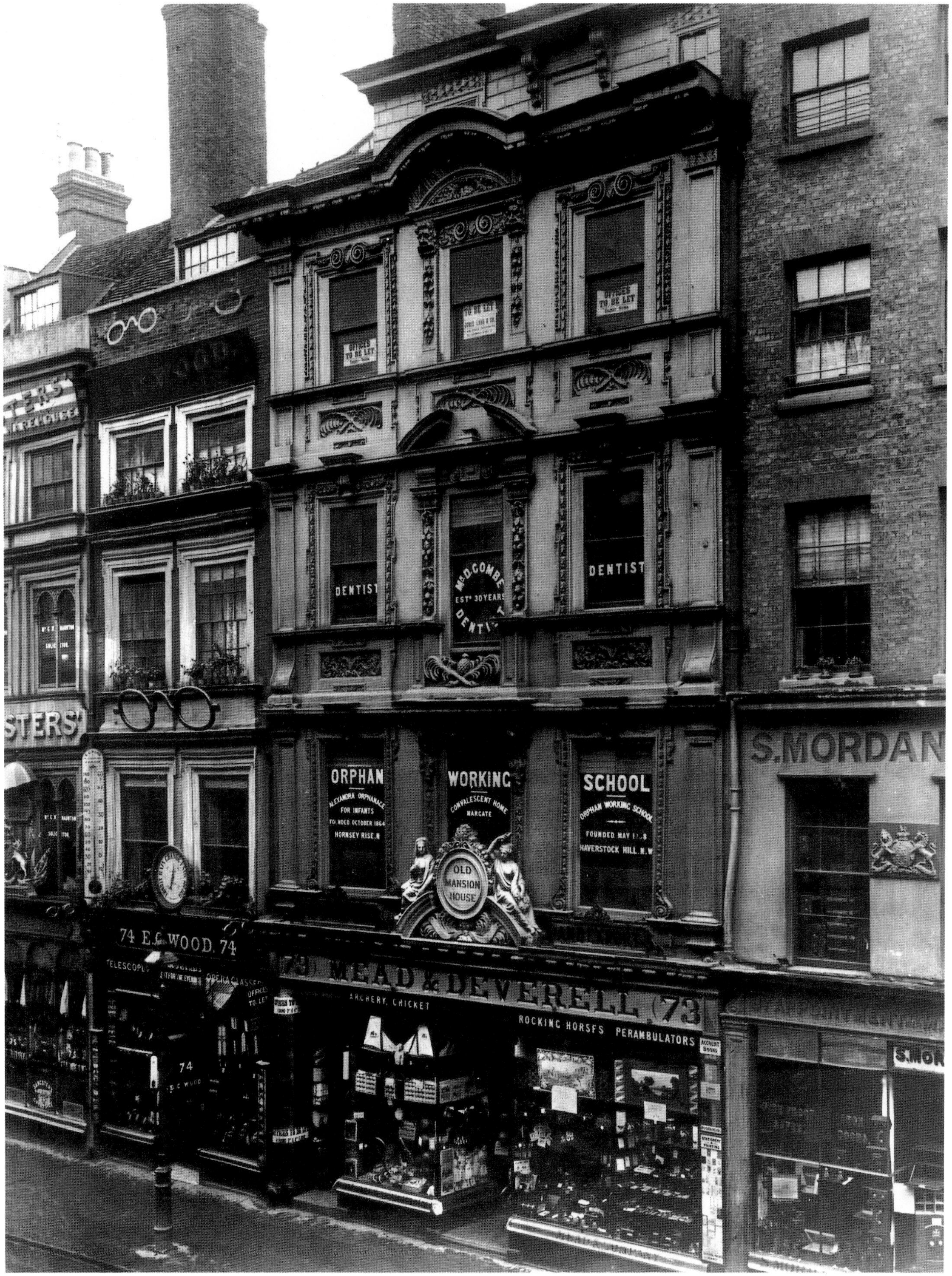

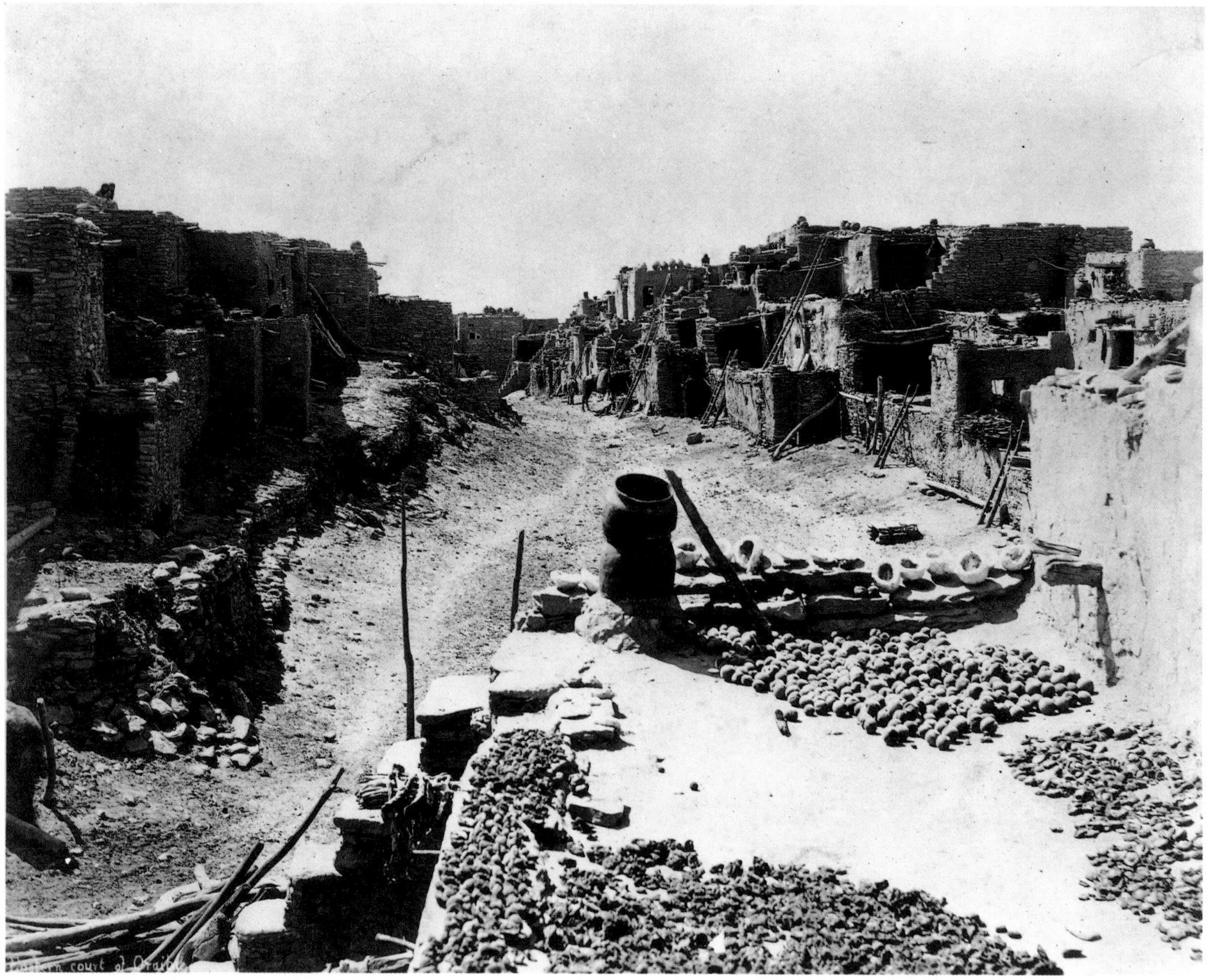

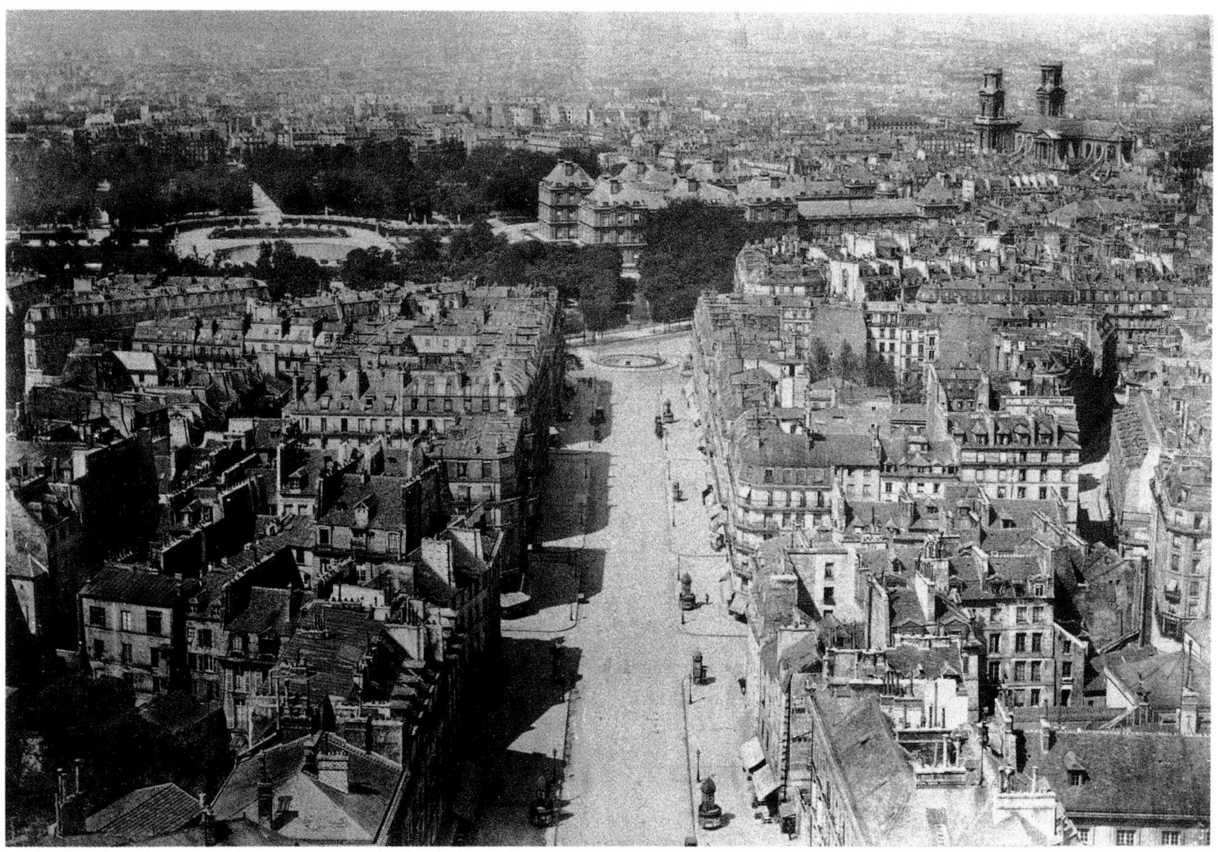

31 *John K. Hillers*

Eastern court of Oraibi, after 1871.
Albumen silver print.
Collections of the Library of Congress.

32 *Photographer unknown*

Paris, panorama from dome of Panthéon, after 1876.
Albumen silver print.
Musée Carnavalet, Paris.

33 *Fratelli Alinari*

Florence, Duomo from dome of San Lorenzo, before 1870.
Albumen silver print.
Courtesy of the Frances Loeb Library, Graduate School of Design, Harvard University.

is the city itself, its density and variety. The contrast is striking between the chaotic, packed roofs of the buildings of the old Sorbonne quarter and the sunlit open space of the recently improved street that leads to the tree-shrouded garden. The redesigning of the rue Soufflot had begun before the inception of Haussmann's work in Paris and was not completed until 1876, five years after the demise of the Second Empire, but it symbolized the effort Haussmann and his colleagues were making to bring light, air, and order to the overcrowded, tuberculosis-ridden city. The photographer used the street to pay tribute to this effort. He paid tribute to another, hardly less important aspect of civic benevolence. The angle of the sun throws into relief not only the regularly positioned street lamps but also the remarkable number of public urinals, nearly one to a corner. This level of amenity is not equaled in the present city. The high visibility given them by the angle of the light leaves no doubt that the photographer saw them as much a contribution to civic well-being as the wide street and leafy park. Sanitary matters were taken seriously at the time. We are in the era of M. de Poubelle, prefect of the Department of the Seine and, in 1884, inventor of the public garbage can.

The bird's-eye view is also valuable in affording an unencumbered view of a large building that is embedded in a city, while at the same time defining the building's relationship to that city. The Alinari photograph of the Florence Duomo taken from the dome of San Lorenzo shows Brunelleschi's great cupola riding above the rooftops (33). Without using extreme, potentially distorting wide-angle lenses, this was the only way to free the cathedral's bulk from its matrix of surrounding buildings. The picture was taken before 1870, when the work began on the new facade. It has the dual merit of showing the entire church while revealing its place in the city and its relationship to the surrounding hills.

Nineteenth-century photographers were somewhat hampered in producing expressive photographs by a certain conservatism in their formal approach. Such modern techniques as tilting the camera upward or downward or using radical perspectives seems to have gone against their sense of what was fitting. Much of the expressive quality of their photographs tended to derive from the things they chose to include or omit from their photographs. This made the device of juxtaposing buildings to buildings or objects to buildings to produce a commentary or interpretation especially welcome. Although deriving from the prephotographic tradition of rendering, it was particularly effective in photography, whose juxtapositions reflected a reality rather than something pasted

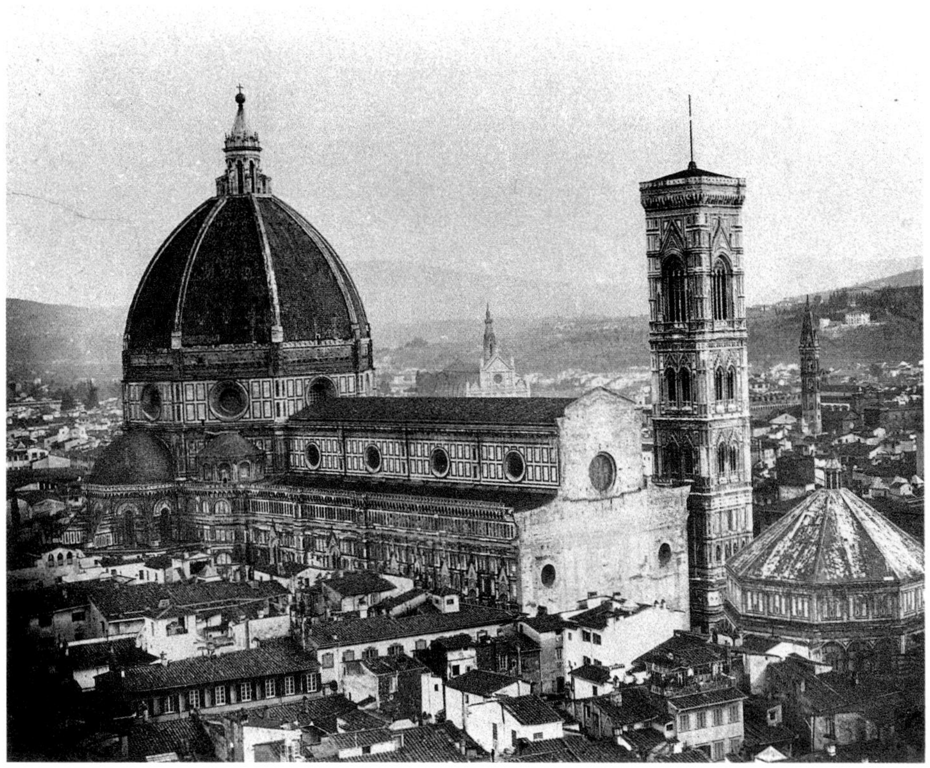

together by artists. Juxtapositions in the period 1839 to 1880 were not as common or as editorially pointed as in our era, but they were part of the armament of photographers from the forties on. The most important form of this technique involved the use of people, as we will see.

In the pioneering era the device can be seen in an 1847 calotype by Fox Talbot of I. K. Brunel's Hungerford Suspension Bridge (1841–45) (34). To the elegant sweep of Brunel's marvel of engineering, Talbot juxtaposed a foreground litter of clumsy sail-powered lighters or river barges, which appear to have been abandoned in the mud. Whatever the reality of the situation being photographed, the contrast depicted in the image makes the statement that the bridge is a revolutionary piece of technology, part of the transport revolution of the age, which has left behind the picturesque but inefficient traditional means of crossing the river. Whether Talbot welcomed the new or regretted the passing of the old is not clear, but the contrast in their forms dramatizes the grace and daring of the bridge.

Juxtapositions could make more specifically architectural statements. A major issue of the period was whether the new "engineer's architecture" introduced by the Crystal Palace deserved the name of architecture. Edouard Baldus's contribution to the discussion is a photograph of an artesian wellhead (1834–41) near the Invalides in Paris (35). The wrought-iron structure with its spiral staircase and Gothic base, typifies the era's desire to find a meeting ground between the new metal construction and the historical forms then considered "art." Atop the structure is a small metal "lantern," an obvious paraphrase of the nearby lantern of the Invalides. Baldus composed his photograph so that the two lanterns are juxtaposed, making their similarity unmistakable. He thus seconds the well designer's claim to architectural status.

As such specifically architectural comparisons are commonplace today, their relative scarcity in the period 1839 to 1880 is surprising, especially since the technique had been established in the public mind through its extremely effective use in Pugin's *Contrasts*. Perhaps the format used by Pugin for contrasting medieval and neoclassical architecture, with two drawings to a page, or facing-page drawings, was hard to adapt to the method of publishing photographs in albums, which emphasized the single image. I have found no clear-cut evidence in books or albums that particular images were meant to be seen in contrast to each other, and the opportunity to make comparisons in a single image is always serendipitous. Photographers apparently were slow to take up

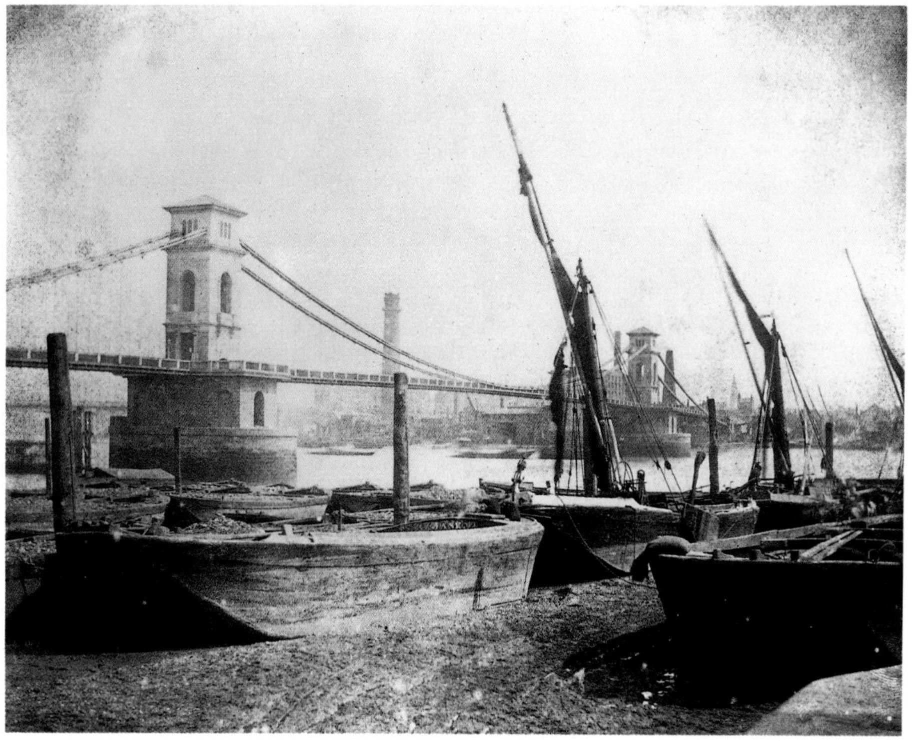

34 *William Henry Fox Talbot*
Hungerford Suspension Bridge, ca. 1847.
Calotype.
Science Museum, London.

35 *Edouard-Denis Baldus*
Paris, artesian well, ca. 1855.
Albumen silver print.
Collections of the Bibliothèque Nationale.

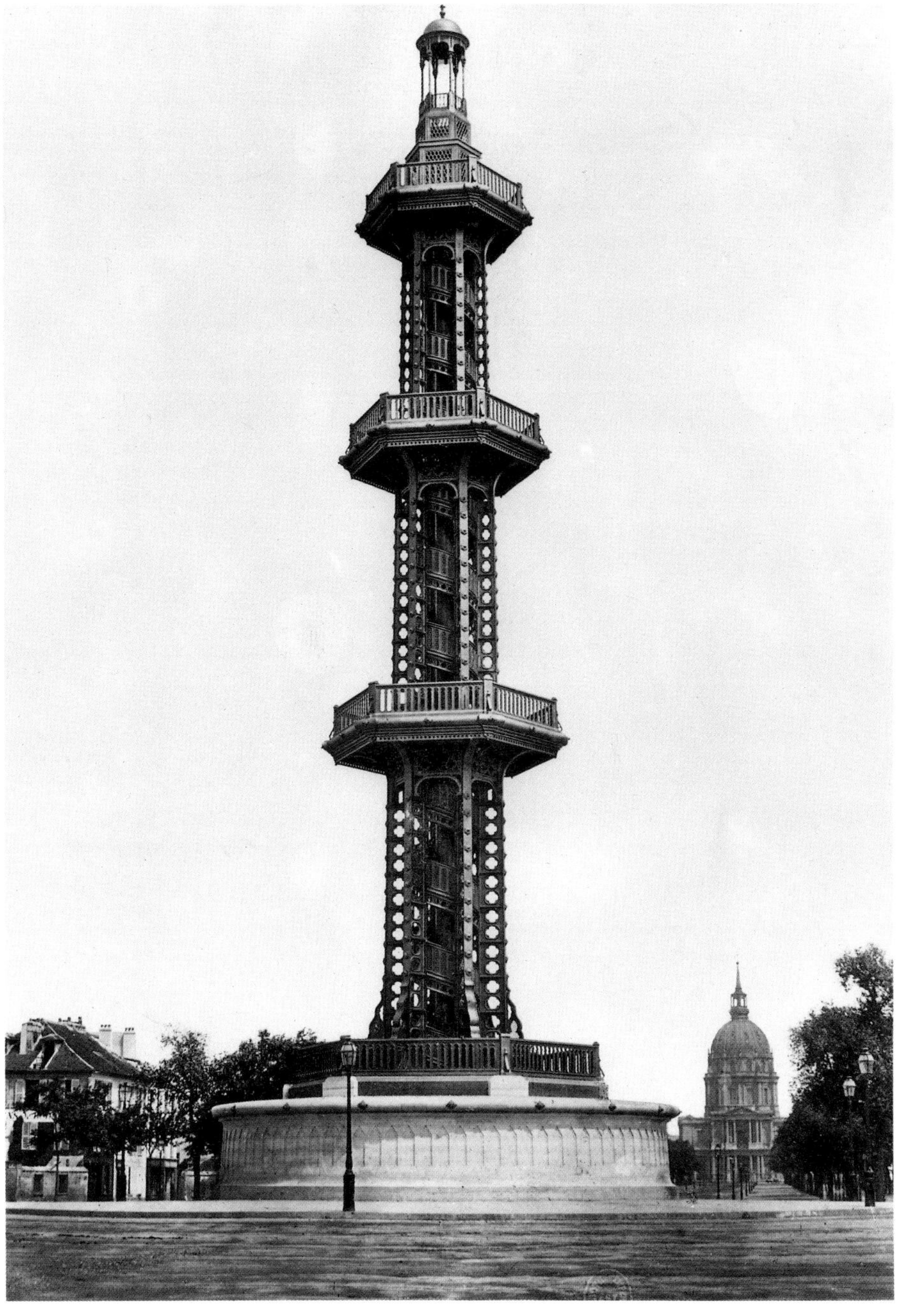

the device, although the twentieth century has more than made up for it. Further research may bring more examples to light.

The "organic metaphor" is a form of architectural comparison that has existed throughout history. Comparisons between architectural and plant forms belong to an ancient tradition going back to the Egyptians but were especially popular in the later eighteenth and nineteenth centuries. John Ruskin championed this approach. In the preface to the second edition of his *Seven Lamps of Architecture*, he stated, "All high art consists in the carving and painting of natural objects" or, as interpreted by Nikolaus Pevsner, "Whatever in architecture is fair, or beautiful, is imitated from natural forms."[20]

Given Ruskin's early interest in photography as a means of documenting architecture, it would be interesting to see the response of photographers to his ideas.[21] In 1862 the English photographer-publishers Cundall, Downes and Co. published a volume, *Wells, Architectural Details of the Cathedral and Close*. Joseph Cundall was well established in the intellectual milieu of photography at this time. He published photographic books and was a founding member of the Calotype Club, with Roger Fenton among others, in 1847.[22] The volume on architecture is accompanied by a volume, *Sculpture of the West Front of Wells Cathedral*, of identical size, layout, and typography. This volume is subtitled "Printed and Photographed for the Architectural Photography Association." As this association was temporarily disbanded in 1861, this is a sort of *opus posthumous*. The association was founded in 1857 by a group of leading architects to improve the level of architectural photography. Its president was Professor Charles Cockerell, and on its board sat, among others, G. G. Scott and Sir James Barry.[23] Presumably, a photographer and publisher like Cundall, who was associating with the leading architectural lights of this era, would have been aware of Ruskin's writings. Indeed, so would have been a large portion of England's literate society.

One of the photographs from *Architectural Details* shows a portion of the nave triforium: the foliate decoration of a spandrel (36). It illustrates perfectly Ruskin's comment on natural objects. It also responds to another of his remarks, that the art of architecture consists in applying to buildings "certain characters venerable or beautiful, but otherwise unnecessary." The leaf is pure applied decoration, without any functional purpose.

Although neither a photographic juxtaposition nor an organic metaphor, another photograph from this volume may have been inspired by Ruskin. It shows the stairs leading to the chapter house at Wells, the famous "sea of

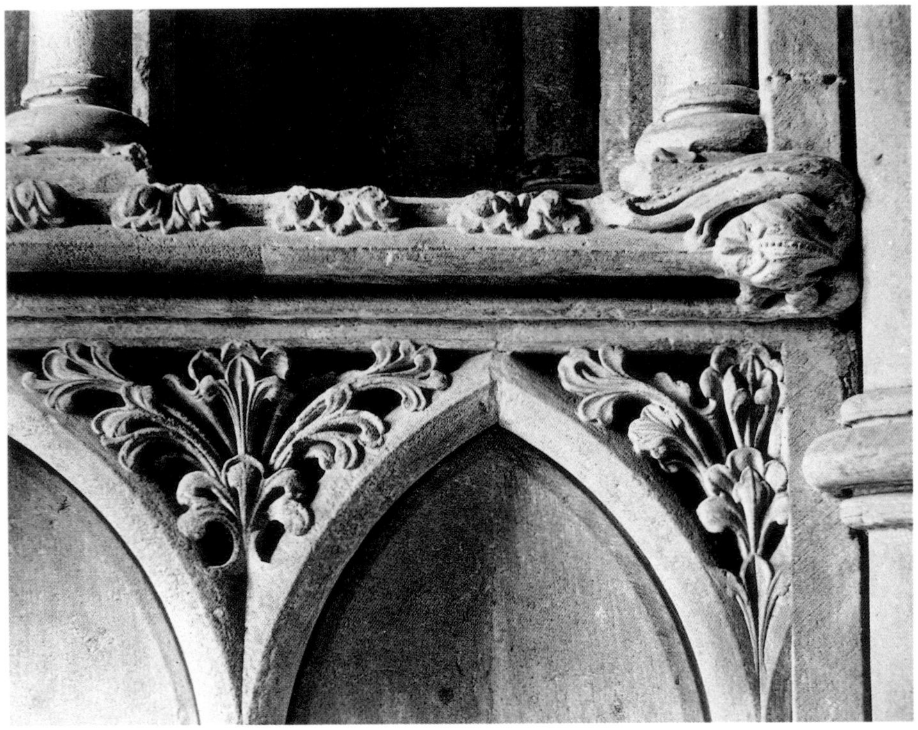

36 *(Joseph) Cundall and Downes & Co.*

Wells, triforium of the nave, detail, 1862.
From *Architectural Details of Wells Cathedral and Close* (1862).
Albumen silver print.
Courtesy of the Board of Trustees of the Victoria and Albert Museum.

steps" later photographed by Frederick Evans (37). Cundall chose a different perspective than Evans. He photographed the steps as though illustrating one of Ruskin's criteria for the true Gothic: ". . . observe if it be irregular, its different parts fitting themselves to different purposes, no one caring what becomes of them, so that they do their work." His photograph depicts that "nonchalance" which to Ruskin was the "sign manual of the broad vision."[24]

The most familiar aspect of nineteenth-century architectural photography probably is the presence of people in association with the architecture. The very ordinariness of the human presence, however, tends to blind us to the complex of meanings it can convey. The role of people in our period belongs to the larger category of juxtaposition and, as with the other aspects of this device, has the purpose of commenting on the architecture or otherwise guiding our perception of it in particular directions.

Innumerable writers on architectural photography have told us that the reason for including people in views of buildings is to establish scale. This frequently is the case, and when it is, the purpose is unmistakable. An example is Désiré Charnay's photograph of the Palace of Mitlá, in the Yucatan (38). This pre-Columbian structure lacks the usual scale indicators of European architecture such as windows, so that the Mexican farmers along its facade are needed to convey a sense of size. They add a touch of local color, but their real purpose is to define scale.

When people stand forth as individuals, or when they clearly represent specific social, ethnic, or occupational types, they carry a weight of meaning that affects our sense of the architecture with which they are associated. They often have been stage-managed by the photographers to provide specific explanations or interpretations of these buildings. That we lack the fine eye for social distinctions that was part of the mental baggage of nineteenth-century Europeans may account for our failure to pick up these meanings. The use of people to convey interpretations of architecture was well established in the graphic arts before the advent of photography. It was, of course, a basic feature of the perspective. Pugin's *Contrasts* provides the most pointed and best-known use of the device, where the age, social class, and demeanor of the people in the engravings manipulates our response to the architecture depicted and is a basic carrier of meaning.

Some indication of the subtlety possible in the use of the human presence is seen in a photograph by Charles Marville, taken in 1860 (39). It shows a man, holding what looks like a measuring stick, standing in the Fontaine des

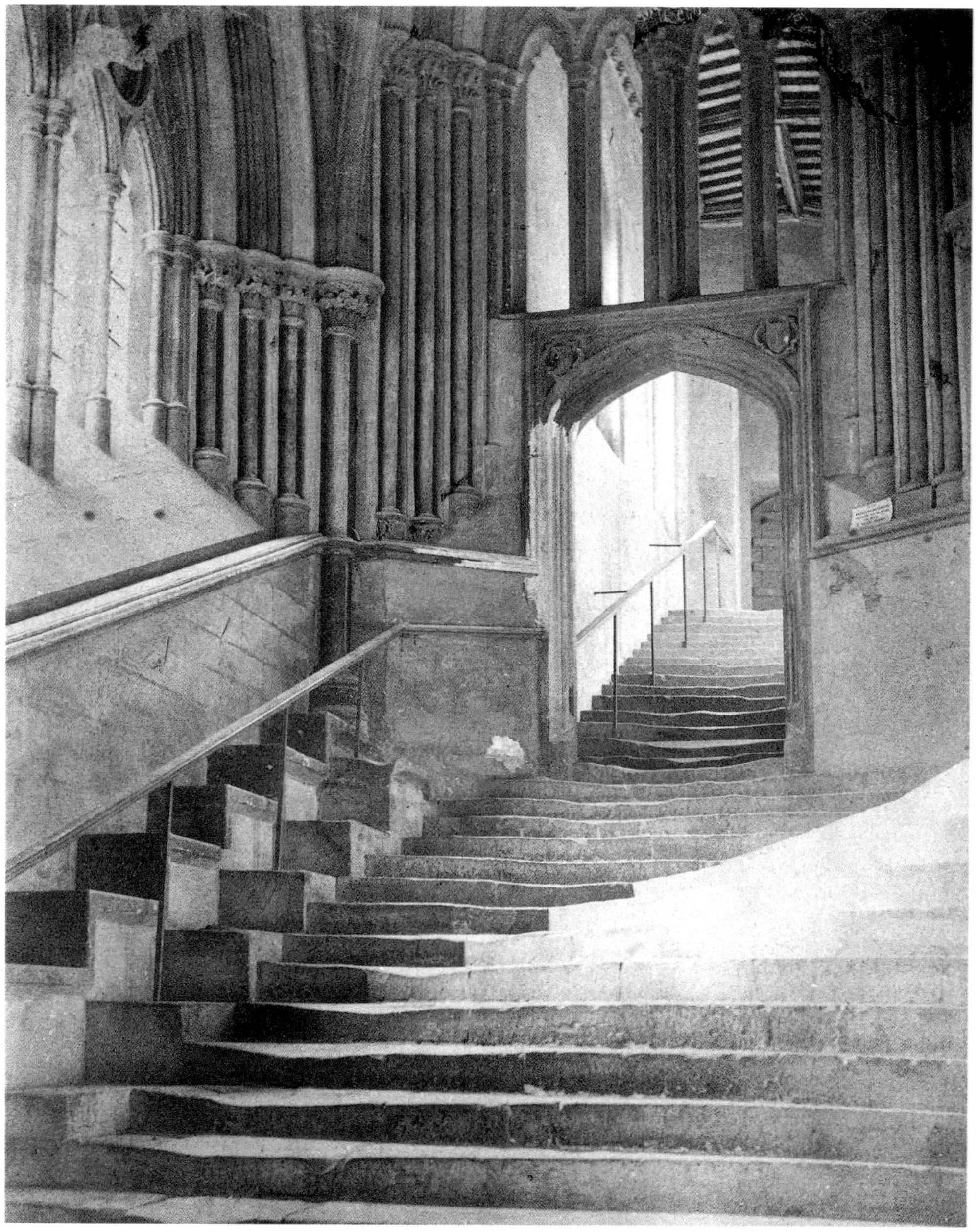

37 *(Joseph) Cundall and Downes & Co.*

Stairs leading to Chapter House, 1862.
From *Architectural Details of Wells Cathedral and Close* (1862).
Albumen silver print.
Courtesy of the Board of Trustees of the Victoria and Albert Museum.

38 *Désiré Charnay*

Palace at Mitlà, ca. 1857–1861.
Albumen silver print.
The J. Paul Getty Museum.

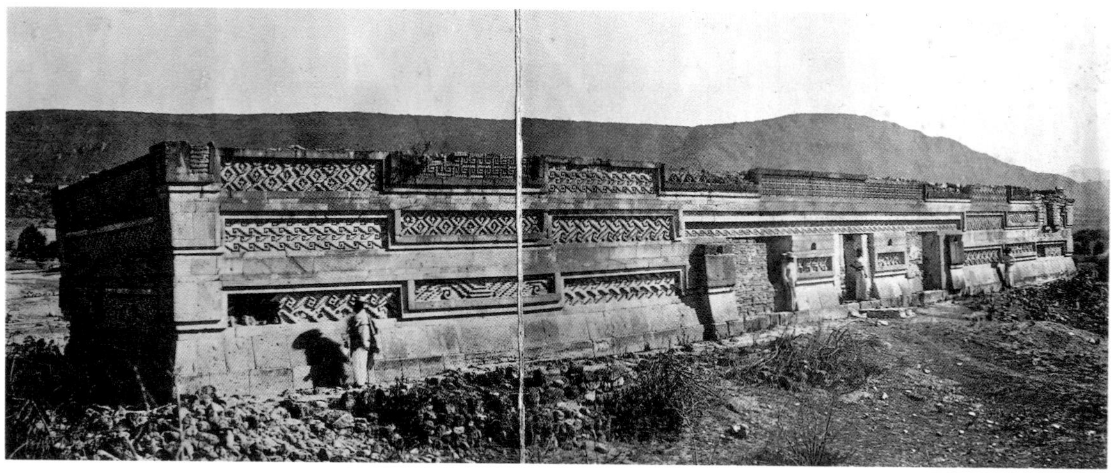

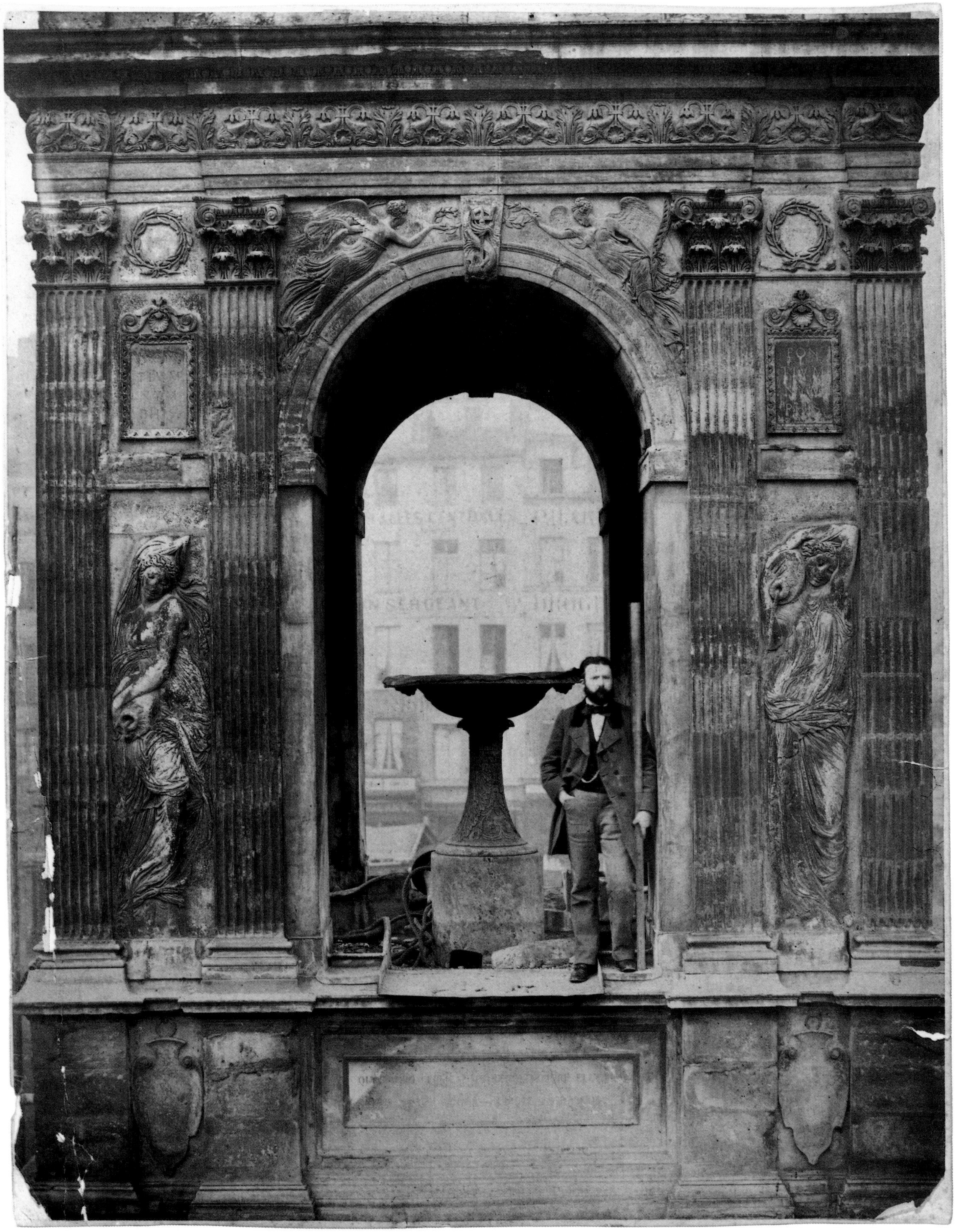

39 *Charles Marville*

Paris, Fontaine des Innocents, ca. 1860.
Albumen silver print.
The J. Paul Getty Museum.

40 *D. O. Hill and Robert Adamson*

Edinburgh, Dennistoun tomb, ca. 1843–1848.
Calotype.
Courtesy of the Board of Trustees of the Victoria and Albert Museum.

Innocents in Paris. The obvious intent was to provide a clear measure of scale. However, the man is no anonymous laborer pressed into service as a scale indicator. He is elegantly dressed and regards us with an air of self-confidence. This photograph was taken during the process of disassembling and moving the fountain in 1860, as is attested by the litter of pipes, ropes, and stone under the arch, and may be part of a series done by Marville of the relocation of the fountain in 1860, of which seven prints are today in the Musée Carnavalet in Paris. Marville, among all the photographers of our period, was particularly fascinated by processes of construction and demolition, as his work eloquently shows.[25] It is most probable that this self-possessed man was, or was meant to be seen as, one of the experts entrusted with the delicate task of moving the fountain and that his measuring stick is a tool of his craft. The photograph is really about the process of moving the structure to its new location and the professional skills required for this process. It fits with a period genre, which shows the workmen and supervisors of a project lined up on a site.

In the forties meaningful juxtapositions of people to architecture were less common and harder to define than in the following decades. D. O. Hill and Robert Adamson's calotype of the Dennistoun tomb in Edinburgh's Greyfriar's churchyard has strong literary overtones, as do many of their photographs (40). The man (Hill?) seated on the tomb copying the inscription is intently watched by two young girls. The dazzling sunlight and the exuberant, baroque tomb contrast with the elegiac mood of the people. The architecture belongs to a distant past but is also part of the ongoing stream of Scotland's history, much as the girls represent ongoing life in the face of death.[26] We cannot be sure if the mood is meant to reflect on the architecture or the architecture is only a foil to help create the mood. In the following decades the uses of people became more explicit and less ambiguous. They help to explain the architecture, to make it more intelligible to the public. This became important as photographers increasingly traveled to exotic places to bring back images of buildings whose form and function were unfamiliar to the audience.

The "local color" approach was relatively modest in intent. It established the geographic or, more specifically, the cultural context of a structure. An example is James Robertson's view of the eighteenth-century fountain of Ahmet III at the entrance to the Old Seraglio in Istanbul (41). This masterpiece of Ottoman craftsmanship has no formal or functional parallels in western architecture. It is placed in the culture that created it, more vividly than by a

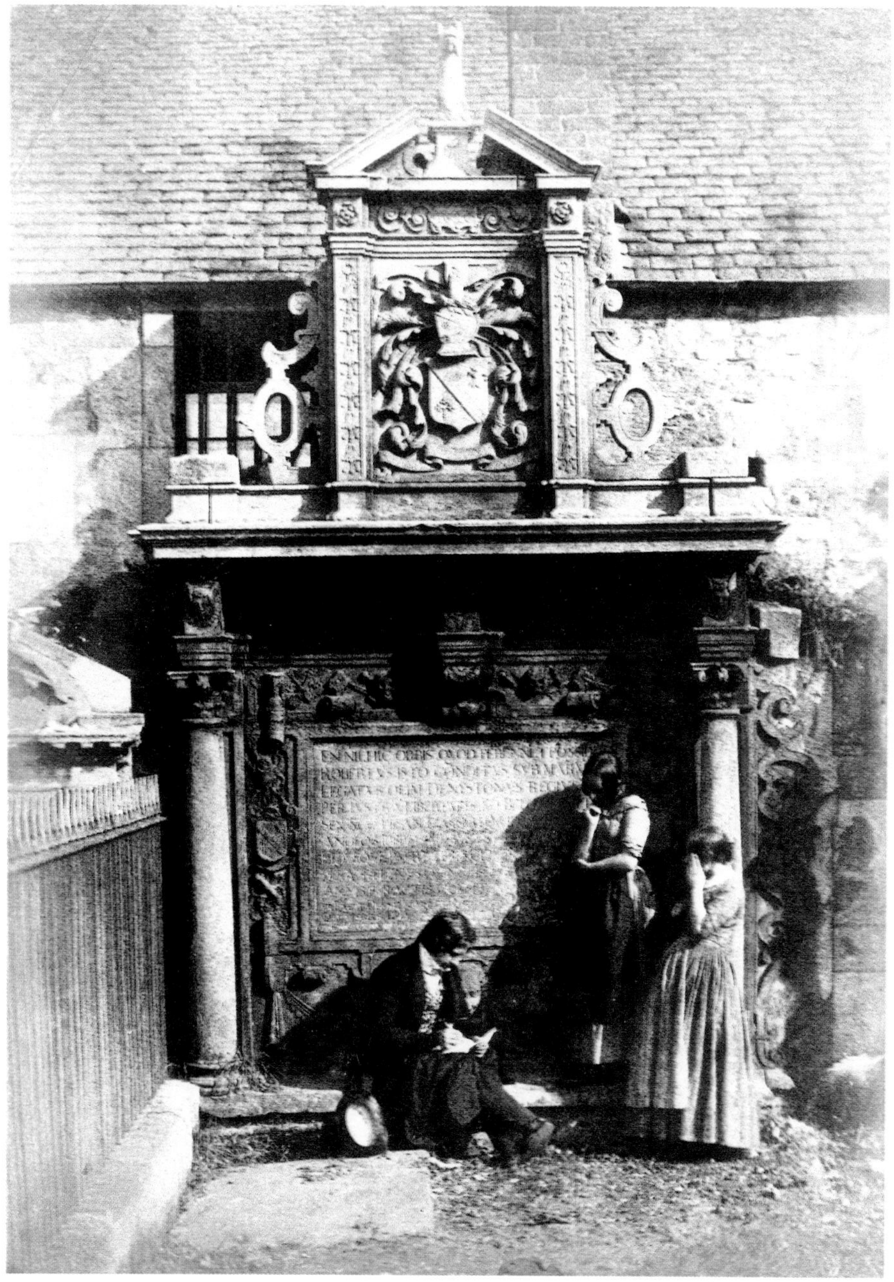

41 *JAMES ROBERTSON*
Constantinople, entrance to Old Seraglio, ca. 1860s.
Albumen silver print.
Courtesy of the Board of Trustees of the Victoria and Albert Museum.

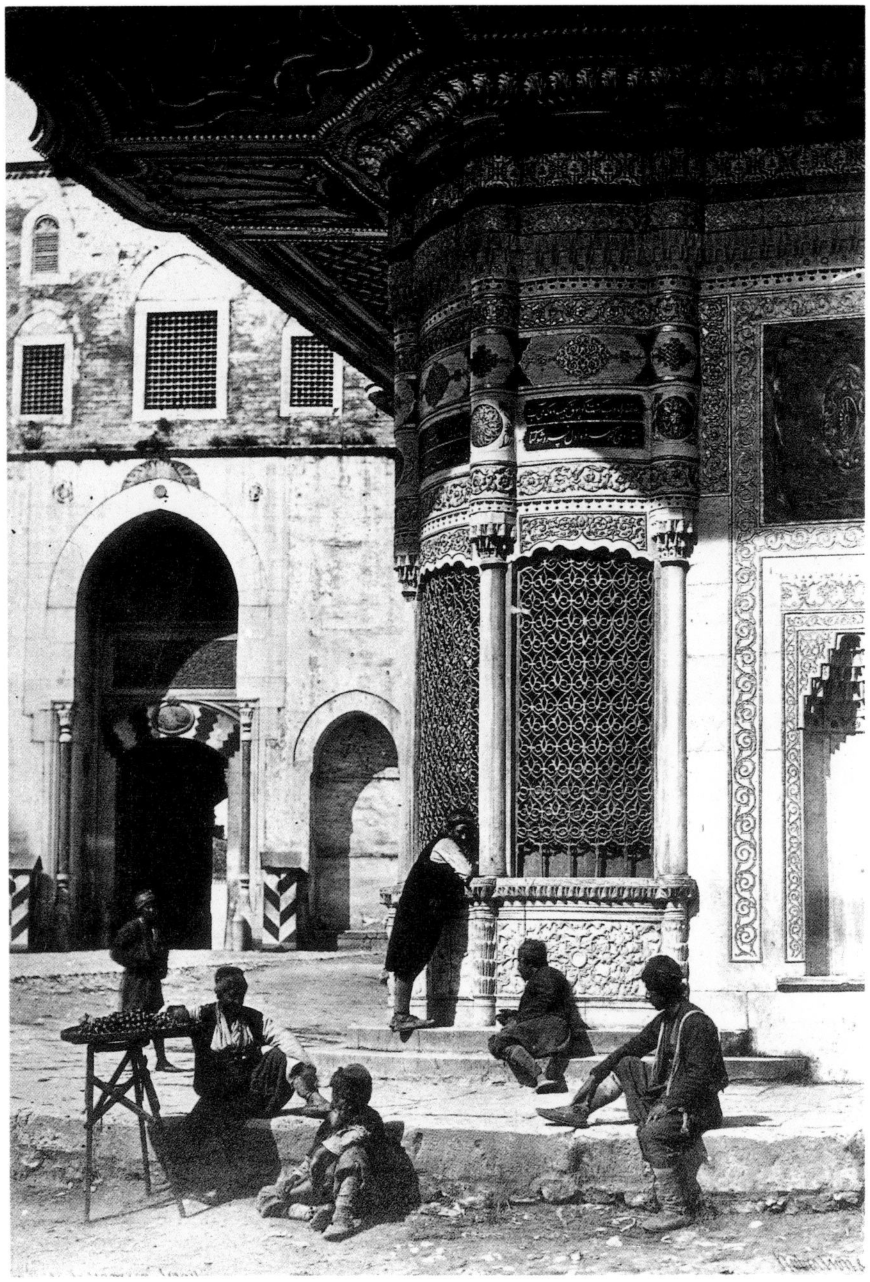

caption, by the Turkish street types carefully posed around it. Some wear the fez, and one offers a tray of (Smyrna?) figs to make the identification more precise. This image has close parallels among Stuart's watercolors on the Acropolis of then-Turkish Athens.

People could also be used to bridge the gap between an alien culture and that of the viewer, thus making a strange building type more intelligible to the audience. No culture seemed more exotic or was more fascinating to mid-century Europeans than Japan, the newly opened land of the "Mikado." Robertson's sometime partner Felix Beato was one of the first western photographers to exploit this fascination, and among those who worked in the orient at this time was one of the most responsive to its cultures. His two-volume study of Japan was published at Yokahama in 1868. The first volume is architectural and topographic; the second one is ethnographic, consisting of posed, hand-colored photographs of characteristic Japanese social and occupational types. Despite their unfamiliar dress and posture, Beato treats them respectfully, as fellow human beings. His approach is exemplified in an image from volume 1 that shows a Japanese couple kneeling in a strange little house (42). Our first impression is of two exotic people in an odd piece of architecture. Beato, however, has used the people to bridge the cultural gap and to link this building to a known western type and social situation. They are a far cry from the rustics found as human furniture in photographs of the period. Beato posed them as an aristocratic couple, the man's Samurai rank proclaimed by the sword hilt at his side. They look out at us with upper-class self-assurance, apparently welcoming us (the lady's mouth is open as if speaking) to the garden of a large house in which the structure is set. This social behavior may be more western than Japanese. By showing this gracious couple receiving us in a manner that reminds us of their aristocratic European counterparts, Beato evokes a recognition of the European equivalent of the little house. It is a Japanese version of a gazebo, that indispensible appurtenance of European noble estates in the nineteenth century.

As we have noted, the most impressive prephotographic use of the human presence in architectural images was in Pugin's *Contrasts,* in which people acted out the contrasting social implications of medieval and the current neoclassical architecture. The piety and benevolence of the Middle Ages which suffuse its "Christian" architecture, as Pugin called the Gothic, was conveyed through people shown in prayer. A photograph dating from before 1882 and found in the collection of Henry Hobson Richardson shows the interior of the

42 *Felix Beato*

Tycoons' halting place on the Tocaido Hasa, 1868.
From *Photographic Views of Japan* (1868).
Albumen silver print.
Courtesy of the Board of Trustees of the Victoria and Albert Museum.

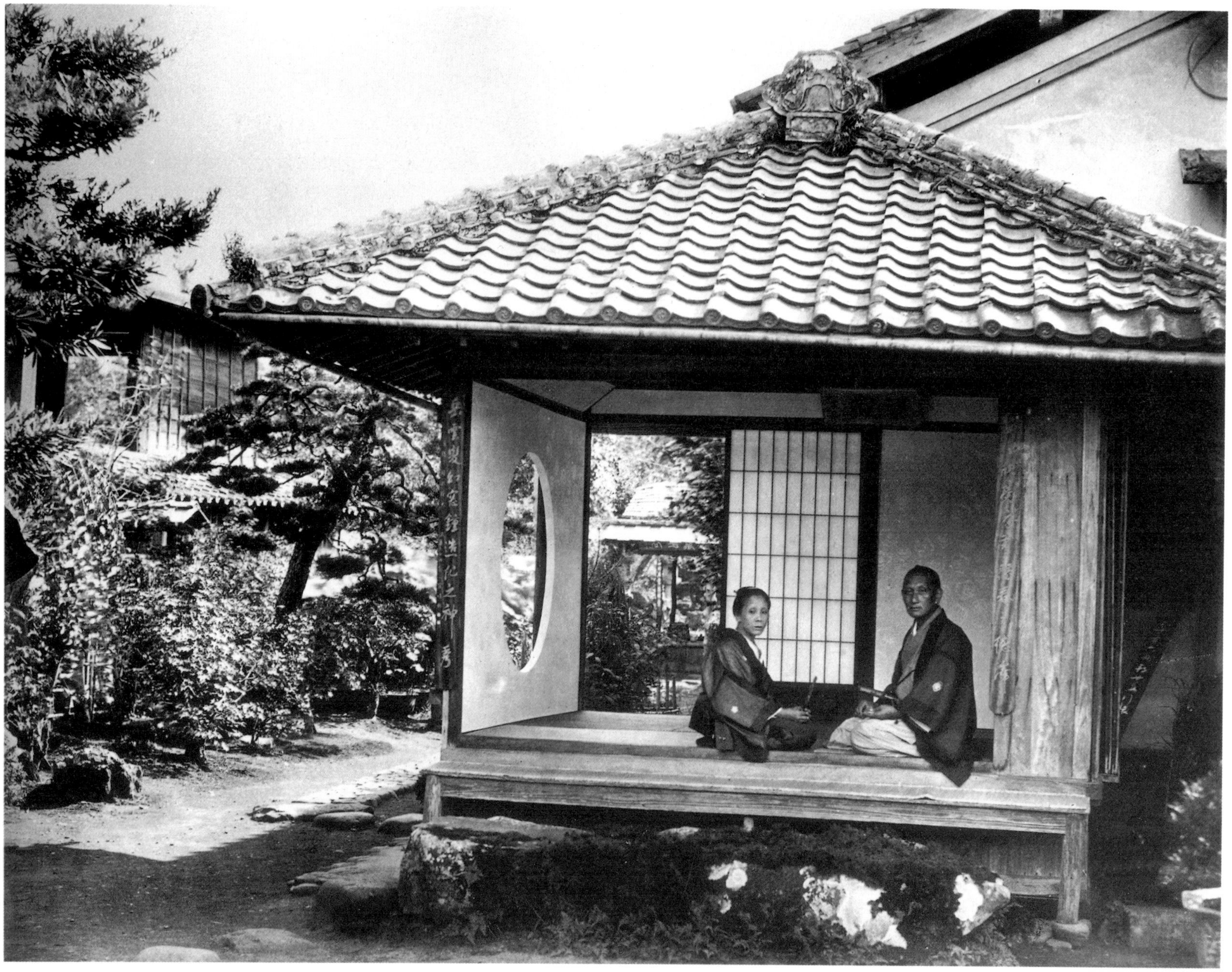

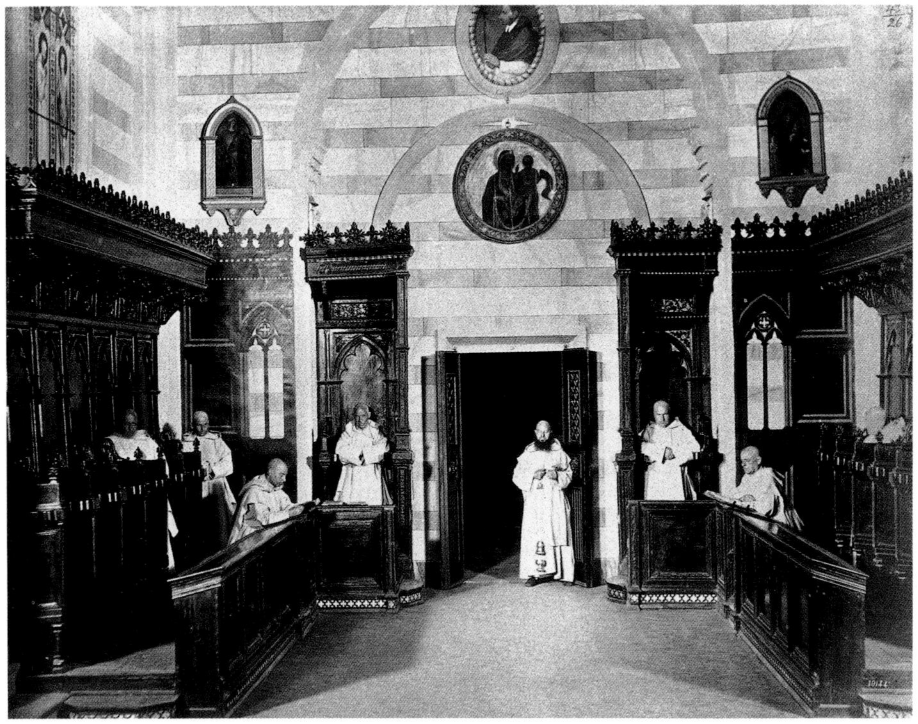

43 *FRATELLI ALINARI*
Florence, Charterhouse, before 1882.
Albumen silver print.
Courtesy of the Frances Loeb Library, Graduate School of Design, Harvard University.

Charterhouse in Florence (43). The chapel's Tuscan architecture and Gothic choir stalls are populated by solemn monks. These relics of the Age of Faith, the Middle Ages, are absorbed in their devotions. They underline the religious vocation of the architecture in the same way as the people at prayer in Pugin's engravings.

An important use of people is intended not so much to comment on the architecture as to convey something about the nature of the photograph itself. Vicarious travel, a major literary genre of the era, played a significant role in the appeal of photography from the time of Lerebours' *Excursions Daguérriennes.* The photograph, with its verisimilitude, could transmit the experience of being in a foreign locale with a directness and immediacy equaled by no other medium prior to the invention of motion pictures. At a time when foreign travel was out of reach of all but the rich, very adventurous, or the desperate, the photograph was a means of bringing foreign places safely home to the firesides of Europe. Many of the books and albums of photography's first decades were also travel books, making available scenes from relatively inaccessible places such as Mexico, China, Egypt, and the Holy Land.

A clear statement of this is found in the introduction to what may be the first book on an architectural subject to integrate photographs and text on the same page, William and Mary Howitt's *Ruined Abbeys and Castles of Great Britain* of 1861: "The publisher has availed himself of the accuracy of photography to present to the reader the precise aspect of the places which, at the same time, are commended to his notice by the pen, . . . so that [he] will be able to feel, when reading of new scenes and lands, that [he is] not amused by pleasant fictions, but presented with realities."[27] Reality, or the sense that no artist's hand or eye has intervened between the thing itself and the viewer of the photograph, was the new medium's great appeal against the traditional forms, which require an artist's interpretation of a scene. In drawings or graphic representations of architecture or topography, a view of the artist at work is not unusual; however, photographs that show the photographer at work are rare. A few show cameras, but they are almost always unattended, as though taking the picture by themselves without human assistance. (In an age of long time exposures this was not wholly a fiction.)

In order to compete with the established and technically virtuosic draftsmen, the photographers had to lean heavily on their version of "truth"—that the photograph was as close as possible to the thing itself—without the distorting intervention of an artist's mind or hand. Conveniently ignored were the elaborate manipulations undertaken by photographers to produce a desired image, including drawing or painting on the negative to enhance or eliminate details. This was a good reason to downplay the photographer's presence, so that the viewer could sustain the illusion that he is confronting "reality" and not someone's invention. Francis Frith's delightful, chatty text in his *Egypt and Palestine* of 1857 weaves a spell that convinces the reader that he is accompanying the photographer on his travels, so that the photographs become the scenes he sees on the vividly described journey.

The substitute presence is a device frequently used to sustain the illusion of the thing itself. Respectable, well-dressed westerners, "people like us," are shown looking at the scene in the photograph, as though they are seeing it for us. This is found throughout the book, which is the source of our quote, the Howitts's *Ruined Abbeys and Castles.* They commissioned some of England's leading photographers to make the small albumen prints that were glued into spaces left in the printed text, which wavers between historical scholarship and touristic description (44). Many of the photographs show a small figure or figures in the foreground, most often with their backs to the camera and looking at the building from the same angle as the lens. They are well dressed in upper-class fashion and stand in attitudes of rapt attention. Unlike the artists in lithographs or drawings, who are seen in the process of creating the image, they are merely looking, so that we may see the scene through their eyes. The objective medium of photography permits us to see it as directly, therefore "truthfully," as they do.

The country house photograph was and is essentially an English genre. Its appeal was at once architectural and snobbish. The country seats of distinguished persons were the usual subject matter, and they are identified in the albums in which these photographs were distributed by the names of their proprietors. These personages were too grand to appear in the photographs, although one might be seen on the lawn astride a fine horse. Lesser mortals (parvenus?) might, however, allow themselves a little self-display. A view of Oakley Hall reflects this. A Tudor style extravaganza built in 1859 by its "present owner," it was photographed a few years later by Beard and Co. of Twyford for their album *Seats and Manors of Berkshire* (45). The long view reveals a stretch of well-trimmed lawn on which the photographer has assembled a number of people, perhaps the proud owner, his family, and selected servants. They lend an air of affluence to the house but, more important, demonstrate that this is a "family seat," with all that that implied for Victori-

his quarters in the abbey. James IV. was the builder of the palace, for the Scottiſh monarchs ſeem greatly to have preferred its ſheltered ſituation to the expoſed one of the caſtle. This muſt have been not later than 1500, for here in 1503, he received

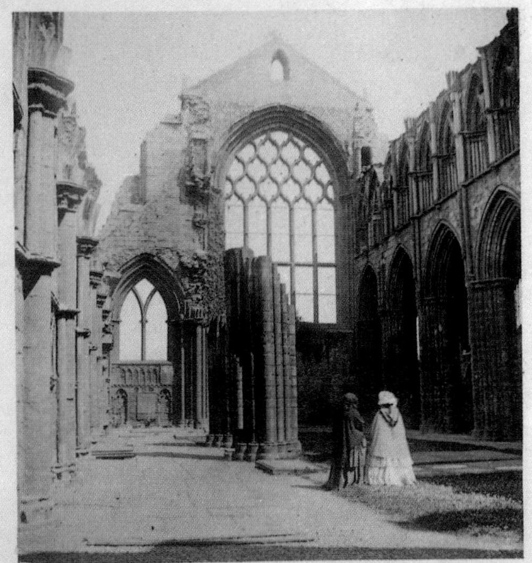

HOLYROOD ABBEY; INTERIOR.

Margaret of England, and here they were married. In 1544, the abbey and palace were burnt by the Engliſh army: this, however, muſt have been with exception of the towers in front. From this time the abbey church ſeems to have become the chapel of the palace—a chaplain being maintained

44 *George Washington Wilson*
Holyrood Abbey, ca. 1861.
From William and Mary Howitt, *Ruined Abbeys and Castles of Great Britain* (1861).
Albumen silver print glued to letterpress-printed page.
Collections of the Library of Congress.

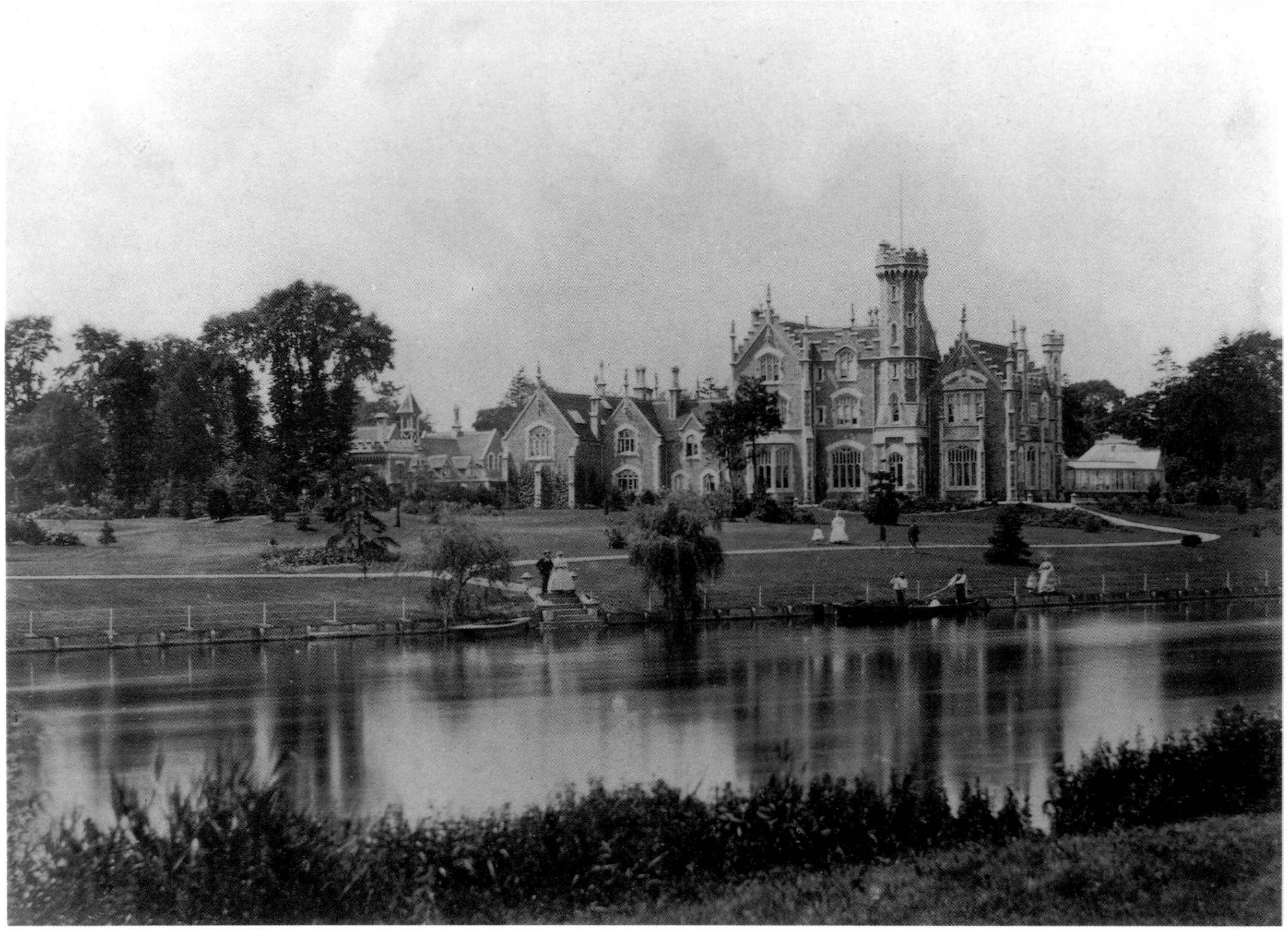

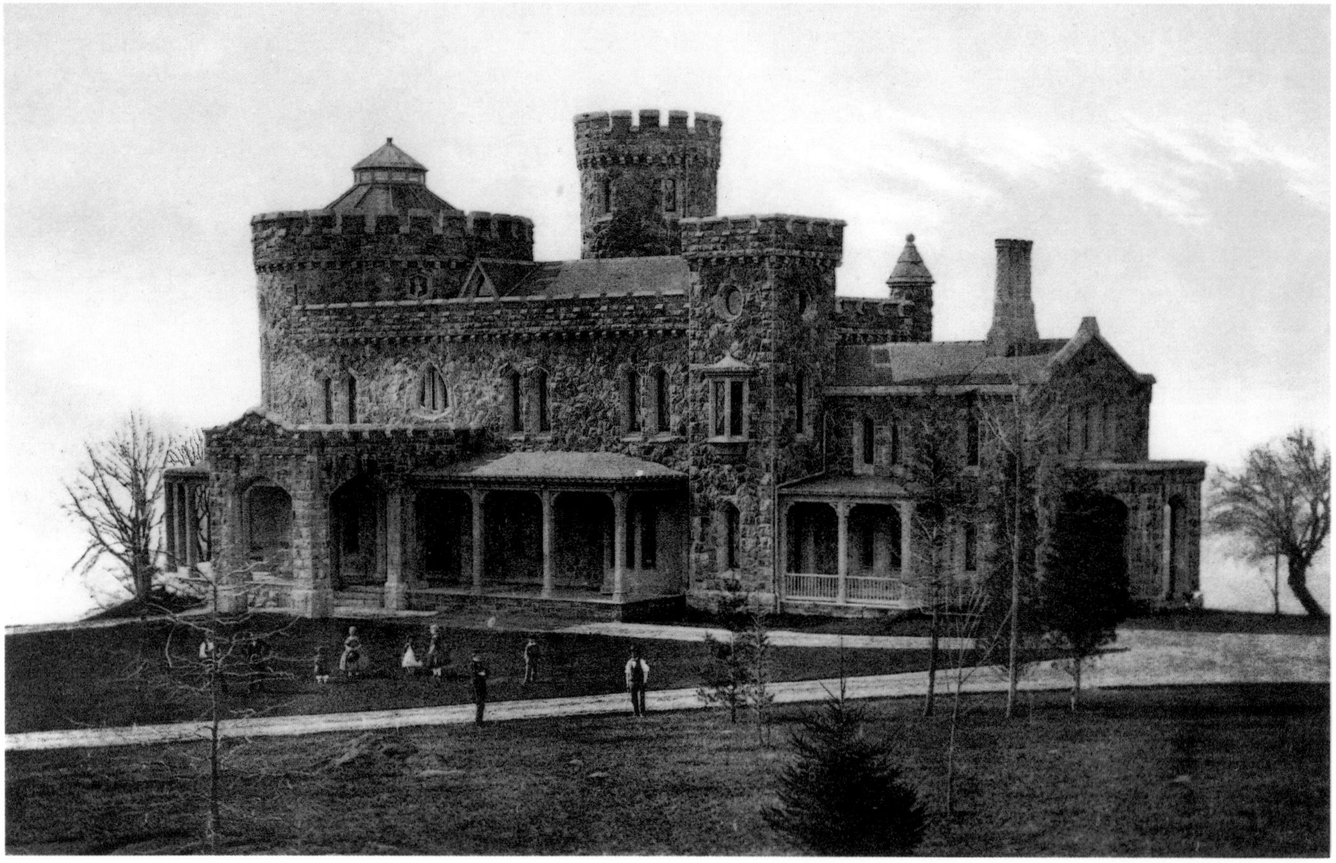

45 *Beard & Co., Twyford*

Oakley Hall, ca. 1860.
From *Seats and Manors of Berkshire.*
Royal Commission on the Historical Monuments of England.

46 *A. A. Turner*

Herrick residence, Tarrytown, N.Y., 1860.
From *Villas on the Hudson* (1860).
Hand-tinted photolithograph.
Collections of the Library of Congress.

ans. A related effect can be seen in a classic perspective of a country house from *Villas on the Hudson,* showing the Herrick residence in Tarrytown, New York (46). A comparison might be made between these and Beato's Japanese "gazebo" (42).

As the nineteenth century's new medium for representing architecture, photography was especially suited to a partnership with the era's newest form of architecture, then called "engineer's architecture." Both were children of the Industrial Revolution and came of age in the pivotal year 1851. Joseph Paxton's Crystal Palace of that year was the first structure to demonstrate the feasibility of a building technique using metal and industrial processes on a large scale. We have already seen the importance of this year to the nascent profession of architectural photography. The new architecture shared with photography the potential of accommodating many people at a significantly lower cost than had been possible with traditional methods by lending itself to industrial methods of production. Paxton's use of factories to turn out modular structural units, units that could be assembled by semiskilled workmen, is comparable to Blanquart-Evrard's partly realized dream of using mass-production techniques to produce quantities of identical, reasonably priced photographic prints.

The new architecture had a more specific appeal for photographers of the fifties and sixties. Although the technical improvements of those years combined with their skill and patience enabled them to overcome most of the limitations of their materials and equipment in photographing static objects, there was one area in which the problems would not be solved for some years: photography in low light levels. Even if adequately corrected lenses of relative apertures comparable to those of modern view camera lenses had been available, emulsions had such low sensitivity that long exposures were still necessary. In the interiors of most masonry buildings, failure of reciprocity would stretch exposures out to impossible lengths. From the forties well into the sixties, the rare interiors photographed tended to be highly luminous Gothic churches with a minimum of stained glass (47). In the later sixties and especially in the seventies as the dry-plate process was perfected, the problem of dimly lit interiors became more manageable, as reflected in Mieusement's albums of French châteaus of the 1870s, which have a large proportion of interior views (48).

The new, greenhouselike exhibition buildings that followed the Crystal Palace, with their great expanses of glass roofing held in thin iron frames, were practically the only buildings of the period lit well enough to permit photographs of large interior spaces. The Paris Universal Exhibition of 1855, housed in such a building, was given extensive coverage by the English team of C. Thurston Thompson and R. J. Bingham (49). They photographed the installation of exhibits of national manufactures in great detail, taking advantage of the bright light transmitted by the iron and glass roof. The process was highly industrialized, with massive hoisting equipment running on rails set into the floor. Thompson and Bingham dwelt lovingly on the complex industrial technology in use. Its interplay with the impressively technological architecture, brought out by the low camera position, implies an early machine aesthetic. C. Thurston Thompson was an important figure in English photography. He photographed for the South Kensington Museum, later to be the Victoria and Albert Museum, and from 1856 on trained a detachment of sappers from the Royal Corps of Engineers to become photographers there. Thompson worked with Captain John Donnelly of the Royal Engineers, who was in charge of the museum's negative store and printing establishment.[28] Captain Donnelly, whose engineering background very likely predisposed him to technological architecture, sponsored an album that documents the building of the South Kensington Museum from 1862 to 1898. It includes a view of the famous "Brompton Boilers" (1856), a pioneering example of metal construction and the provisional home of the museum (50). The most systematic album of this type was presented to the museum by Sir Charles Dilke. It shows the construction of the buildings for the London Exhibition of 1862. Each image is dated on the plate so that the "progress of the building" can be followed with precision (51, 52). Techniques of construction—the raising of trusses, the cleating of the cast-iron piers into the subfloor, and the laying of drains—are studied in great detail. This album served as a reportage on up-to-date methods of construction technology in 1862. It prefigures the Chevojon photographs of Dutert and Contamine's Galérie des Machines by twenty-seven years.

Exposition buildings were not the only representatives of "engineer's architecture" in the period. The railroads, which had emerged as the greatest force in the area of transportation, were major patrons of this form of construction, from the train sheds of urban termini to the bridges and viaducts that carried the right-of-way over rivers and into cities. The latter were the subject of some of the century's best-known photographs. Less familiar but as important were certain specialized building types that were developed to meet the needs of the railroads. A. Collard's 1858 photograph of a locomotive roundhouse is elo-

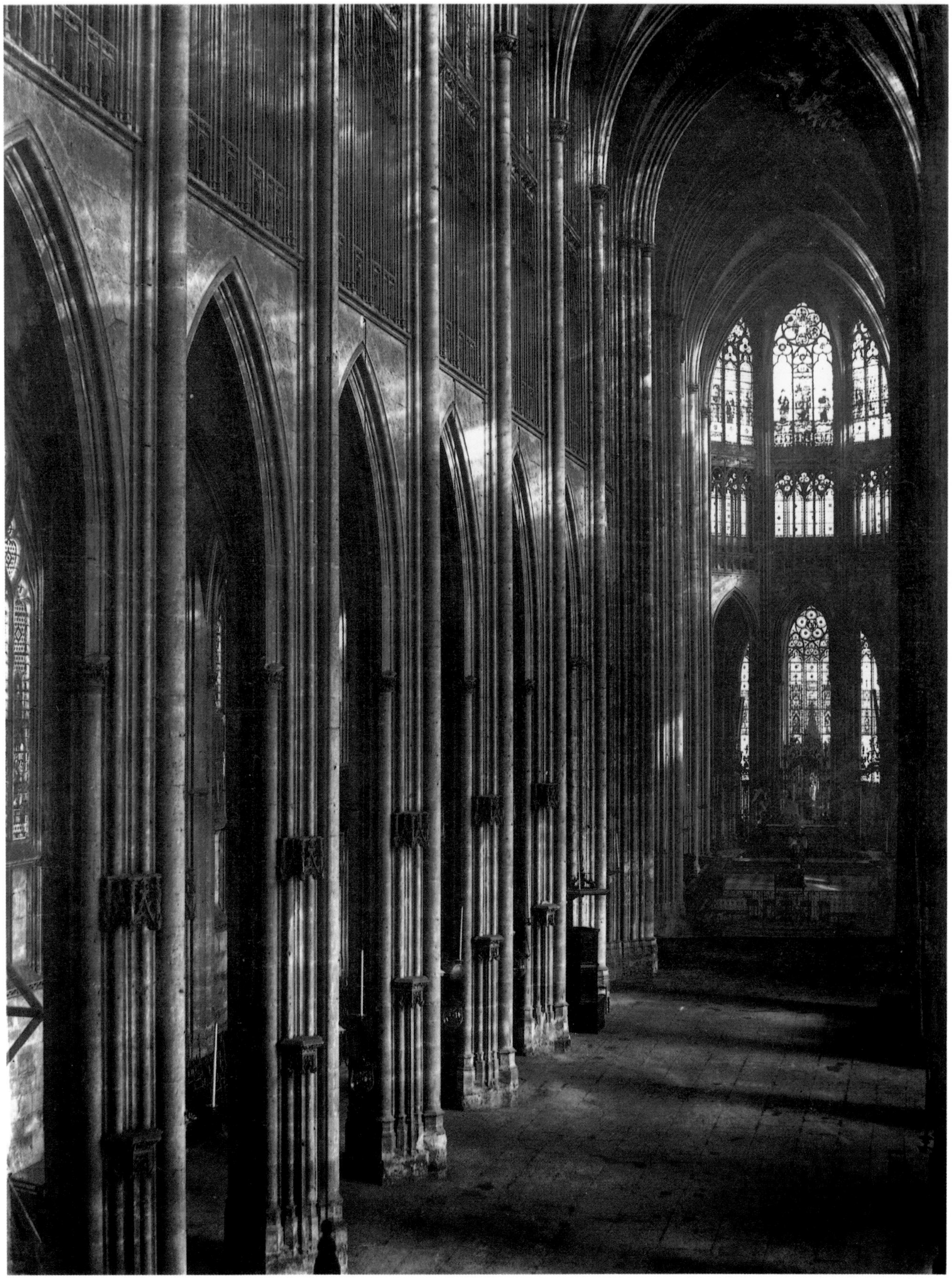

47 *Bisson Frères*

Rouen, St.-Ouen, interior, ca. 1855.
Albumen silver print.
The J. Paul Getty Museum.

48 *Mieusement*

Chateau de Blois, meeting hall, ca. 1875.
From *Chateau de Blois* (1875).
Woodburytype.
Collections of the Bibliothèque Nationale.

49 *R. J. Bingham*

Paris Universal Exhibition, state of the arrangements on the first of May, 1855.
From C. Thurston Thompson and R.J. Bingham, *Paris Universal Exhibition of 1855*.
Albumen silver print.
Courtesy of the Board of Trustees of the Victoria and Albert Museum.

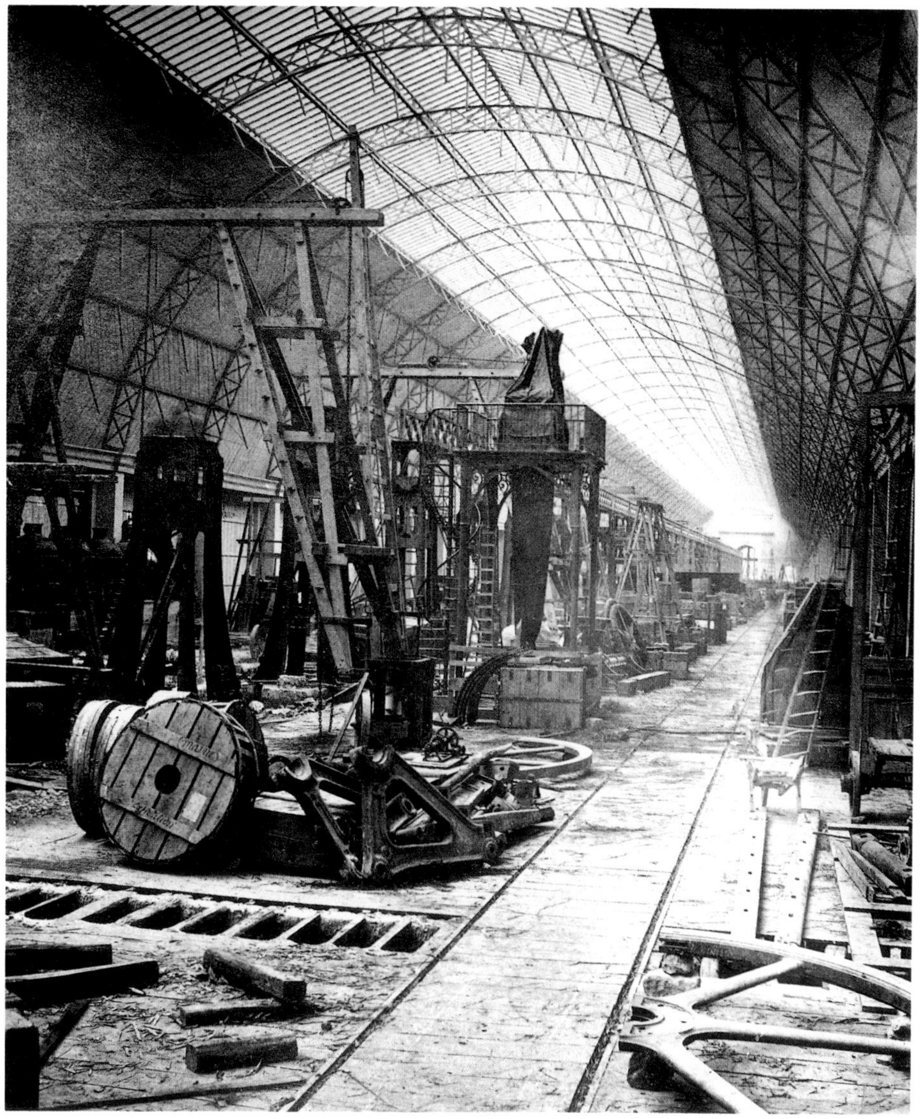

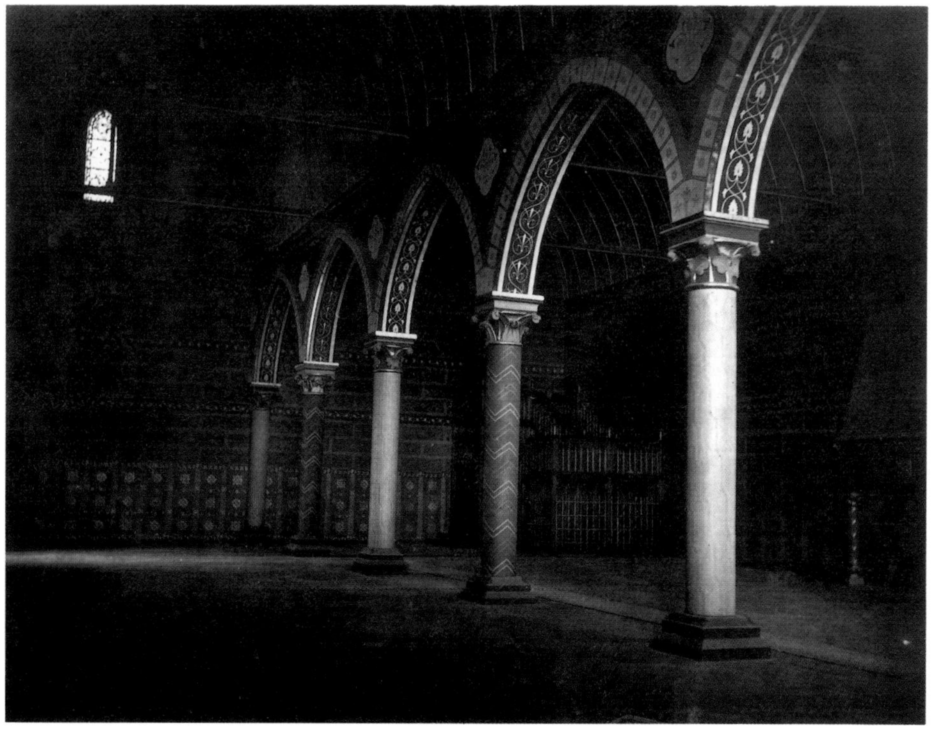

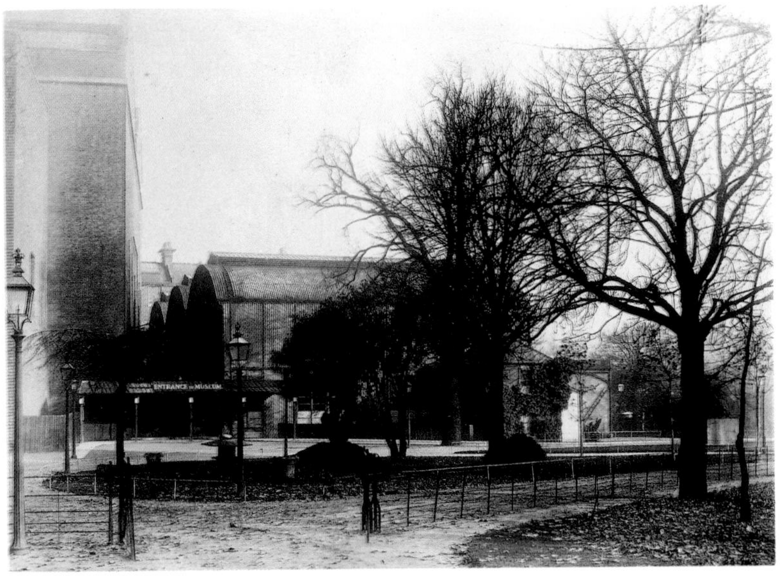

50 *PHOTOGRAPHER UNKNOWN*

Brompton boilers.
From *Donnelly Album, Construction of the South Kensington Museum, 1862–1898*, n.d., 1860s.
Albumen silver print.
Courtesy of the Board of Trustees of the Victoria and Albert Museum.

51 *PHOTOGRAPHER UNKNOWN*

Hoist of nave rib, 21 October 1861.
From *The Exhibit of 1862*, presented by Sir C. W. Dilke.
Albumen silver print.
Courtesy of the Board of Trustees of the Victoria and Albert Museum.

52 *PHOTOGRAPHER UNKNOWN*

Base of nave columns with drains and bracing, 8 February 1862.
From *The Exhibit of 1862*, presented by Sir C. W. Dilke.
Albumen silver print.
Courtesy of the Board of Trustees of the Victoria and Albert Museum.

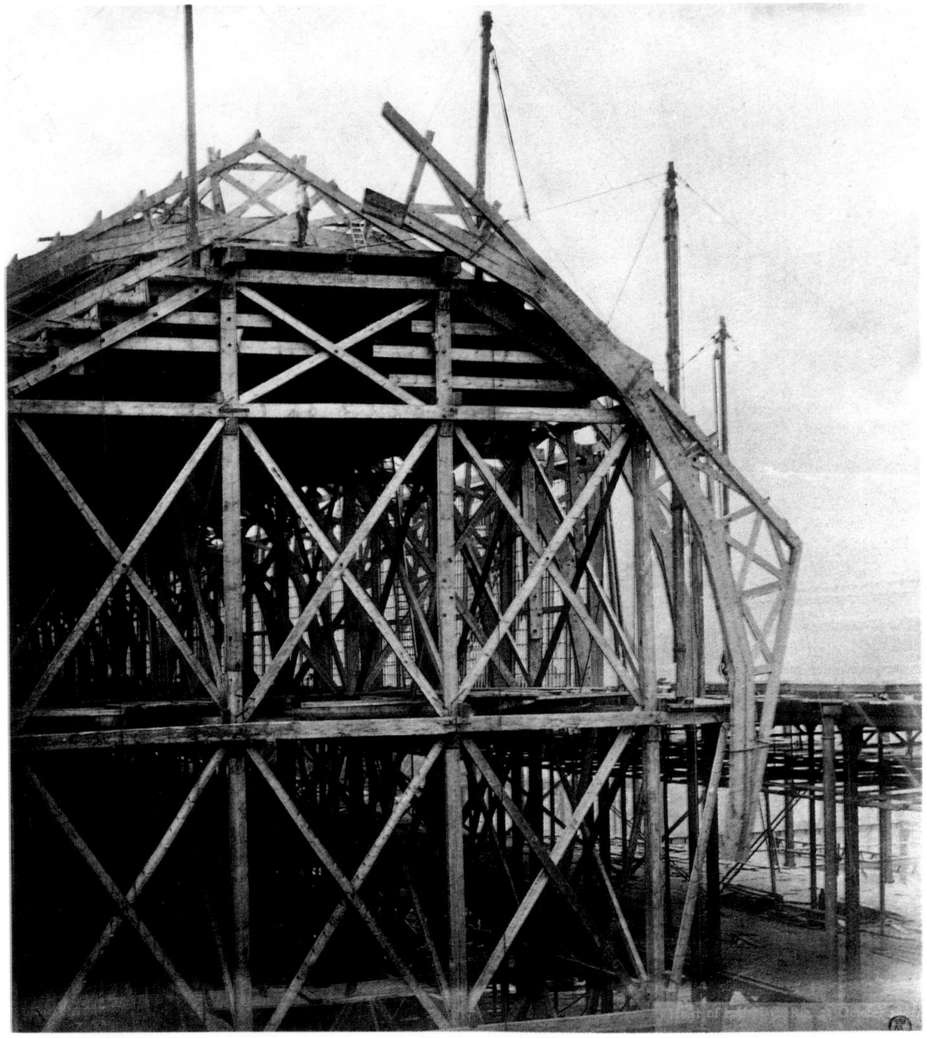

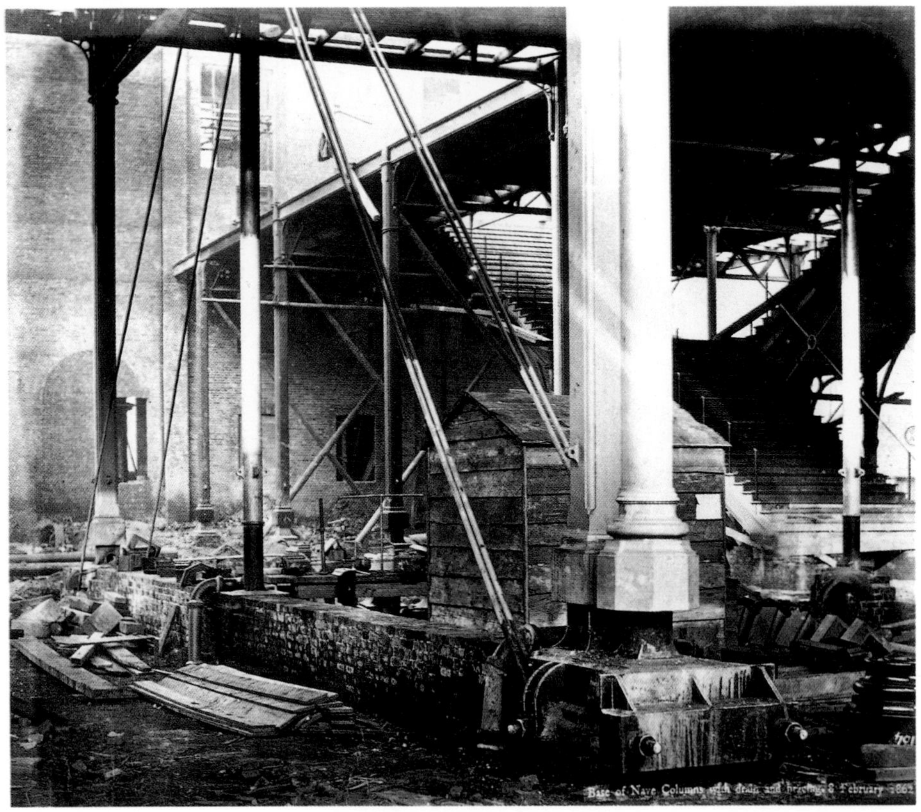

quent of the fascination of these structures (53). He was known to have been a contract photographer for the French government's civil engineering department: L'Administration Nationale des Ponts et Chaussées.[29] It is not known if this photograph was taken under its auspices, but Collard did photograph railroad bridges for the Administration. The photograph shows the immaculate iron and glass roof of the roundhouse with its exposed girders and the neatly numbered locomotives standing "docile and omnipotent" in their stable ("remise"). Each one is drawn up under an ingenious funnel arrangement which, by drawing smoke out of the building, avoided the pitting and staining of the glass roof, which was a major problem of early railroad structures. A superb marriage of engineering and architecture, it is photographed with a fine appreciation for both its grace and utility. The engineer was a heroic type of the period, as typified by the romantic and tragic figure of I. K. Brunel. Fox Talbot gave us an early appreciation of the appeal of such creations as his in the view of the Hungerford Suspension Bridge discussed earlier.

Traditional masonry construction, however, was not ignored. In the forties Talbot had photographed the construction of London brick houses, and in 1846 or '47 Hill and Adamson followed the construction of the neo-Gothic Walter Scott Memorial and the neoclassical National Gallery of Scotland, both in Edinburgh. Although the mandate of the 1851 Mission Héliographique did not encourage the depiction of restoration in progress, being more concerned with prerestoration states, a large number of restoration photographs survive from the period. The daguerreotypes Viollet-le-Duc had commissioned from Lerebours of Notre-Dame in Paris as a preparation for his work there have not surfaced. This lengthy restoration project became a favorite topic for Parisian photographers, although no one appears to have followed the work in the systematic way we saw in the engineering albums. Charles Marville showed an educated interest in processes of construction of traditional masonry buildings. His Fontaine des Innocents photographs are examples among many. Noteworthy is his photograph of one of the era's greatest projects using traditional masonry construction, the completion of the nave and transept of Cologne Cathedral (54). It was published by Blanquart-Evrard in 1853 or 1854. The view across the mason's yard shows the cut stone ready for installation and the complex scaffolding needed to place it. It is an illuminating study of nineteenth-century masonry techniques as applied to medieval style buildings.

Photographs showing processes and sequences of construction of all types of architecture would have appealed to a dual audience. As journalistic records of buildings in the public eye they would have attracted amateurs of architecture for whom they would have had an educational function. For architects, engineers, and contractors, they would have supplemented the engravings regularly published in professional reviews and general-circulation magazines such as *Scientific American* to illustrate articles on technical subjects and thus would have been an important source of technical information.

Although their role in nineteenth-century architectural photography was not as important as construction photographs, images of demolition of the intentional or inadvertent variety were an important aspect of the period's work. Dynamite, which was to raise the demolition of buildings to the level of a fine art, was not yet widely used for that purpose, but the era managed to produce a rich variety of techniques for destroying structures.

The systematic tearing-down of buildings to erase chaotic street patterns was an essential ingredient in Baron Haussmann's redesign of the center of Paris. This massive demolition project may have been the first to attract the attention of photographers. There was no unanimity of opinion on the virtue of this work. Preservationists mourned the passing of picturesque and historic quarters, while the advocates of progress and social change welcomed the healthier and more orderly capital that emerged. Demolition was an indispensable component of the changes that were taking place, and photographers saw it as worthy of documentation. Only two years after his involvement with the eminent preservationists who sponsored the Mission Héliographique of 1851, Henri Le Secq witnessed some of Haussmann's earliest clearances on the Île de la Cité. His response places him, as we might expect, among the advocates of preservation. From the usual high window, he photographed two Renaissance *hôtels* making their last stand (55). The orderly and inexorable process of destruction had arrived at the thresholds of these profoundly Parisian buildings, one with a fine late Gothic *tourelle* of a type once common in central Paris. Le Secq's characteristically careful choice of light in this perspective view brings out the sooty ghosts of the chimney races, an eternal feature of Paris demolition, and throws into relief the delicate tracery of the *tourelle,* creating a lasting image of the disappearing structures.

Charles Marville responded to similar scenes in his own way, in his photographs of the demolitions for the *percement* of the avenue de l'Opéra, around 1860 (56). Marville was concerned with the actual processes of demolition. Typically for him, he immerses us in the scene. He also included chimney races and staring windows but was more interested in the neat sorting and

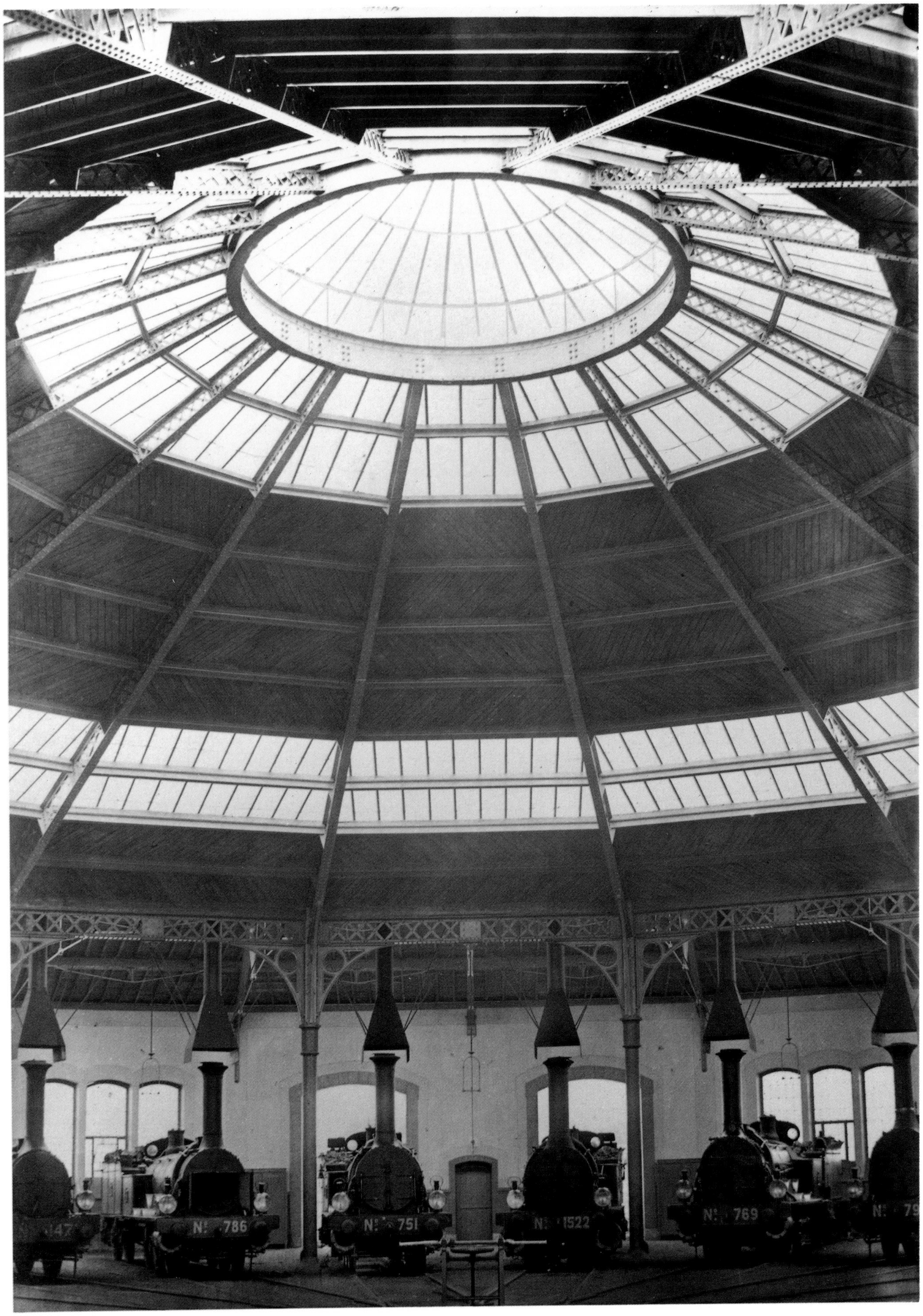

53 *A. Collard*

Nevers, roundhouse for 32 locomotives, ca. 1860.
Albumen silver print.
The J. Paul Getty Museum.

54 *Charles Marville*

Cologne Cathedral, south portal, ca. 1853–1854.
From *Les Bords du Rhin* (1853–1854).
Albumen silver print.
Collections of the Bibliothèque Nationale.

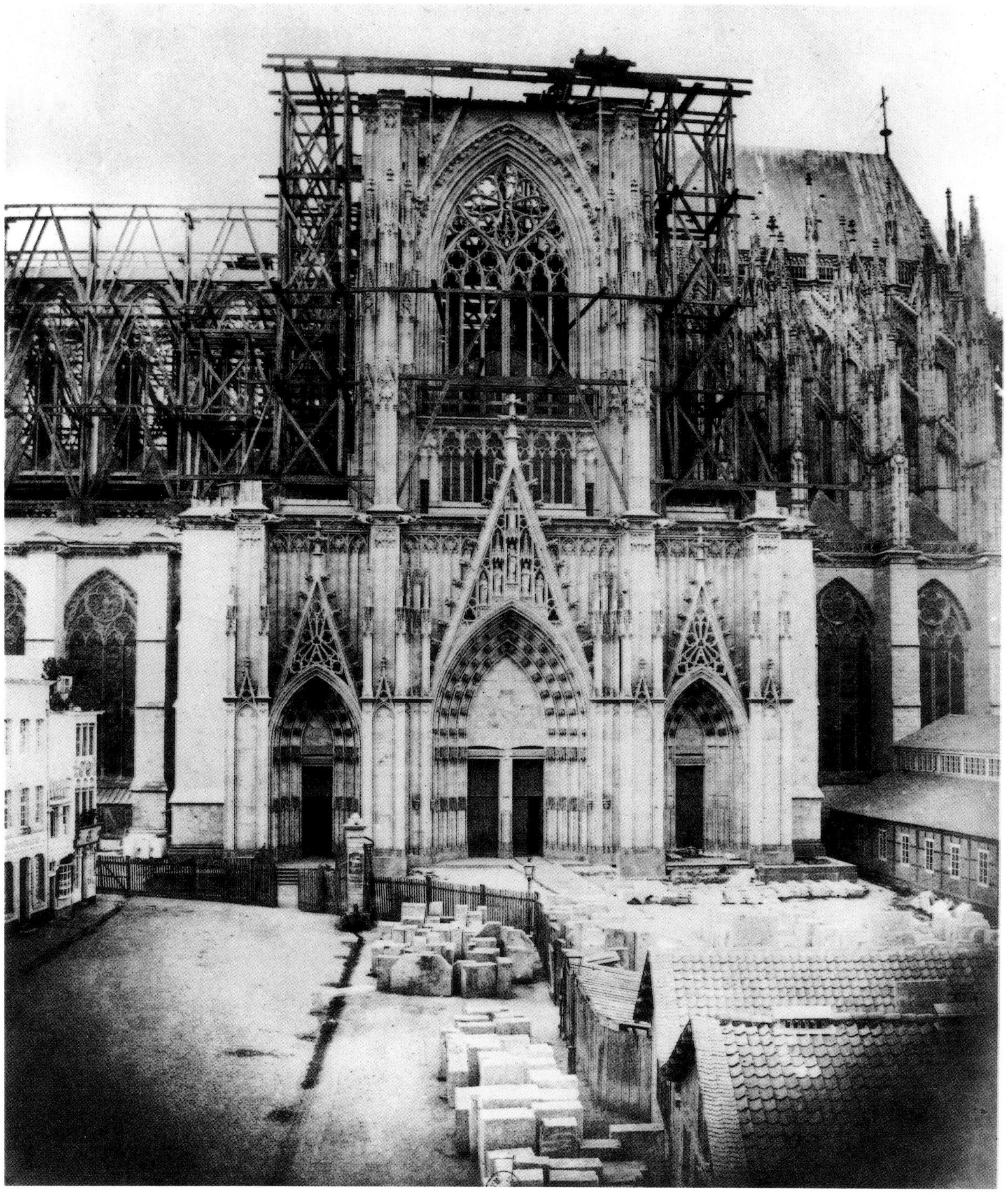

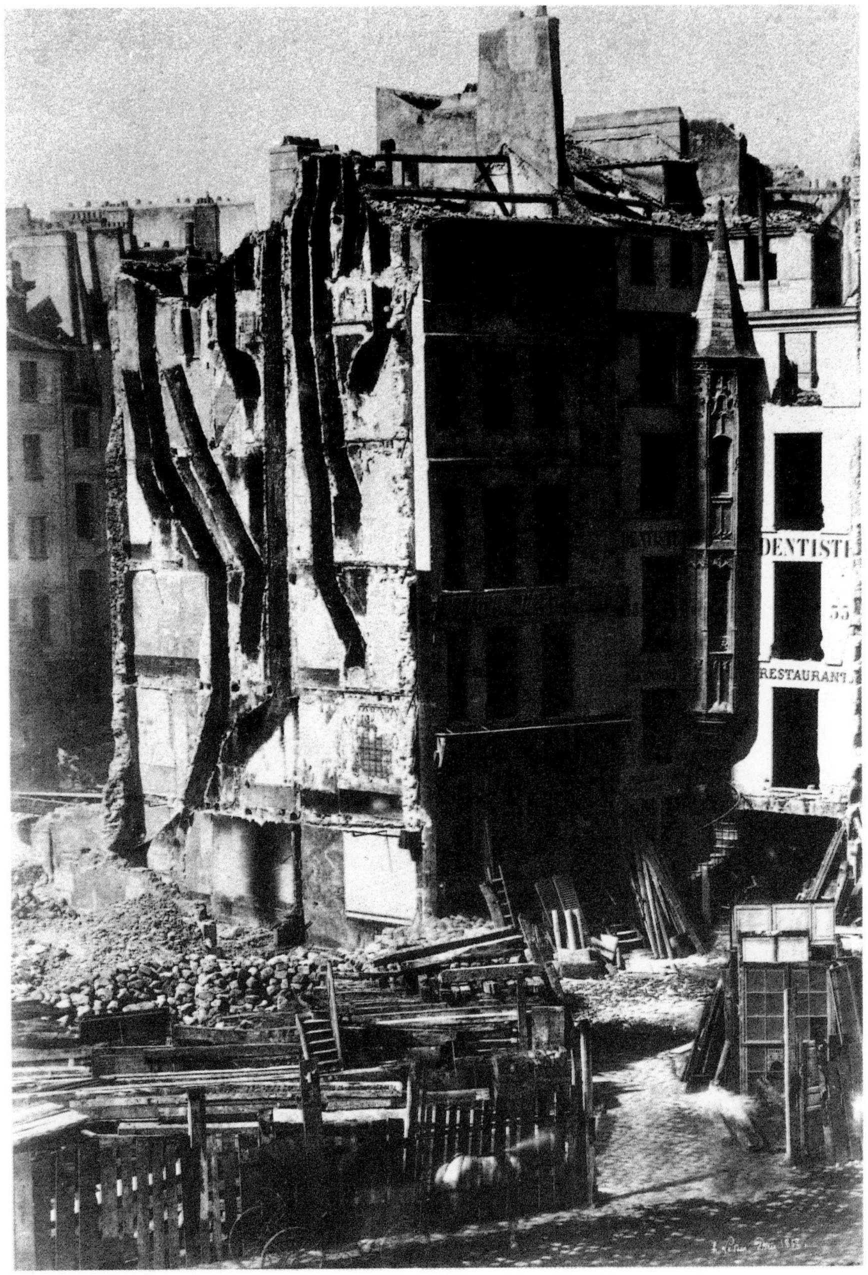

55 *Henri Le Secq*

Demolitions on the Île de la Cité, 1853.
Albumen silver print.
Musée Carnavalet, Paris.

56 *Charles Marville*

Piercing of the avenue de l'Opéra, ca. 1875.
Albumen silver print.
Musée Carnavalet, photo Lauros-Giraudon, Paris.

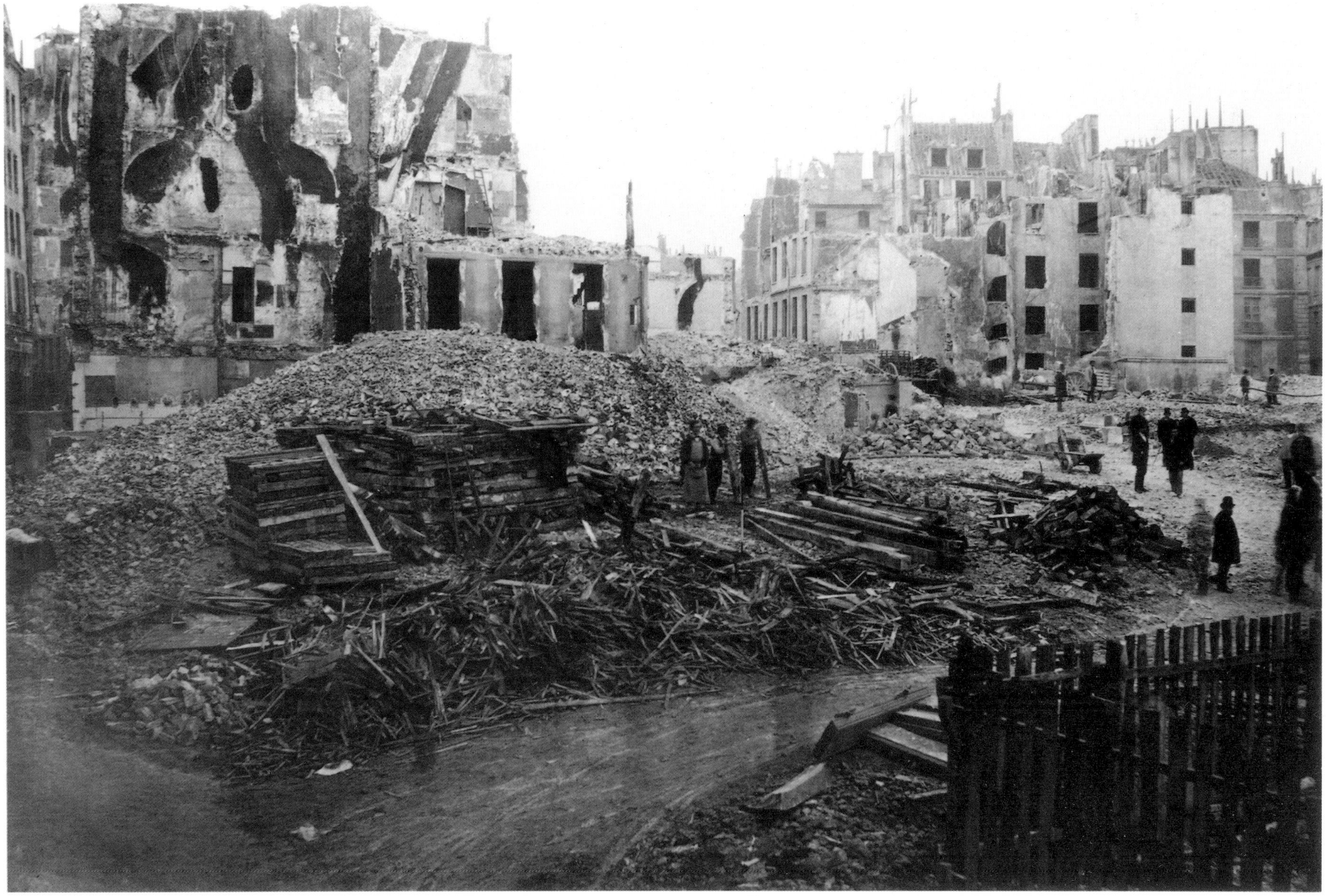

57 *J. W. Black*
Boston fire of 1872, 60 Pearl Street.
Albumen silver print.
Boston Athaneum.

58 *George Barnard*
Ruins in Columbia, S.C., 1864.
From *Photographic Survey of Sherman's Campaign* (1866).
Albumen silver print.
Collections of the Library of Congress.

stacking of rubble and the well-placed safety fence. Marville was especially concerned that we see the men responsible for the work: both the shirt-sleeved laborers and top-hatted supervisors whose collaboration made this huge project feasible.

Although systematic demolition played an important role in the period, inadvertent destruction was even more common. The concentration of population in cities resulting from the Industrial Revolution and the slow growth of civic institutions capable of dealing with these masses had created a situation in which the disasters that had always been a part of urban life took on enormous magnitude. Edouard Baldus's 1856 photographs of the floods on the Rhône River give eloquent testimony of the devastation natural forces could wreak on ill-protected towns. The most spectacular threat to the era's overpopulated, ill-organized cities was fire, especially in the United States where a succession of conflagrations became famous catastrophes. Chicago's in 1871, Boston's in 1872 were the most notorious. Photographs by J. W. Black in the aftermath of the Boston fire testify to the power of these conflagrations in their scenes of total desolation (57). Only bits of buildings are left standing, their stones charred as if they were wood. These photographs anticipate images of devastation that in our century total war has made familiar.

This form of warfare was beginning to appear back then. Sherman's March to the Sea during the Civil War may have seen the first appearance of a total warfare in which the horrors of the battlefield, themselves magnified because of improvements in ordnance, were brought home to the civilian population. George Barnard followed Sherman's armies to produce a series of images of the devastation resulting when the munitions of war are turned on houses and cities (58). The wreckage of solid buildings testifies to the power of the new munitions. Barnard's brilliant technique and matter-of-fact approach can lend a chillingly clinical aspect to his photographs. Images of military installations demolished by exploding artillery shells were already known, but this may be the first series to show their impact on civilian buildings.

The emergence of the halftone process after 1880 as an economical and visually satisfactory means of reproducing photographs prepared the way for a shift away from the photographic print as the most frequently used means of distributing photographic images. In the nineties mechanically reproduced images, whether by halftone or other processes, began to become commonplace. The integration of photographs into the texts of books and articles, which halftone facilitated by allowing them to be printed on the same plate, was to

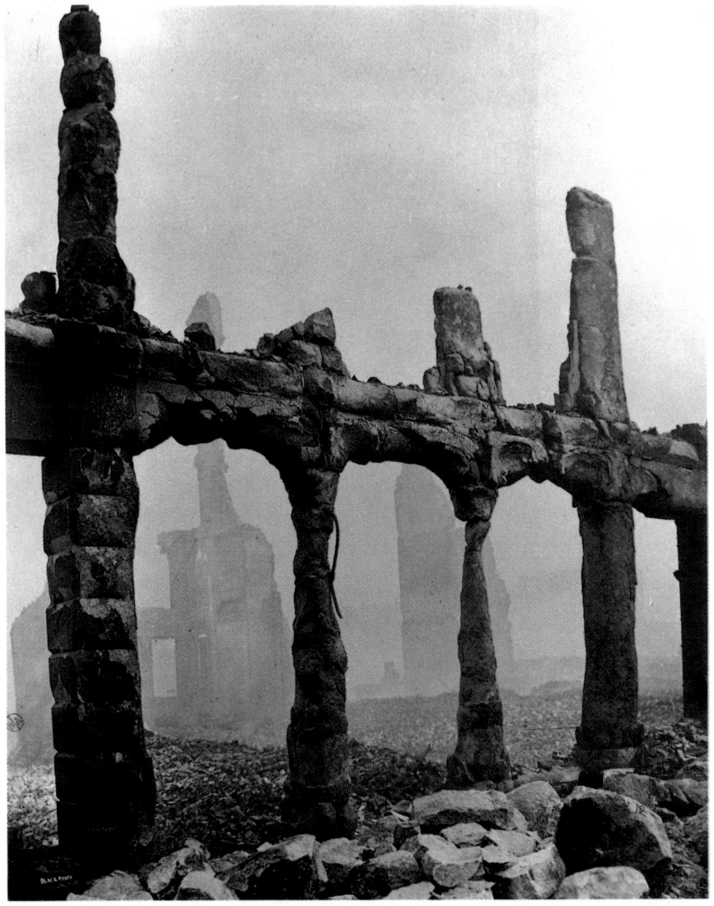

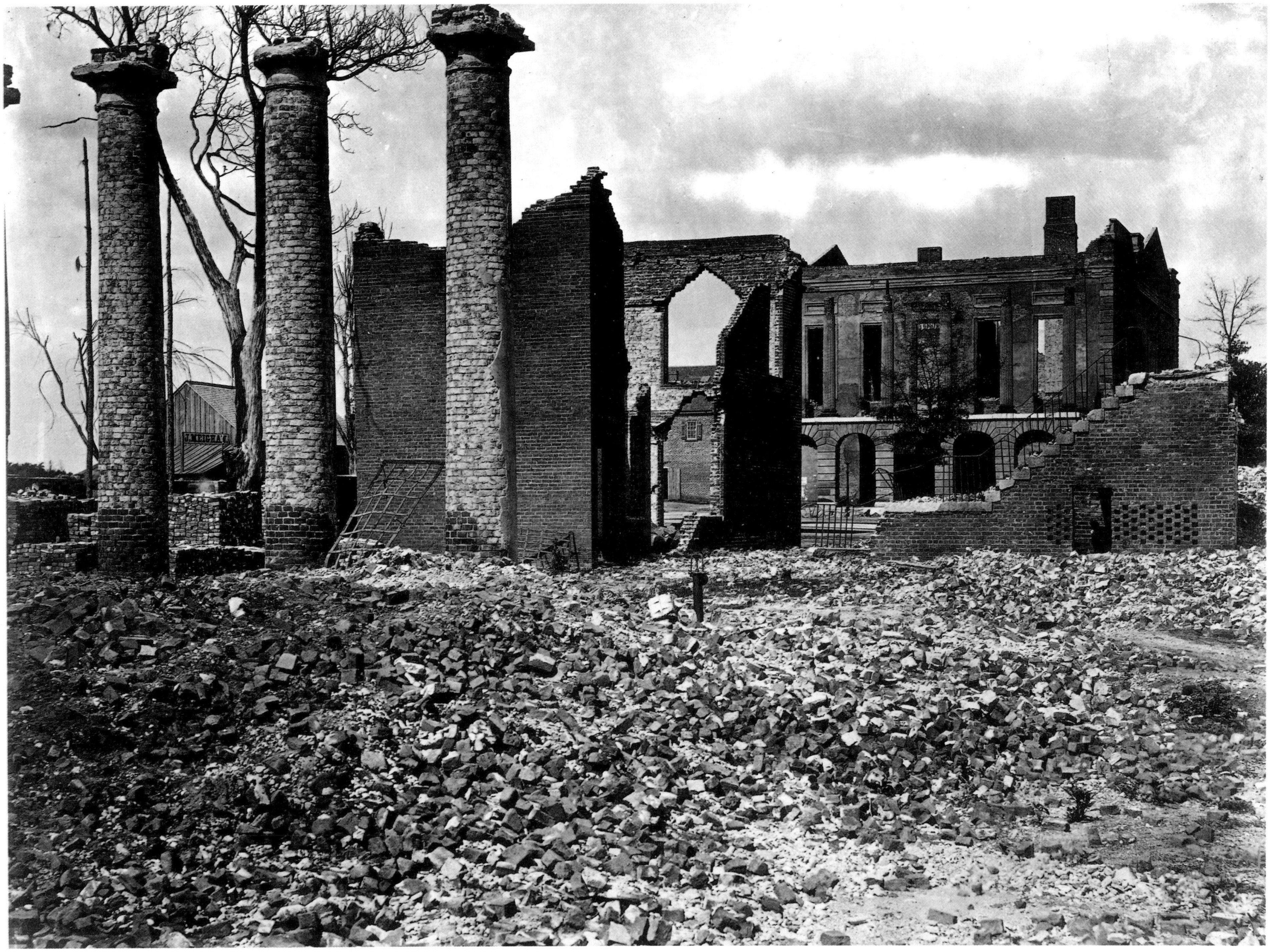

become the norm rather than the exception. The emphasis shifted from the individual photograph standing on its own to the suite of photographs illustrating a text. By this time a language for photographing architecture had become current. It was only natural that it would have its roots in the older media of architectural representation that were based on drawing, but the unprecedented immediacy and accuracy of the photograph, its ability to "place" the viewer in a scene or before a building, gave photography a unique advantage. It gradually came to stand on its own as a medium of architectural representation.

By 1880 this had largely been achieved, and the succeeding years saw photography begin to overshadow the older forms. These developments will be the province of the essays to follow.

1. See André Jammes and Eugenia Parry Janis, *The Art of the French Calotype* (Princeton: Princeton University Press, 1983), 9–16; Direction des Musées de France, *La Mission héliographique, photographies de 1851* (Paris, catalog, 1980), 8; Joseph Maria Eder, *History of Photography*, trans. Edward Epstean (New York: Dover Publications, Inc., 1978), 345–347.

2. Helmut Gernsheim, *The Origins of Photography* (New York: Thames and Hudson, Inc., 1978), 205–207.

3. See *Mission héliographique.*

4. Isabelle Jammes, *Blanquart-Evrard et les origines de l'édition photographique française* (Geneva: Librairie Droz, 1981), 42–44.

5. *Mission héliographique*, 15–16.

6. Jammes and Janis, *French Calotype*, 91.

7. Eder, *History of Photography*, 676.

8. Helmut Gernsheim, *Focus on Architecture and Sculpture* (London: The Fountain Press, 1949), 21.

9. John Harris, Jill Lever, Margaret Richardson, *Great Drawings from the Collection of the RIBA* (New York: The Drawing Center, 1983), 7; John Wilton-Ely, "The Rise of the Professional Architect in England," in *The Architect*, Spiro Kostof, ed. (New York: Oxford University Press, 1977), 193–197.

10. William Clark and Joel Herschman, *Un Voyage héliographique à faire* (New York: Queens College Press, 1981), 9–10.

11. Jammes and Janis, *French Calotype*, 48–49.

12. Quoted in: Nikolaus Pevsner, *Some Architectural Writers of the Nineteenth Century* (Oxford: Oxford University Press, 1972), 112.

13. Wilton-Ely, "Professional Architect," 195; Harris et al. *Great Drawings*, 8, 47.

14. See David Van Zanten, "Architecture," in *The Second Empire, 1852–1870, Art in France under Napoleon III* (Philadelphia: Philadelphia Museum of Art, 1978), 39–40.

15. Gernsheim, *Origins*, 111.

16. James F. O'Gorman, "On Vacation with H. H. Richardson, Ten Letters from Europe, 1882," *Archives of American Art Journal* 1, 1979, 8–9.

17. Bonnie Grad and Timothy A. Riggs, *Visions of City and Country* (Worcester: Worcester Art Museum, 1982), 65–132, *passim.*

18. Marie de Thézy, in Bibliothèque Historique de la Ville de Paris, *Charles Marville, photographe de Paris de 1851 a 1879*, (Paris: catalog, 1982), 21; for related developments in Germany see: Ursula Peters, *Stilgeschichte der Fotografie in Deutschland* (Cologne: Dumont Büchverlag, 1979), 125–131.

19. Recently Marville's modernism has been emphasized, although a measure of ambivalence is admitted. See de Thézy, *Marville*, 20–21; Maria Morris Hambourg, *Charles Marville* (New York: French Institute, 1981), 10–11. I would lean toward the ambivalence.

20. John Ruskin, "Preface to 2nd Edition of *The Seven Lamps of Architecture*," in *The Collected Works of John Ruskin*, eds. E. T. Cook and A. Wedderburn (New York: Longmans, Green & Co., 1903–1912), vol. 8, 11. Quoted in Pevsner, *Some Writers*, 149–150.

21. Phyllis Lambert, in Richard Pare, *Photography and Architecture, 1839–1939* (Montreal: Canadian Center for Architecture, 1982; The MIT Press, 1985), 10. See especially Michael Bartram, *The Pre-Raphaelite Camera* (Boston: Little, Brown, 1985), 52–53.

22. John Hannavy, *Roger Fenton of Crimble Hall* (Boston: David R Godine, 1976), 17.

23. Gernsheim, *Focus*, 21.

24. From John Ruskin, "The Nature of Gothic," in *The Stones of Venice: Works of Ruskin*, vol. 10, 268. Quoted in Pevsner, *Some Writers*, 151.

25. See *Marville* (Paris), 8.

26. The theme is expressed in a poem by the photographers' favorite writer, Sir Walter Scott: poem 2 of *Patriotism*, "Nelson, Pitt, Fox;" stanza 1.

27. William and Mary Howitt, *Ruined Abbeys and Castles of Great Britain* (London: A. W. Bennett, 1861), preface.

28. John Physick, *Photography and the South Kensington Museum* (London: Victoria and Albert Museum, 1975), 2–10.

29. Metropolitan Museum of Art, *After Daguerre*, (New York: catalog, 1980), entry 44.

Part II

1880 to 1930

In the half century from 1880 to 1930 photographers—thanks to an increasing use of reproduction in books and magazines and an increasing acceptance of the optically correct but conventionally odd perspective that the camera often seemed to give—at first refined a factual style that had existed since the midcentury. Then, starting in the 1890s, and for several reasons in addition to a simple turn in taste away from the factual style, they were led to give a more fragmentary and experiential view of their subjects, often revealing an embarrassment that subjects in photographs had to be specific and not generalized as in other arts. Finally, in the 1920s photographers redirected their attention to specific subjects while still maintaining the air of self-conscious artistry learned in the pre-war years. These fifty years also saw the gradual but unevenly paced evolution of photography, from being a medium in which an especially perspicacious architect—H. H. Richardson—could see the value, to being in the twenties the medium by which new buildings were almost universally presented.

The manner in which a photographer can approach a building has always been constrained by the nature of the subject and its surroundings. He cannot decide to take all buildings in one way, head on and from a fixed distance, for instance. Many times something in the way will prevent him. He takes the pictures he can. Yet an age may find itself especially drawn to a particular kind of view, to one perspective, and pictures of that sort will carry special conviction and deserve special attention. In this way in the late 1870s and the 1880s a picture that seems specially characteristic presented a generally free-standing building from a distance and with a startling precision. A photograph of H. H. Richardson's Trinity Church (1877) in Boston, which appeared in the form of a collotype in *American Architect and Building News* in 1877, set the style for this sort of view (though it did not in every way exemplify it) (59). This picture shows the church and parish house under construction as seen from the southeast with Richardson's earlier Brattle Square Church (1873) tower in the distance on the far right and Cummings and Sears' New Old South Church (1875) on the far left. The considerable distance between the camera and Trinity gives an air of objectivity to the picture, and the space allowed around the building suggests the completeness of the information given. How this picture differed from later examples of the style was in its placing of the secondary church towers at the left and right edges of the picture (but the subject compelled that) and in the muted contrast and detail of the reproduction. The magazine pioneered in the use of the collotype, which was soon to be characterized by the enhanced sharpness of its images. In contrast, some forty-five years later, the most compelling among Arthur Köster's pictures in *Wasmuth's Monatshefte für Baukunst* of architect Erich Mendelsohn's newly completed Einstein Tower (1921) in Potsdam showed only a fragment of the building, a curved surface punctuated by window and door openings and water spouts, seen obliquely and in a moody light (60). The earlier picture gives much the sort of information that an architectural drawing to scale would have. We could easily make a conjectural plan of the building from the photograph; moreover it shows us convincingly the facts of how the building looked as built. The later picture gives us a compelling impression of the plastic character of the Mendelsohn building but virtually no information of its internal organization or its use. This picture may well tell us how the building is to be remembered, but the sight of the actual building, after a previous acquaintance only through this picture, would probably surprise us. The stylistic difference between the two pictures, a development of the "elevations" and "perspectives" of the early decades of photography, illustrates a revolutionary change in sensibility that had occurred in the interval between the taking of each, the change representing a split that would begin to be reconciled in the late 1930s.

Although the publication of original photographs mounted on bound pages was common before the eighties, reproduction systems that allowed photographs to be printed quickly, cheaply, and permanently in ink made feasible in the late seventies and eighties the publication in books and magazines of one category of photograph that had hitherto been slighted, that of pictures of new nonmonumental architecture.

The most significant reproduction systems were collotype and photogravure. Other systems, precursors of halftone, which gave reproductions made up of fine parallel lines of widths that varied or of vermiculated patterns (rather than the dots of halftone), were also common, but collotypes—which have been known under many names, among them Albertypes, gelatine prints, heliotypes, Lichtdrücke, phototypes—and photogravures were clearly of higher quality. The latter, which were remarkable for pearly highlights and velvety blacks, involved considerable handwork, visible as retouching, in the making of the plates from which reproductions were printed. No such handwork was involved in the preparation of the gelatine plates from which collotypes were printed. In that respect the collotypes, though not likely to be confused with originals, were undistorted versions of the photographs from which they were made.

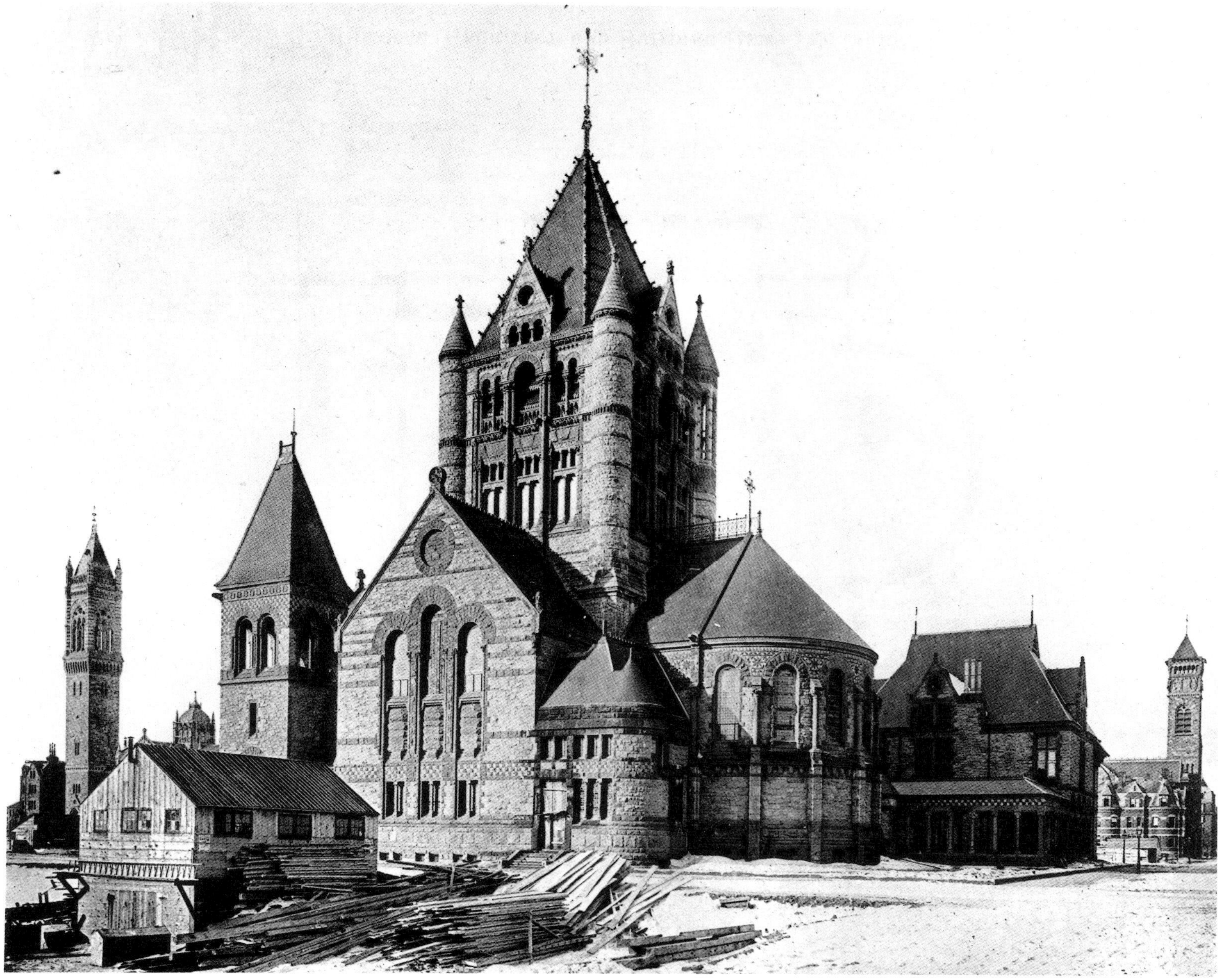

59 *Photographer unknown*

Boston, Trinity Church.
From *American Architect and Building News* (1876).
Collotype.
Metropolitan Museum of Art, New York.

60 *Arthur Köster*

Potsdam, Einstein Tower, ca. 1923.
Technische Universität, Berlin.

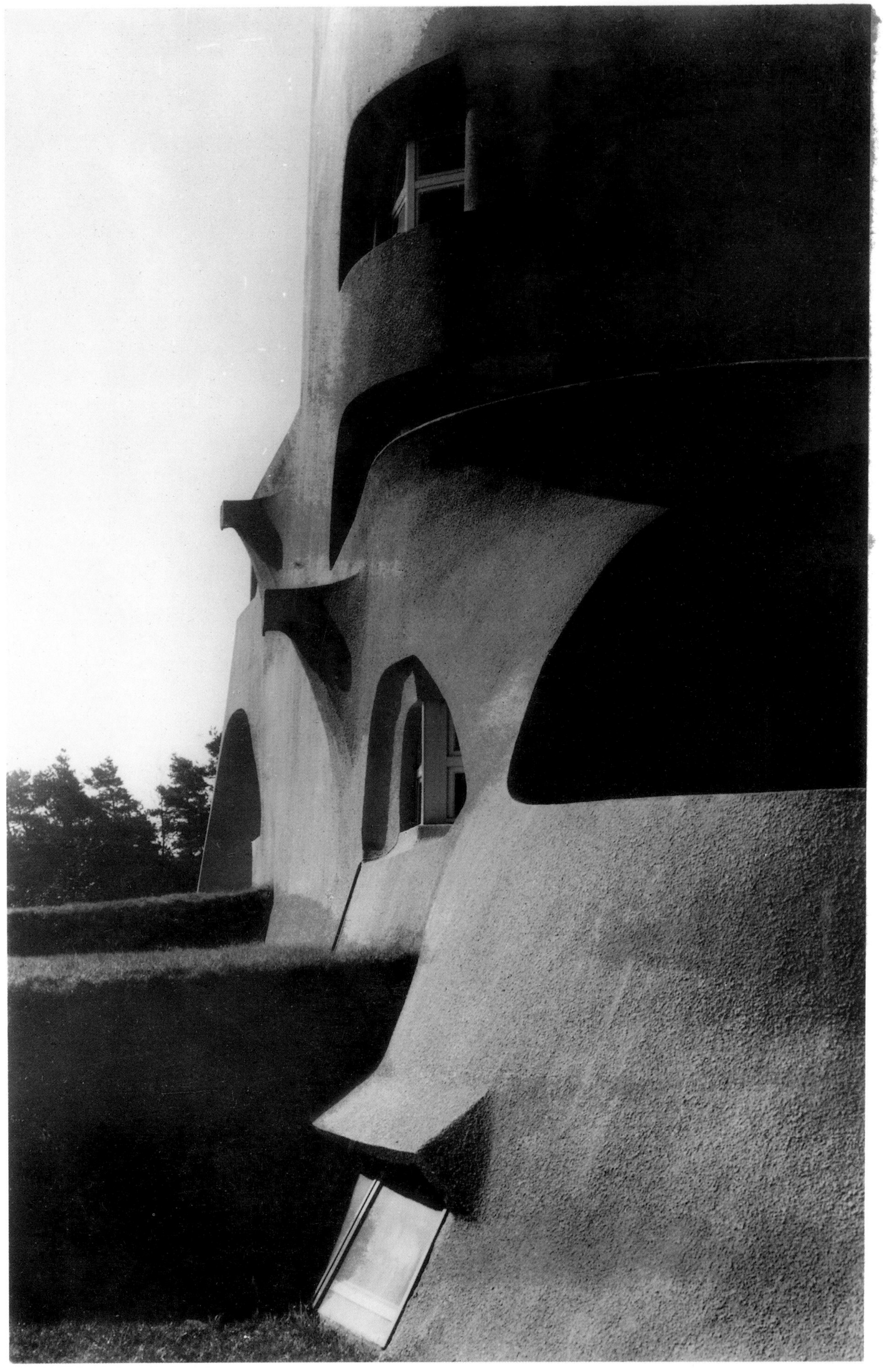

The collotype process, and apparently some varieties of photogravure, generally produced an exaggerated contrast at the edges between tones in a picture, an effect analogous to one we associate in the late twentieth century with "high acutance" films, with reproductions made from plates produced by laser scanning, and with the "image enhancement" of photographs made from satellites. The effect was most remarkable for the manner in which lettering on signs, edges of shingles and tiles, the lines of tree branches, and blades of grass stood out, resulting in reproductions that seem infinitely detailed. It is not by chance that collotype was the medium through which most of the nineteenth-century photographs in Vincent Scully's *The Shingle Style* were available to him.

The books in which these new buildings appeared, George William Sheldon's *Artistic Country Seats* of 1886–87 and D. Appleton's *Artistic Houses* of 1883–84, and the early *Monographs of American Architecture*, such as that on H. H. Richardson's buildings at North Easton, of 1886, provided a first systematic view in published photographs of contemporary architecture. Architects' own albums had characteristically been filled with photographic prints of historic buildings, ones they had collected individually to serve as sources for details of their own buildings (a practice for which American architects were especially known, in contrast to their European colleagues who were more likely to make sketches). Present also in these albums were occasional sets of photographs of contemporary buildings by others, included presumably because the buildings were of special interest or the prints had been gifts from their designers. Otherwise, an architect would have known of contemporary work only from having seen it as it had been published in the form of drawings or firsthand in his travels. Many of these drawings published before the reproduction of photographs became common in the 1880s had themselves been made from photographs and looked it, but reproductions directly from photographs held a special conviction that no drawing could. The more a viewer of photographs knew about photography, and therefore the better he knew how it can distort, the better he also knew how to interpret it, so that authenticity was not lost by familiarity. In addition, as reproduced, photographs were printed as separate plates, for the most part one picture to a plate, with a full burden of significance placed on each photograph, a practice that set them apart from drawings that often mixed the factual with a decorative border or had the character of fragmented collages of sketches (61).

Just as publishers of photographic prints in the early decades of photography often neglected to give credit to photographers, publishers of reproductions also neglected to do so, partly one can guess because the photographers were their employees or perhaps due to the impersonal, magisterial style of the photographs themselves. Like other new technologies, photography was both regretted (for its literalness) and welcomed (for its authenticity) but was in any case unavoidable, and its offspring, reproduction processes, were coveted before it was fully apparent how they might be useful. Several times at the end of the nineteenth century the acquisition of a printing plant was wedded to an inclination toward the subject of architecture, and these motivated the founding of a magazine that published architecture. This was true of the *American Architect* as later of *Country Life*. In Germany on the contrary the collotype plates for *Blätter für Architektur und Kunsthandwerk* in the late 1880s and the nineties were made by the same firms of photographers who took the pictures that were being reproduced, and separate credits were given to the photographers and to those who prepared the plates, who often proved to be the same people.

Whether or not they were credited, these photographers of the eighties demonstrated a consistent style. In court photographers Römmler & Jonas's photograph of Gottfried Semper's Royal Art Gallery (1854) in Dresden, published in 1889, the building's central pavilion is shown head on and precisely on its axis with the Matthäus Pöppelman's eighteenth-century Zwinger, visible beyond a rakish figure, one of two in the central archway (62). Although the whole building facade does not appear in the picture, the pavilion facade that does is completely described, and the picture is clearly in the line of descent from Baldus's pictures of the Louvre. But a significant difference is that Römmler & Jonas have worked from pavement level rather than the height from which the earlier photographer worked. By the use of a rising front they have dropped the horizon sufficiently to include the pavilion cornice and roof. It was not just the increasing availability of wide-field lenses in the eighties that made this possible but a cautious relaxation in the face of wide-angle perspective. Perspective distortion can be described in different and contradictory ways even in our day. By several such definitions it would be agreed that the distortion was least where the Zwinger falls in this picture, which therefore displays an increased confidence but a most cautiously exploited one.

Constantin Samhaber accepted an inevitably oblique view but returned to Baldus's high camera position in his view of the parish church of St. Maria at Bamberg (collotype by Georg Büxenstein of Berlin, also a photographer) in

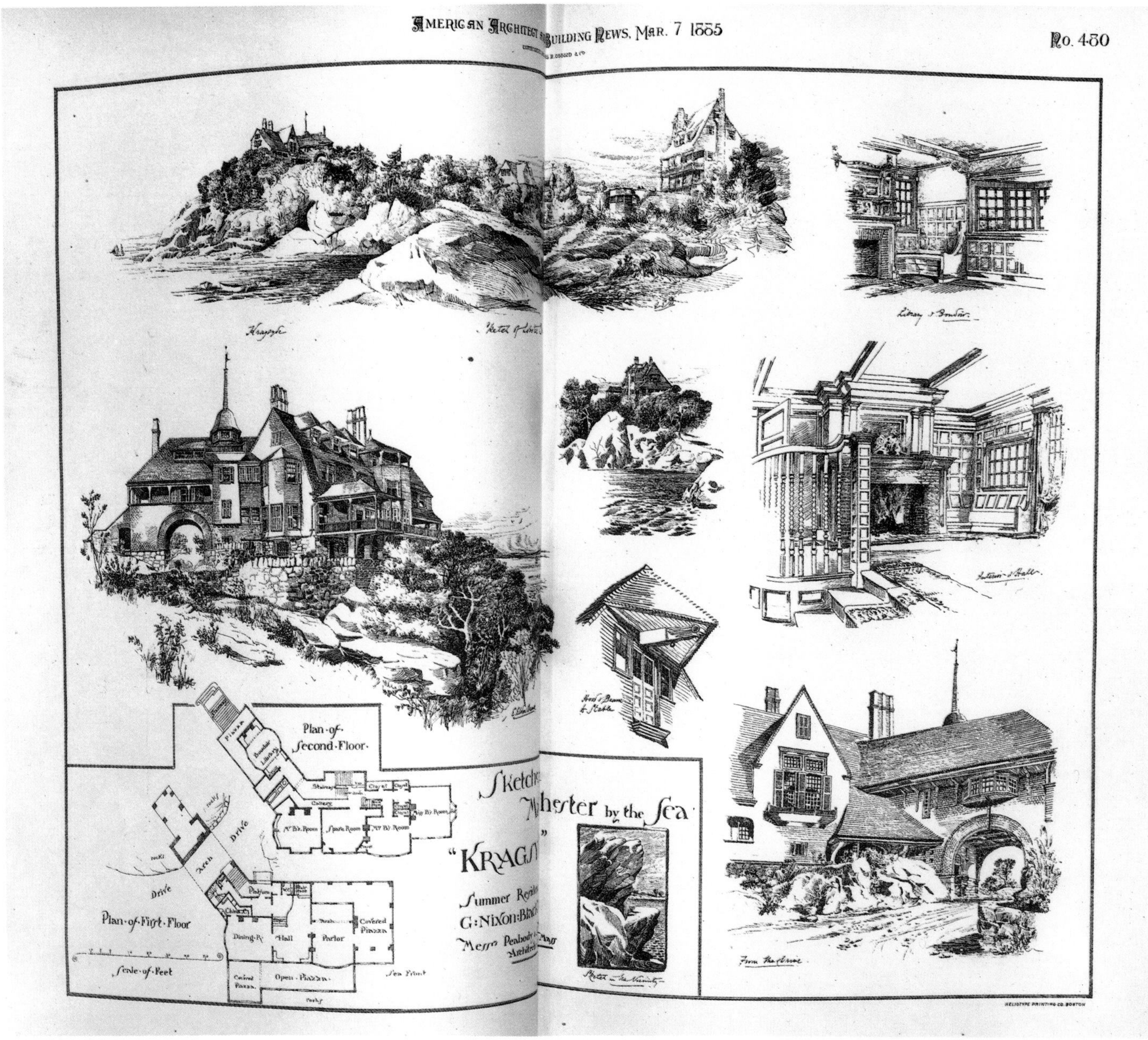

61 Layout from *American Architect and Building News* (March 7, 1885). Metropolitan Museum of Art, New York.

62 *Römmler & Jonas*

Dresden, Royal Art Gallery.
From *Blätter für Architektur und Kunsthandwerk* (1893).
Collotype.
Avery Architectural Library.

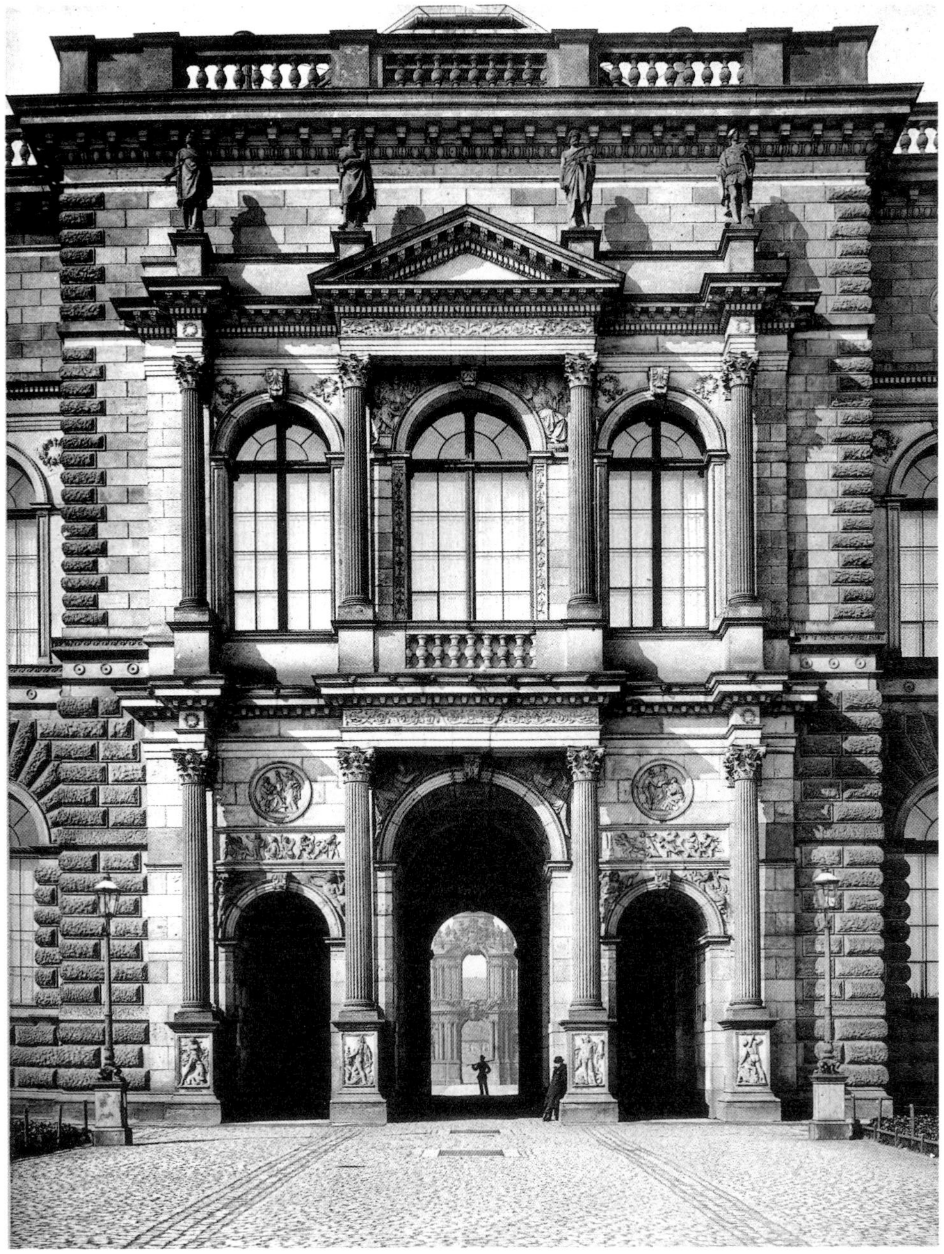

which the building stands free and whole within the picture rectangle and a crucifix at the base of the building appears head on in the Zwinger position behind a group of children who watch the photographer (63).

Looking at a reproduction of the eighties, though we can clearly observe that it was taken on a sunny day (or was not), we see that the feeling of the kind of day is minimized. This is partly because reproductions, while exaggerating the edges—the edges of shadows of course as well as of objects—also dampened the difference between sunlit areas and areas in shadow. Furthermore the largely blue-sensitive plates of the 1880s (and of the earlier and following decades for that matter), rendering blue sky as white, reduced the difference in photographs between sunlit surfaces and shadowed ones lit by the sky. The consequences were an emphasis in the reproductions on substance and on voluminous details, gained at the expense of much sense of ambient light.

This is not to say that photographers taking these pictures could ignore light. It is clear from their pictures that they were quite as artful in the use of it as any subsequent photographers. A set of pictures taken by an anonymous photographer and reproduced by the Heliotype Printing Company of Boston in 1886 of H. H. Richardson's library (1879) and Ames Memorial Building (1881) in North Easton, Massachusetts, illustrates this. The set was taken in early spring on a cloudless day (as we can see from the quality of the light on the buildings and from the alacrity with which the photographer was able to move from one picture to the next). His job was to photograph two related buildings standing a short distance apart. Just as he would nowadays, the photographer made a clockwise circuit of the buildings following the sun as it rotated around them through the day, lighting them favorably first from the east, then the south, and later the west. He started with a general view of both buildings from the south with a light that was somewhat too flat (64). Thereafter, starting with a view of the library from the east, he worked his way around first the library, then the Memorial Building until he reached the south corner of the latter, where he fell behind the sun: he had decided to take a view down the loggia while the sun was still shining into it from the southeast (65, 66, 67). In doing so, he lost the sunlight he needed on the main southeast facade of the building for two subsequent pictures (68). Up to that point he had worked quickly (though not quickly enough to have taken all the pictures he wanted in good light), but after making the two facade pictures, he stopped (for lunch? to take the two interiors of the library that were published?) and only resumed work on the exterior of the Memorial Building when the sun had moved considerably onto its rear facade (69). His last pictures were of the rear of the library and a general view, perhaps the best he took in the day's work, of the two buildings from the northeast, looking like two ships in a heavy sea (70). This character comes from the buildings and the hill on which they stand; the pictures themselves maintain an air of distance and objectivity.

Like the earlier books on whose pages original photographs had been glued, books with reproductions were published on many categories of building. The impetus to use reproductions was clearly twofold: to lower the cost of pictures and to make them more permanent than the silver images of photographs. But it is not clear that it was economically feasible to publish something in reproduction form that had not been feasible before that time. Some of the books we have were certainly not financial successes. The book of views of Moscow, mentioned later, published in the late eighties was exported from the U.S.S.R. in the form of fresh copies in the 1930s. The book had not sold out in almost a half century.

In the 1880s and 1890s books were published on waterside warehouses at seaports, post office buildings, manor houses, and castles, but the most significant of such topics were topographic portraits of towns that depended on a belief that a town or city could be summed up by its architecture and natural features. This conviction was soon to be destroyed by two developments. One was the urban growth that followed the electrification of trolleys and made towns less visually coherent in shape. The other was the introduction of halftone reproduction which made for a fragmentation of the subject of cities into topics (such as "the criminal classes") and away from topographic views. In the period before this revolution occurred, a portrait of an American town would include the main street, the principal public, business, manufacturing, and religious buildings, selected private houses, river frontages, parks and graveyards. Where topography allowed, a picture would be taken to begin the series that encapsulated an ideal balance between nature and town. In one such picture of Leominster, Massachusetts, a town under the thrall of the mansard roof, the buildings have the typical eighties character of being objects set out in the open space just as the churches in the picture that featured Trinity Church appeared (71). The earliest and best of these portraits of towns were produced in collotype, photogravure, or a pigment process, as were the Leominster pictures. Pigment prints of various sorts resembled albumen prints of the day more closely than did other reproductions but, like other facsimiles, suffer, as compared to photogravures and collotypes, from the fact that the more closely

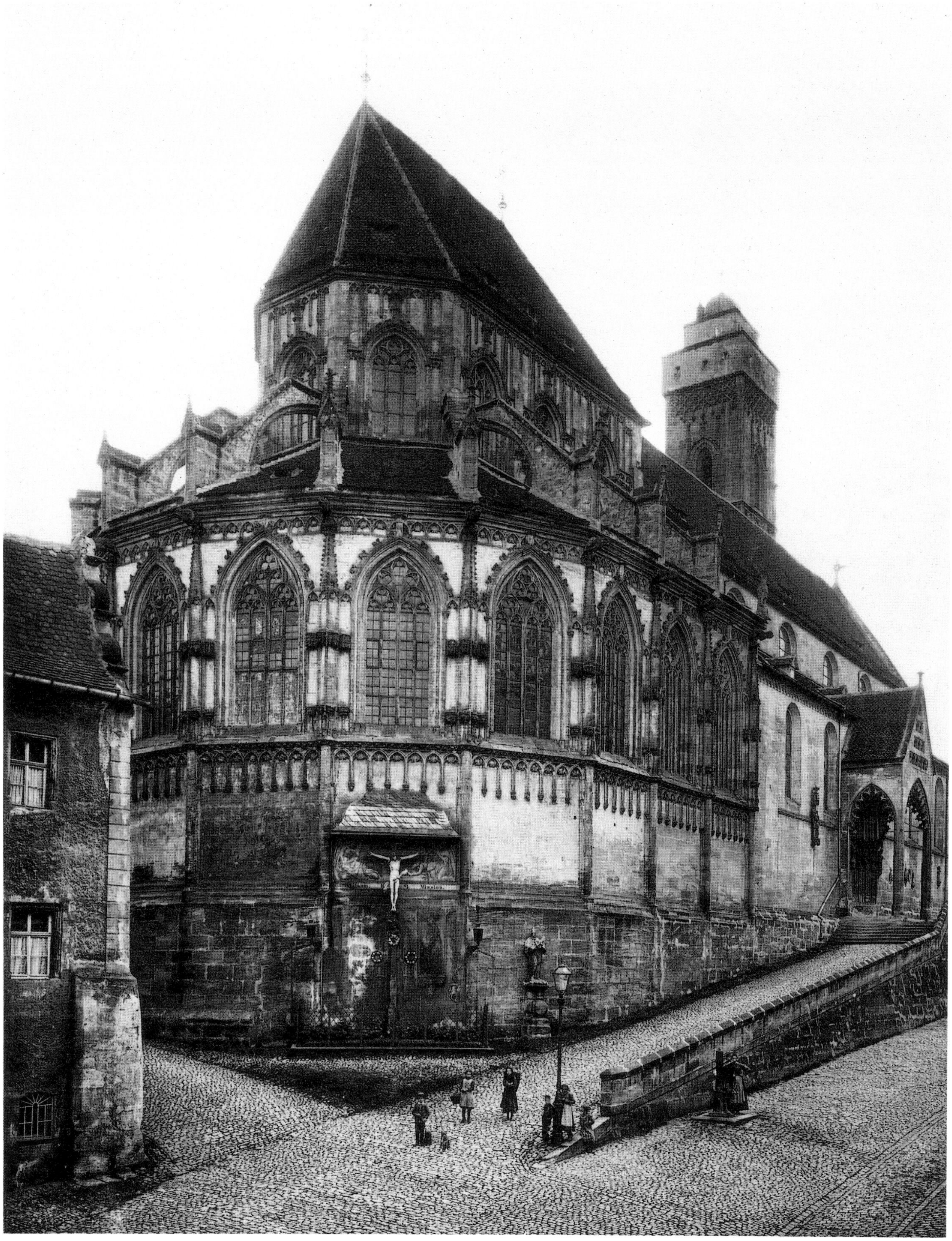

63 *Constantin Samhaber*

Bamberg, upper parish church of St. Maria.
From *Blätter für Architektur und Kunsthandwerk* (1893).
Collotype.
Avery Architectural Library.

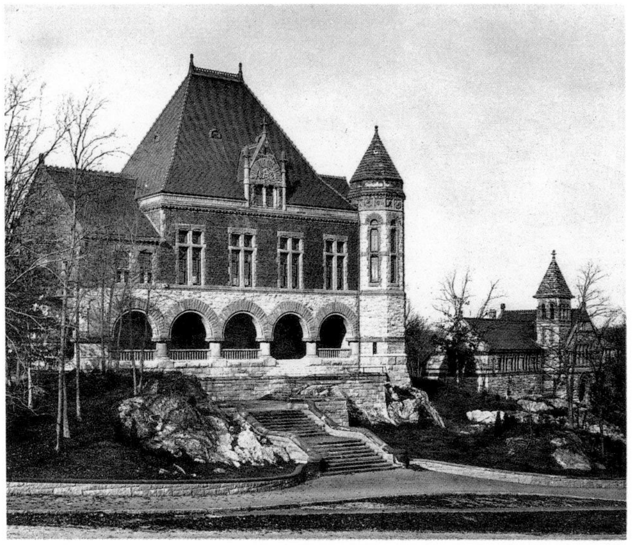

66 *Photographer unknown*

North Easton, Ames Memorial Hall.
From *Monographs of American Architecture* (1886).
Collotype.
Avery Architectural Library.

67 *Photographer unknown*

North Easton, Ames Memorial Hall.
From *Monographs of American Architecture* (1886).
Collotype.
Avery Architectural Library.

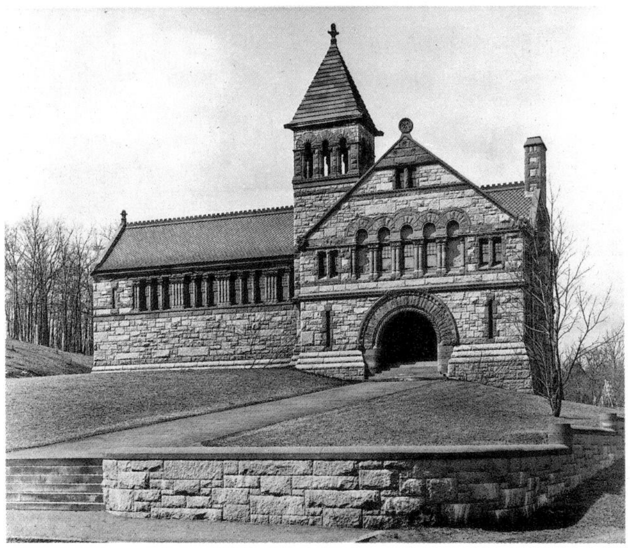

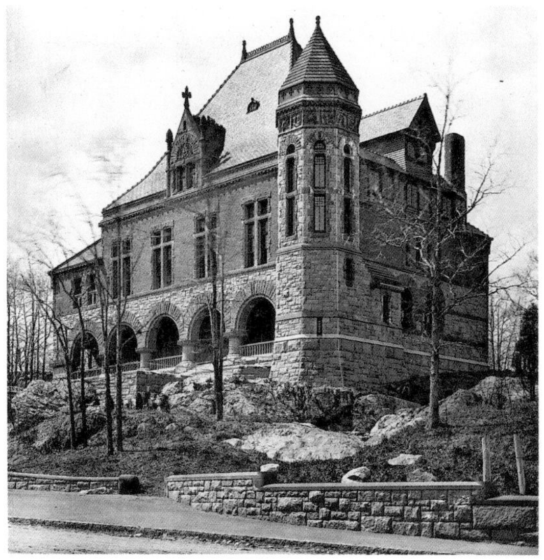

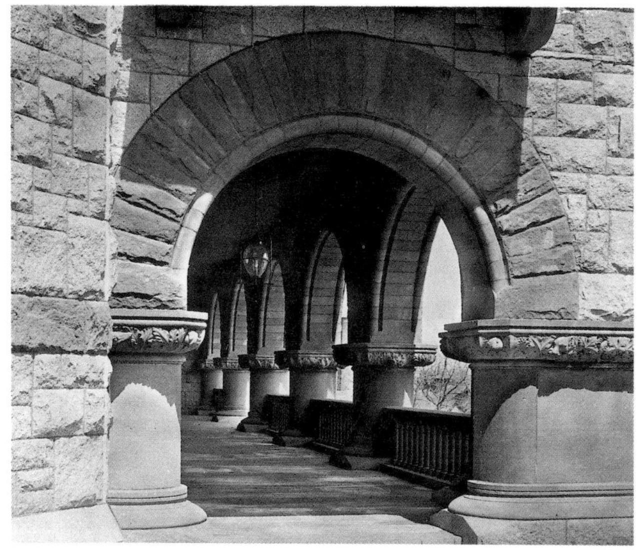

64 *Photographer unknown*

North Easton, Ames Memorial Hall and Library.
From *Monographs of American Architecture* (1886).
Collotype.
Avery Architectural Library.

65 *Photographer unknown*

North Easton, Ames Memorial Library.
From *Monographs of American Architecture* (1886).
Collotype.
Avery Architectural Library.

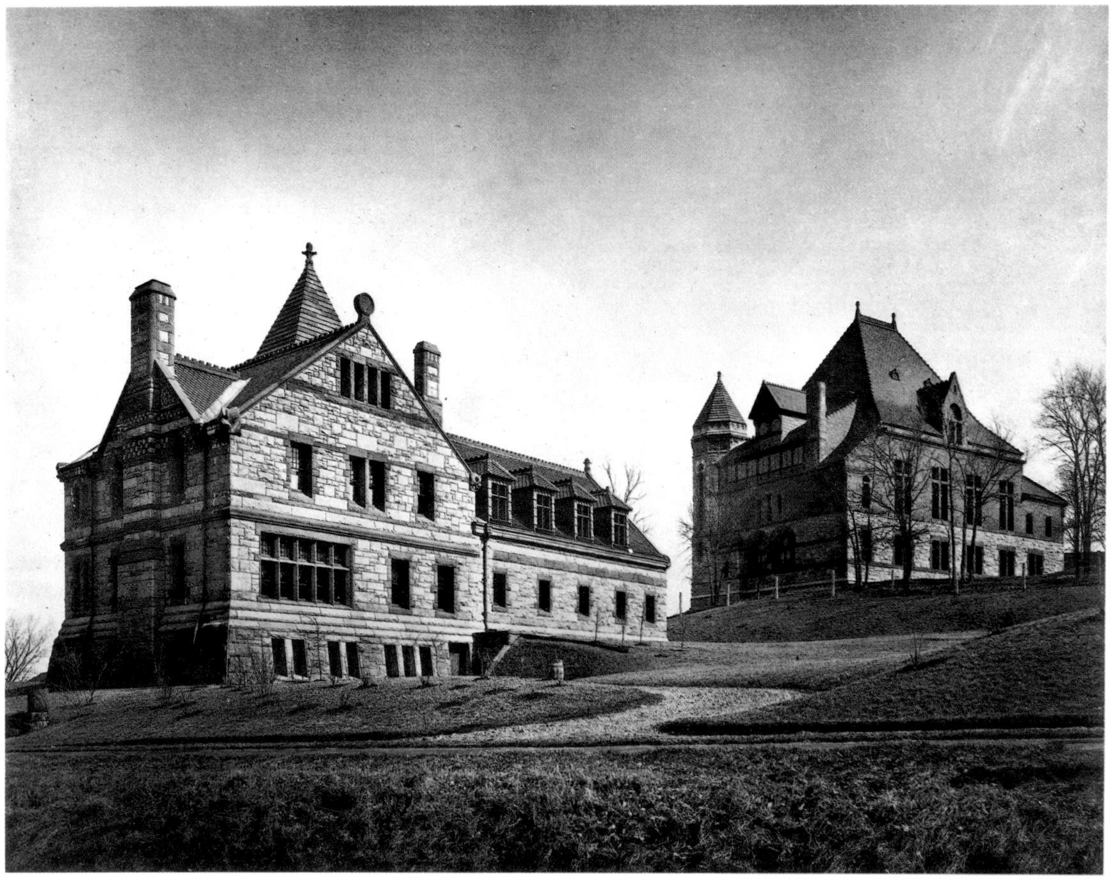

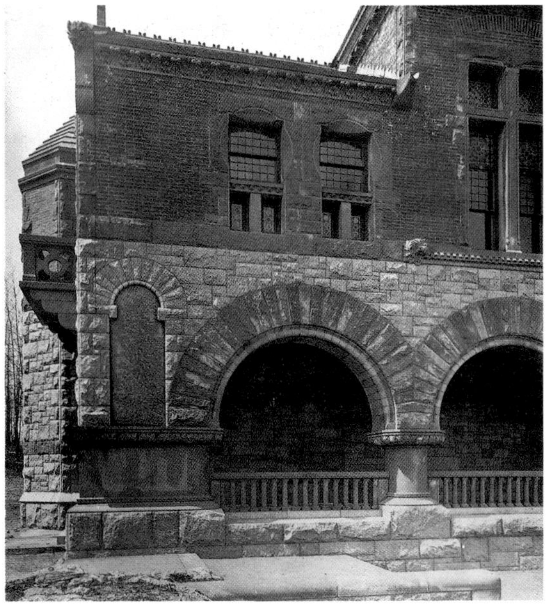

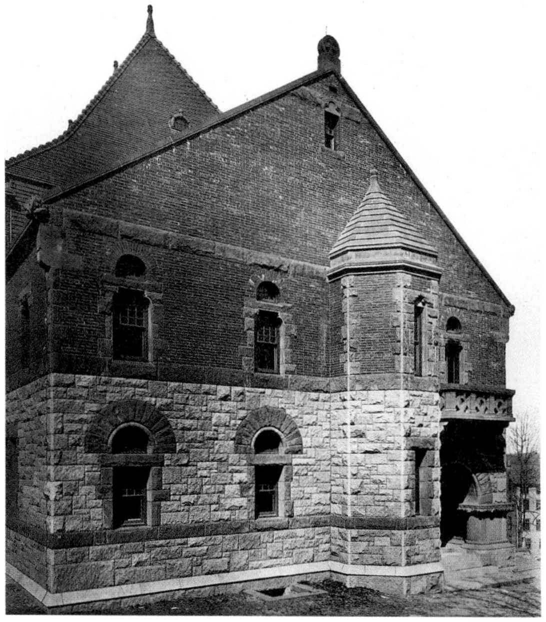

68 *PHOTOGRAPHER UNKNOWN*

North Easton, Ames Memorial Hall.
From *Monographs of American Architecture* (1886).
Collotype.
Avery Architectural Library.

69 *PHOTOGRAPHER UNKNOWN*

North Easton, Ames Memorial Hall.
From *Monographs of American Architecture* (1886).
Collotype.
Avery Architectural Library.

70 *PHOTOGRAPHER UNKNOWN*

North Easton, Ames Memorial Hall and Library.
From *Monographs of American Architecture* (1886).
Collotype.
Avery Architectural Library.

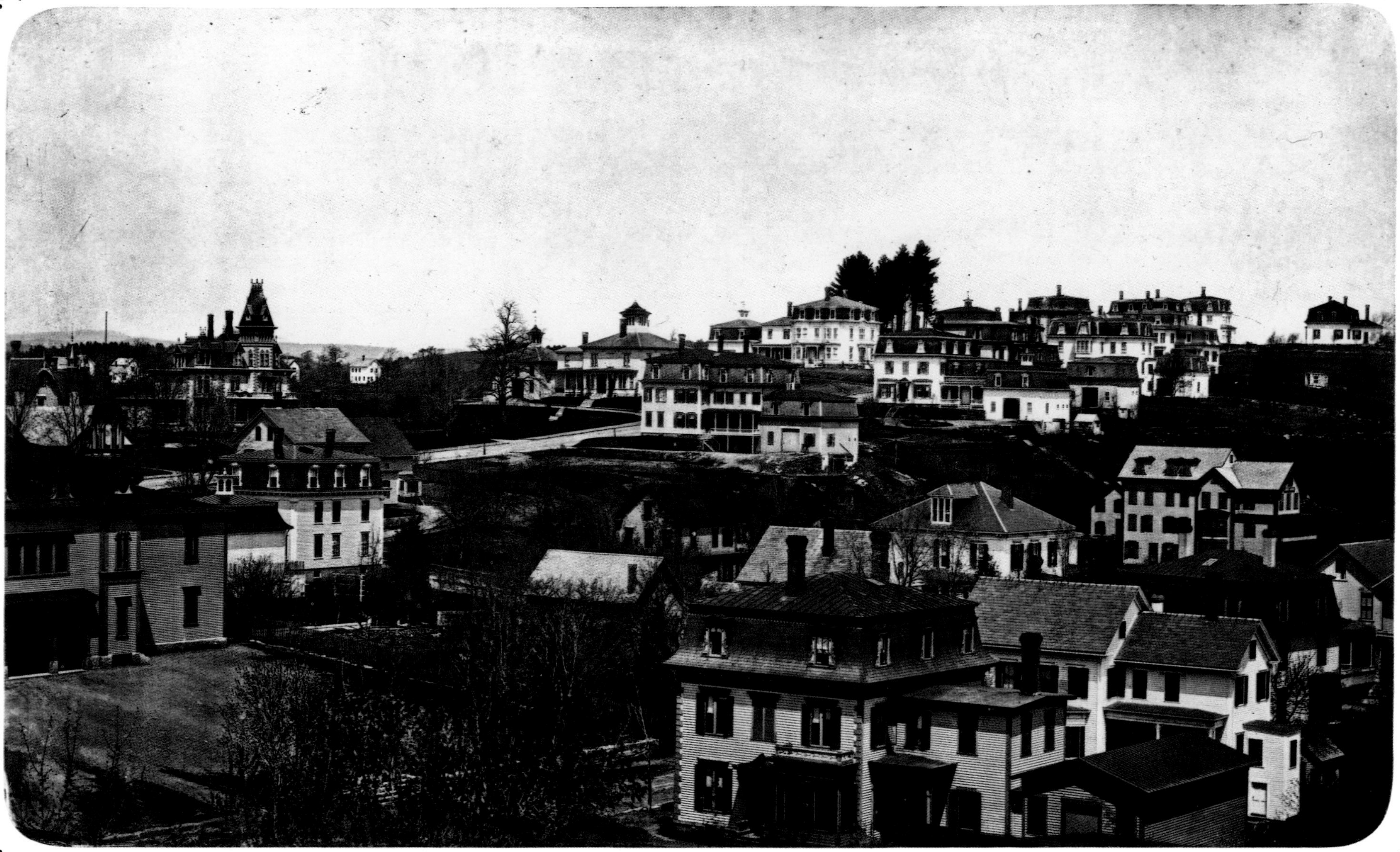

71 *Photographer unknown*

Leominster, Massachusetts, "Grove Avenue from Unitarian Church." From *Leominster Illustrated* (1880s). Pigment process. Avery Architectural Library.

they resemble the real thing, the more disappointing the few remaining disparities become.

Another example of this genre was a book of views of Moscow (1884–1891) in three volumes by N. A. Naidenov, the first two in photogravure and the third in collotype. The first volume is largely of individual buildings; the later two are made up of views taken across open spaces or the Moskva River of major buildings or urban groupings, including commercial streets. These pictures are made loosely in the sense that they are not only not closely cropped but freely incorporate surroundings of their proper subjects as though meant on principle to be unselective. But they are not carelessly comprehensive. We are given the same sense that some pictures taken in the 1970s give us that they are intended to be inclusive and therefore trustworthy rather than selective and probably biased. We view them with the conviction that we can see through them with extraordinary accuracy how Moscow looked in the 1880s, a city then of approximately the population of present-day Baltimore, Maryland, and one in which a building of over four stories stood out by its height (72).

Parallel to these efforts to publish architecture was that of Albrecht Meydenbauer (1834–1921), founder of photogrammetry and of the Königliche Preussische Messbildanstalt, of which he was director from 1885 to 1909. Meydenbauer's institution made precise photographs of German and Near Eastern historic architecture, 40 centimeter-square pictures from which measured drawings could be derived, a process he outlined in his *Handbuch der Messbildkunst in Anwendung auf Baudenkmäler- und Reise-Aufnahmen* of 1912. These pictures, often identifiable by index marks at the midpoints of their sides, were taken in the magisterial style of the 1880s: they managed whenever a subject allowed it—as the cathedral at Aachen does, shown here in a Messbild print that includes one whitened index mark uncropped by the Library of Congress at its bottom— to keep an objective distance from their subject and to show the whole of it, not a part; they rigorously maintained the square proportions of the camera format, as photographs would often cease to do in the decades to come; and they followed the tenets of traditional perspective rendering by the use of lens shifts to keep vertical lines parallel (a practice that would later be abandoned by photogrammetrists) (73). But to contemporaries these pictures would have seemed revolutionary, had they not probably been acceptable, only because of their highly technical purpose. The Messbild cameras used extremely wide wide-angle lenses and their photographers allowed the consequent perspective lines to show, as they do in the porch of the cathe-

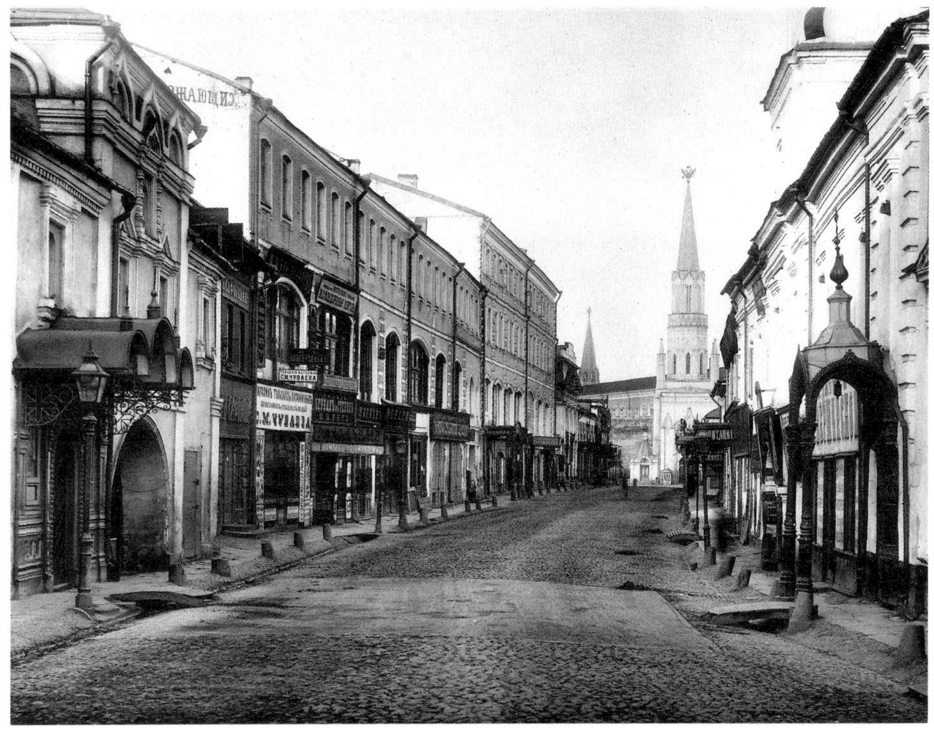

72 *PHOTOGRAPHER UNKNOWN*

"Moscow, view of Nikolskaya Street (from Bogoyavlenskaya Street to the Kremlin)."

From N. A. Naidenov, *Moskva* (1886).

Photogravure.

Avery Architectural Library.

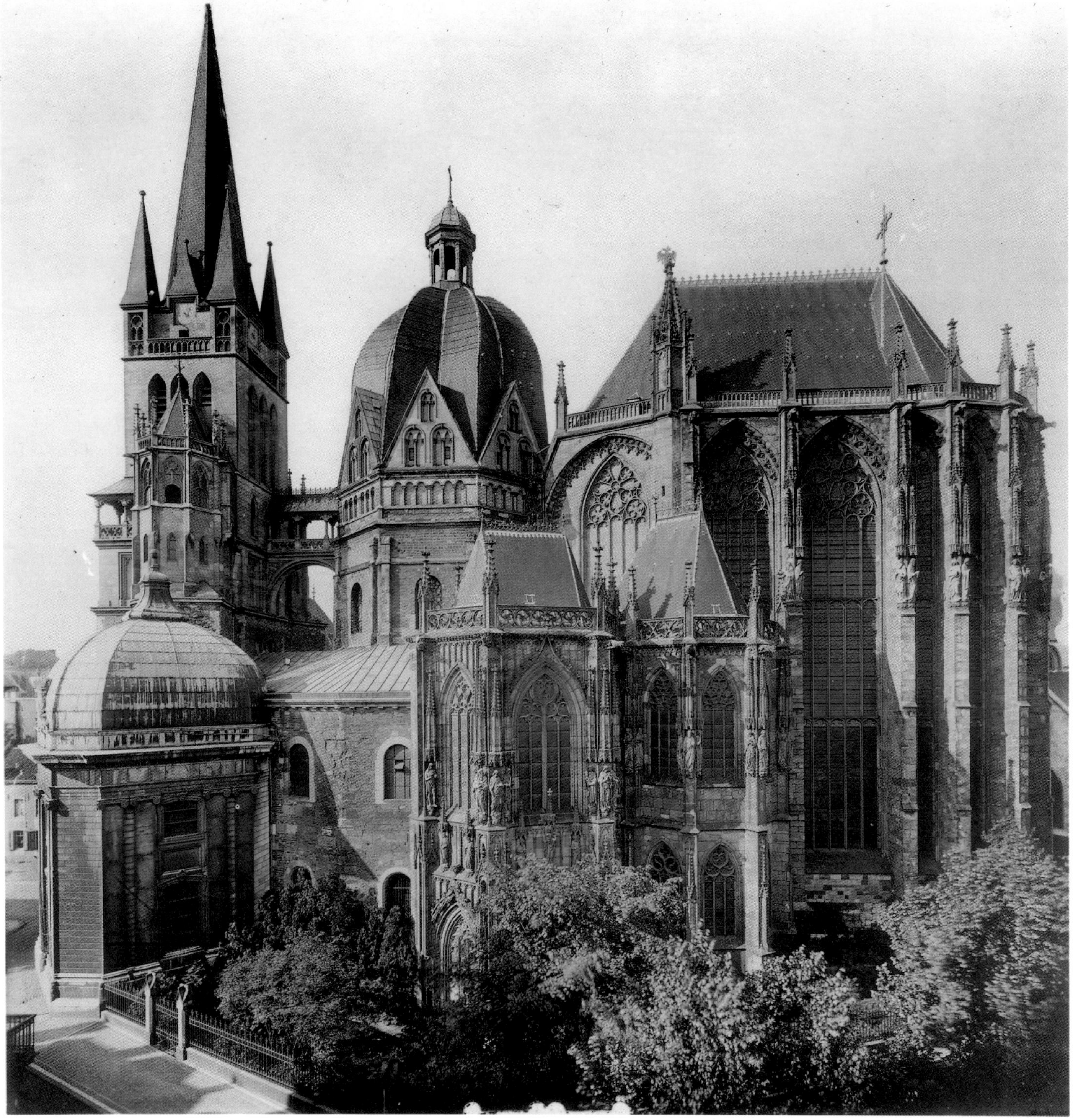

73 *PHOTOGRAPHER UNKNOWN*

Aachen Cathedral. From Königliche Preussische Messbildanstalt (1890s?) Collections of the Library of Congress.

74 *PHOTOGRAPHER UNKNOWN*

Erfurt Cathedral. From Königliche Preussische Messbildanstalt (1880s?). Collections of the Library of Congress.

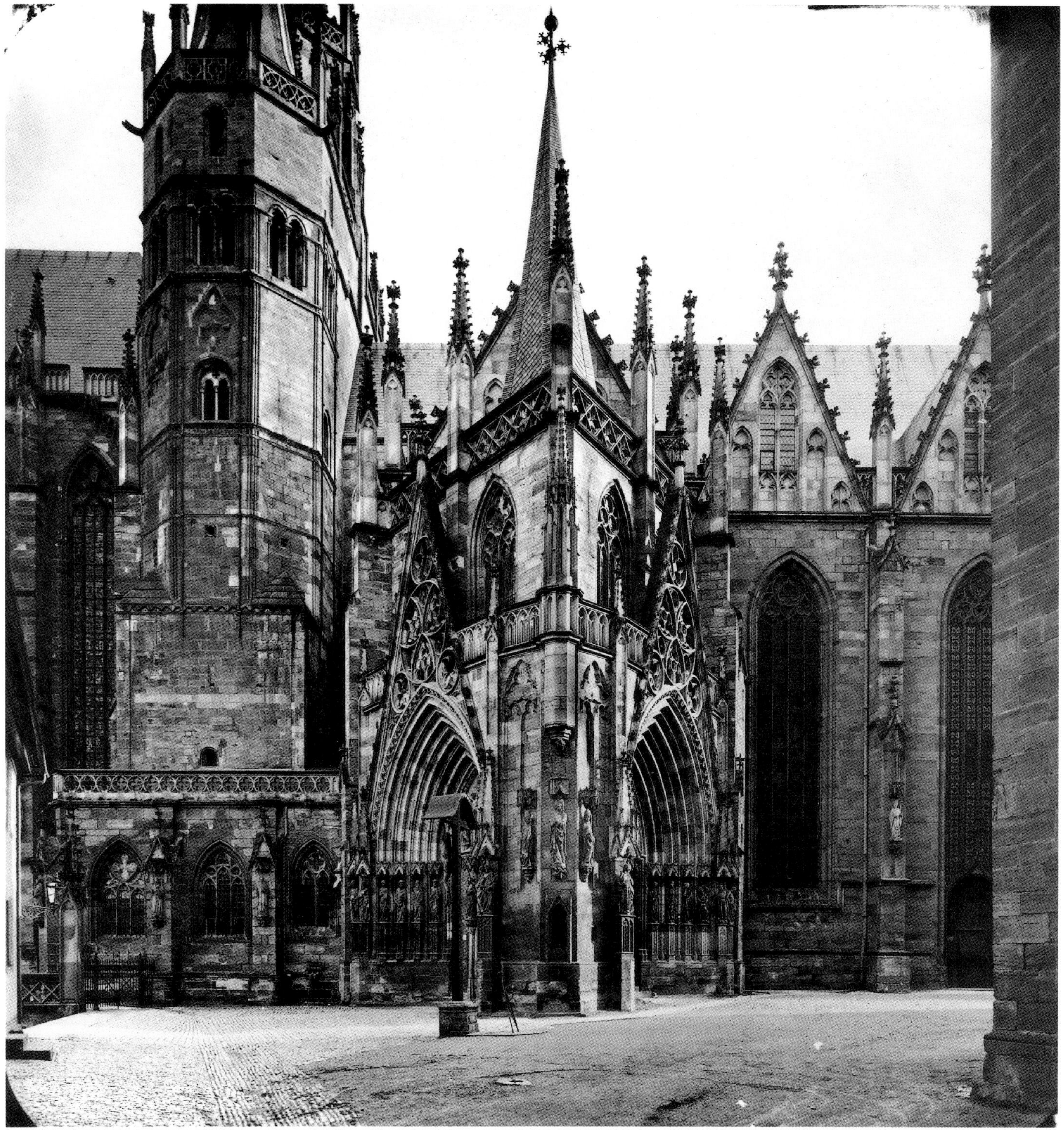

dral at Erfurt where the short focal length used can be read by eye from the two vanishing points on either side of the porch (74). The documentary intention behind these pictures represented the ultimate position in the stylistic spirit of the eighties. To our eyes, some of the Messbild pictures, particularly close-in, oblique ones, have a surprisingly modern look because of this acceptance of wide-angle distortion. Meydenbauer also devised photographic plate processing techniques that were intended to produce results analogous to the edge-enhancing, contrast-dampening effects of collotype. These were designed to reduce automatically the enormous contrast ranges encountered in some of his subjects (and were revived after World War II by American landscape photographers as part of what they named "the zone system").

In the 1890s and the first decade of the new century there was a turn away from the style of the eighties, which came to seem dated. Not only was there a simple change in taste—in some ways back to the emphasis on light in early calotypes—but a disparate set of influences worked against the older style, among them innovations in reproduction techniques and in camera and lens design. The turn was to a style that emphasized both light and a fragmentary view of the world. Pictures gave a feeling of the ambient qualities surrounding a subject, often of the light falling on it, and emphasized the selective aspect of picture taking, the quality photographs had of being rectangles plucked out of a larger piece of subject matter. If pictures in the eighties had promised the viewer facts, the most extreme of the new pictures gave the viewer a selected view and a sense of atmosphere at the expense of providing any precise information about the specific building that was the subject of a picture—one cannot even say the "nominal" subject, since sometimes the particular subject was not identified and it was clearly a point of embarrassment that a photograph had unavoidably to be of one particular thing rather than a generalized one.

The watershed between the new and the old styles is illustrated by C. D. Arnold's (1844–1927) photographs of the World's Columbian Exhibition of 1893 in Chicago, which put forward a set of buildings that would sell America on a classicizing revival, buildings that were most appropriately photographed in the old manner, as many of their progeny would not be. The exhibition buildings were free-standing structures whose visible roofs gave them a plastic coherence that the buildings constructed under their influence, most of them city row houses with a single facade on a street, generally lacked. Arnold's pictures are similar to the photographs of Richardson's buildings in that they too show free-standing buildings in a context of other free-standing buildings, as does, for instance, his view of George B. Post's Manufacturers and Liberal Arts Building taken from Machinery Hall (75). In this picture, as in the others in the style, the space allowed on either side of the building suggests the inclusiveness and completeness of the information given. In it, unlike many other pictures in the style which included broad areas of blank white sky above the subject and empty ground below it, the full proportions of the camera plate are rationalized by the rostral column on the right, and the paved area with planting and a balustrade at the bottom provide a base for the picture. However, two suggestions of a newer attitude appear in at least some of Arnold's pictures. The first is the presence of human figures looking at the view in pictures taken from high vantage points on the Manufacturers and Liberal Arts Building; in the instance illustrated here, there can be seen a woman in a light-colored dress, a descendant of many earlier figures contemplating views who would often in these years upstage the view behind them (76). The second suggestion of things to come was the use of platinum paper for these pictures; its use represented a fresh awareness of print media.

The posed people in such pictures point to a new emphasis on experience in photographs. Four years earlier a picture had been taken at the top of another exhibition building, the Eiffel Tower, whose height was made palpable in the picture by the presence of a man's figure on a spiral staircase to the very tip of the building and by the absence of any concrete details of the city in a haze behind him. But such pictures were not restricted to exhibition buildings. A picture that could be described in very much the same way was taken by Fratelli Alinari at the top of the tower of Florence's Palazzo Vecchio showing a man, again in the process of ascending a spiral staircase, with the Duomo only partially visible in the distance beyond him (77).

Though human figures in such photographs emphasized the experiential nature of the pictures, they tended to carry full significance just as it first became possible—perhaps because of an increase in emulsion speed—to pose them in some particular way. Later, when such pictures lost their novelty or when photographers could include such people without posing them, the sense of significance was always lost. As it seemed to happen, the energies of photographers suddenly able to work in light that had previously been too dark soon turned not to stopping motion but to rendering the special qualities of light.

As characteristic was a fresh confidence in showing partially what previously would have been shown wholly. This is illustrated in a construction photograph of Paul Wallot's Reichstag building (1894) in Berlin, a detail of a

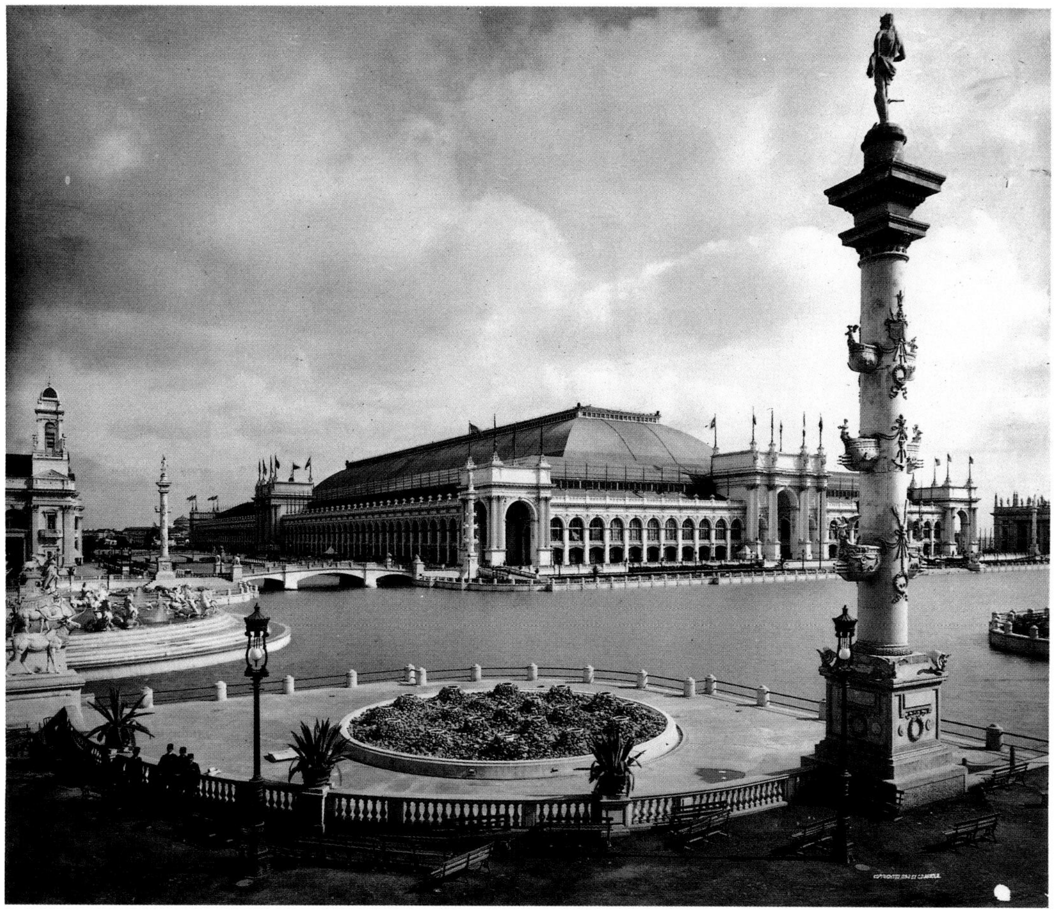

75 *C. D. Arnold*

Chicago, Manufactures and Liberal Arts Building, 1893.
Platinum.
Avery Architectural Library.

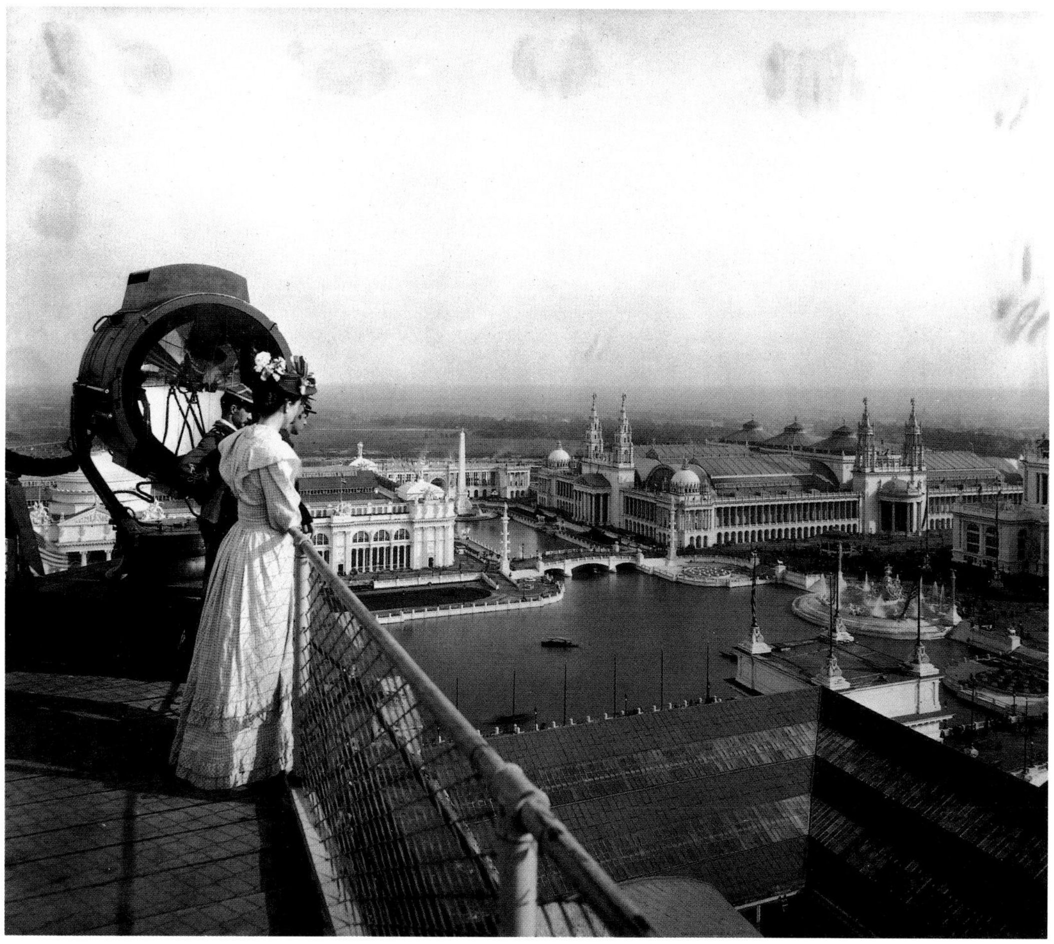

76 *C. D. Arnold*

Chicago, view from the Manufactures Building, 1893.
Platinum.
Avery Architectural Library.

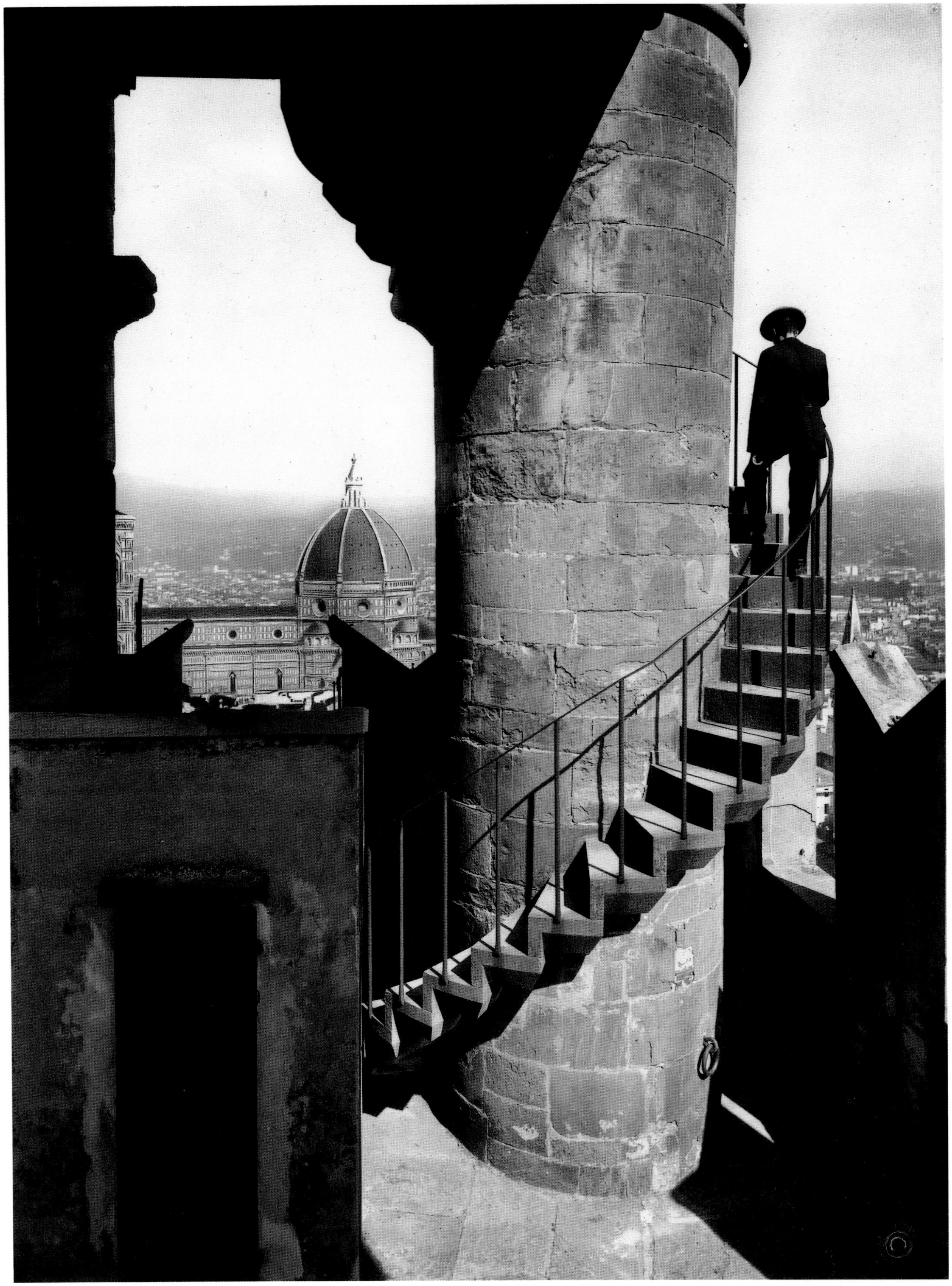

77 *Fratelli Alinari*

Florence, Palazzo Vecchio, ca. 1890s.

78 *Photographer unknown*

Berlin, Construction of Reichstag building.
From *Blätter für Architektur und Kunsthandwerk* (1893).
Collotype.
Avery Architectural Library.

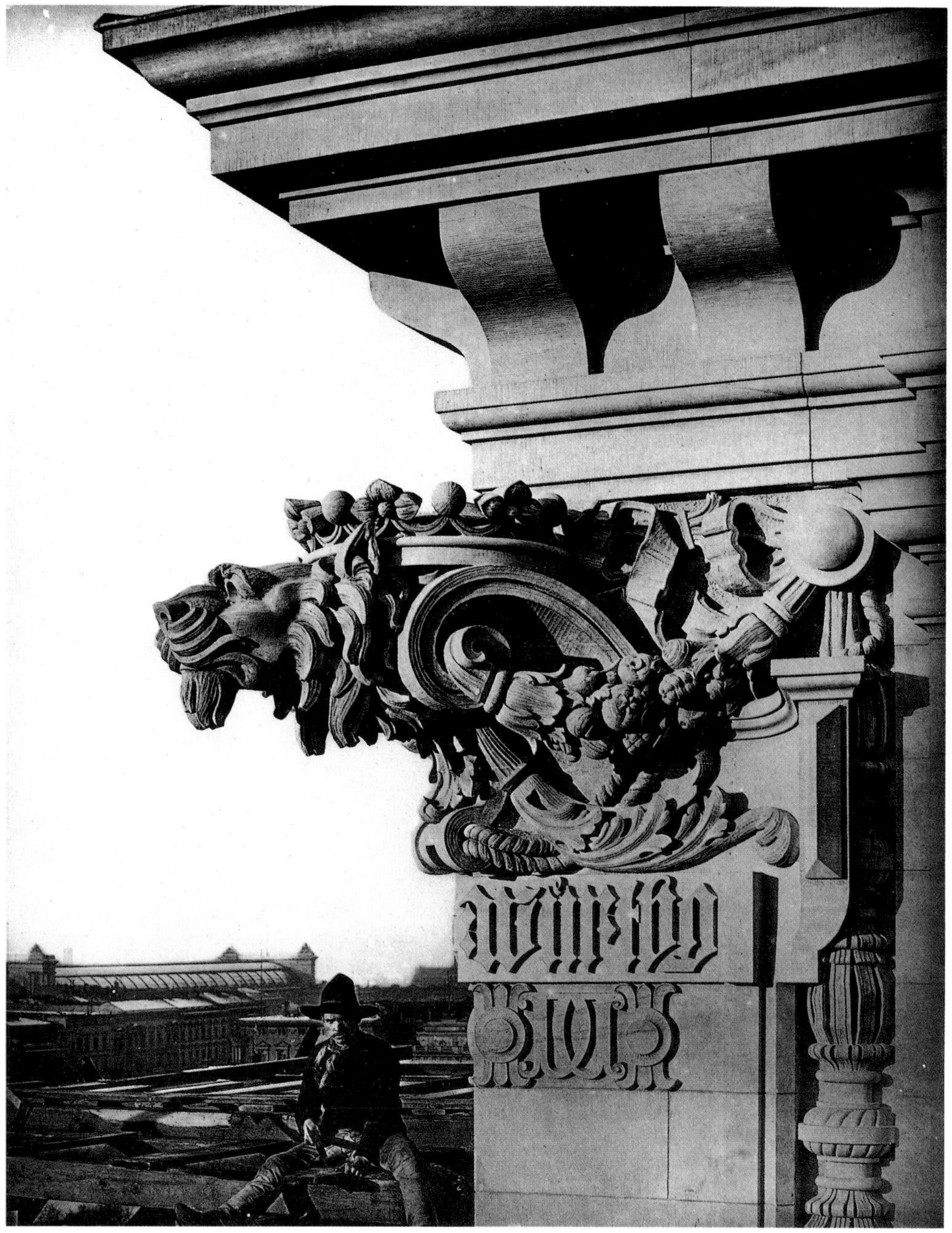

cornice that includes a human figure looking at the camera, a worker in a cowboy hat (78). Both the fragmentary view of the building and the ambiguous shift in emphasis that comes from the role the worker plays in the picture are fresh if not new (there are similarities between this picture and one by Charles Nègre of Henri Le Secq on Notre-Dame). In another photograph, reproduced like the Reichstag picture in *Blätter für Architektur* in the 1890s, a view of Milan Cathedral by Georg Büxenstein, the southwest corner of the building isolated in the picture frame, rather than the more common view of the whole building from the southwest, brings a surprising freshness and urgency to the subject, while the waiting carriage at the bottom of the picture provides not only scale but invites the viewer to participate (79).

A still earlier taste for cropped views of pedestrians and vehicles derived, as Aaron Scharf has pointed out, from what had happened at the edges of stereographs. Smaller cameras can have faster lenses, and some of the first equipment to stop the motion of pedestrians and vehicles had been stereoscopic cameras. Because of the interval that passed between the time the apparatus was set up and the ground glass focusing screen at its rear observed under a black focusing cloth, and the time a plate holder could be introduced (when the image on the screen would no longer be visible), a photographer had at best to guess which pedestrians and vehicles were inside his picture's edges and which were outside. Some inevitably were halfway in, and this led to a taste—in paintings, for instance—for such clipped subjects. In the nineties a similar taste was apparent in architectural photography for the cropping of subjects that would not have moved. This was encouraged by changes in reproduction technology and in lens and camera design.

The innovation in reproduction was the successful development of halftone reproduction by letterpress, a process by which the middle tones of photographs were represented by dots of ink of varying sizes on a regular grid, one whose virtues were that pictures could be printed in the same press run with texts, whereas collotypes and photogravures were printed in separate press runs on what was likely to be a different paper from texts. Some magazines that started up in the nineties, such as *Architectural Record* and *Country Life*, made use of the new process from their inceptions. The predictable conjunction of text and illustrations both made possible and encouraged two things: first, the publication of buildings of which one did not necessarily approve—it was implicit in the older plate system that what was published was approved of, else why would it be published—and, second, the fortuitously odd juxtaposition of pictures on a page. *Architectural Record* could feature its "Architectural Aberrations" that joined a photograph of a building to a text saying why it was bad architecture, only because its innovative method of printing ensured that picture and hostile text would be reliably next to each other. The odd juxtapositions of pictures on a page in many magazines developed in their readers a taste for such combinations that would become significant in the 1920s.

With the introduction of halftone some of the special characteristics of the older processes became more apparent. In practice both the boundaries and the tonal quality of two examples of what was ostensibly the same collotype reproduction could vary widely, one perhaps having especially good middle tones and another giving more detail in highlights or shadows. Any photographer who was used to having his pictures reproduced by such a process would have learned to expect the edges of his pictures to be approximate so that any important detail should be well inside them; he would also have learned to expect a loss in the feeling of light in his pictures and a gain in a sense of minute detail.

In contrast to this, the edges of a halftone were more precisely fixed and, even more significantly, had often been adjusted to fit among areas of text—as original photographs mounted in earlier books had rarely been—a process of editing that had sometimes made the pictures more incisive. That is, they had been cropped where text demanded it and the subject allowed, and this sometimes could improve the photographs. The photograph of a bathhouse from a page of a 1902 issue of *Baumeister* is cropped high and narrow to fit between two columns of type (80). Simultaneously lines on either side of the picture by their conjunction with its edges lend a purposefulness to the picture that might well have been lost had the building been shown in the older style, in its totality with room to spare. A second difference that halftone brought was that it had none of the tone-dampening action of earlier processes, and so the character of light in photographs was more directly transmitted. But halftones seemed inferior in several ways as well. Their quality was often intentionally run-of-the-mill since they did not require the special papers of other processes. And the structure of dots that made up their grey tones was always slightly apparent and made them seem more mechanical than earlier reproductions. As a further consequence of the pattern of dots, halftones were themselves difficult to reproduce by a screened process without producing an unpleasant secondary moiré effect. The advantage of the process made it unavoidable, but its disadvantages, mostly coming from its screened nature, made all the earlier pro-

79 *Georg Büxenstein*

Milan Cathedral. From *Blätter für Architektur und Kunsthandwerk* (1897).
Collotype.
Avery Architectural Library.

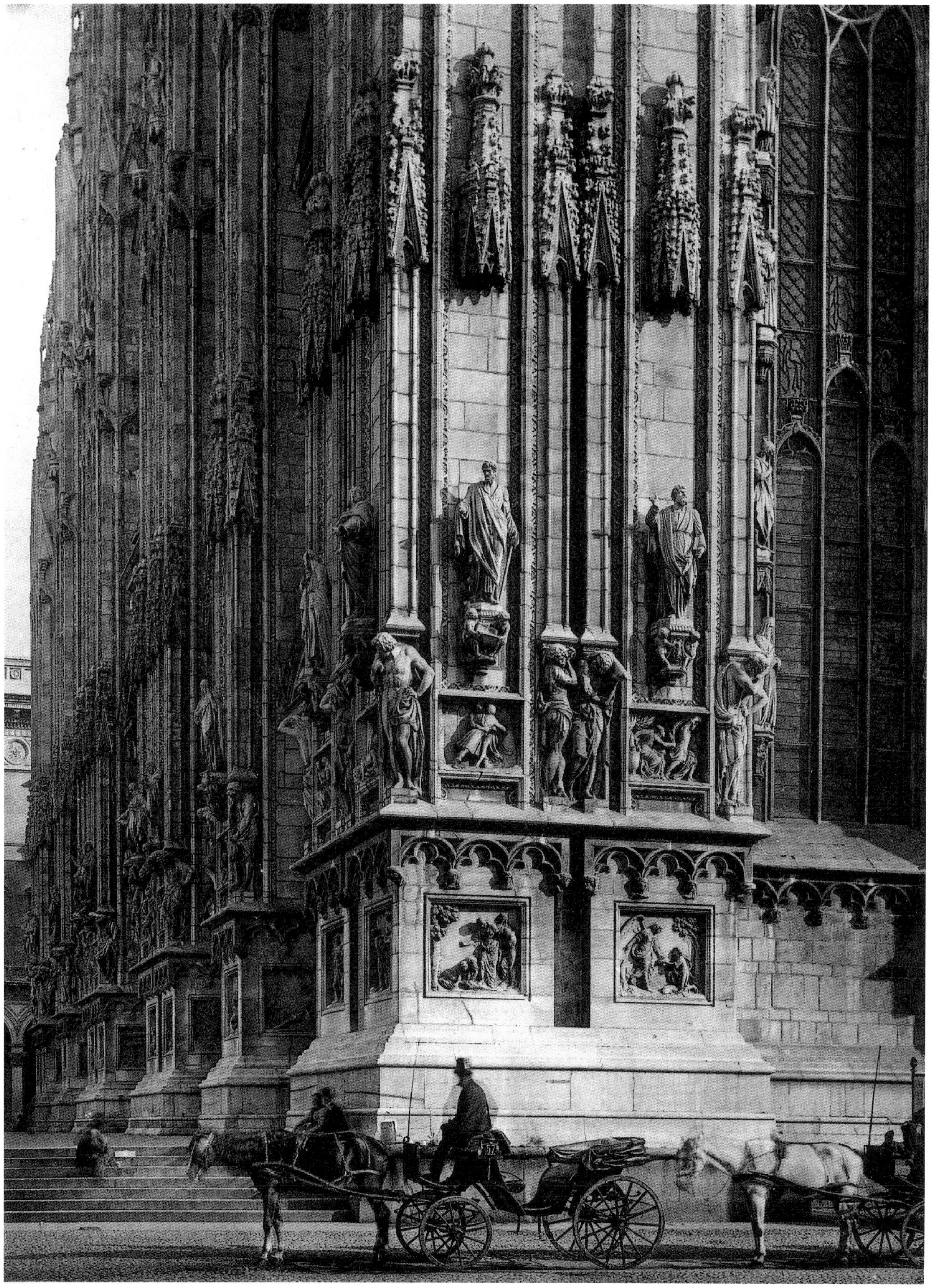

80 View of a German bathhouse.
From *Baumeister* (1902).
Halftone.
Avery Architectural Library.

81 *CHARLES LATHAM*
Cheshire, Little Moreton Hall.
From *In English Homes* (1904).
Halftone.

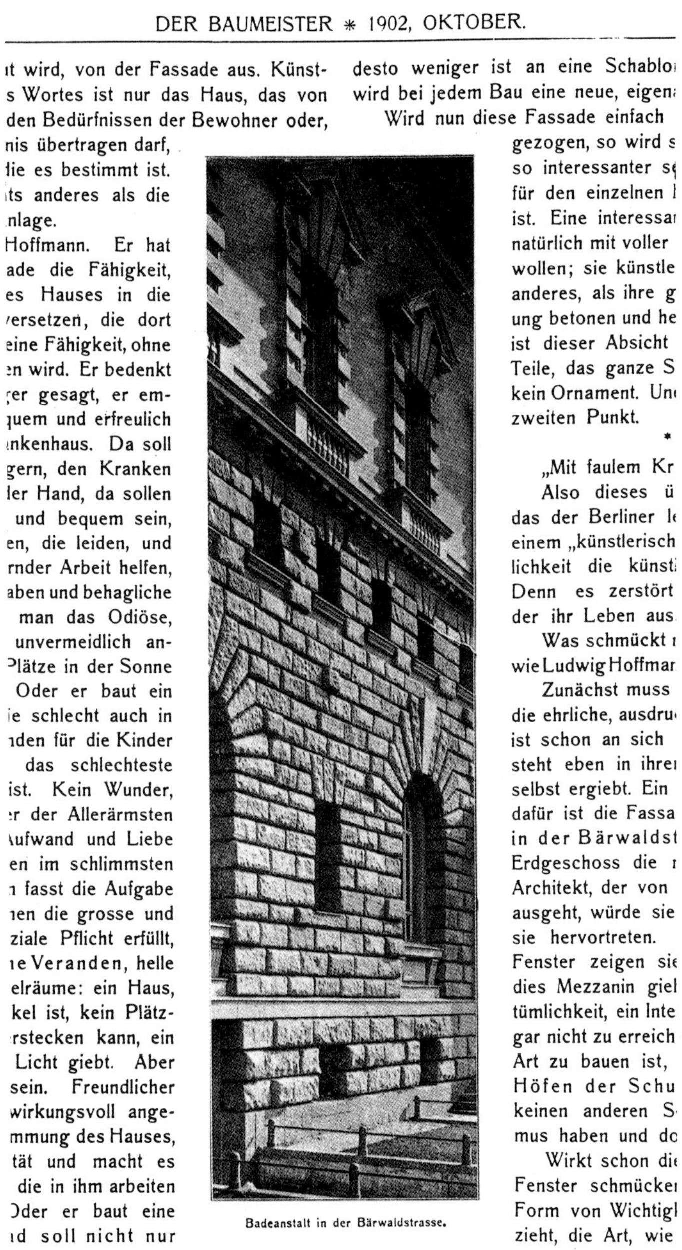

DER BAUMEISTER ✻ 1902, OKTOBER.

ıt wird, von der Fassade aus. Künst-
s Wortes ist nur das Haus, das von
den Bedürfnissen der Bewohner oder,
nis übertragen darf,
lie es bestimmt ist.
ıts anderes als die
nlage.
Hoffmann. Er hat
ade die Fähigkeit,
es Hauses in die
'ersetzen, die dort
eine Fähigkeit, ohne
ın wird. Er bedenkt
ꞔer gesagt, er em-
ʇuem und erfreulich
ınkenhaus. Da soll
gern, den Kranken
ler Hand, da sollen
und bequem sein,
en, die leiden, und
rnder Arbeit helfen,
aben und behagliche
man das Odiöse,
unvermeidlich an-
Plätze in der Sonne
Oder er baut ein
ie schlecht auch in
ıden für die Kinder
das schlechteste
ist. Kein Wunder,
ır der Allerärmsten
ufwand und Liebe
en im schlimmsten
ı fasst die Aufgabe
ıen die grosse und
ziale Pflicht erfüllt,
ıe Veranden, helle
elräume: ein Haus,
kel ist, kein Plätz-
rstecken kann, ein
Licht giebt. Aber
sein. Freundlicher
wirkungsvoll ange-
mmung des Hauses,
tät und macht es
die in ihm arbeiten
Oder er baut eine
ıd soll nicht nur

desto weniger ist an eine Schablo
wird bei jedem Bau eine neue, eigen
Wird nun diese Fassade einfach
gezogen, so wird s
so interessanter s
für den einzelnen I
ist. Eine interessa
natürlich mit voller
wollen; sie künstle
anderes, als ihre g
ung betonen und he
ist dieser Absicht
Teile, das ganze S
kein Ornament. Un
zweiten Punkt.

„Mit faulem Kr
Also dieses ü
das der Berliner I
einem „künstlerisch
lichkeit die künst
Denn es zerstört
der ihr Leben aus
Was schmückt
wie Ludwig Hoffmar
Zunächst muss
die ehrliche, ausdru
ist schon an sich
steht eben in ihre
selbst ergiebt. Ein
dafür ist die Fassa
in der Bärwaldst
Erdgeschoss die
Architekt, der von
ausgeht, würde sie
sie hervortreten.
Fenster zeigen si
dies Mezzanin giel
tümlichkeit, ein Inte
gar nicht zu erreich
Art zu bauen ist,
Höfen der Schu
keinen anderen S
mus haben und dc
Wirkt schon di
Fenster schmücke
Form von Wichtig
zieht, die Art, wie

Badeanstalt in der Bärwaldstrasse.

cesses and other unscreened processes that might be devised, as well as original prints—particularly ones that resembled the earlier reproductions as Arnold's platinum prints had resembled photogravures—seem the more special.

The work of two photographers who contributed to *Country Life* illustrates several aspects of the newer style. In a photograph of windows on the courtyard of Little Moreton Hall, Cheshire, by Charles Latham, reprinted in the photographer's book *In English Homes* of 1904, the bays fill the picture, bellying out into the viewer's space as they would not have done if the edges of the plate had not been brought close to them (though the confined nature of the courtyard was clearly a contributing reason to Latham's taking them in this manner) (81). The work of Frederick H. Evans (1853–1943), a bookseller-turned-photographer, illustrates this fragmentary approach and other aspects of the new style as well. His "A Sea of Steps," when compared to Cundall and Downes's earlier view of the steps to the chapter house at Wells Cathedral, illustrates the effect of concentrated attention that comes to a view that eliminates all that is inessential (though what now seemed inessential had seemed part of the facts of the staircase in the eyes of the earlier photographers—Ruskin's "different parts fitting themselves to different purposes") (82). The picture demonstrates again the experiential emphasis that comes from a surface—that of the steps—that is thrust forward toward the viewer and demonstrates the manner in which light, here characteristically for Evans layered between the near and distant parts of the picture, becomes part of the experience of the subject and not, as in the earlier style, a means for showing objects with clarity. Another picture by Evans, of Bourges Cathedral, illustrates his inclination to give us the atmosphere of a building at the expense of telling anything concrete about its formal organization (83). Not only could we not make a conjectural plan from this picture, but Evans does not make clear which fragment of the building we are looking at. We get the impression that he thinks such information would distract us from his true intention. Evans retained all of the wariness of earlier photographers in regard to the camera's perspective with wide-angle lenses. In an essay in the *Practical Photographer* of 1904 he wrote, "It would be a good plan for the worker who desires pictures rather than views . . . to take a long lens and compel himself to find subjects to suit it . . . it is, of course, the golden rule . . . always to use the longest focus lens that existing conditions will permit. . . ." He went on to recommend keeping the camera as low as possible to keep the floor from "being *apparently* that of a steep incline." In general, Evans's work demonstrates a new

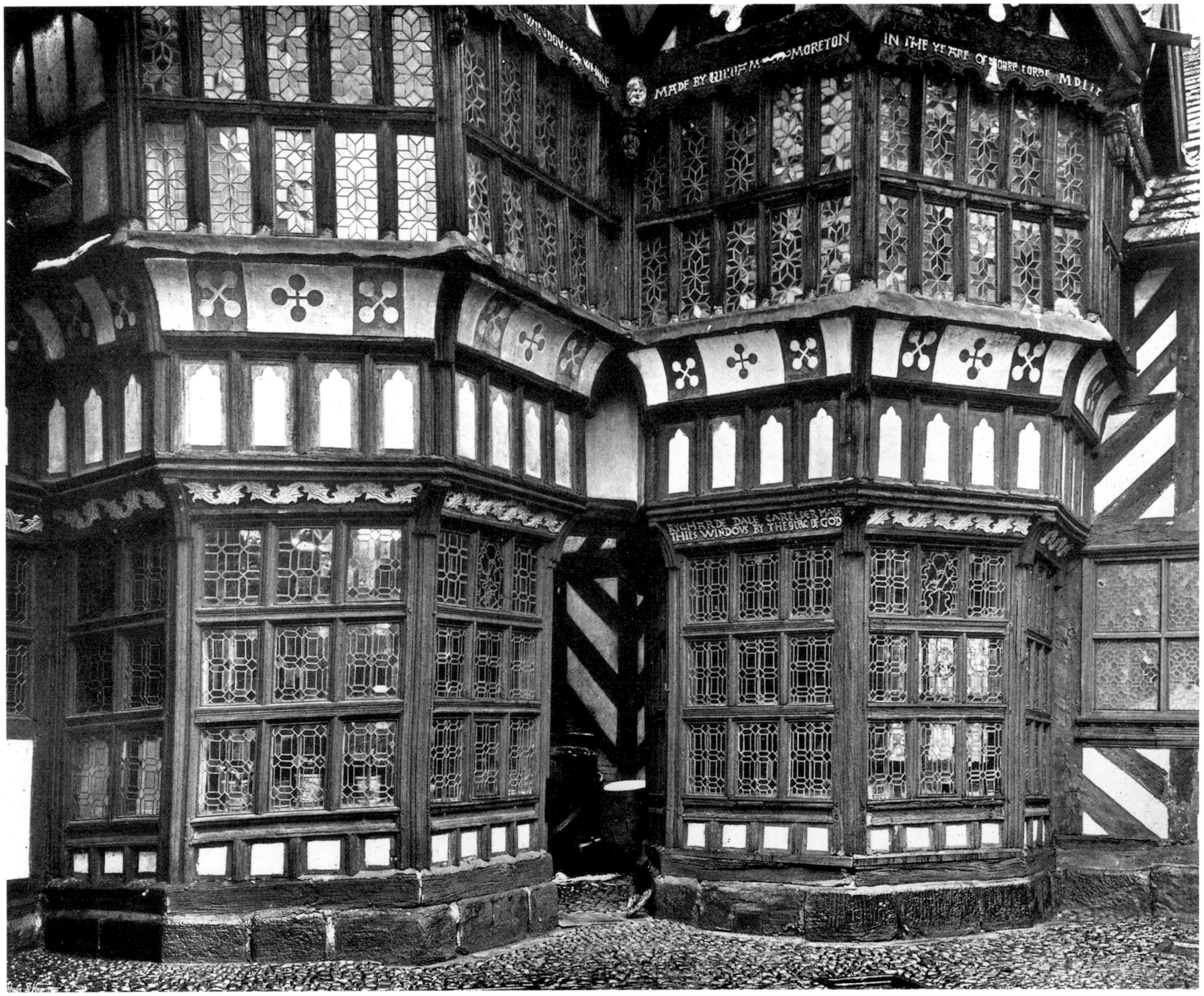
MADE BY
MORETON
IN THE YEARE
RICHARDE DALE
MADE
THIES WINDOVS BY THE
GOD

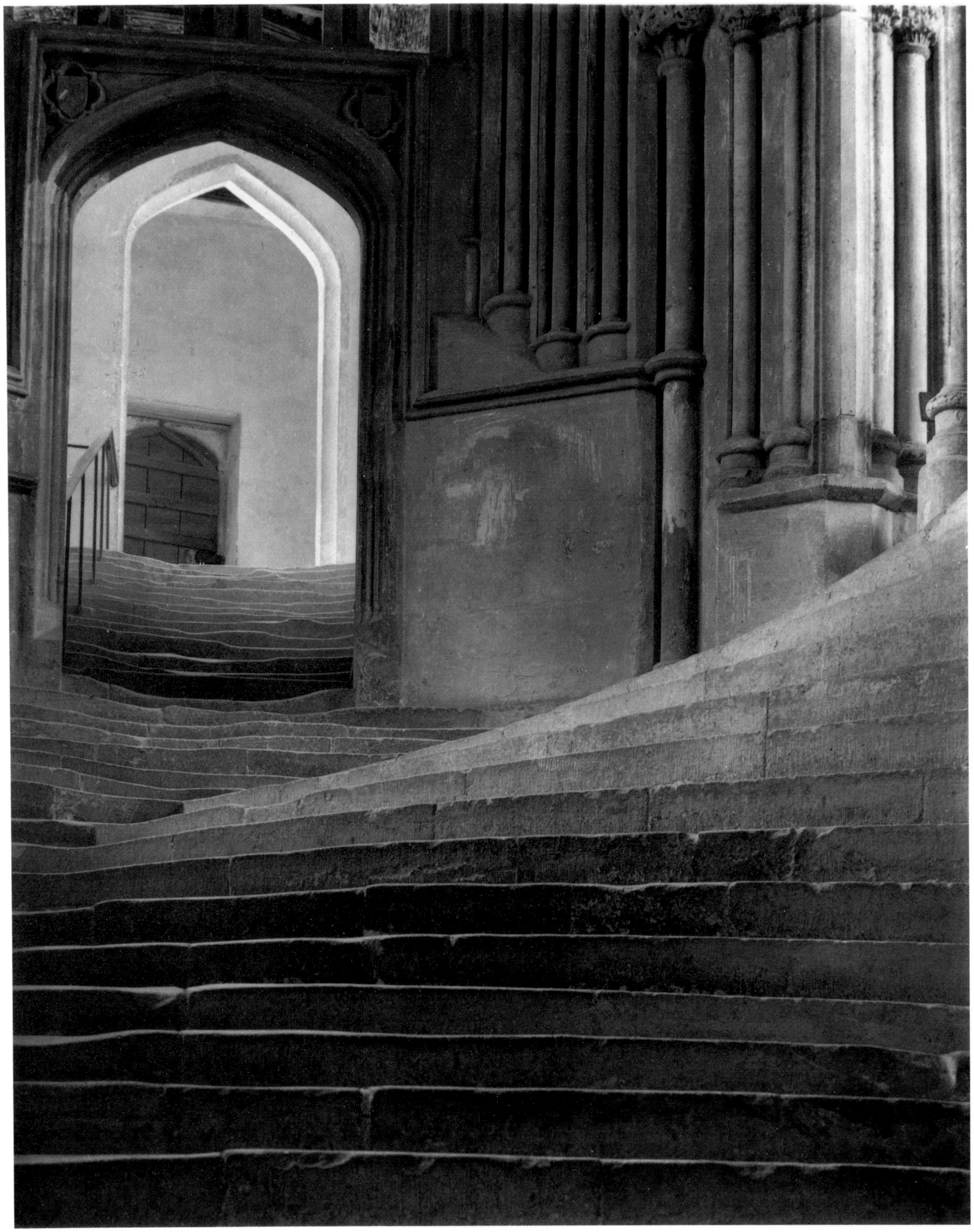

82 *FREDERICK H. EVANS*

Wells, "A Sea of Steps," 1903.
International Museum of Photography at George Eastman House.

83 *FREDERICK H. EVANS.*

"Height and Light in Bourges Cathedral," 1903.
Platinum.
Metropolitan Museum of Art, New York.
The Alfred Stieglitz Collection.

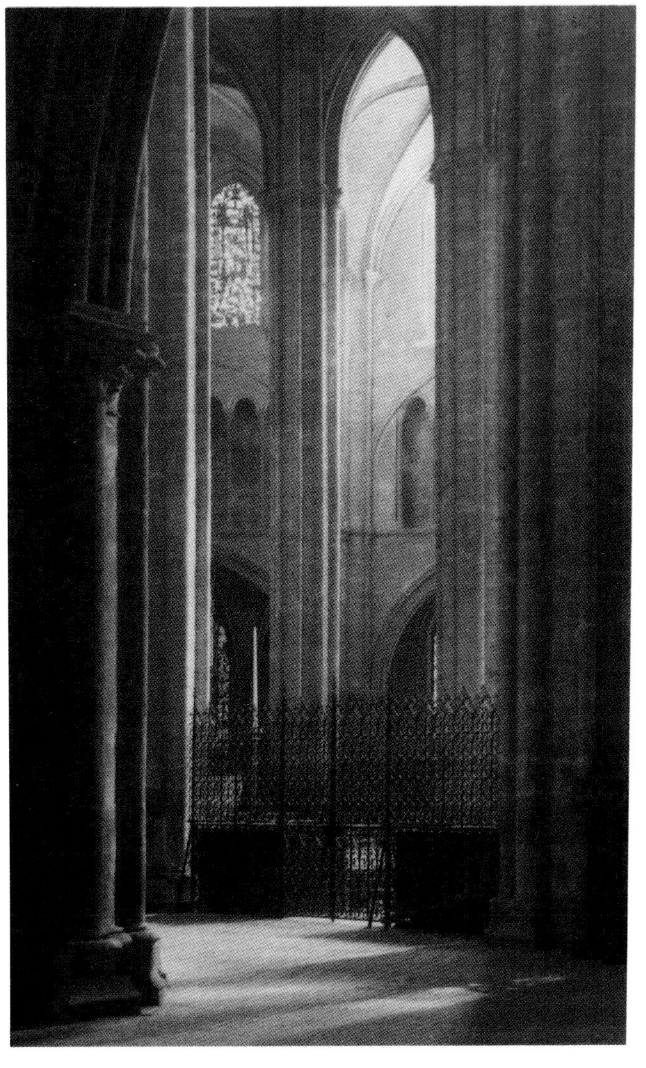

commitment to a limited range of subject matter, in his case, medieval churches, that brought its own characteristic and desirable forms and atmosphere, whereas workers in the earlier style had a more professional attitude. He also showed a new consciousness of medium by his preference for prints on platinum paper, which, rather than reproductions, he clearly thought of as his end product.

The manufacture of platinum paper was intended to provide a print material more permanent than silver. Its physical character was similar to earlier photogravures (at this time gravures were sometimes screened, and therefore more mechnical than the earlier ones), setting such prints at a desirable remove from both halftones and common, glossy photographic prints.

Of the three characteristics of the newer style, fragmentary views, an emphasis on qualities of light, and an inclination to use special printing media, the first two were the most significant. Choice of special papers or printing techniques was largely a question of packaging and therefore superficial. The use of such media was an easy way of setting one's work apart from that of the hordes who used more common papers or printing techniques; the first two were choices made at the time a picture was taken and were therefore more essential. A more significant aspect of work in these years, and one parallel to the self-consciousness of printing on special paper, was a sense that certain subject matter might be a given photographer's most appropriate material. Just as Evans became associated primarily with medieval subjects, others showed a comparable awareness in their choice of subjects.

The French actor-turned-photographer Eugène Atget (1857–1927) managed to find—or to create—a France largely untouched by the hand and awareness of the twentieth century. An early view like that of St. Maclou at Pontoise shows his generation's characteristic emphasis on light and its willingness to cut off part of a subject and run other parts—the gargoyles—dangerously close to the edge of a picture (84). By comparison an earlier photograph by an unknown photographer of Amiens from the collection of the architectural firm of Leopold Eidlitz shows the lengths to which the previous generation of photographers would go in order not to cut off part of a subject (85). In order to include the tops of the towers, he is willing to abandon the standard requirement that a building's vertical lines be rendered as parallel in a photograph. (In fact the angular field of his lens is only wide enough just to include the whole church in this tipped perspective, and the diameter of the field is not even great enough to cover his plate.) If Atget was willing to cut off part of a

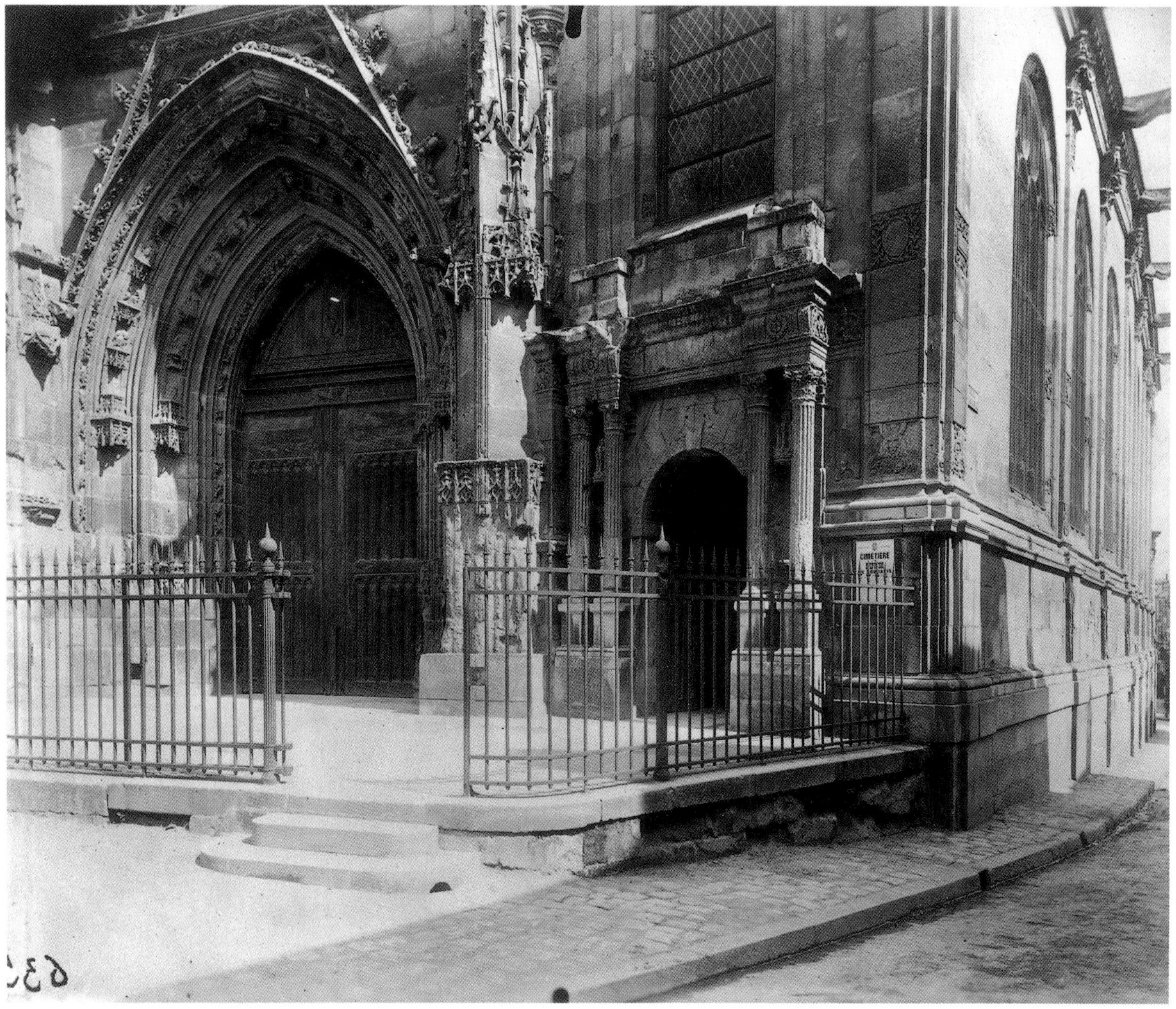

84 *Eugène Atget*

Pontoise, Church of St. Maclou, 1902.
Museum of Modern Art, New York.
The Abbott-Levy Collection.
Partial gift of Shirley C. Burden.

85 *Photographer unknown*

Amiens Cathedral, n.d.
From Collection of Leopold Eidlitz.
Avery Architectural Library.

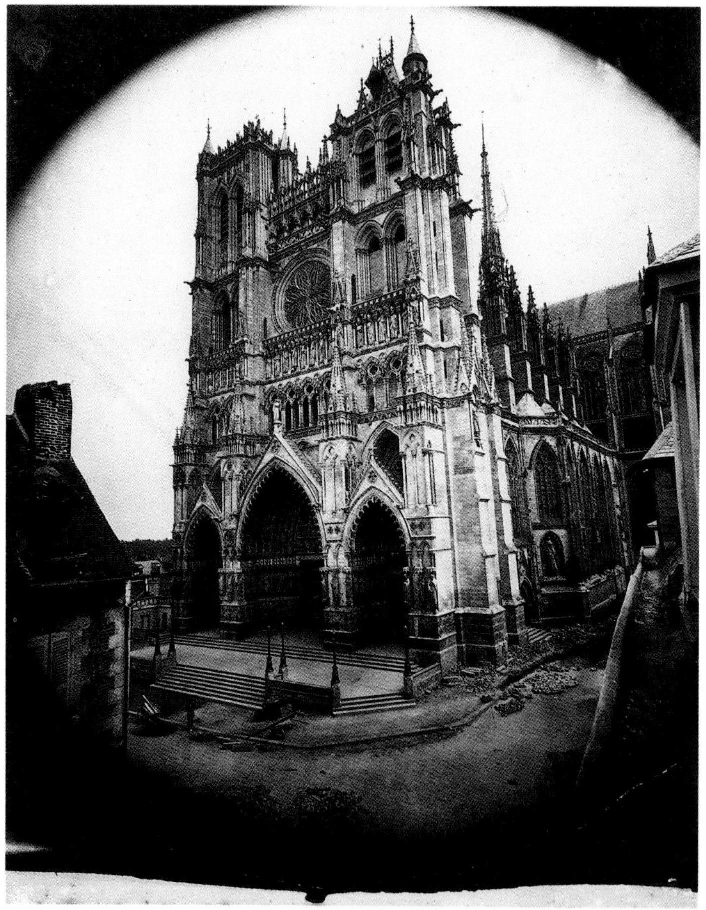

subject, he did not do so in order to use a longer lens that would give him more "correct" perspective. He did so while using a standard (for him) relatively short lens. One of the reasons for his appeal to us is his complete acceptance of the perspective of such a lens, and his consistent use of it gives his work both unity of style and modernity in our eyes.

Some photographers worked in the newer style without abandoning old forms of reproduction and without specializing in one genre of subject. In 1910–12 there appeared an elegant publication in plate gravure of Paul Vitry's *Hôtels et maisons de la renaissance française* consisting of photographs by Chevojon Frères, pictures that were not outside the range we associate with Atget. In one photograph arched openings and brackets are selected from the facade of the Maison de la Coquille at Orléans (86). The camera is close enough to show sculptural details with clarity and far enough from the subject to give us a clear idea of the role the details play in the facade. The relationship of building details to the edges of the picture—the architrave and flowerpots at the top, the capitals at the bottom, the endings of the molding courses on the left, and the door paneling on the lower right—lend a sense of intentionality to the picture and, as a consequence, a new and aggressive sense of confidence in picture making. In another, of the courtyard of the Hôtel de Réynès at Albi, we get very much the same pleasure we do from an Atget photograph except that the architectural interest of the subject is more specific and greater than it would be in an Atget and that the photographer, because as a professional he means to take the best possible picture of the object of preservation before him, even if it means intruding his presence on it, has wetted down the pavement in order to reduce glare from it (87). But it would be a mistake to associate only this subject matter with the firm of Chevojon Frères, for their earlier picture—of Contamin and Dutert's Halle des Machines in 1889 in Paris, in the newer style because it juxtaposes a close detail of a three-hinged arch's support at ground level with a whole arch seen in the distance—betrays a quite contradictory taste (88). Chevojon Frères were generalist professionals.

Frances Benjamin Johnston (1864–1952), an immensely energetic if often undisciplined photographer of many kinds of subjects, took, in partnership with Mattie Edwards Hewitt (1870–1956) from ca. 1909 to 1917, highly skilled pictures of architectural interiors, and after the war became a photographer of, among other things, gardens. The picture shown here from among her photographs of Hampton Institute, though taken in the late nineties before her turn to the subject of architecture proper, illustrates the manner in which human figures with their attention turned to the subject of a picture, can heighten our sensual awareness of it (89). We feel the surfaces of the woodwork of the staircase as an unpeopled picture could not have made us do. Johnston demonstrated that she—or perhaps her age—thought interiors and gardens particularly appropriate for a woman; indeed women had made specialties of these two forms of design. The photographing of architectural interiors had flourished since the 1880s, when each of D. Appleton's *Artistic Houses* had been represented by a single interior taken in a stylized fashion by flash illumination. Such photographs are by their nature experiential because they are always partial views; no interior can pretend to be the complete, distanced record that had been sought from exteriors taken in the older style.

The cropping of subjects and emphasis on qualities of light had also been encouraged by innovations in lens and camera design. These were the introduction of faster lenses, notably the Zeiss Tessar, in the early years of the new century, and of cameras that could exploit them to the full, cameras that might be used either on tripods or hand held, pointed with one of two kinds of reflex finder from waist level. One of these finders was a through-the-lens type similar in principle to those on many present-day cameras. It was usable with a longer lens than was appropriate for architectural photography. The other kind of camera had a finder mounted close to the lens and often combined with a level to give a small, bright, and approximately outlined version of what the lens could see.

One response to the introduction of this sort of equipment was travel pictures taken by architects, for instance, those made in 1911 by Charles-Edouard Jeanneret. Taken with a camera of minimal flexibility that offered a limited ability to look up while maintaining parallel verticals, these pictures inevitably emphasized surfaces at the photographer's feet, like the pavements and steps from Prague and Pisa illustrated here, just as the Rolleiflexes used by British editors in the 1950s at waist level emphasized similar pavements and street furniture as well (90, 91, 92). Relatively fast equipment and plates that allowed pictures to be taken in poor weather encouraged ones in which rain, say, seems an integral part of the subject. And the ease with which the small equipment could be employed encouraged views of surfaces seen at hitherto unexpected angles that further emphasized the experiential nature of the pictures.

Jeanneret's compatriot, Fred Boissonas (1858–1946), was also taking voluminous pictures of eastern Mediterranean subjects in an often experiential style

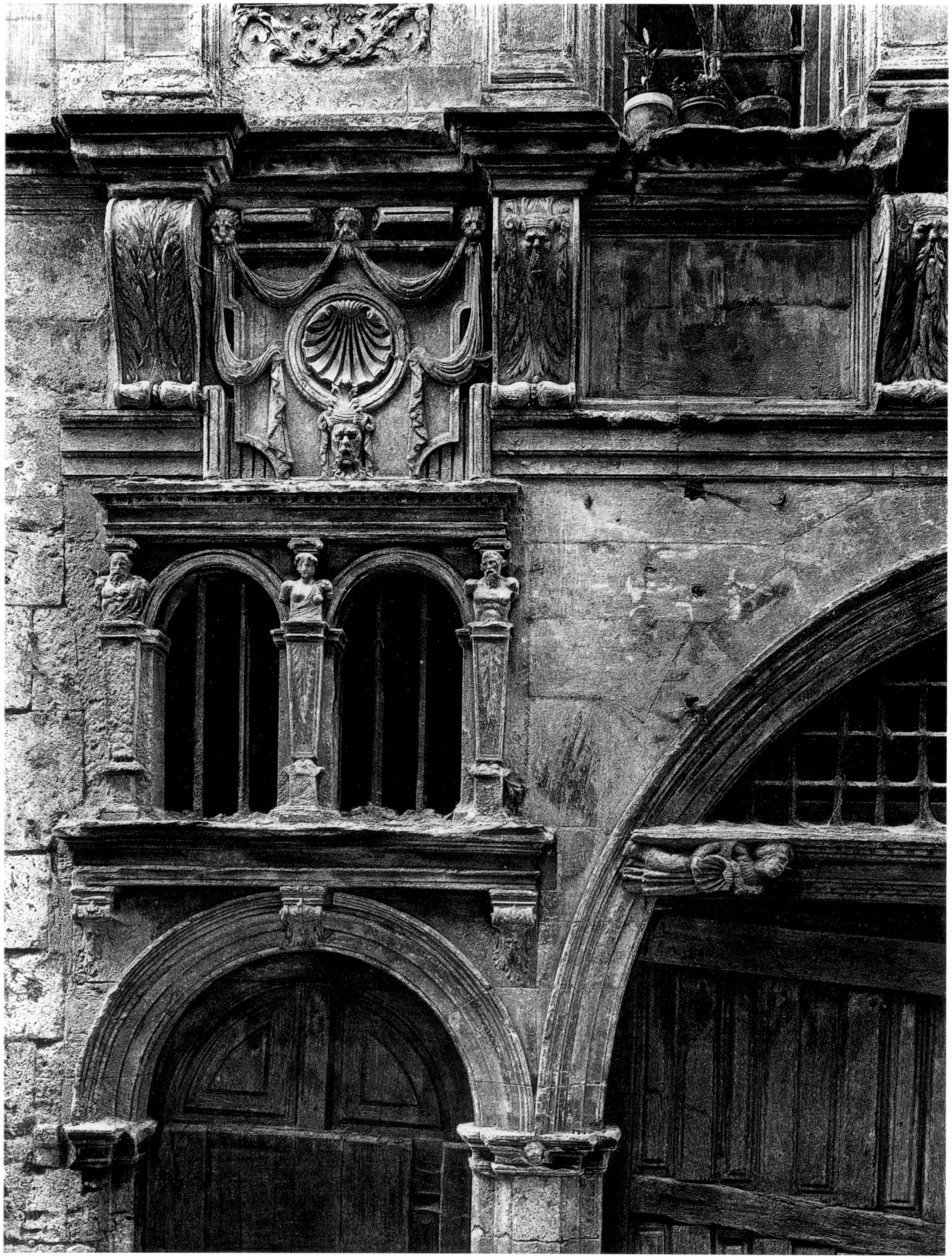

86 *Chevojon Frères*

Orléans, Maison de la Coquille. From *Hôtels et maisons de la renaissance française* (ca. 1910).
Photogravure.
Avery Architectural Library.

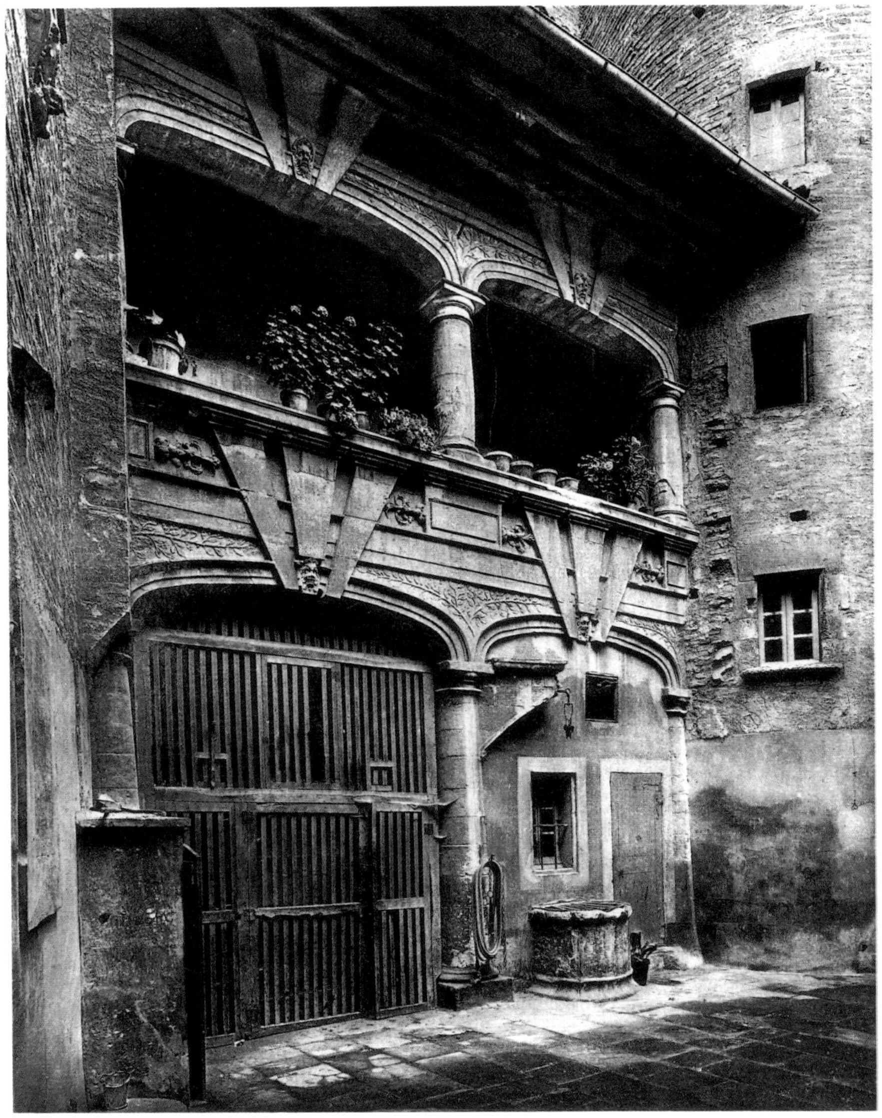

87 *Chevojon Frères*

Albi, Hôtel des Réynès.
From *Hôtels et maisons de la renaissance française* (ca. 1910).
Photogravure.
Avery Architectural Library.

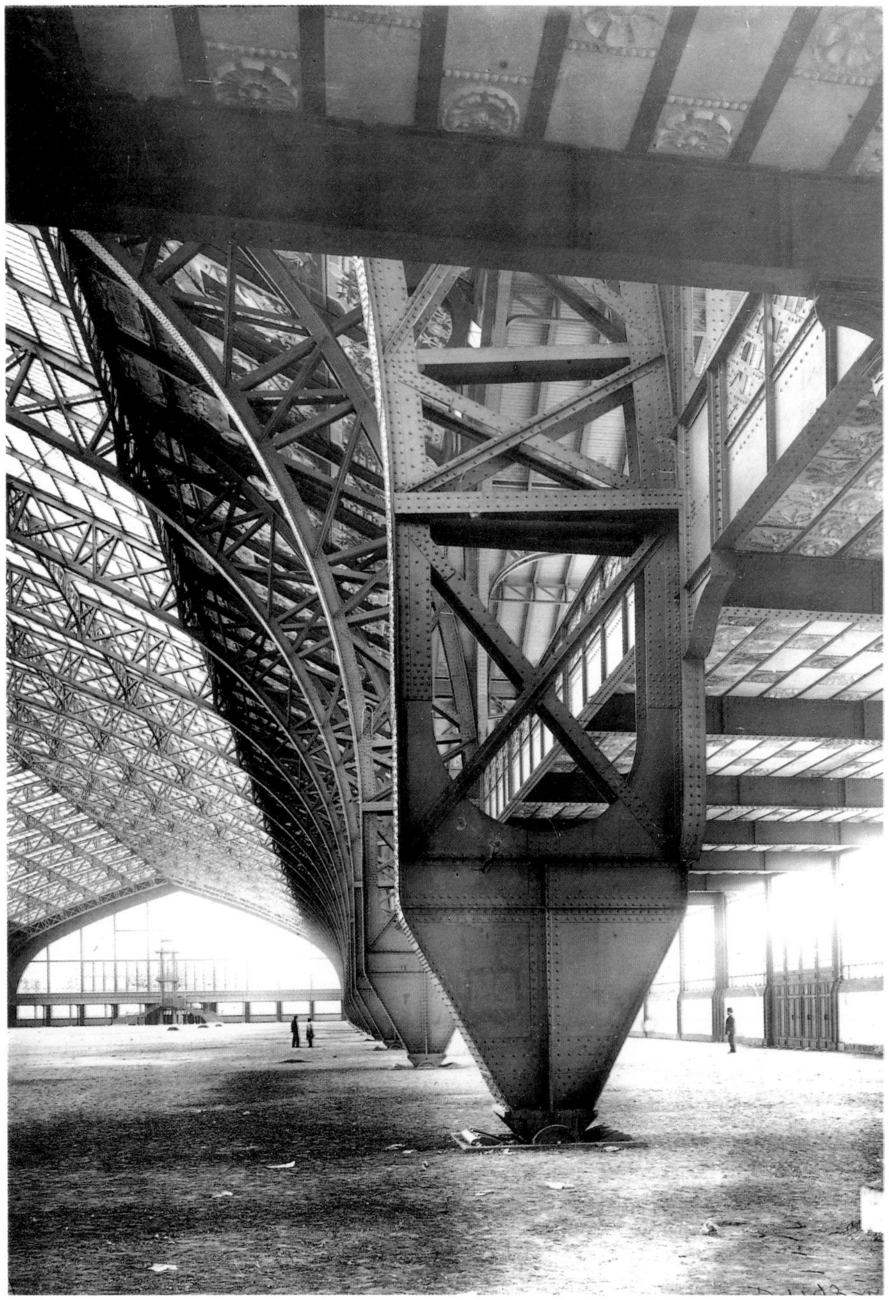

88 *Chevojon Frères*

Paris, Halle des Machines, 1889.

89 *FRANCES BENJAMIN JOHNSTON*
Stairway of treasurer's residence, students at work.
From an album of Hampton Institute (1899–1900).
Platinum.
Museum of Modern Art, New York.

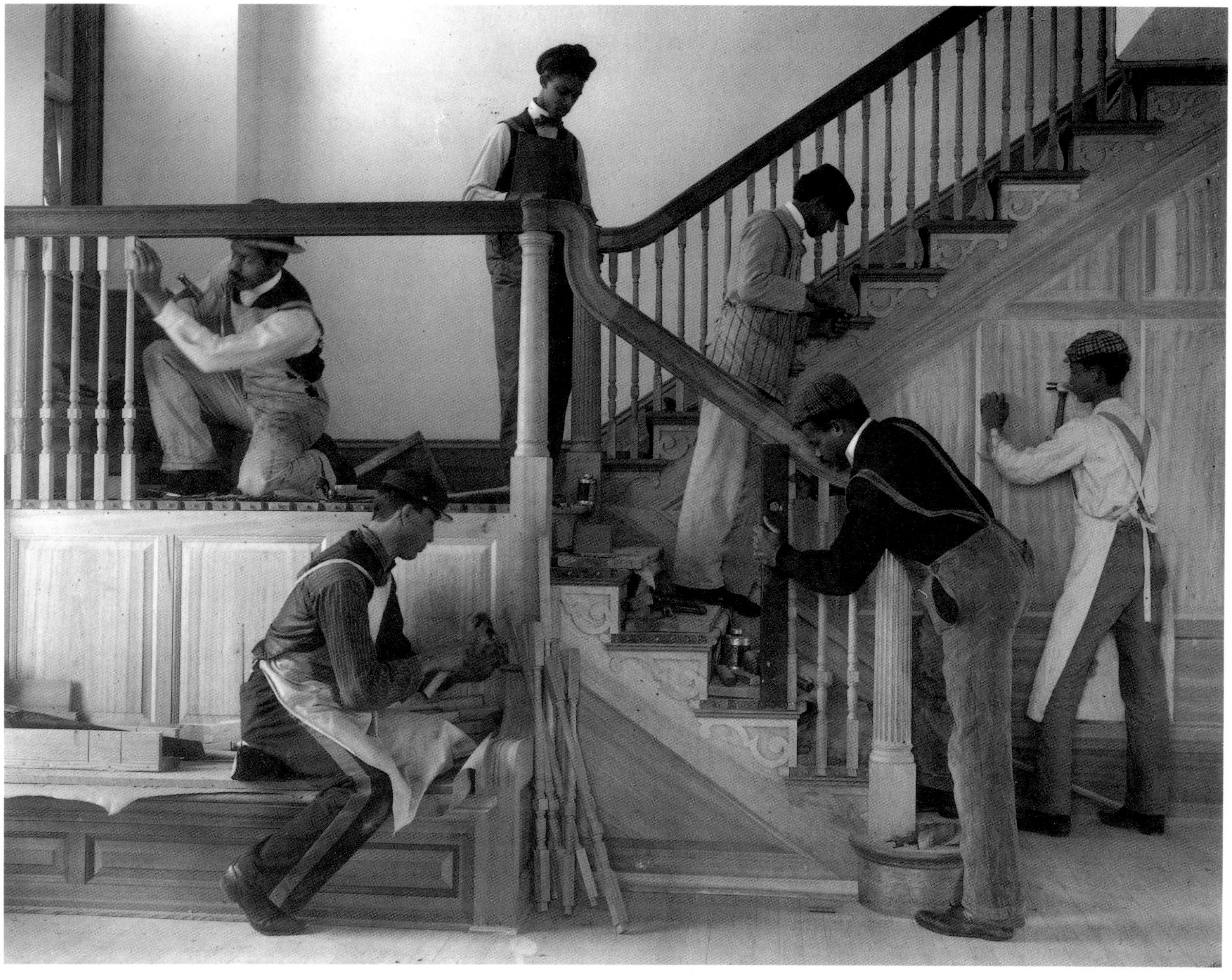

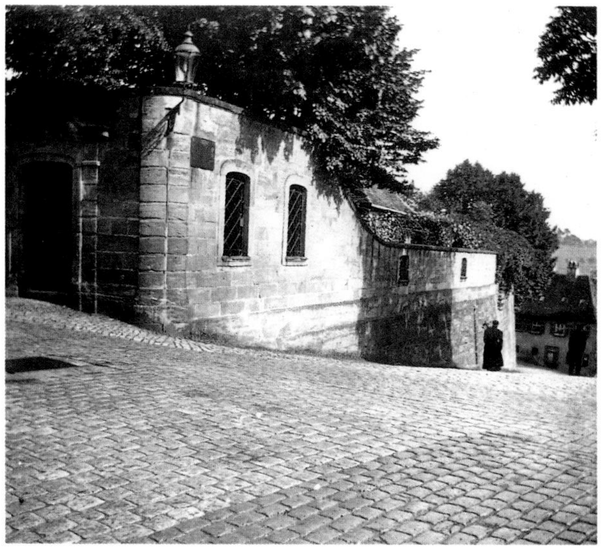

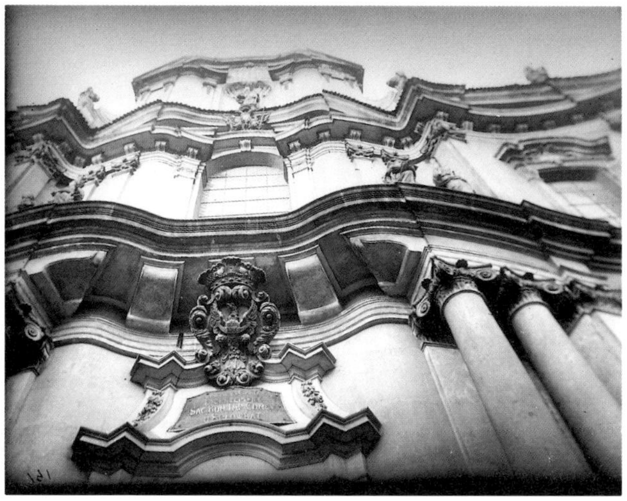

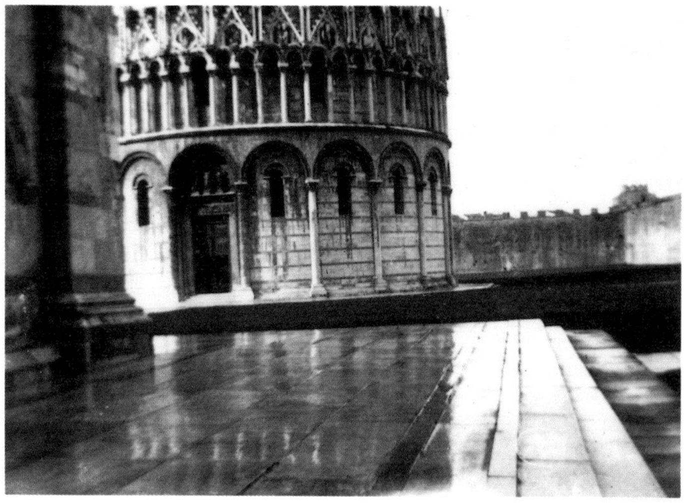

90 *Charles-Edouard Jeanneret*

Prague, ascent to castle, 1911.
Bibliothèque de la Ville, La Chaux-de-Fonds.

91 *Charles-Edouard Jeanneret*

Prague, St. Nicholas on the Kleinseite, 1911.
Bibliothèque de la Ville, La Chaux-de-Fonds.

92 *Charles-Edouard Jeanneret*

Pisa, baptistry from north transept, 1911.
Bibliothèque de la Ville, La Chaux-de-Fonds.

in these years and in the early twenties, pictures that he published himself in booklets to be sold as souvenirs. But he had also photographed with "W. A. Mansell & Co." in a factual manner for a lavish French publication of 1910, *Le Parthénon: l'histoire, l'architecture et la sculpture* (with an introduction by Maxime Collignon). When in the twenties Jeanneret/Le Corbusier used his compatriot's photographs of the Parthenon in *Vers une architecture,* the pictures he chose were not the experiential later ones—the most experiential he used in the book illustrated an "impeccable adjustment to the law of optics"—but the earlier, tense, head-on, factual ones. By the twenties the architect's taste had changed.

Architects were not the only amateurs of photography who exploited the new lenses and cameras. Their use was apparently common among the photographers encouraged by Alfred Stieglitz. Edward Steichen's use of such equipment to take his "The Flatiron" of 1904 is clear (93). This is a dusk view that a new fast lens made possible. Its use at full aperture led to characteristic lack of definition at the edge of the field of the lens where the top of the building falls, and the loss of the top of the building is probably due to the inaccuracy of the finder but in any case conformed to the new style and served to make the building seem taller. Such views made at dusk or in the rain or the snow, which would come to be condemned as trite and hackneyed by the 1930s, seemed fresh and innovative at the time they were taken.

Considerable embarrassment was apparent among Stieglitz's group at both the sharp, nonhandworked quality of simple photographs, which seemed to them unartistic, and the reluctance of photography to generalize. "Artistic" handwork is apparent in many of the pictures Stieglitz encouraged, including the Steichen shown here and one of an unidentified Italian building by the Austrian Hugo Henneberg (1863–1918) (94). Both are "gum prints." This interest in special printing techniques was paralleled by Stieglitz's interest in the older reproduction techniques he often used in preference to halftone in his periodical *Camera Work.* Indeed, the artistic printing techniques of photographers probably bore the same relationship to the older reproduction techniques as, in traditional printmaking, monotypes bear to engravings and etchings.

The wish that photography would generalize led other photographers than Henneberg to leave subjects unidentified. Viewing these photographs in an age that is not only not embarrassed by photography's specificity but is likely carefully to record the address of the most banal subject, we would like to know which villa this is and another photographed by Henneberg and identified as "Italienische Villa im Herbst." Stieglitz's own photograph "Old and New New York" includes an unidentified metal-framed skyscraper under construction on an unidentified New York avenue, a way of presenting subject matter that would have totally changed by the 1920s (95).

It is clear that these photographers adopted their styles of printing in order to separate their work from more traditional pictures. It is also clear that they paid a very high price for what seems in retrospect a small gain. In recent decades photographers have at times felt that only pictures taken with certain sizes of camera were to be regarded seriously. The black rebate edges characteristic of eight-by-ten sheet film or 35mm films have been made apparent in printing to separate the few pictures made "seriously" from the many that were not. But photographers who have used either of these sizes of film have gained some real advantages: with an inobtrusive, fast camera they have been able to take what it may not have been possible to take before; with a large camera they may have regained some of the detailed, factual quality apparent in early photographs. If the pre-World War I photographers achieved a sense of quality of light or time of day, they did so as often as not through handwork, not through the camera, and in the process they paid a dire price in loss of clarity of statement.

Stieglitz's group called itself the "Photo-Secession," some of its members were Austrian, and it would be gratifying to find that the Austrian Secession, fruitful in so many areas of art, had also developed a strong style of architectural photography. But the vigorous character of Secession perspective rendering—and the virtuoso perspective rendering technique of the Expressionist School of Amsterdam as well—with their evocations of kinds of weather and of time of day apparently left no room for an innovative photography. Pictures of Secession buildings were either leftovers from the older style showing awkward samplings of decorative wall detailing, or they represented a pale version of the standard perspective rendering techniques and took second place to stylish book design, sometimes to the extent of being printed in colors of ink that echoed those of their subjects, though they were black-and-white photographs. Much the same thing might be said of pictures of Belgian and French Art Nouveau architecture. In general, a compelling perspective rendering technique seems to have inhibited photography, which could capitalize most on a situation in which the standard drafting technique for publication was, as was the case in Germany, that of elevations or one in which, as in the United States, photographs frequently formed the basis for perspective drawings.

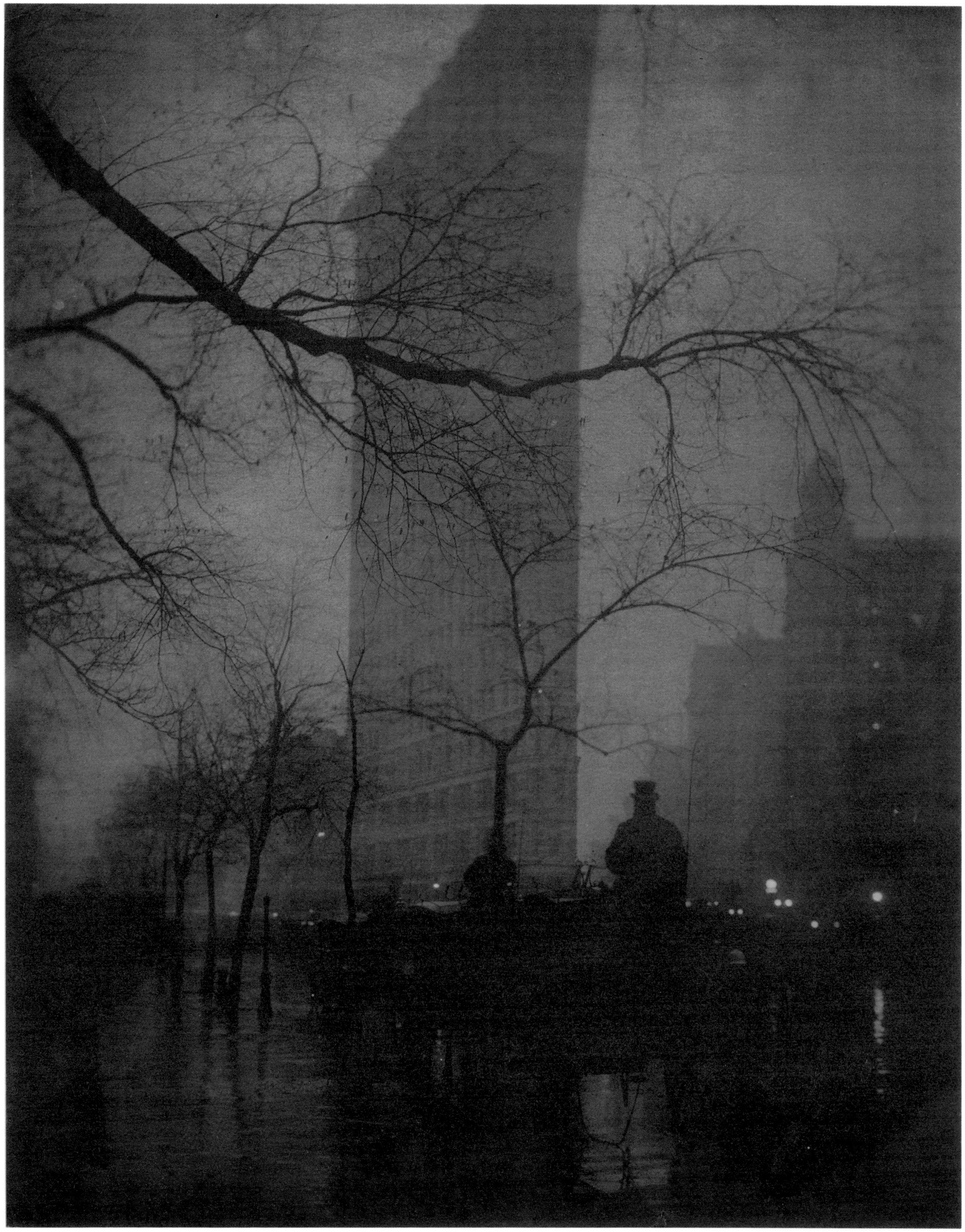

93 *Edward Steichen*

New York, "The Flatiron," 1904.
Gum print.
Metropolitan Museum of Art, New York.
The Alfred Stieglitz Collection.

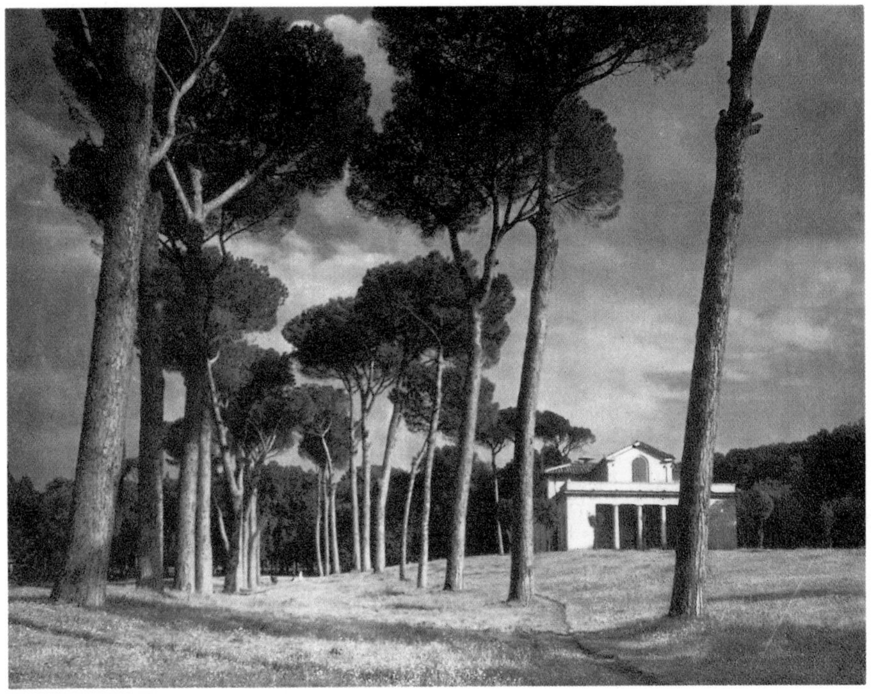

94 *Hugo Henneberg*

An Italian villa, 1898–1900.
Brown-pigment gum-bichromate.
Metropolitan Museum of Art, New York.
The Alfred Stieglitz Collection.

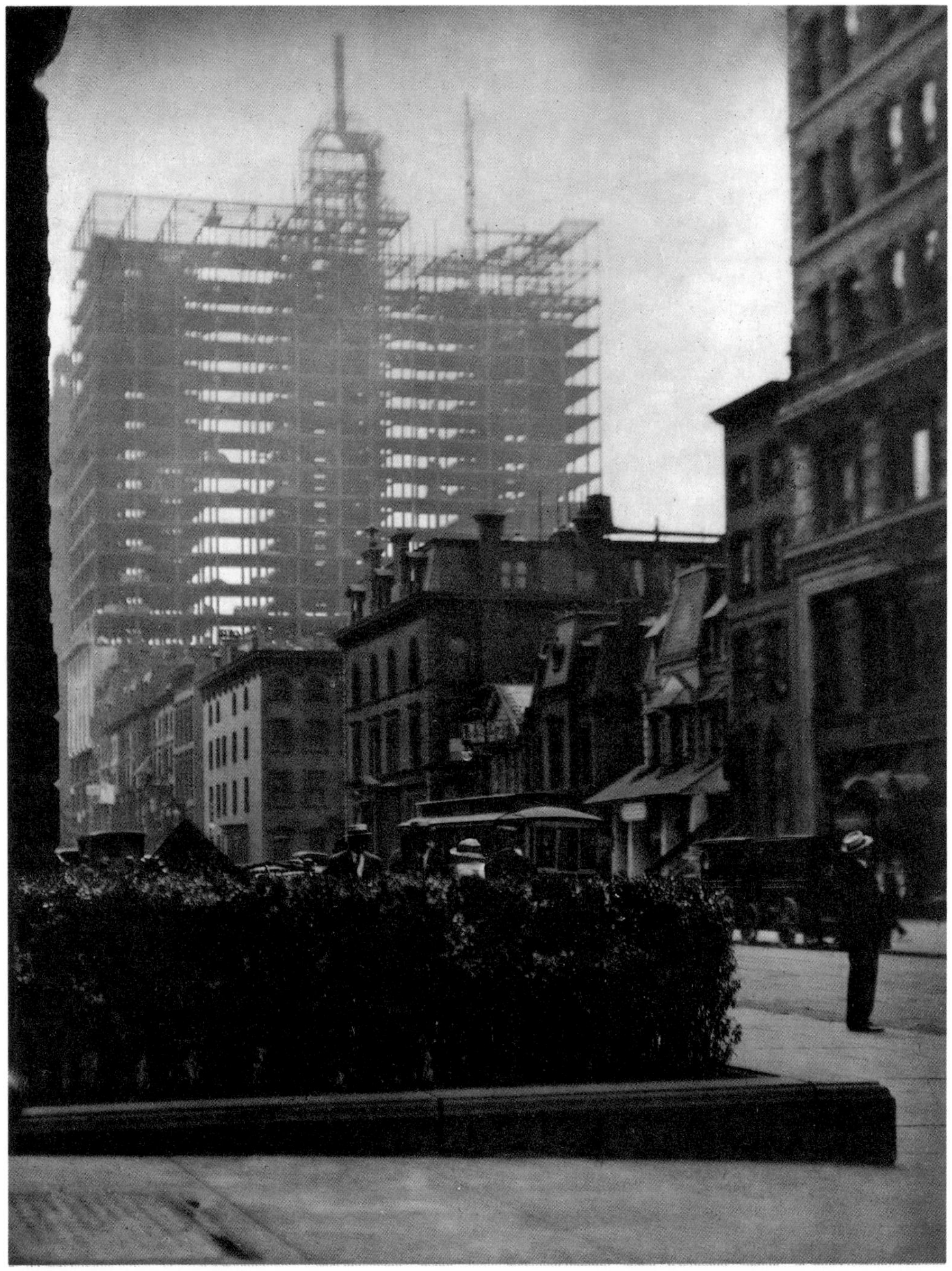

95 *Alfred Stieglitz*

"Old and New New York," 1910.
Photogravure.
Centre Canadien d'Architecture/Canadian Center for Architecture, Montreal.

Hugo Schmölz (1879–1938) took pictures of Walter Gropius and Adolf Meyer's pavilion for the Deutscher Werkbund exhibition of 1914 in Cologne that were either determinedly head-on and on axis or as determinedly (though often pointlessly) oblique. While a general view of the set of buildings from the southeast and a view of the Machine Hall and Deutz Pavilion taken from the roof of the office block are clearly justified because they explain the relationship between the buildings, other pictures in the 1915 *Jahrbuch des deutschen Werkbundes* were a head-on view of the front of the office block so determinedly axial that it obscured the entrance of the building with the sculpture that was on axis in front of it and a pair of nervously oblique views that showed the courtyard facades of the office block and Machine Hall while avoiding the sheds that were on either side (96). That is, they were oblique but gained nothing by it. In the 1950s when Schmölz's pictures were reused in books on Gropius, it was a head-on, courtyard view of the office block (along with the general exterior from the southeast) that became the obligatory views because the glass curtain wall, unrelated to the other buildings, had come to seem the central issue (97).

In its early decades Frank Lloyd Wright's Larkin Administration Building (1906) was frequently represented by a picture that Clarence Fuermann (1883–1983) had taken from the Seneca Street sidewalk in which the metal fence in front of the building ran close to the camera to give a sense of experiential immediacy that the other photographs lacked (98). The picture was used in the 1908 *Record* to illustrate Wright's article "In the Cause of Architecture," in the second Wasmuth volume of Wright's work (1911), in the special issue of *Wendingen* on his work (1925), and in Erich Mendelsohn's *Amerika* (1928). After the twenties it almost dropped from sight, presumably because Wright's work was accepted and something more objective and informative seemed called for. Wright in Fiesole in 1910, preparing drawings for the first Wasmuth volume, chose another of Fuermann's photographs that had been taken from across Seneca Street to copy to show the front of the building. (For the rear view he took the low brick wall from a less incisive photograph of the rear by Fuermann—redesigning the wall as he drew it—and copied the main office block from the photograph reproduced here, its fence removed and the windows of the opposite building flank drawn in.) My point is not that this was an appropriate or inappropriate way to make drawings or use photographs. It is that some of the special quality of the sort of experiential photographs that were being made with new confidence after 1890—like the one shown here—

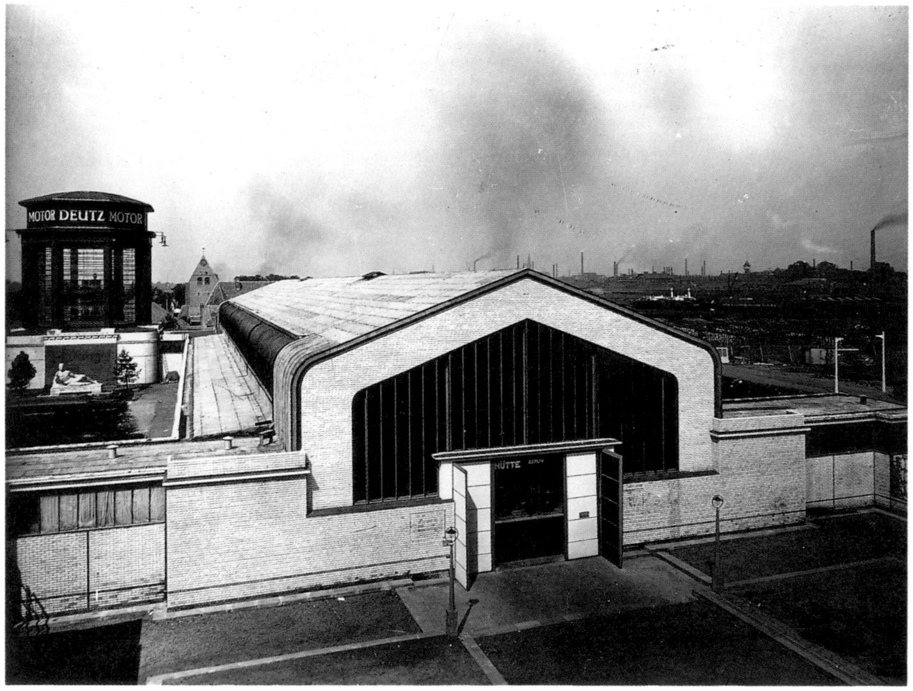

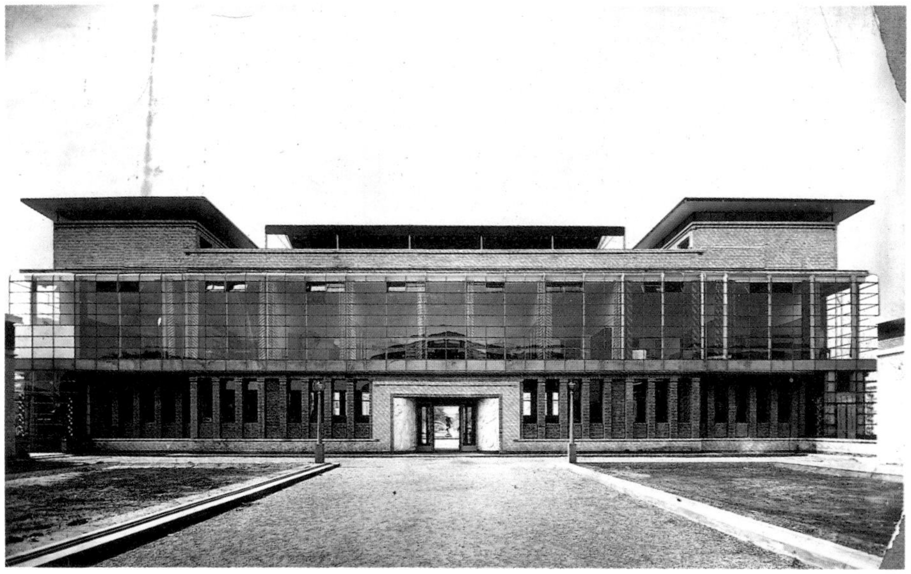

96 *Hugo Schmölz*

Cologne, Deutscher Werkbund machine hall with Deutz Pavilion, 1914.
Bauhaus-Archiv, Berlin.

97 *Hugo Schmölz*

Cologne, Deutscher Werkbund office block, 1914.
Bauhaus-Archiv, Berlin.

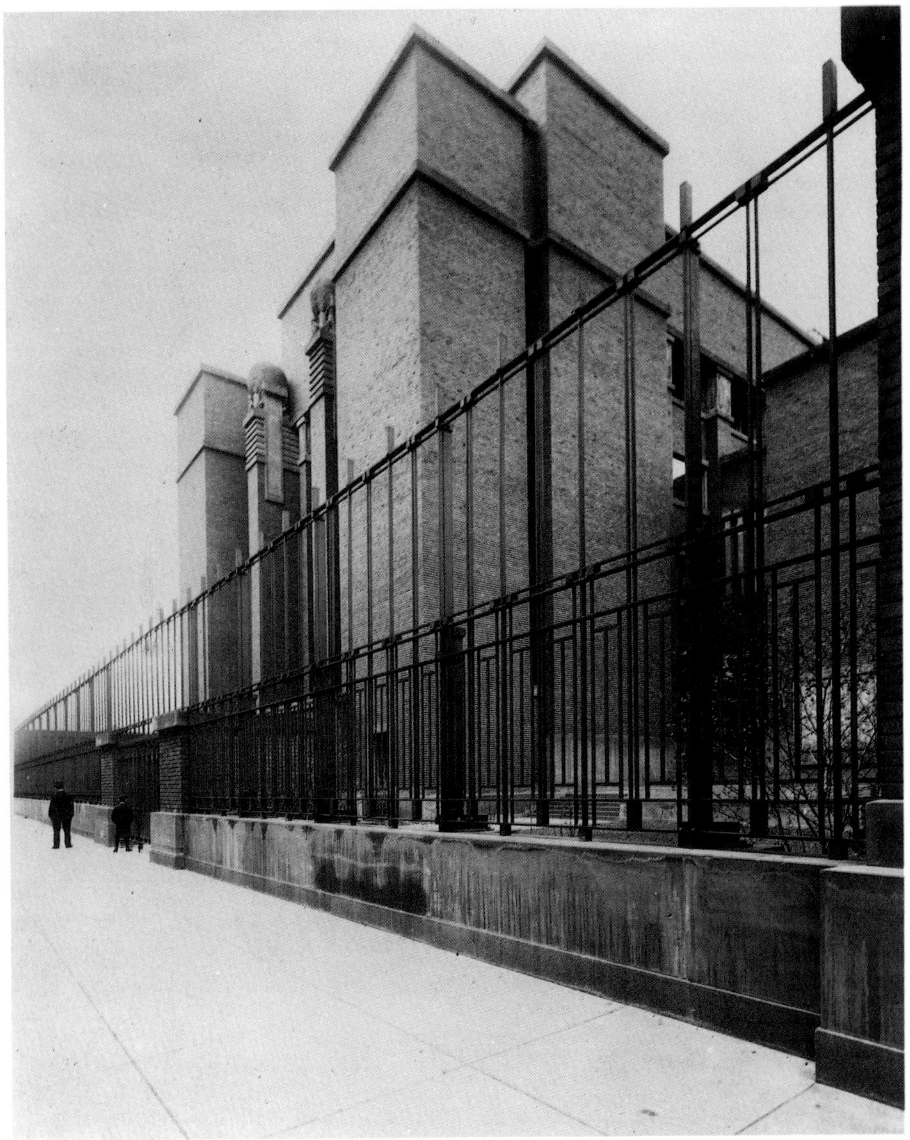

98 *CLARENCE FUERMANN*
Buffalo, Larkin building, ca. 1904.
Metropolitan Museum of Art, New York.

was that they emphasized the act of the photographer in taking them, his arbitrariness, his willfulness, even where this special quality was accompanied by a loss of considerable information about the ostensible subject. Clearly one of the reasons Fuermann took this photograph as he did was to avoid a telephone pole that was just to the left of his camera, and, as clearly, one of the reasons Wright chose to copy the view from across the street was that he could remove the telephone poles and wires in his drawing. But the success of the photograph, despite its obscured view of the building, comes not only from the immediacy of the subject but the palpable act of the photographer, a feeling that was present in a drawing simply because it was drawn. Photographs in the long run had the advantage over drawings because of their evident authenticity. In the meanwhile they had to try harder.

The factual style suited a general view of Wright's Coonley house (1908) at Riverside, Illinois. Fuermann took several views of the garden front, most of which include the Coonley child, sometimes regarding the camera, sometimes playing beside the pool. In one, a head-on view with the child at the pool, the Coonley parents are seen inspecting an ivy plant, thereby demonstrating the pleasurable experience of living in such a house (and thereby echoing the Japanese family in the Beato photograph of their house) (99).

In the postwar decade of the 1920s photographers returned to an acknowledgment of the specific and ungeneralized character of their subjects. At the same time they retained some of the "artistic" goals of the pre-war period: prints delivered to architects were often printed, mounted, and signed as though they were for exhibition. But now the experiential quality of pictures was often tempered by a "new objectivity" and by an emphasis on the formal traits of their subjects.

Arthur Köster's iconic picture of the Einstein Tower is also a typical experiential photograph in the line of Frederick Evans's "A Sea of Steps" (60, 82). The building's stuccoed brick surface comes toward the viewer in the same compelling way as do the steps in the earlier picture (or the fence in front of the Larkin building). To make the building's message single-minded, a fragment is shown, where a more complete view could have dissipated the picture's impact, and there is a clear impression of light, in this case morning light from a hazy sky. The picture has proved significant in part because it was "artistic" and in part because it summed up the building's spirit in a way that other, more general views did not.

99 *Clarence Fuermann*

Riverside, Illinois, Coonley house, ca. 1908.
Museum of Modern Art, New York.

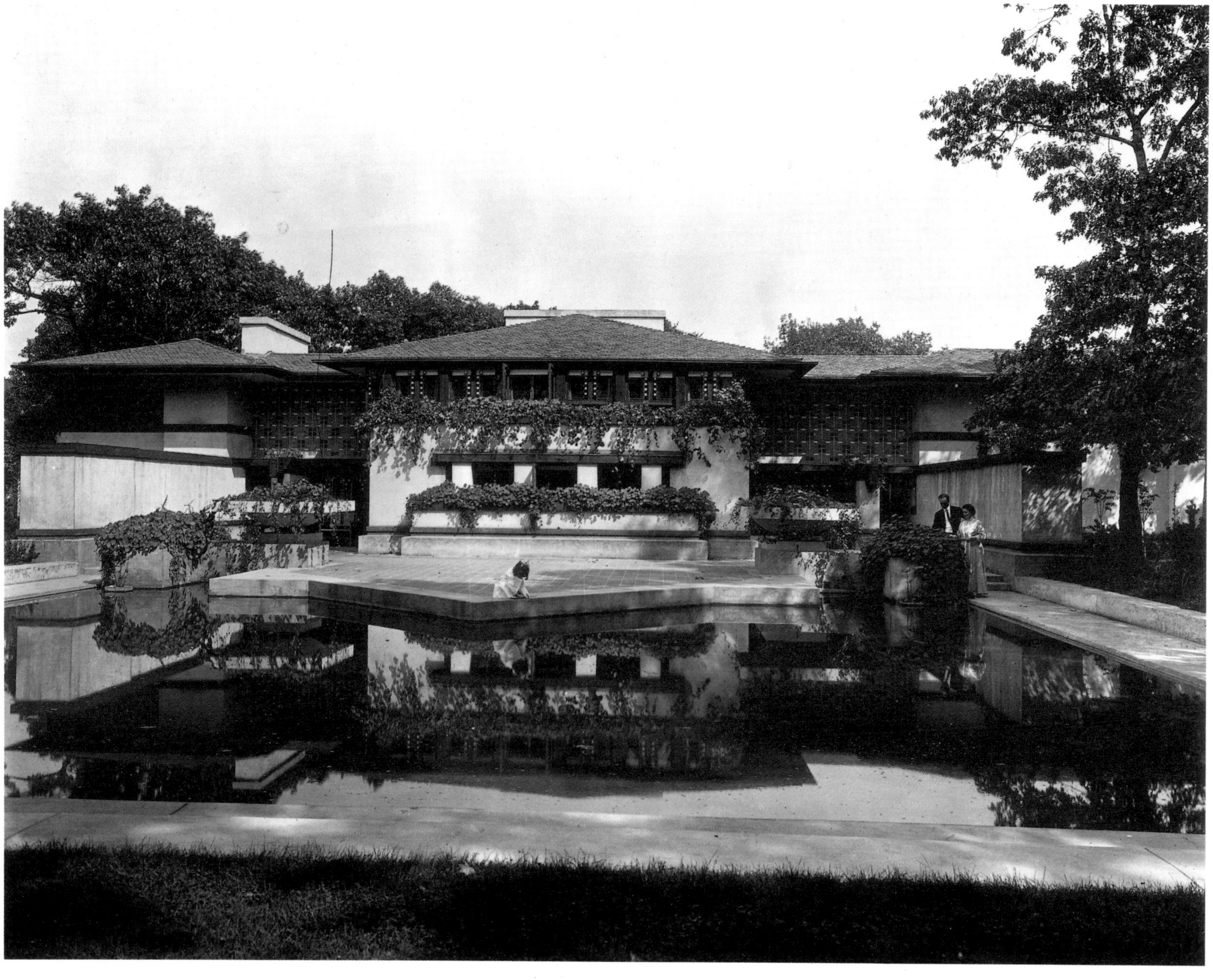

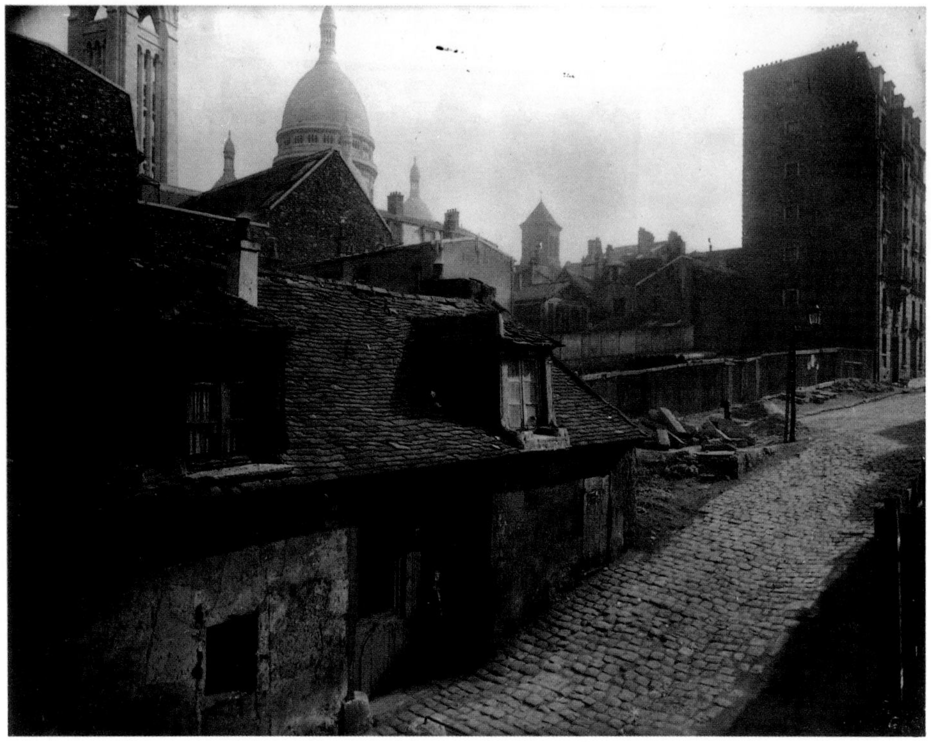

100 *Eugène Atget*

Paris, Montmartre, rue de Mont-Cenis, 1923.
Museum of Modern Art, New York.
The Abbott-Levy Collection.
Partial gift of Shirley C. Burden.

101 *Eugène Atget*

Paris, Arc du Carrousel, n.d.
Caisse Nationale des Monuments Historiques et des Sites, Paris.

102 *Charles Sheeler*

Chartres Cathedral, buttresses, 1929.
Museum of Modern Art, New York.
Gift of the photographer.

In the twenties Eugène Atget, in the last years of his life, turned from views that had often seemed fragmentary to a kind of composition that harked back to the stage sets of his youthful life as an actor. These were views of Paris in which a foreground that invited a dramatic presence (but was generally empty of people) was enclosed by architecture that offered something like stage exits in the form of a distant perspective down a street on one side of the picture and overlapping structures at the center, which was sometimes capped by a vista of the top of a major building in the distance. In a picture of the rue du Mont-Cenis of 1924 the distant, major building is the Church of Sacré-Coeur, and as in much of Atget's work, there is an emphasis on quality of light, a hazy side lighting in this instance, that did not come inherently from the photographic materials available to him (though it is shared by Köster in his picture of the Einstein Tower) (100). Atget's earlier picture of St. Maclou had included the distant side vista and some of his pre-war pictures of former royal parks had seemed composed of pieces of stage property set on largely empty stages. If it were argued that this dramatic quality of buildings and light was simply the way Paris came, that argument can be refuted with Marville's earlier pictures. Just as Marville's achieve their most convincing character in head-on perspective, Atget's occasional head-on views reveal his total lack of interest in them (101).

Photographers other than Köster and Atget adopted a style that was more disinterested and analytical—disinterested in that, though they presented their subjects as very specific ones, feelings associated with particular places or times of day played no role in their pictures; analytical in the sense that in these pictures they often showed forms as functional or as abiding by a desirable geometry. Charles Sheeler (1883–1965) demonstrated this in his pictures of Chartres Cathedral taken in 1929, in which he confined himself to exteriors, views of buttresses seen as structural, and therefore functional, elements, views in which these buttresses also formed patterns on the photographic print that reflected the interest in repeated or fountain- or plantlike forms of the Art Deco years (102). In these pictures Sheeler used light articulately but for the purpose of precise description, not the evocation of a time of day or kind of weather. Where Frederick Evans had summed up the whole of a building in terms of an interior detail and ambient light, Sheeler was interested only in a functional part and its formal possibilities. Margaret Bourke-White (1904–1971) also found forms that appealed to an Art Deco sensibility in the Niagara Electric Company, among other industrial subjects. A photograph of the com-

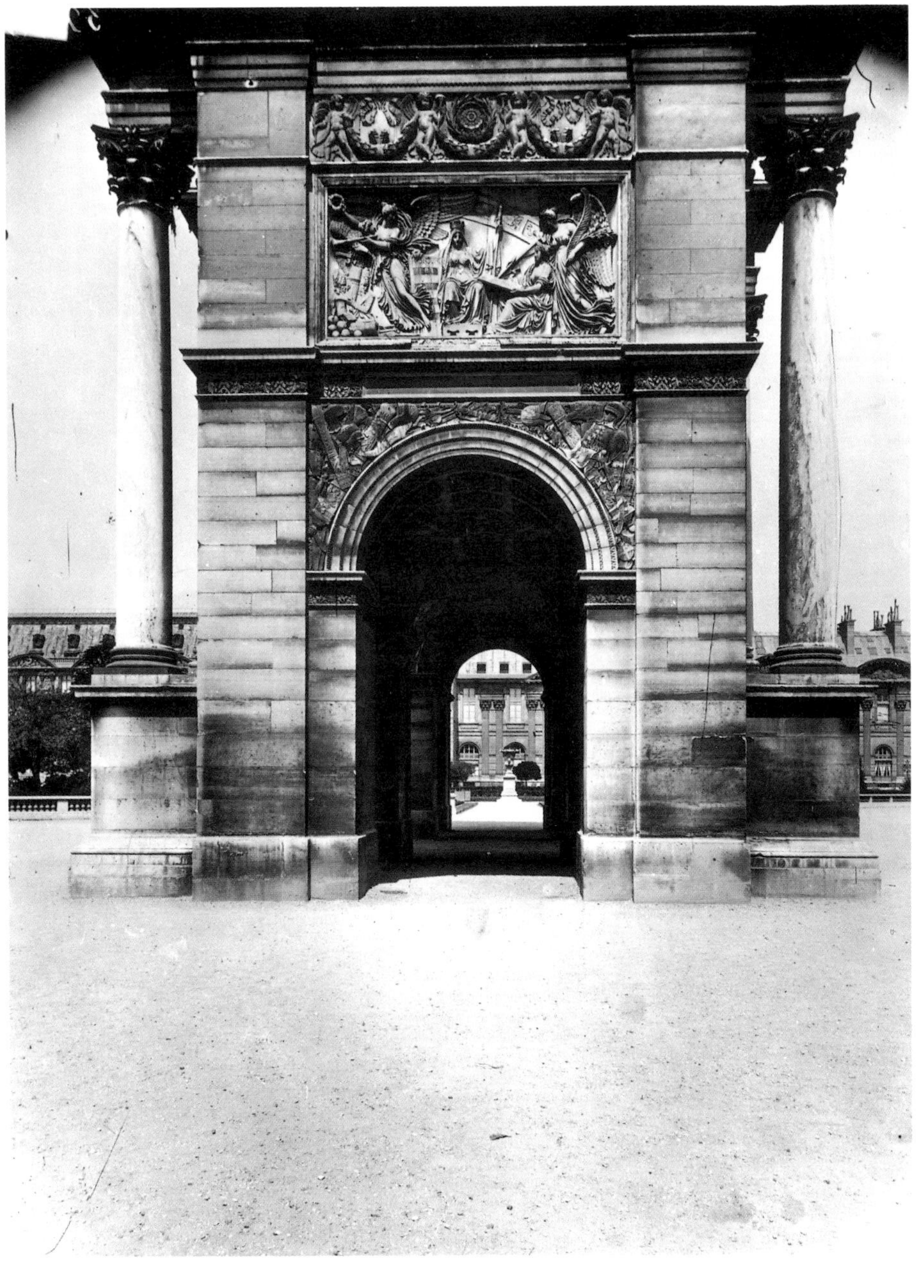

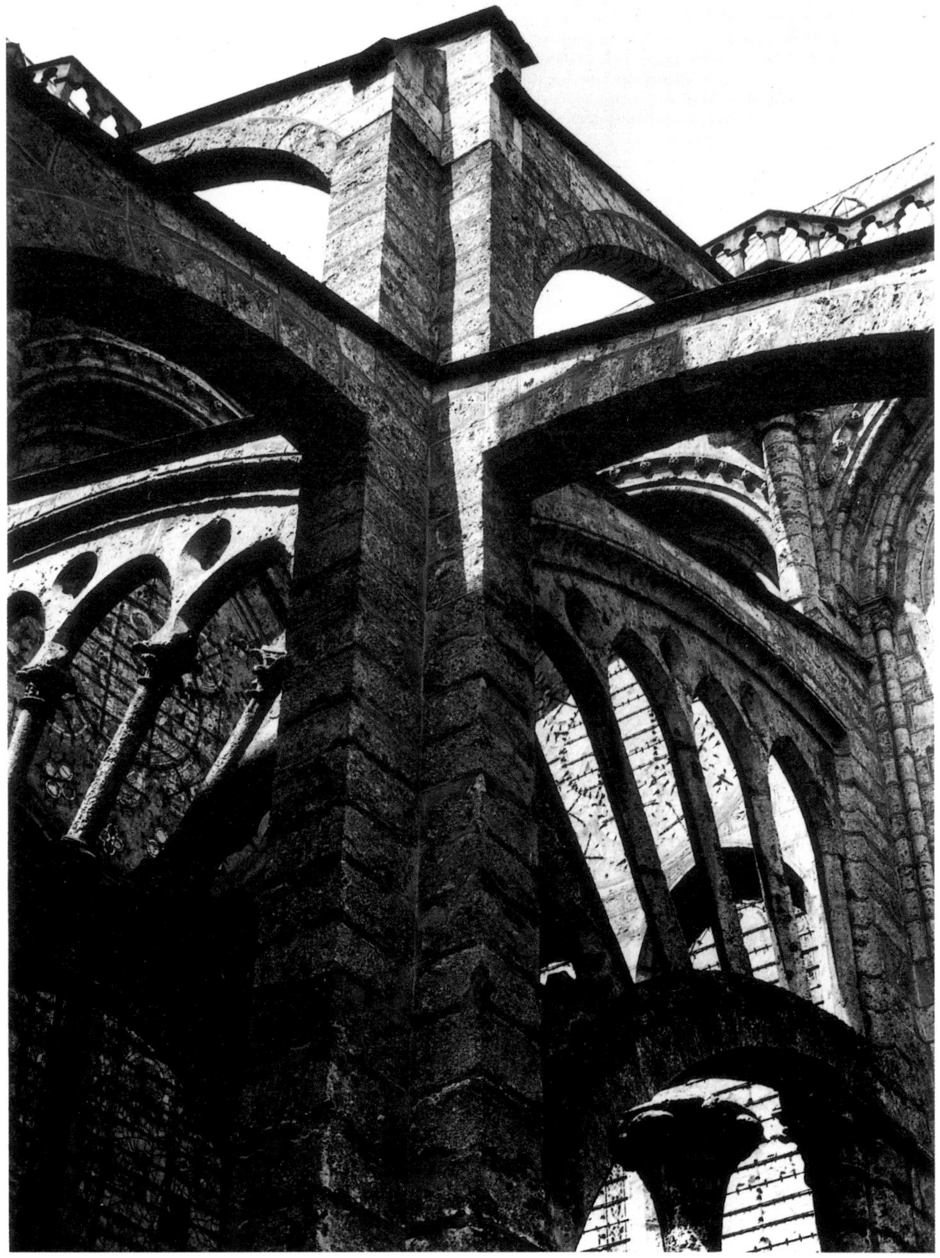

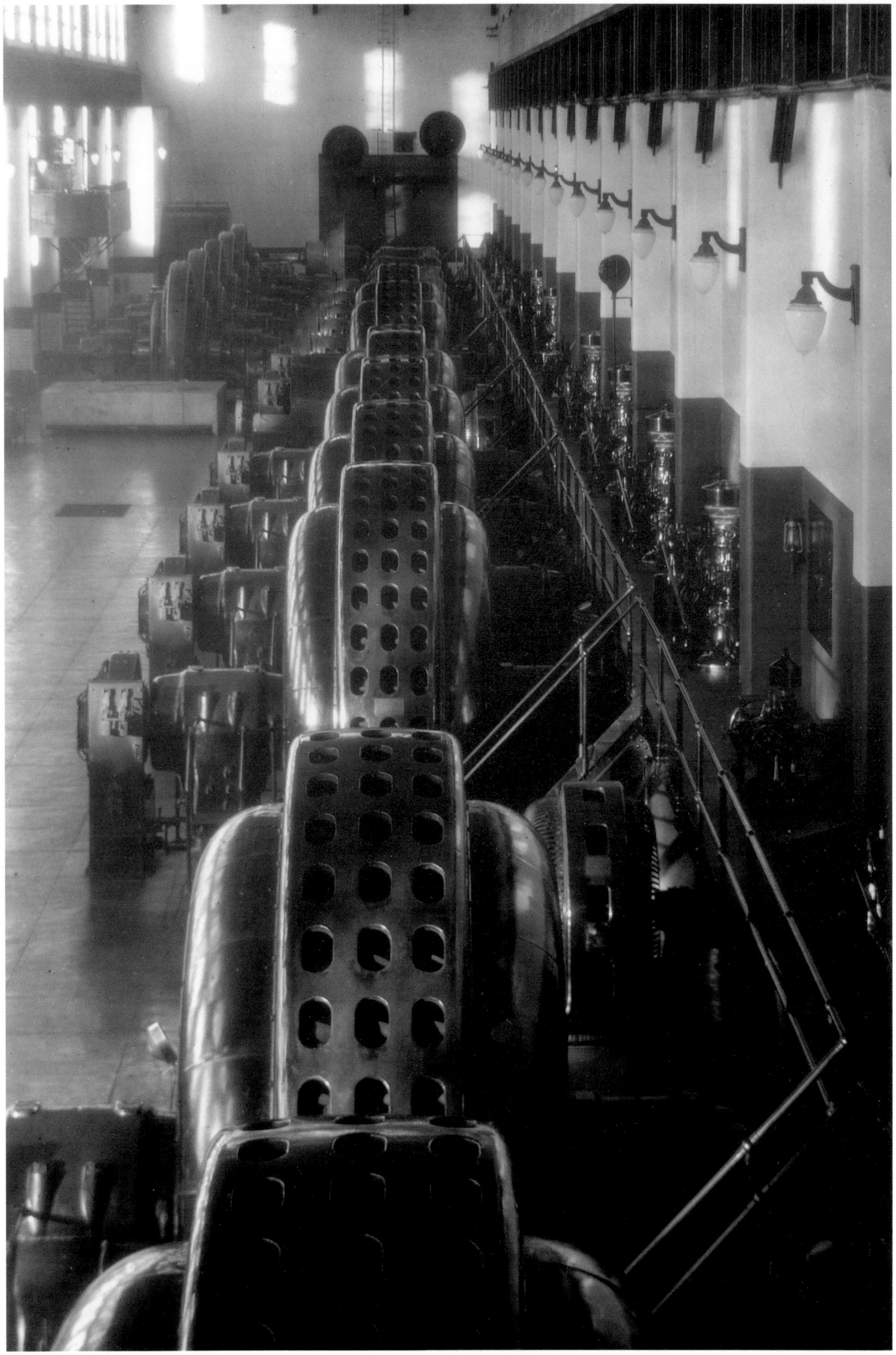

103 *Margaret Bourke-White*

Niagara Electric Company dynamos, ca. 1929.

Margaret Bourke-White Collection, George Arents Research Library for Special Collections at Syracuse University.

pany's dynamos (with a railing that passes neatly to the right margin of the picture and then returns to the lowest dynamo) appeared in a portfolio of her work in a 1929 issue of *Architectural Record*, and a slight variant on it appears here (103).

Conventional perspective as produced by an architectural photographer's view camera by what is known as "perspective control" assumes a world of rectilinear buildings whose principal facades are the subject of photographs—or at least a world in which buildings are symmetrical about a principal axis. Just after the First World War several buildings were built in forms that were not always rectilinear. A circulation area in Hans Poelzig's Grosses Schauspielhaus (1920) in Berlin taken by an anonymous photographer shows an example (104). The picture is successful rather than chaotic because the nearby column (described as *Säule mit Beleuchtungskörper*) and the wall opening to the left, as well as the two more distant columns, form axes upon which the space, as the camera sees it, can be organized. The Einstein Tower too is an example of this sort of building, and the success of Köster's picture is in part due to his keeping the axis of his camera parallel to that of the building.

Though few such curvilinear buildings were built, an interest on the part of photographers in structures that had no flat, principal facade continued throughout the 1920s. This was probably encouraged by the interest the architectural community took in the plant photographs of Karl Blossfeldt (1865–1932), whose subjects can be looked at as variations on the theme of organized structure without facades. His winter horsetail, reproduced in *Wasmuth's Monatshefte* in 1928, recalls, if it did not provide a model for, Poelzig's lobby (105). Both the buttresses photographed by Sheeler and the dynamos taken by Bourke-White are facadeless forms too. But such forms as those of Willkomm's saxifrage or Bourgati's Eryngo were more nearly paralleled by the naves and buttresses of Gothic churches (106). Through the second half of the 1920s and into the 1930s Albert Renger-Patzsch (1897–1966) produced a series of books on church buildings, cities, and industry whose message seemed to be that the forms of a church, say, were both organic and no different in nature from those of industry. He took the nave and buttresses of the Marienkirche at Lübeck from a level above which the church would normally be seen, in a view that removes it from its urban context and that emphasizes the inherently organic form of its east end, the emphasis being the stronger because he has lopped off the tops of the west towers and the spire (107). In a view of the Sandkirche at Breslau, shadows on buttresses, between some of which apses project, emphasize an abstract formal pattern rather than the urban space of the street (in which pedestrians are irrelevant blurs) (108). When Renger-Patzsch photographed medieval vaulting, he showed patterns of ribs that were plantlike or the forms of the tops of vaults seen under a church roof as stalagmitelike. Medieval piers and industrial smoke stacks are shown in very much the same spirit, and in his books he could shift from a religious structure to an industrial one in a manner that gave an impression of tough mindedness and passion in both (109).

Those photographers whose work has seemed to sum up a time or a society or a world have always held a special appeal. Generally, such a photographer's work can be seen to have fallen into all three categories, architecture, portraiture, and landscape, and to have maintained a style that unified them. Renger-Patzsch's *Die Welt ist Schön* of 1928 proposed no less than eight categories of subject (and lumped people with animals). The remaining subjects, besides landscape and architecture, were plants, materials, technics, the variegated world (*bunte Welt*), and symbols. Of these he was clearly most comfortable with materials and technics, and both the scheme and the book as a whole are not convincing.

A portrait of *Amerika* that the architect Erich Mendelsohn put together in 1925 and revised in 1928 from his own snapshots and those of a few friends is more successful. The subjects are cityscapes and details of New York City, Chicago, and Detroit seen on a trip of 1924. The book is less remarkable for the dynamism of style one might hope to find in Mendelsohn's own pictures than it is for the dynamism apparent in these cities as he sees them, largely drawn from the figures of pedestrians he includes, and from the mixture of subjects he considers relevant, which include not only major buildings and major streets, such as Fifth Avenue, Broad and Wall Streets, and Times Square, but back streets, advertising posters, and grain elevators (110, 111, 112). As a view of the actual world that lay between major publishable works of architecture, *Amerika* was a forerunner of what would become the second interest of architectural journalism after new buildings in the late thirties and after World War II, namely townscape.

An alternative approach to travel photography was demonstrated by F. R. Yerbury (1885–1970), a long-time secretary of the Architectural Association in London, who photographed an extraordinary number of new or recent buildings in the twenties, in particular, ones that seemed significant to the Modern Movement, and who saw his pictures published in a series of books. Inherent

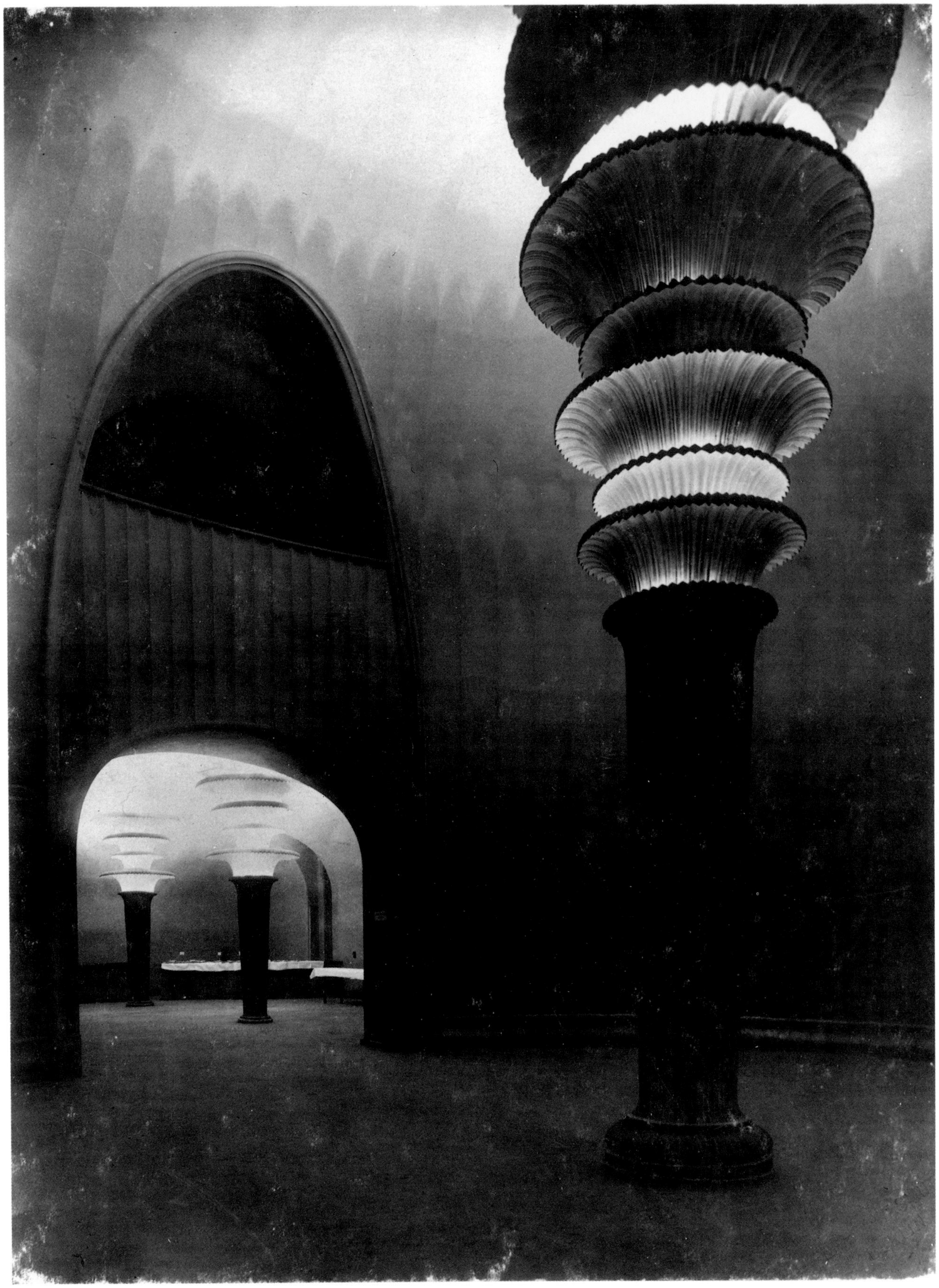

104 *Photographer unknown*

Berlin, Grosses Schauspielhaus, ca. 1920.
Technische Universität, Berlin.

105 *Karl Blossfeldt*

Equisetum hiemale (winter horsetail), n.d.

106 *Karl Blossfeldt*

Saxifraga willkommniana (Willkomm's saxifrage), n.d.

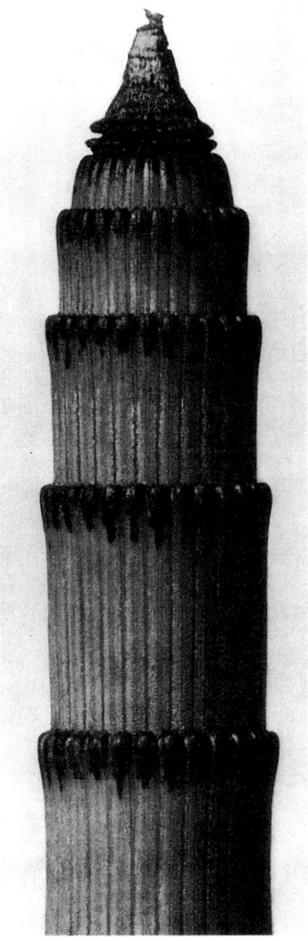

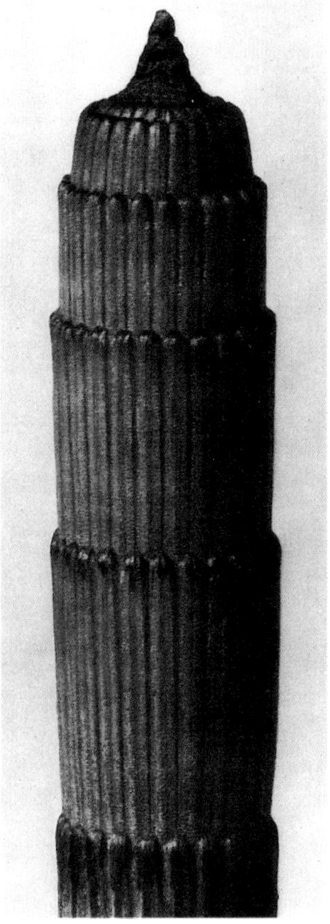

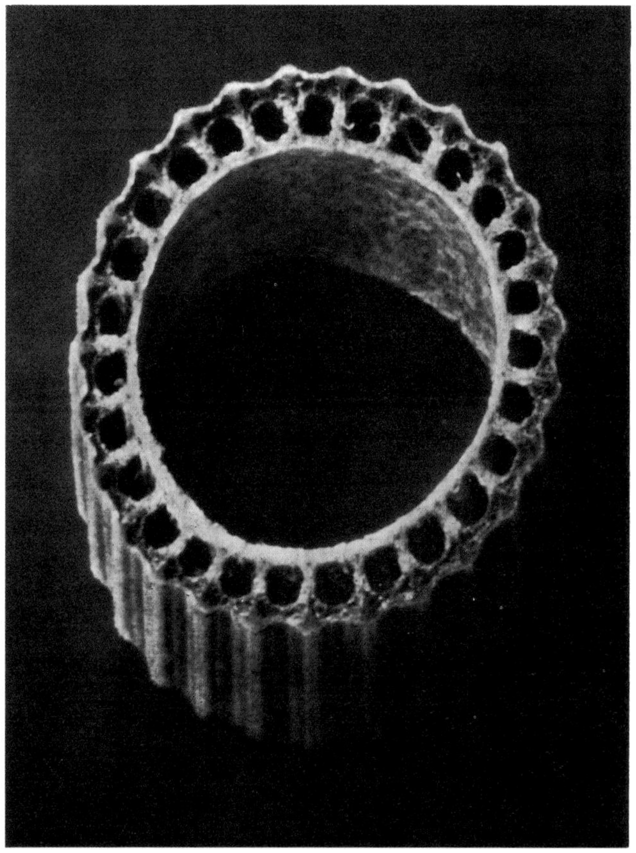

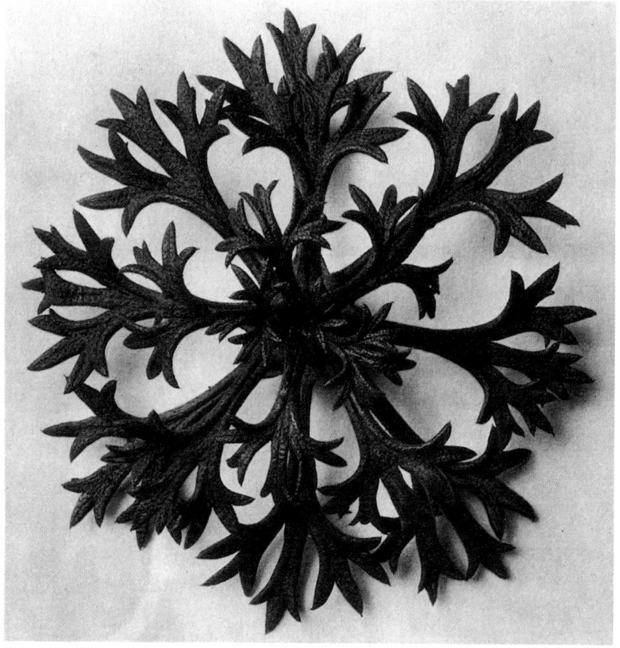

107 *Albert Renger-Patzsch*

Lübeck, Marienkirche, 1927.
Galerie Wilde, Cologne.

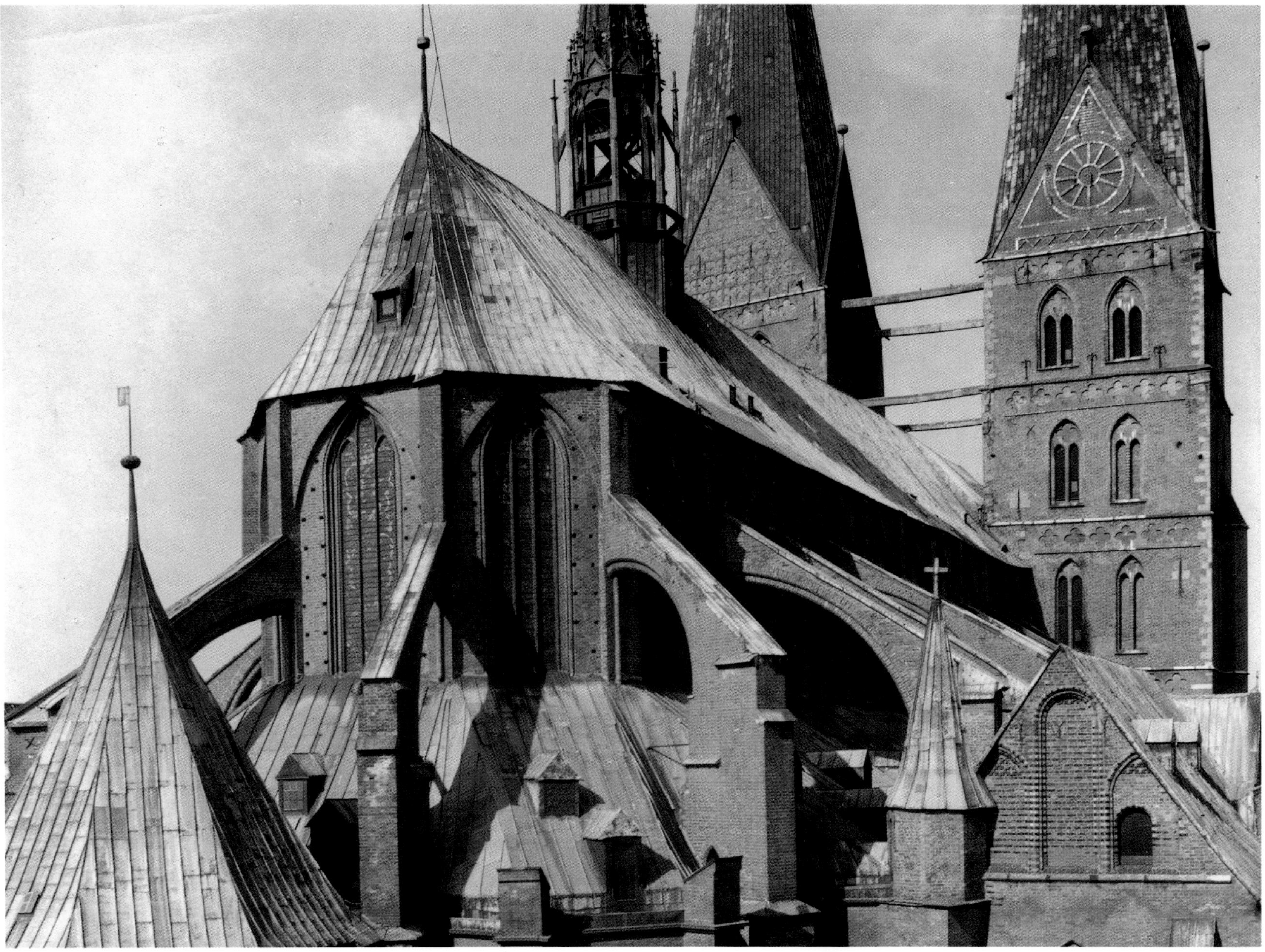

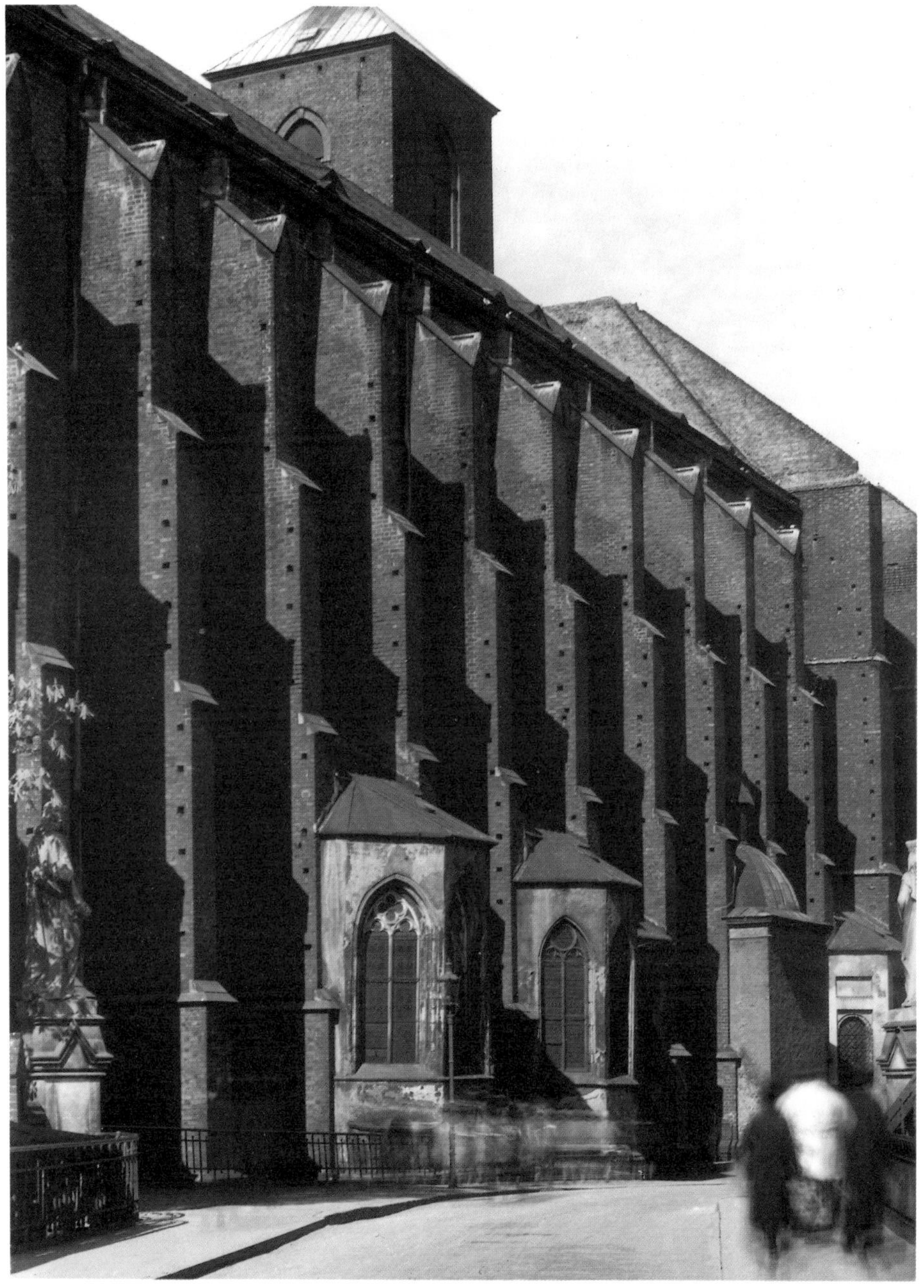

108 *Albert Renger-Patzsch*

Breslau, Sandkirche, 1928.
Galerie Wilde, Cologne.

109 *Albert Renger-Patzsch*

Hamburg, giant crane in harbor, 1929.
Galerie Wilde, Cologne.

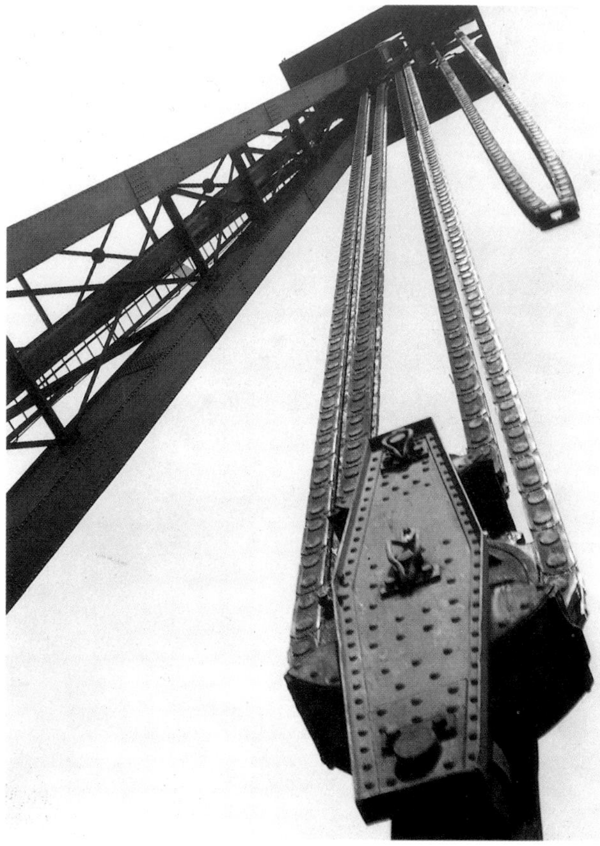

110 *"Mein Chef-Architekt Karweik"*

New York, Times Square, ca. 1924.
From *Amerika* (1924).
Avery Architectural Library.

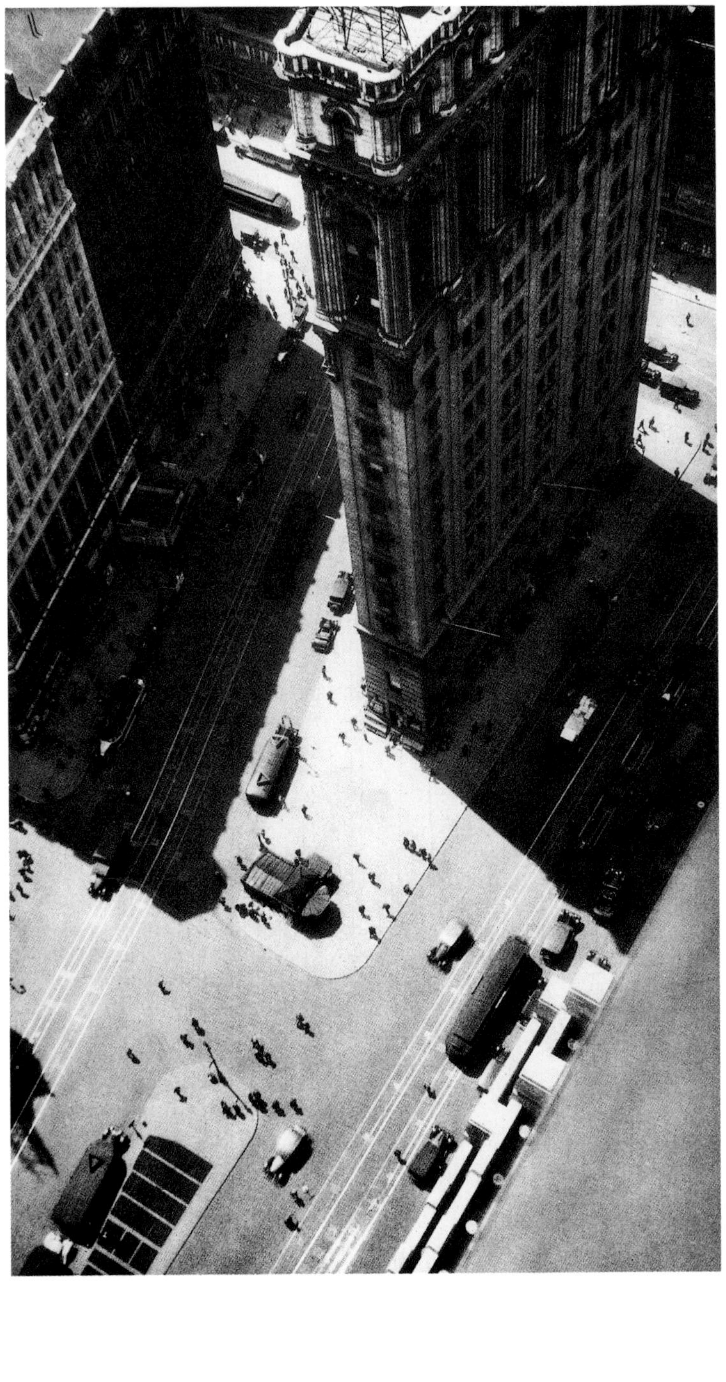

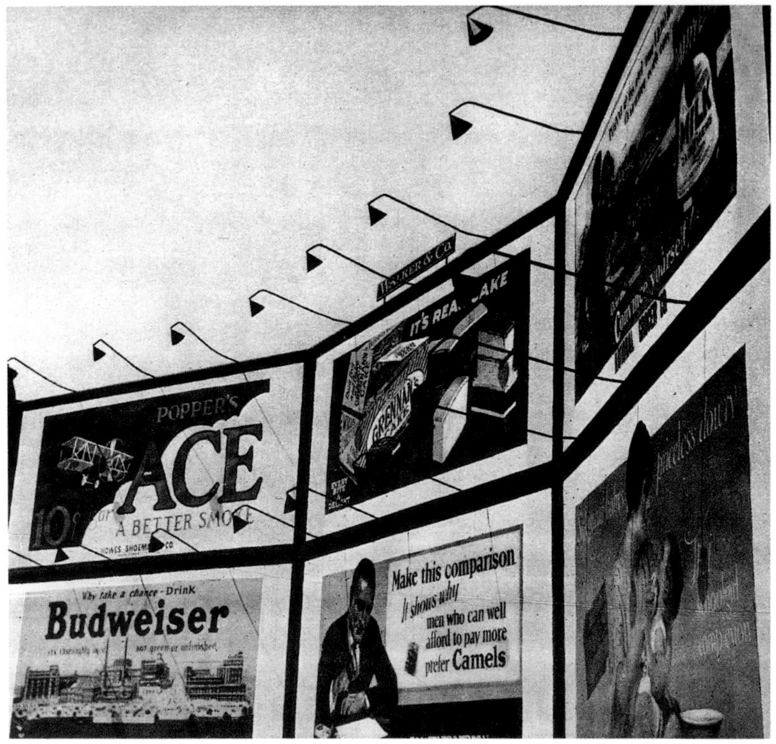

111 *Lönberg-Holm*

Detroit, billboards, 1924.
From *Amerika* (1924). Avery Architectural Library.

112 *Erich Mendelsohn*

Chicago, conveyers to grain elevators and distributor bridges, 1924.
From *Amerika* (1924).
Avery Architectural Library.

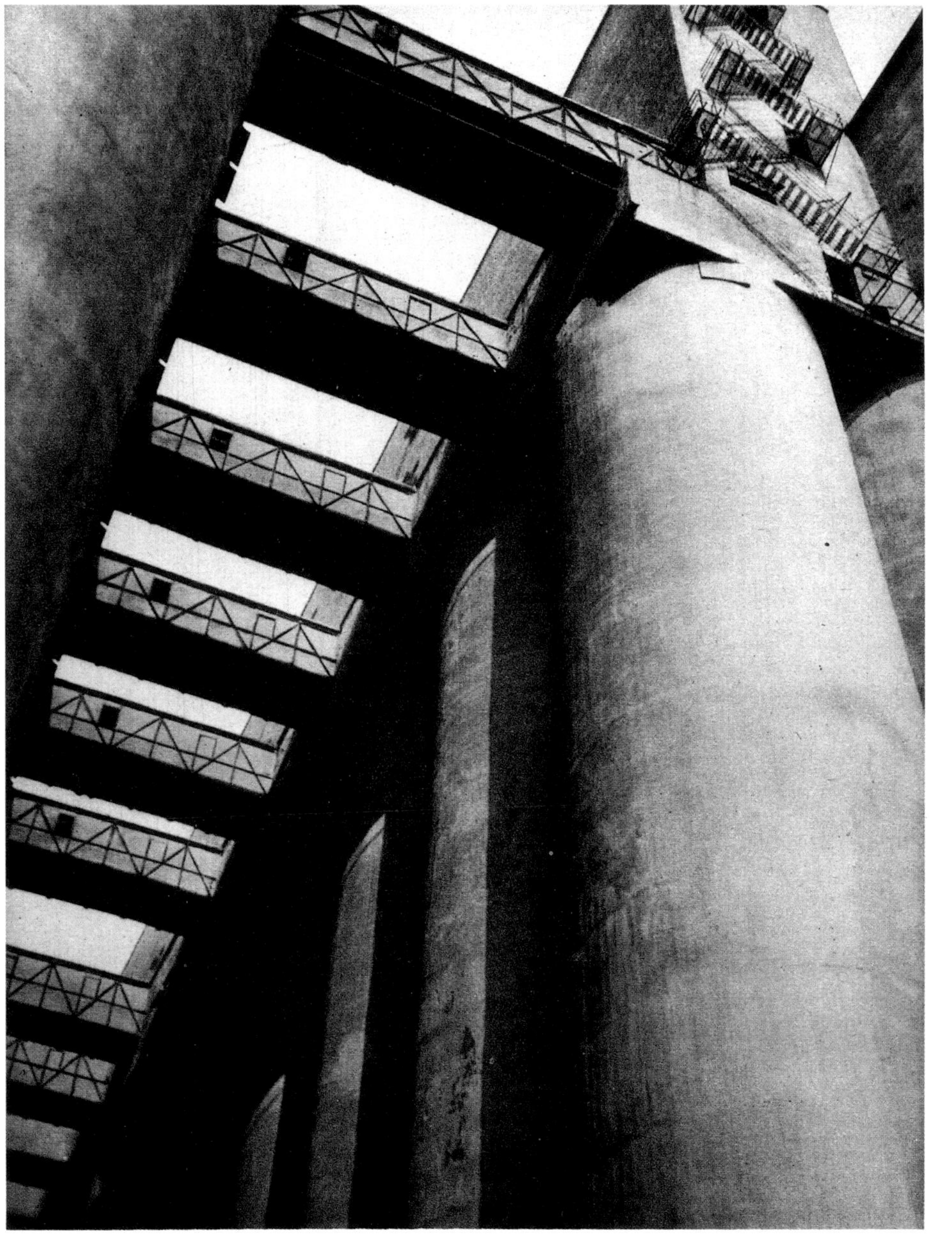

in such a task of photographing many relevant buildings for publication in what amount to catalogs is that none will seem to have been taken with a particular purpose in mind. The inevitable result is pictures that are decent but dull. An exception among Yerbury's pictures is one that might be said to be of the front porch of the Einstein Tower, an afternoon shot that takes in somewhat the same area of the building as Köster's picture but does not have its concentrated force both because it gives us more information—the form of the porch steps and the recess for foot scraping below them for instance—and because it distracts us with this information (113). What Yerbury attempted would be developed into an elegant manner of travel photography by the architect G. E. Kidder Smith in the late 1940s and 1950s.

Photographers of the middle and late twenties whose purpose it was to take the definitive pictures of new buildings, whether they worked in Dessau or New York, faced new problems. In Dessau Gropius and Meyer's new Bauhaus building (1926) taken in a general view from any direction seemed to be taken from the wrong direction. Later a view with the workshop block in the foreground (with the name "Bauhaus" on it) came to seem the most satisfactory, but that was in part because that block, due to its glass walls, appeared the most significant. But in the early days the most satisfactory way to photograph the buildings was to take each from a vantage point beside another, and the one of these partial pictures that summed up the building best was one by Lucia Moholy that appears in several respects to have been quite casually taken (114). It illustrates the structure of the workshop wing and its curtain wall as well as the reflectivity and transparency of the building's glass in general, but the picture's core is an automobile parked in shadow across the street from the entrance to the technical-school wing. This car, positioned in the picture so that its windshield is just free of the basement wall and its rear all but lined up with the edge of the curtain wall above, provides a focal point and a feeling of potential energy to the picture, which would have been merely vacant without it. The vehicle was probably included not to suggest modernity and functionalism as it would be in many pictures of Le Corbusier's buildings and in the pictures of the 1930s by the Chicago photographer Ken Hedrich since cars do not turn up in other pictures that Lucia Moholy took. If it was included on purpose, it was probably to imply that the Leopolddank was a functioning street. Nevertheless, this seems to be the first picture of a modern building in which a vehicle plays an energizing role that was to become common in the following decade.

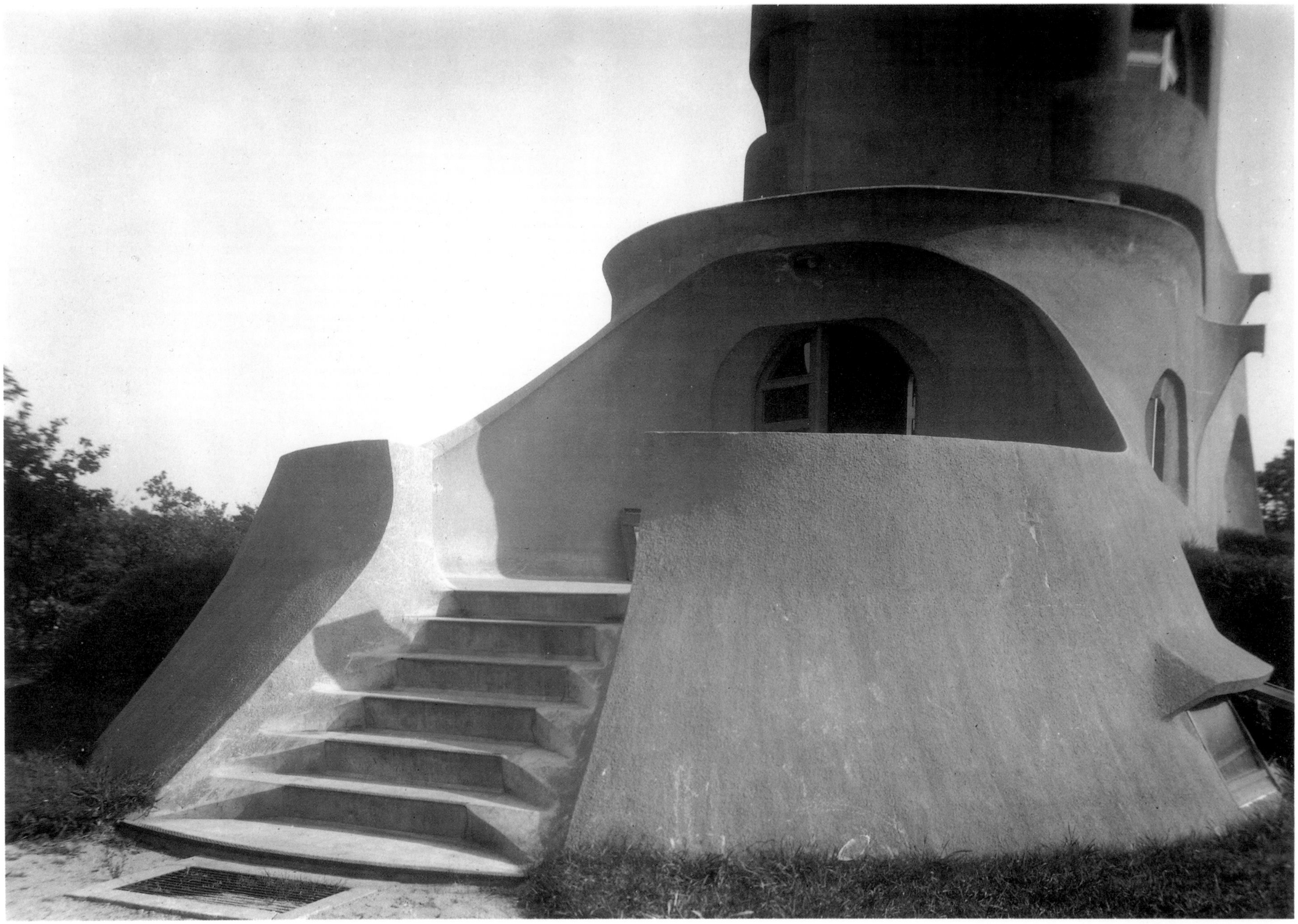

113 *F. R. Yerbury*

Potsdam, Einstein Tower, 1920s.
Architectural Association, London.

114 *Lucia Moholy*

Dessau, Bauhaus buildings, ca. 1926.
Museum of Modern Art, New York.

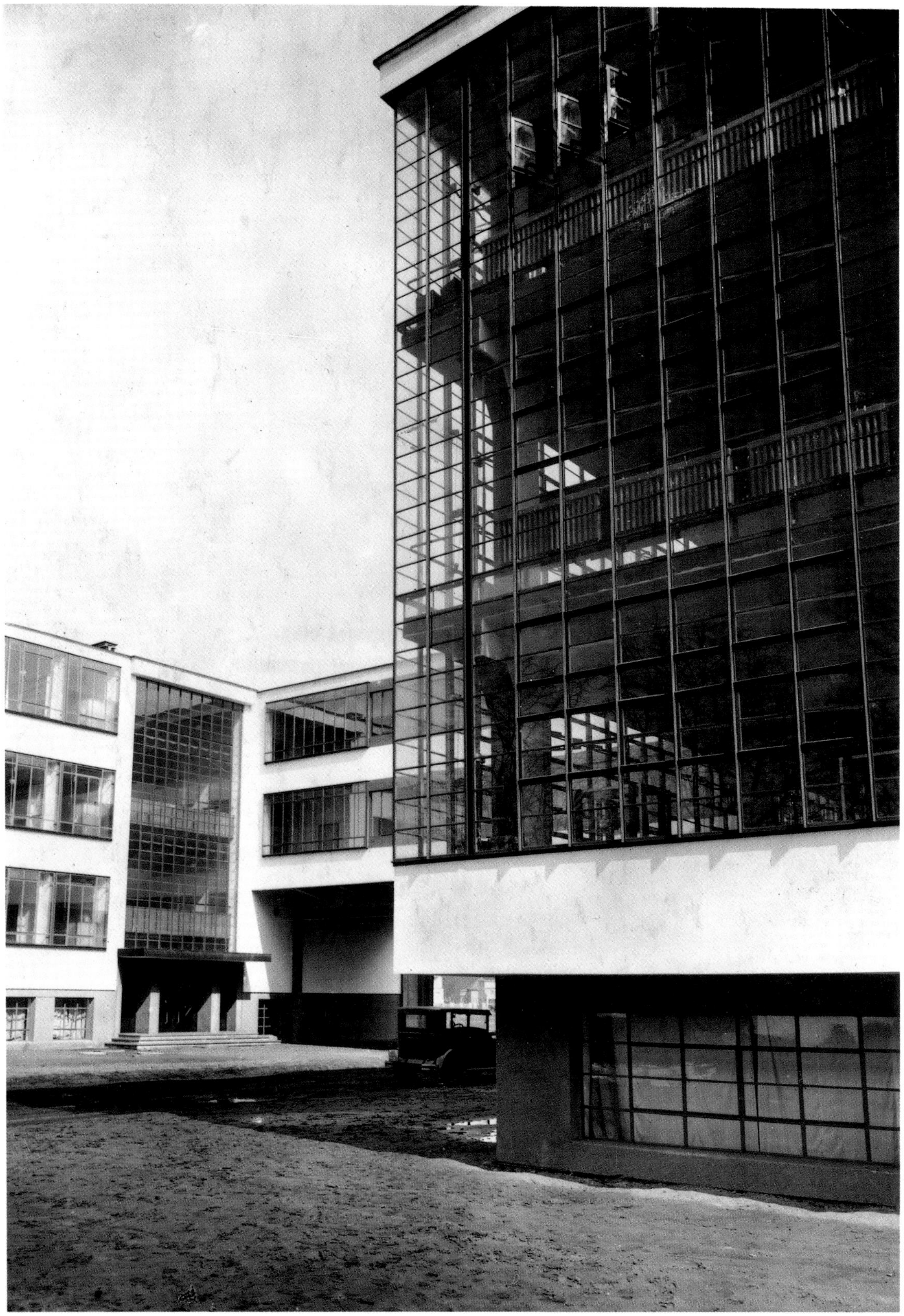

115 *SIGURD FISCHER*

New York, Barclay-Vesey Building, 1923.
Courtesy Haines Lundberg Waehler, successor to McKenzie, Voorhees & Gmelin.

116 *SIGURD FISCHER*

New York, Western Union Building, 1930.
Courtesy Haines Lundberg Waehler, successor to Voorhees, Gmelin & Walker.

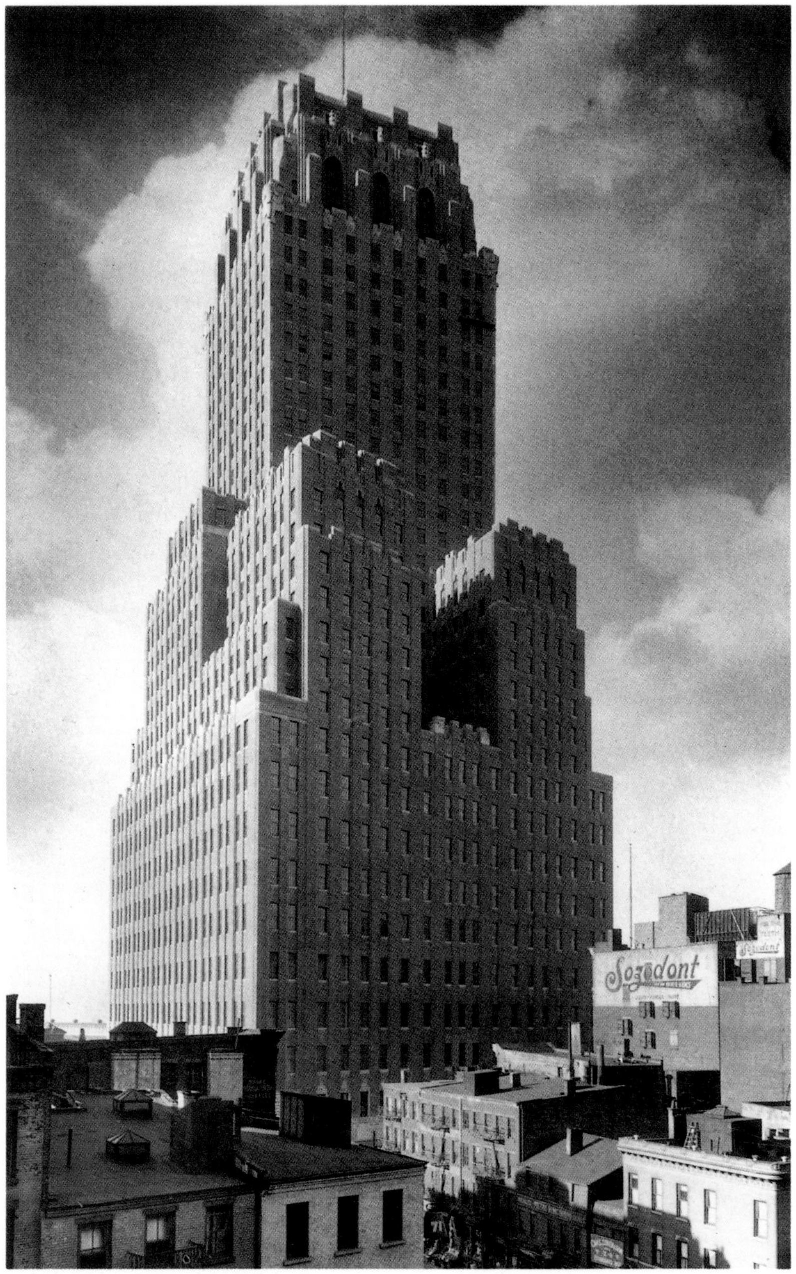

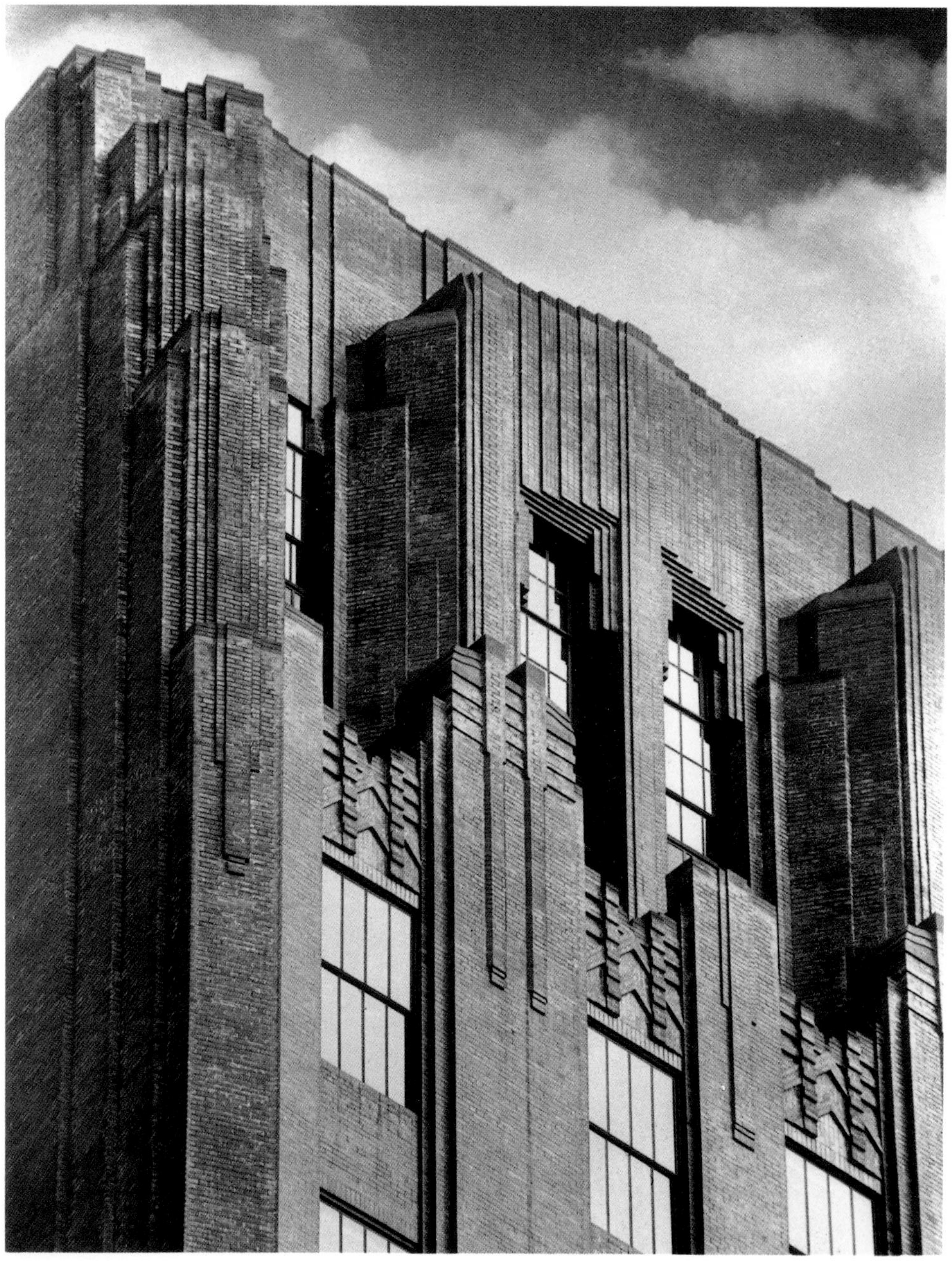

117 *F. S. Lincoln*
Brooklyn, New York Telephone Company, Long Lines Division, 1931. Courtesy Haines Lundberg Waehler, successor to Voorhees, Gmelin & Walker.

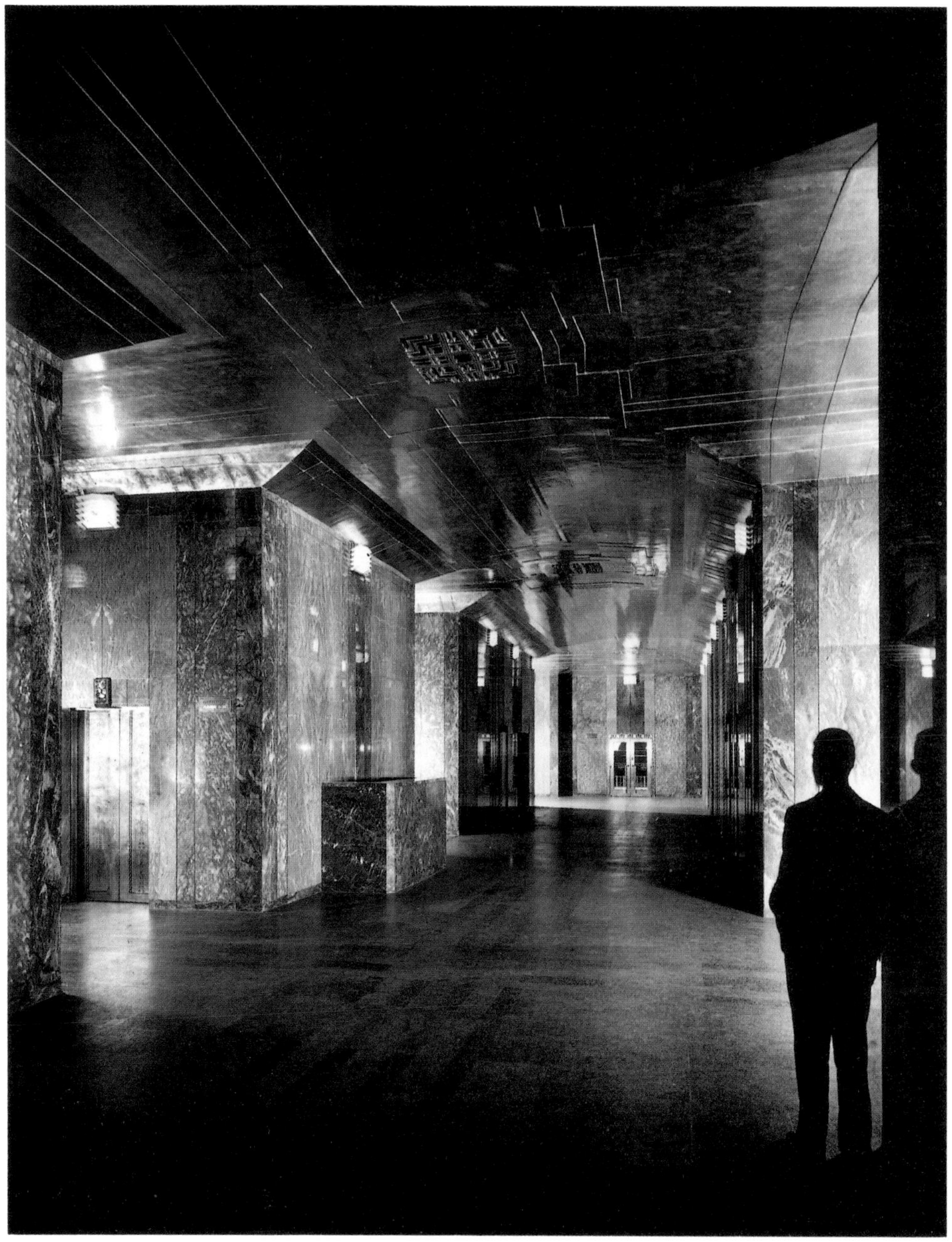

One of two problems New York photographers faced was the great height of some new buildings and the small scale of the decoration on them; the other lay in the difficulty of photographing interiors lit in the new manner, indirectly. That they did not entirely solve the first problem is demonstrated by two photographs by Sigurd Fischer. One is a general view of McKenzie, Voorhees & Gmelin's Barclay-Vesey Building (1923) and shows that such a view reveals nothing of the decorative sculpture—elephant's heads, and so forth—on the building; the other is a detail of the top of the successor firm, Voorhees, Gmelin & Walker's Western Union Building, which demonstrates that when such detail was taken with a long lens, its function on the building as a whole was lost (115, 116). Several photographers solved the problem of taking interiors that had low-intensity indirect lighting by adding lights that paraphrased the effect of indirect illumination, reduced the great contrast between ceiling and lower walls, and revealed decorative materials there (117). Three firms were especially successful in photographing such spaces: Dell & Wainwright in England, Hedrich-Blessing in Chicago, and Nyholm & Lincoln in New York, especially the last, whose craftsmanship in picture taking and printmaking set new standards for the profession. But all three of these firms had a more significant impact in the thirties than in the twenties.

Part III

1930 to 1970

In the 1930s photographers shed much of the artistic self-consciousness of the previous decade and its disinterestedness. Photography became a purposeful tool. The thirties and the decades after World War II continued to be marked by the same split that had started in the 1890s between professional and amateur, between those whose work was skillful, technically conservative, and predictable but versatile—in the sense that one picture might serve many illustrative purposes—and those whose work was awkward, artistically progressive, limited in its purposes, and sometimes innovative in subject matter. In the thirties, as happens in times of economic stress, there was a stock taking of the older built world as it then existed. The awkward—instead of photographing new skyscrapers as they had before the First World War—took the vernacular and older world as their subject; the skillful and conservative adopted the architectural profession's utopian views and photographed new buildings to illustrate the glowing future that was to come.

This schism that fell between those who took pictures of vernacular and historical buildings and those who took contemporary architecture might fall between some photographers who took pictures "for themselves" and others who worked for the architectural profession or might fall between magazine editors who took occasional pictures they used and the professionals they hired to take the rest. Professional work was marked by the use of large (eight-by-ten-inch, "whole-plate," or eighteen-by-twenty-four-centimeter) cameras and clever perspectives; the other by the use of naïve perspectives (head-on, say) with either large cameras or small cameras intended for amateurs. Two photographs, one by Walker Evans, the other by Ken Hedrich, illustrate the split in style. In the first a vernacular wooden building appears head on and very much in the manner of the 1880s except that the sides of the building are brought close to the edges of the picture frame (118). In front of the house is a Ford Model T. It was clearly the juxtaposition of car to house that supplied the occasion for the photograph (we assume Evans found his juxtaposition and did not create it). The point of the picture seems to be in large part the formal resemblance between the car and the house. We may also be inclined to see the building as a Model T of houses, but it is hard now to know what connotations the car can have had to Evans. In 1931, when the picture was taken, the Model T had been out of production for only three years; on the other hand, the design was one of 1908. The important thing here is the existence of the significant juxtaposition and the fact that neither car nor building plays a secondary role.

The second picture is one of Albert Kahn's Dodge Half-Ton Truck Plant (1938) in Detroit (119). It shows a facade obliquely that might well have been photographed in more recent years head on. The perspective gives the building a more dynamic air and emphasizes the glassiness of the facade. We are presented with the experience of the building, not just the facts about it. In the left foreground of the picture is the front of a new Dodge automobile whose purpose, we see, is partly to enliven the space in front of the building and partly to serve as a metaphor: the car is the latest in streamlined design for one purpose, the building is a comparably exciting and up-to-date design for another purpose. The car nudges us in the direction Ken Hedrich, Albert Kahn, and the original publishers of the picture want us to go. It tells us how to interpret the picture and how to think of the building.

Each picture uses juxtaposition as part of its structure, and the building that is the subject of each is not only specific but so individual that we feel we would recognize it if we came upon it even today. But one picture gives us its equivocal message as a matter of simple, awkward fact; the other wants to seduce us with the experience of the building that is its subject (though it is a building type few of us are likely to encounter) and thereby to propagandize the new architecture.

The propagandizing style that had developed among professional photographers by the end of the thirties remained a useful one through the 1960s. The alternative, more amateur manner increasingly explored the real world that lay between publishable modern buildings, and it became an essential part of the language of architectural journalism. For reasons that have to do with the scheduling of photography, architectural photographers did not succeed in bridging the gap between amateur and professional as some fashion photographers have, who used the one manner for unflattering portraiture and the other for seductive fashion statements. In architecture two groups have kept their distance one from the other for five decades, a practice that has often been to their mutual disadvantage since each had much to learn from the other.

The roots of the new style lay superficially in the evolving technology of photography and more profoundly (as they had in the 1890s) in changing practices in photomechanical reproduction. Surprisingly this new language that was triggered by the need to sell modern architecture arose not in the countries that had developed the new architecture but in those that welcomed it as an import, England and the United States.

118 *WALKER EVANS*

Westchester, farmhouse, 1931.
The Estate of Walker Evans.

119 *KEN HEDRICH*

Detroit, Dodge Half-Ton Truck Plant,
export building, 1938.
Courtesy Hedrich-Blessing.

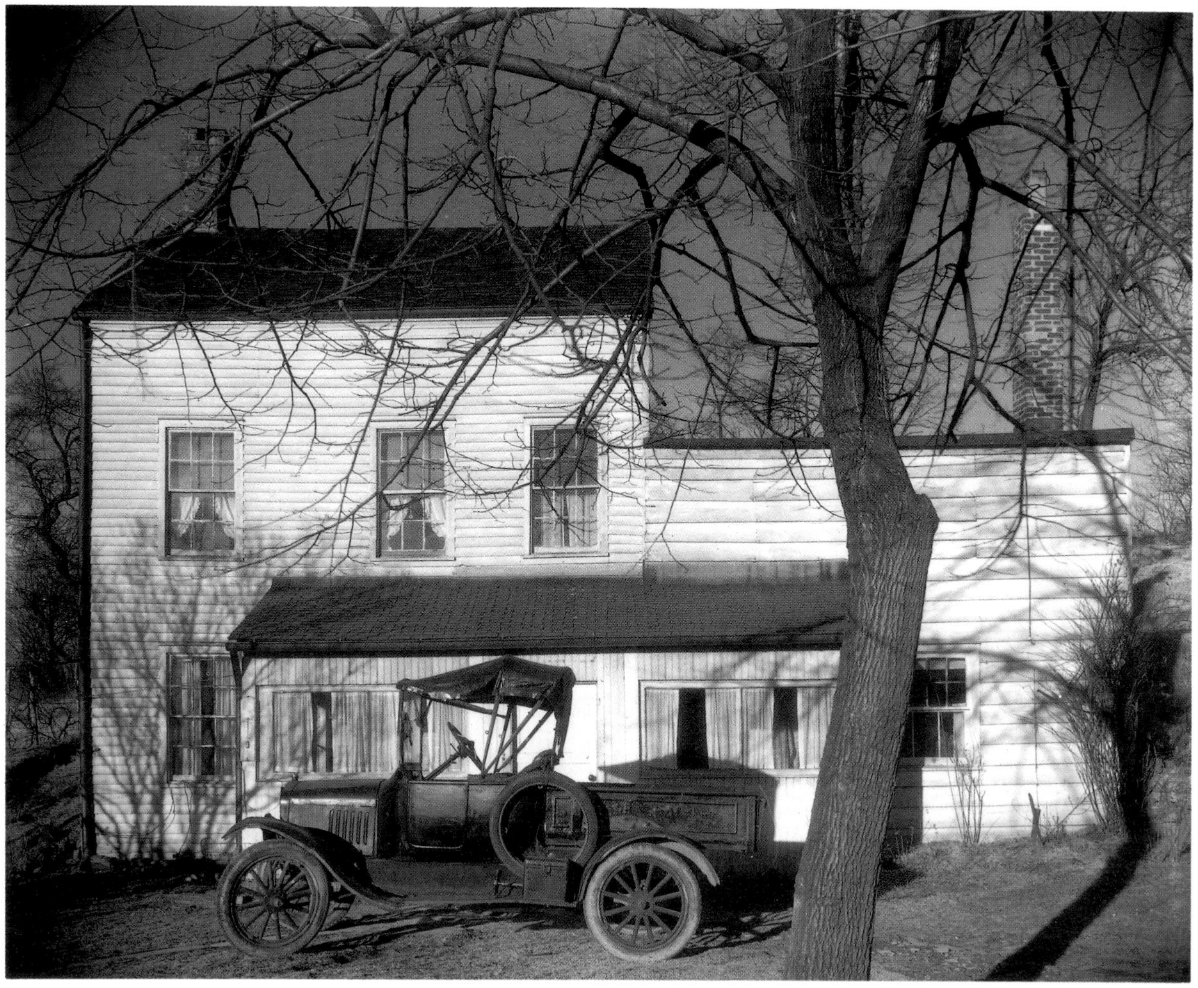

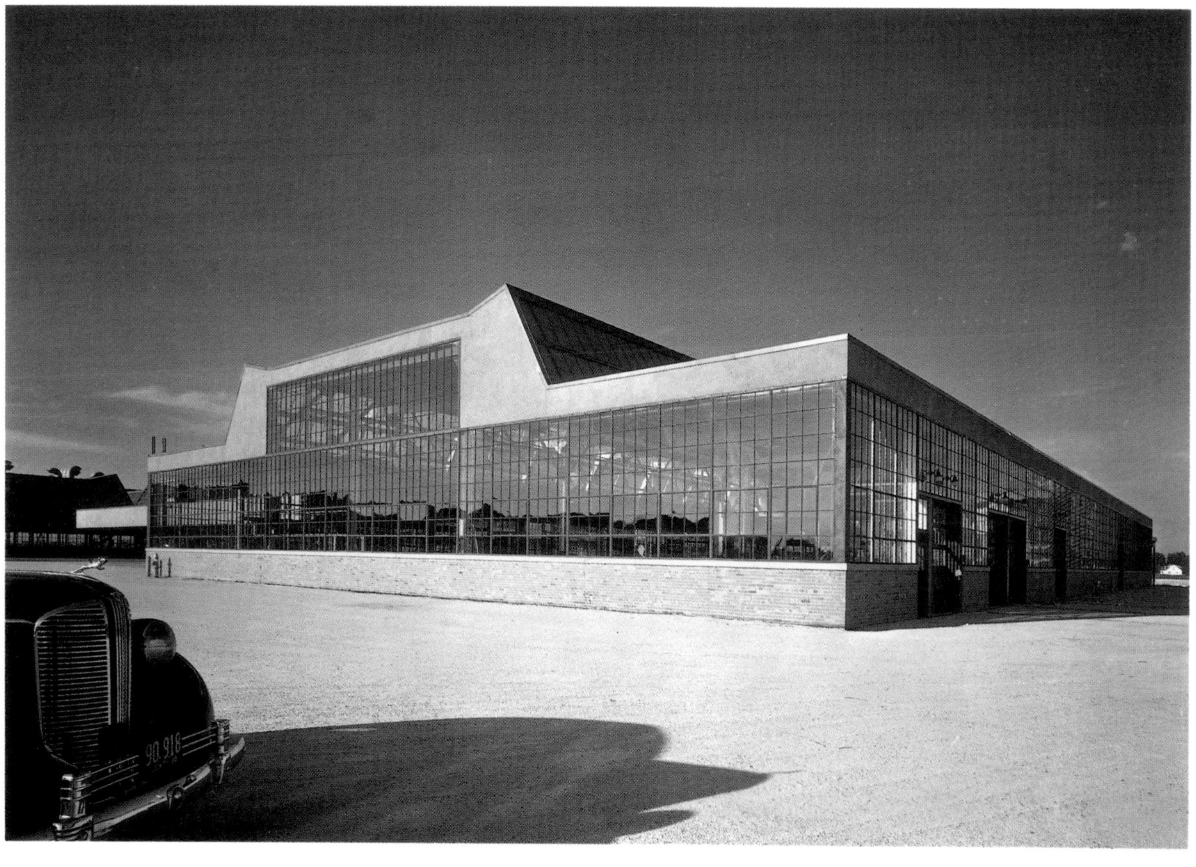

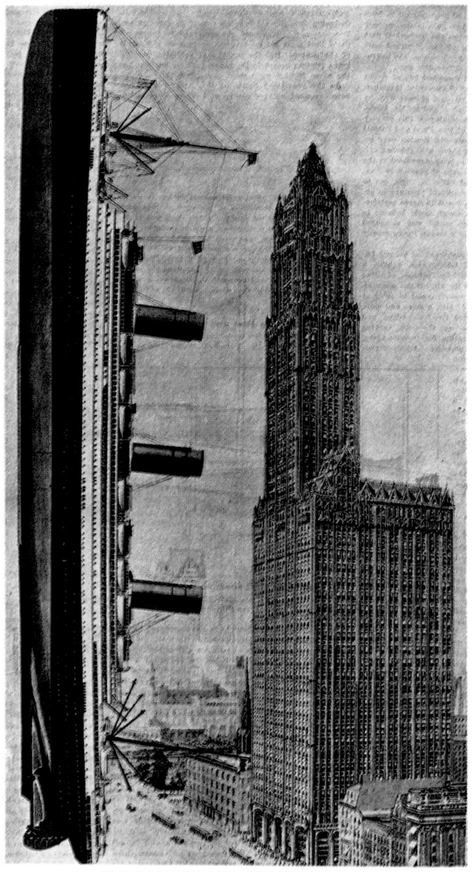

The "Imperator" 900 feet. Woolworth Building 730 feet.
THE LONGEST SHIP AND THE TALLEST BUILDING

Superficial changes brought about by new photographic technology are easy to see. To those who worked in the thirties the exciting aspects of the new photography were its tipped worm's- and bird's-eye views, which they saw as deriving from the influence of motion pictures and the use of small still cameras. Yet the architectural photographs taken in those perspectives were made, like most architectural pictures to this day, not with hand cameras but with large ones set up in a time-consuming process on tripods. Also the generation that turned forty in the 1930s had been brought up on popular magazines that had not only set discordant pictures next to each other (the significance of each being explained in a caption or a text) but might in a drawing juxtapose the image of a skyscraper and a transatlantic steamer set upright on its stern to compare their relative lengths (120).

Starting in the twenties, progressive architectural journals and books on the continent propagandized the new modern architecture, and a significant aspect of the subsequent turn to modernism in England and the United States in the thirties consisted in the exploitation of new uses for photographs that would have been suggested to editors by, say, the juxtaposition in a Bauhaus publication of a silk hat, the wizened face of an old man, and a rotten apple (121). This fresh sensitivity to juxtapositions made photographers increasingly conscious of the structure of their pictures—that is, to the elements that might compose them and the manner in which these could be combined. During the thirties it became apparent that the experiential and the factual perspectives that had started out in the mid-nineteenth century as versions of two kinds of architectural drawing and of which the first, the experiential, had become by the beginning of this century the perspective of "artistic" expression, had again changed their meanings and would begin to change them once more in the forties. In fact during the thirties the head-on perspective was adopted by the artist while the oblique, experiential perspective was used to sell the International Style. The two perspectives were brought together during the forties in the supple style in which the proliferating new architecture of the postwar period would be presented.

The task of an ambitious architectural photographer at the beginning of the 1930s was much what it had always been and continues to be to our day: to produce a print of sufficient physical quality that one's work is taken seriously, to get ahead of the pack of one's fellow photographers by some aesthetic act, and to remain in the public eye thereafter with a recognizable, individual style.

120 “The longest ship and the tallest building, the ‘Imperator’ 900 feet, Woolworth Building 750 feet.”
From *Scientific American*, September, 14, 1912.
Columbia University Libraries.

121 From Moholy-Nagy, *Von Material zu Architektur* (trans. as *The New Vision*) (1929).

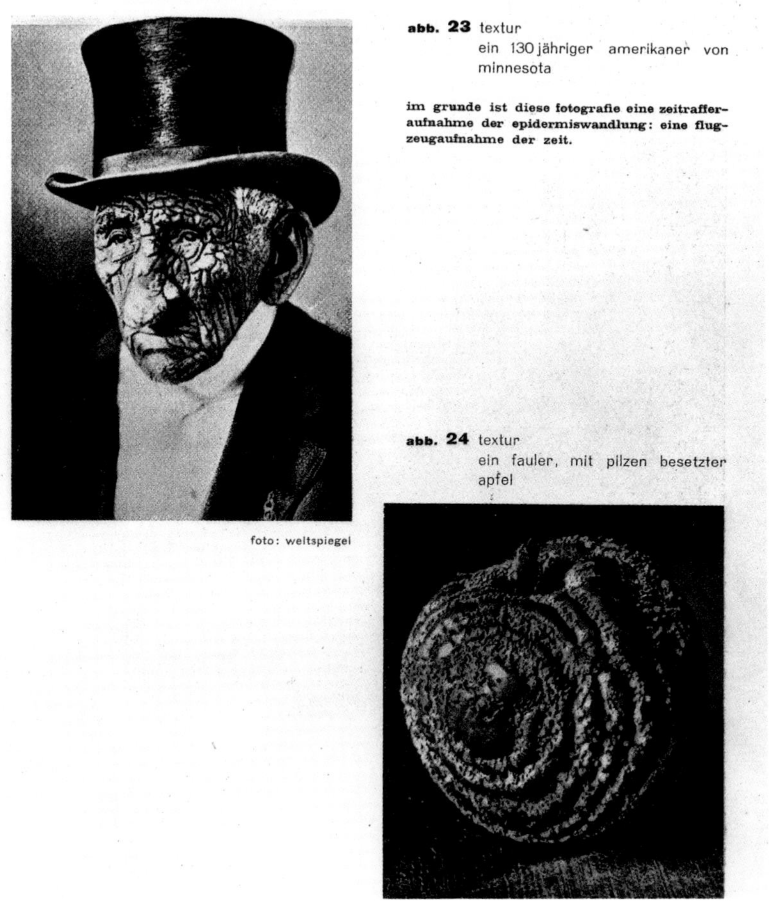
abb. 23 textur
ein 130jähriger amerikaner von minnesota

im grunde ist diese fotografie eine zeitrafferaufnahme der epidermiswandlung: eine flugzeugaufnahme der zeit.

foto: weltspiegel

abb. 24 textur
ein fauler, mit pilzen besetzter apfel

The photographers of the countries that developed the new modern architecture, the Netherlands, Germany, and France, did not—despite the contributions of Arthur Köster and Lucia Moholy—develop a new style for photographing it. In Germany the manner in which a classicizing house of the years just before the First World War might have been taken or a modern house in the late twenties or a pitched-roof cottage just before World War II was the same. This was in large part because modernism was closer to being part of a continuum of progressive architecture in Germany than it was in England or the United States. When Hugo Schmölz took pictures of a Catholic church (1931) by Dominikus Böhm on the island of Norderney on the Baltic coast, he was photographing a building by a major architect whose work fell slightly, but decisively, outside the canons of the International Style (though that is less obvious now than it was twenty years ago) (122). The character of the entrance and stairs, as well as of the hanging bell and the cross sets this building apart from the purism demonstrated by contemporaneous International Style buildings. The picture neither emphasizes the building's elevation by handling it head on nor its experience by bringing a surface close to the camera and does not construct a metaphor by juxtaposition; rather, it treats the building the same as if it were a classicizing building or a cottage. This is a trait that persists among German photographs of this period. It seems that German photographers may have been too locally oriented to achieve a distinctive style. Each German city—Berlin, Cologne, Stuttgart, Nuremberg, Hamburg, Munich, Frankfurt, Breslau, and Düsseldorf among them—had its share of skilled photographers. But their names were too closely linked to their home bases—E. Wasow-München, Max Krajewsky-Berlin—for them to have been independent of the architects they worked for. A healthy playing off of architects against journals has in other places nurtured the most vigorous photography. The fact that we have recently seen wide publication of the work of the Cologne photographers Werner Mantz (b. 1901), August Sander (1876–1964), and Hugo Schmölz has less to say about their preeminence as architectural photographers than it does about the fortuitous preservation of their negatives or prints and the contagious fame of Sander as a portraitist. Finally, the Modern Movement in Germany was largely over before photographers had fairly gotten started on it, unlike the United States where they had some fifteen or twenty years to learn and prepare.

German photographers could distinguish themselves by helping to fill a national demand for picture books on German cities—in particular on their

122 *Hugo Schmölz*
Norderney, Catholic tourist church, 1931.
Courtesy Karl-Hugo Schmölz.

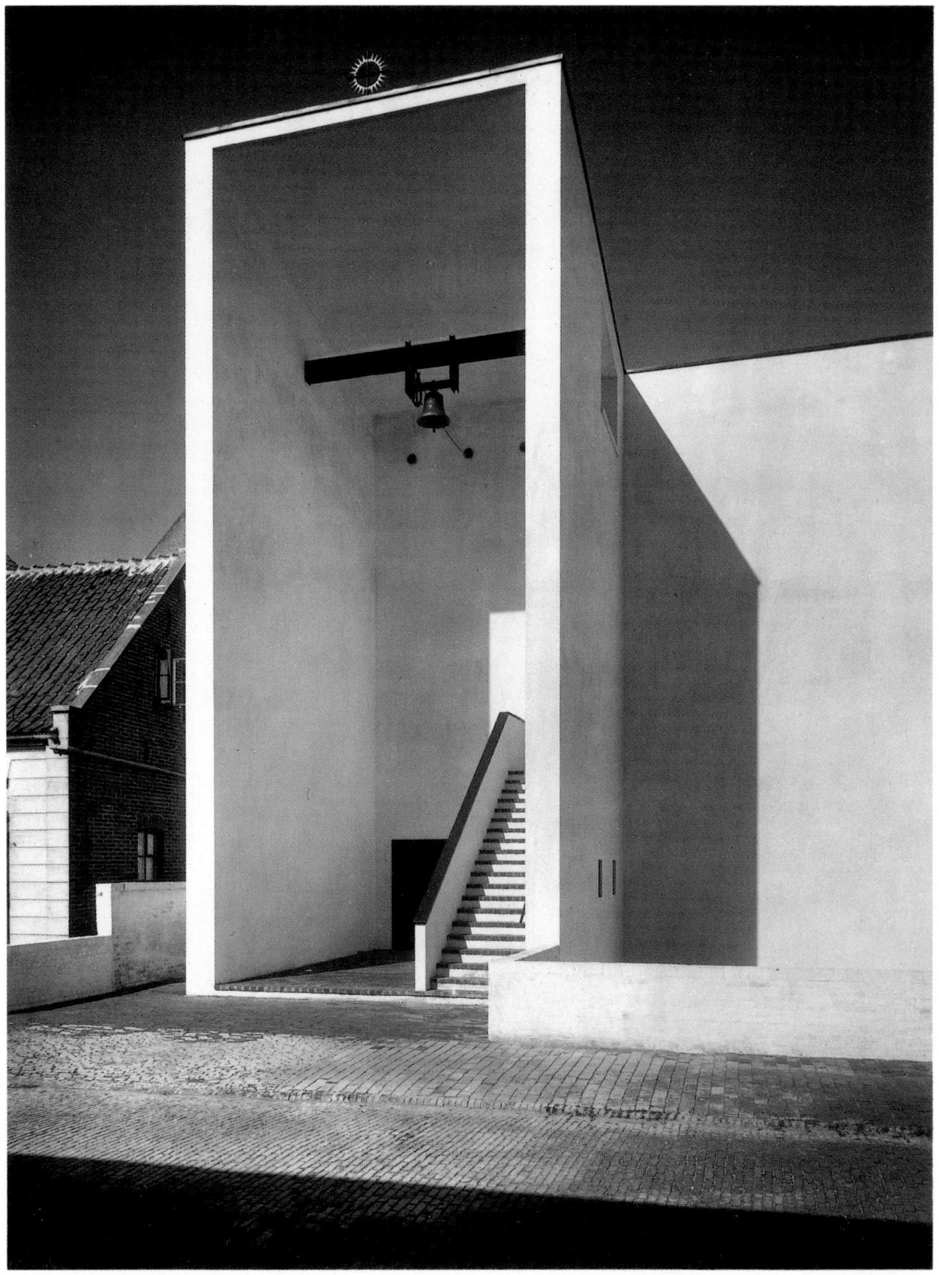

cathedrals—and on Italian and Greek architecture. The advantage to a photographer in doing this lay in his being able to show his full expressive range within the covers of each volume. But a frequent weakness in these books was that many of the pictures on any one subject, say, a cathedral or the Acropolis, were so similar in content to others that the whole bore an impression of uncertain editing or padding. This was less true of the books that Albert Renger-Patzsch continued to produce through the thirties but was true of those by Walter Hege (1893–1955), many of them done for Deutscher Kunstverlag which may therefore share the blame.

There remains the question of style in Arthur Köster's pictures of Erich Mendelsohn's buildings, not only that of the Einstein Tower but later ones, tipped worm's-eye views of housing published in the early thirties. It is clear from his drawings and his book *Amerika* that the architect suggested to Köster the dynamic manner in which his buildings could be taken.

The Netherlands were sufficiently small that two names, E. M. van Ojen and Jan Kamman (1898–1983), are associated with much of the International Style work there and in Van Ojen's case with the Expressionist School of Amsterdam as well. One photograph of Kamman's, whose negative and apparently all prints were destroyed in the bombing of Rotterdam, did combine elements in such a way as to achieve a picture in the full thirties style. In this picture, taken on the roof of Brinkmann, Van Tijen, and Van der Vlugt's Bergpolder apartments (1934) in Rotterdam, a child beside a tubular steel chair looks into a planter; to the right the picture includes a spiral staircase and in the distance, through a glass windscreen, we see two ocean liners at dock. The photograph through the presence of the child, the vegetation, and the ships thus links youth, nature, and functionalism to the new architecture (123).

Some four years earlier a comparable message, but more intellectualizing, had come from France. The most significant photographers were based in Paris, where some eight of them made the well-known pictures of new buildings of the late twenties and the thirties though none managed to stand out particularly from his fellows. Alain Salaün took Le Corbusier's own apartment at the Porte Molitor and André Lurçat's school at Villejuif; both J. Collas and G. Thiriet took the exhibition rooms Le Corbusier, Pierre Jeanneret, and Charlotte Perriand designed for the Salon d'Automne in 1929; Chevojon Frères did buildings of Henri Sauvage and August Perret; Maurice Tabard (1897–1984?) took Siclis's Théâtre Pigalle; Claude Gravot did the Villa Savoye, the Pavillon Suisse, and the de Beistegui apartment; R. Levy took Le Corbusier's Salvation Army Hostel; and Marc Vaux took Lurçat's Villa Guggenbuhl.

The significant message came in a picture of the Villa Savoye taken by Claude Gravot for Le Corbusier. For this picture the camera was set up outside an unglazed window opening at the solarium level and looked inward across a table surface upon which, front and center, were several objects of the architect's that played a larger role in this picture than did the coat and hat that often appeared in pictures of his houses in order to make them look inhabited (124). Clearly Le Corbusier had set these significant Phileban forms or *objets types* in front of the camera, where they could upstage his building, in order to tell us how we should interpret the forms of the house that was the nominal subject of the picture. They proved to be the ancestors of many carefully chosen things—everything from office furniture to brandy snifters—set out in front of cameras for fifty years to come. However, there is evidence that in their first use here they were neither placed with utter assurance by the architect nor received with any enthusiasm by the journal that published Gravot's pictures, for a second photograph was taken with the objects apparently placed nearer the camera, and when this second picture was reproduced in *L'Architecte* in January 1930 the objects had been cropped out.

Another ingredient of the new style, at least into the forties, was the tipped perspectives of bird's- and worm's-eye views, which could be used in two quite different spirits, one arising from the problem of photographing skyscrapers, the other from the freedom that the hand camera allowed. New buildings of the late twenties, many of them in the Art Deco style, had often been too high and thin and too cramped by neighbors to be taken in traditional perspective with parallel verticals. One obvious solution had been to give up trying to keep verticals parallel and to point a camera up at a tower from the street below it. Such a worm's-eye view could serve as a bridge between an overall view and pictures of a building's details. These worm's-eye views became associated with the romance of skyscraper cities. An example of this Art Deco approach to buildings is one of the pictures Edward Steichen made for Eugene Schoen's New York State Exhibition at the Chicago Century of Progress Exhibition of 1933–1934. It is a double exposure of Shreve, Lamb & Harmon's Empire State Building (1930) and comprises a tipped worm's-eye view from directly across Fifth Avenue and a subsequent three-quarter view from the corner of Thirty-Third Street, untipped and taken just before the sun passed from the west side of the avenue (125). Though taken in 1932, it still

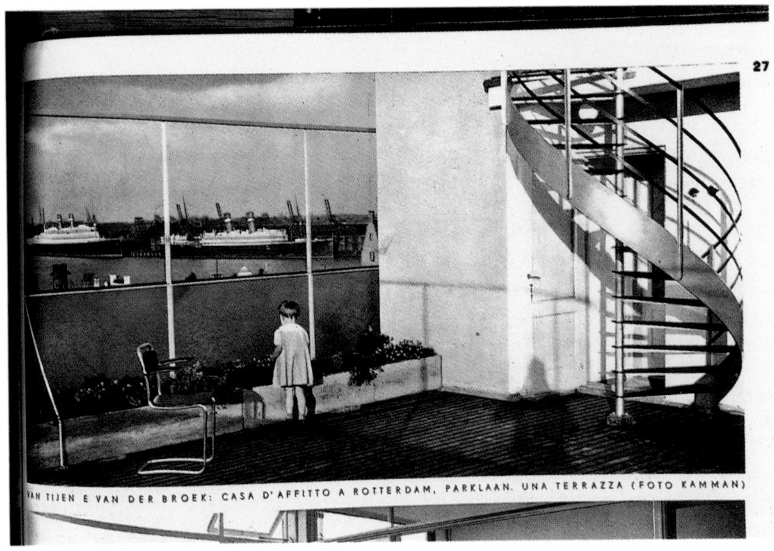

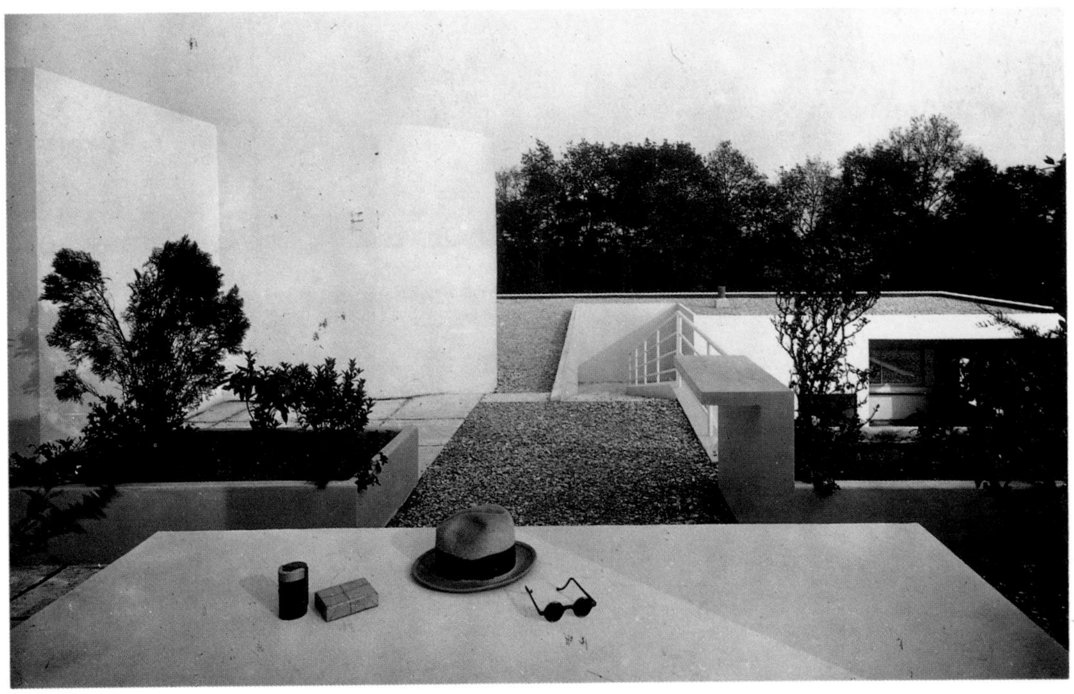

123 *JAN KAMMAN*

Rotterdam, Bergpolder apartments.
From *Casabella* (1938).
Avery Architectural Library.

124 *CLAUDE GRAVOT*

Poissy-sur-Seine, Villa Savoye, 1929.
Museum of Modern Art, New York.

125 *EDWARD STEICHEN*

New York, "The Maypole," 1932.
Museum of Modern Art, New York.
Gift of the photographer.

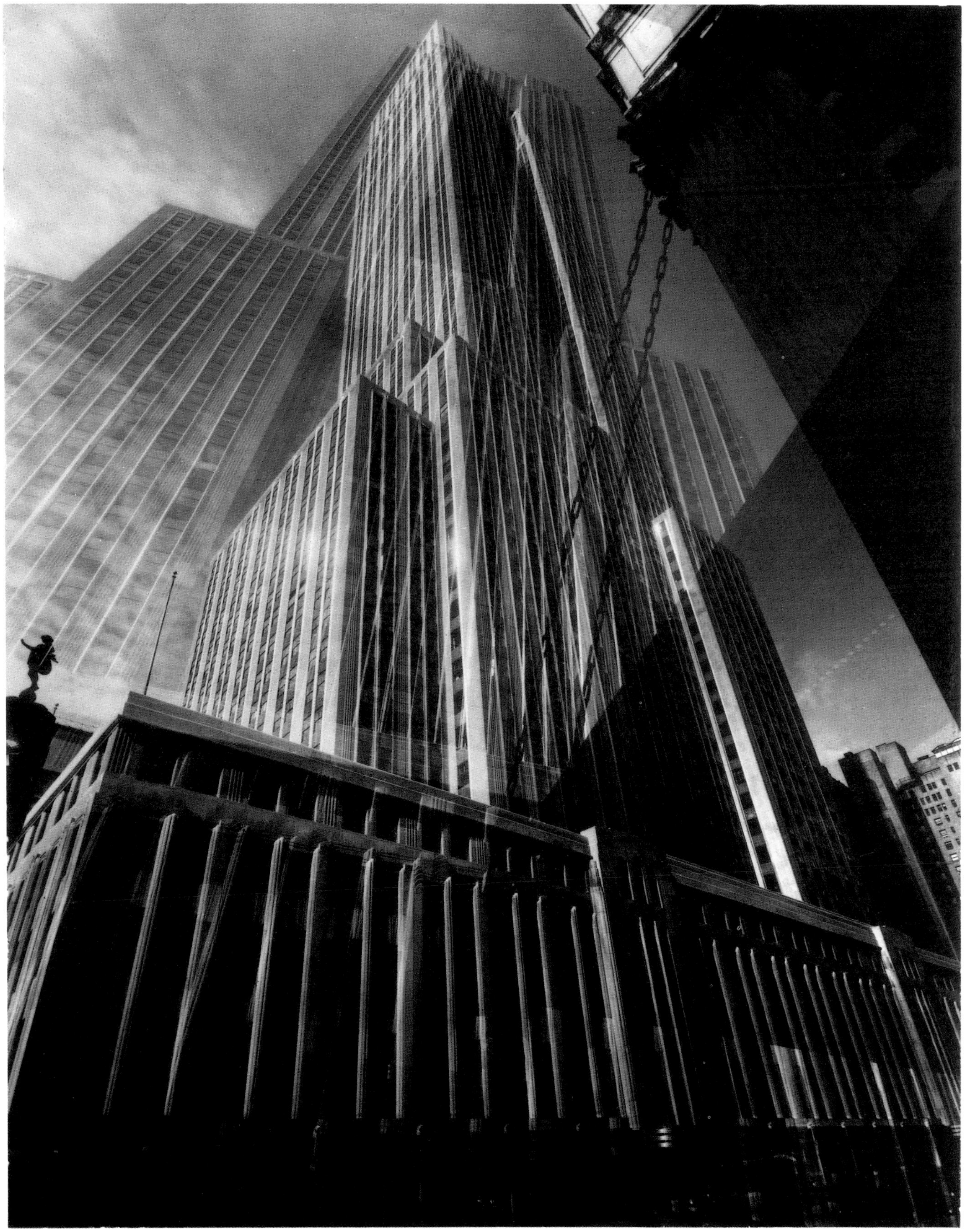

maintains the tendency of photographers of the twenties to emphasize formal patterns.

Bird's-eye views also took on some of the technical glamour of aerial photographs. In Germany in the twenties Laszlo Moholy-Nagy in *Von Material zu Architektur* (1929) had advanced both worm's- and bird's-eye perspectives as characteristic of the modern vision, a new way of seeing the world encouraged by the new hand camera and air flight. Thus the views adopted because of the limitations posed by the urban skyscraper introduced a perspective that suggested heady, unquestioning optimism while the techniques of aerial surveillance suggested freshness and exploitation of new technology.

Though the confluence of these two influences could make a sometimes mindlessly decorative Art Deco perspective acceptable to modernists, the new style was not as simple as that. The schism between amateur and professional played a role at this point. In about 1930 the British journal, the *Architectural Review,* became a convert to the Modern Movement and adopted an appropriate style of photography. But when it mentioned photography, an odd split was revealed. In an article of January 1934 P. Morton Shand wrote:

> The two fields in which the spirit of our age has achieved its most definite manifestations are photography and architecture. Did modern photography beget modern architecture, or the converse? It is an interesting point. But since their logical development was simultaneous, and their interaction considerable, it hardly matters much . . .
>
> Without modern photography modern architecture could never have been "put across." In the early nineteen-twenties architectural photography was as unimaginatively true to "life" and conventional perspective as any other sort of photography. Men with the cultural equipment of beach photographers walked round buildings at a respectful distance like policemen on their beat flashing lanterns on the impeccably obvious. But the new sort of architects had their buildings taken by the new sort of photographers. A revolution in the technique of architectural photography resulted, which has revolutionized architectural criticism.

The article, though it seems to be about the photographing of International Style buildings, is illustrated with some pictures by Moholy-Nagy, who did not photograph modern buildings (unlike his wife Lucia). The pictures are a bird's-eye view of a city street pavement with trolley tracks and a bicyclist, a view from above of stacked circular tables at a roof-top cafe, and a view from below of the thin, curved vaults of a "concrete airplane hangar" under construction. And the illustrations for a subsequent article on the new photography were of subjects that a tourist might have taken on a holiday on the continent—demonstrations of the possibilities of hand-camera photography.

The fact is that Shand's disdain reveals the split betwen amateur and professional and that something like his "beach photographers," though now often using other than conventional perspective, would continue to take new buildings in an honorable fashion while others (who had Shand's "cultural equipment") would turn their tourist energies to increasingly useful purpose.

The standard to which the *Review*'s pictures of new buildings lived up was set by the photographers M. O. Dell (d. 1959) and H. L. Wainwright, who became the magazine's official photographers in about 1930. Their style was a straightforward, unremarkable one punctuated, especially in their early years, by occasional worm's- or bird's-eye views, whose purpose was partly expressive and partly functional. Besides allowing them to imply that Ellis & Clarke's and Sir Owen William's Daily Express Building (1931) was a skyscraper, which it was not, a view up from Shoe Lane allowed Dell & Wainwright to emphasize the modernist glass skin of the building, to remove from sight the Art Deco detailing of the ground-floor lobby, and to juxtapose the new building to the spire (1703) of Christopher Wren's St. Bride, Fleet Street, in order to locate it and to suggest its quality (126). The low viewpoint also allowed them to isolate their subject from any of its environment they did not want to show. And the tipping suggested controlled excitement. Where a diffuse giddiness had been conveyed by Steichen's picture of the Empire State Building in which edges of the building were not aligned with either margin of the picture, here the window washer's rail is aligned with the right margin; not only the excitement inherent in the new architecture but its purposefulness were conveyed as a result. Such perspectives provided an extreme position to which a responsible photographer could occasionally go to express his position on such new buildings.

The *Review* had a broader range of interests than we expect of architectural magazines today. Among them was one in the qualities of vernacular design. Articles on a lack of quality in the ordinary world outside of publishable buildings had begun to appear in the late twenties in the form of sets of snapshots or stock photographs, supported by mocking captions, on such subjects as gas station design and the impact of billboards on the appearance of motor roads. In the thirties one stock photograph so popular with the editors that it was used not once but twice showed part of a bathroom: bathtub to the right, sink

126 *Dell & Wainwright*

London, Daily Express Building, ca. 1931.
Courtesy Architectural Press, London.

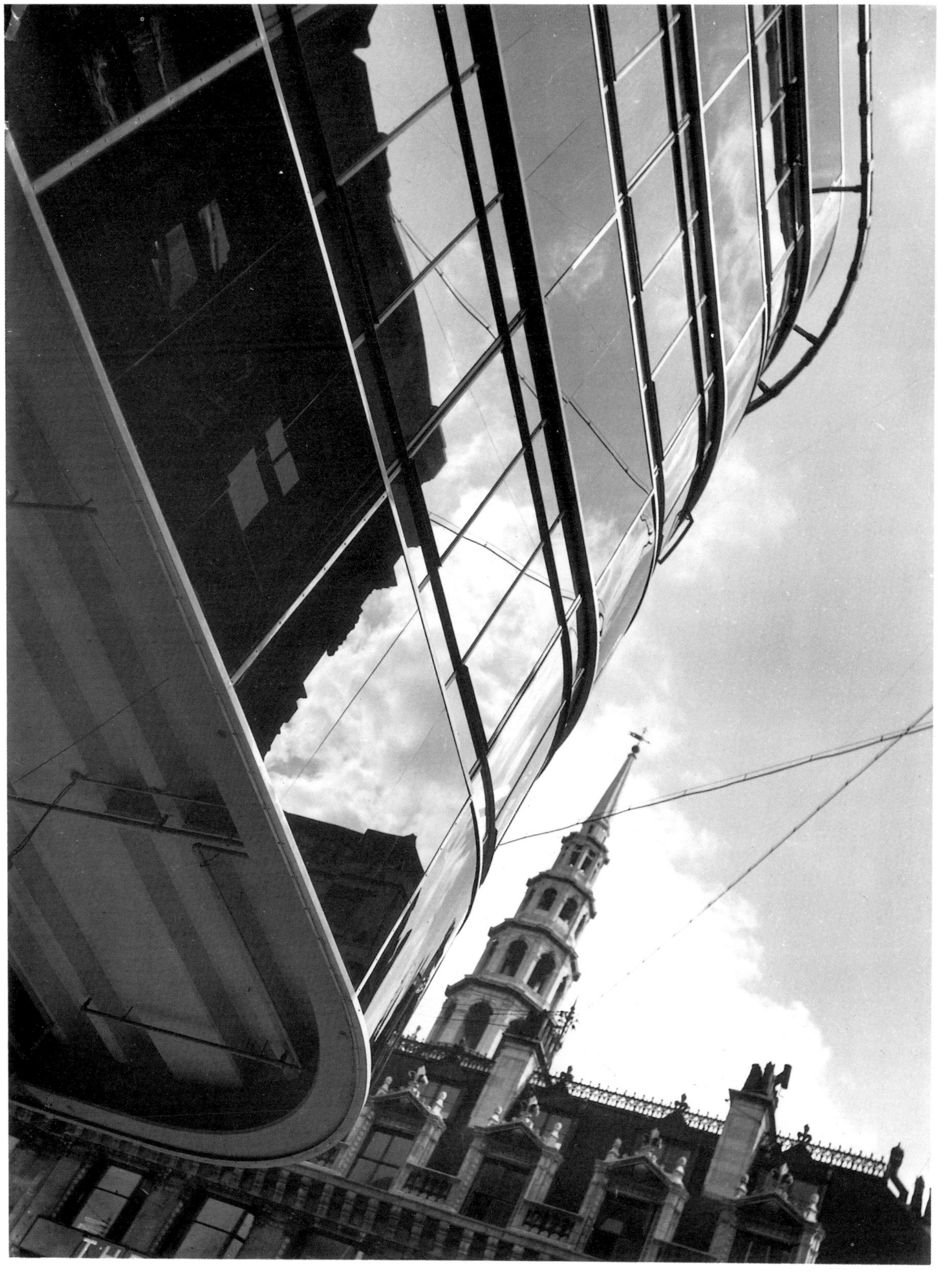

above, and a toilet seat (experientially) close to the camera on the left, the suite joined by an extraordinarily elegant example of British lead plumbing (127). By the late thirties this tradition had developed into an appreciation of older vernacular forms presented in the form of an essay of instructional analysis and a set of captioned pictures taken by the author, who was often an editor of the magazine. Two such articles of 1937 and 1938 described the qualities of "The Nautical Style" of design on England's seasides and "Black-and-White," a British tradition of painting utilitarian structures in those two colors (and therefore a tradition particularly suited to illustration in black-and-white pictures). A photograph by John Piper from "The Nautical Style" shows that these photographers did not hesitate to pluck a piece out of a larger whole (in the pre-World War I style) in order to make all the more tangible the quality and substance they were talking about (128). It was not the total lighthouse that was Piper's and J. M. Richards' subject but the spirit in which the parts had been assembled and maintained; the flagpole, halyards, and fence have as much of a role in this as the lighthouse proper. A consequence of the change from subjects that were mocked to those that were presented as exemplary was the new care that went into showing the latter. The argument that something is in bad taste may even be furthered by an inept photograph of it, but virtuous subjects need simple, direct, and convincing pictures.

Thus British journals had one language to propagandize the new architecture and another to illustrate the useful lesson of older traditions. Pictures of new buildings were taken by skilled craftsmen whose work the magazine could describe as by its "official photographers"; pictures of vernacular structures, visibly less skillful, were taken by editors or sometimes by painters, that is to say, by amateurs. The first pictures were polished but in the end predictable; the second were innovative in subject matter and in the way the pictures were used but showed no more competence than necessary. Both were nicely adjusted to the needs of a magazine whose interests were as varied and attractive as the merchandise in a department store.

American photographers operated differently. If the British tended to polarize between predictable professional and innovating amateur, Americans tended to become either commercial photographers or those who took pictures "for themselves," the latter with many conservative traits and a conviction that they were artists, the former rather hoping to be told they were. And on occasion Americans also accomplished a synthesis between the two British traditions of the innovative amateur and the skilled craftsman—most obviously in photojournalism.

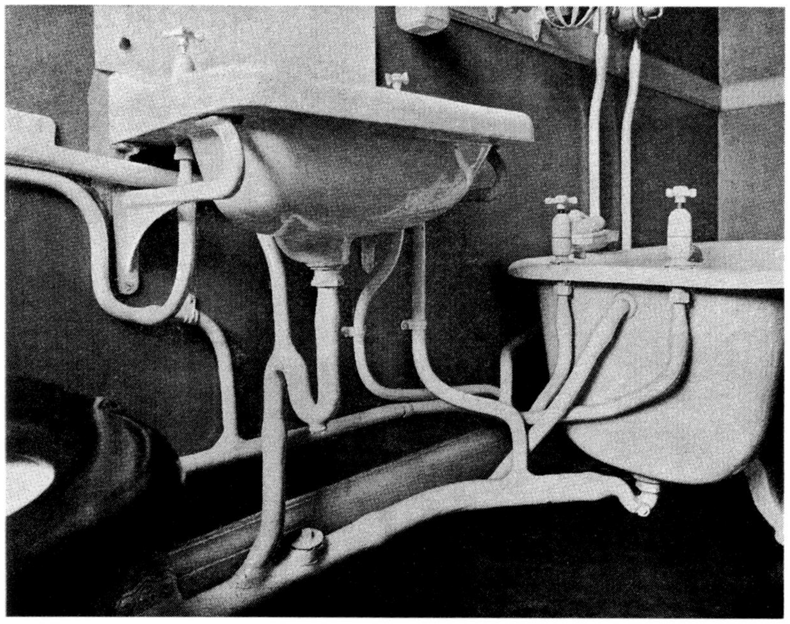

127 British bathroom plumbing.
From *Architectural Review* (1935).
Avery Architectural Library.

128 *John Piper*

Portland, lighthouse. From "The Nautical Style." *Architectural Review* (1938).
Avery Architectural Library.

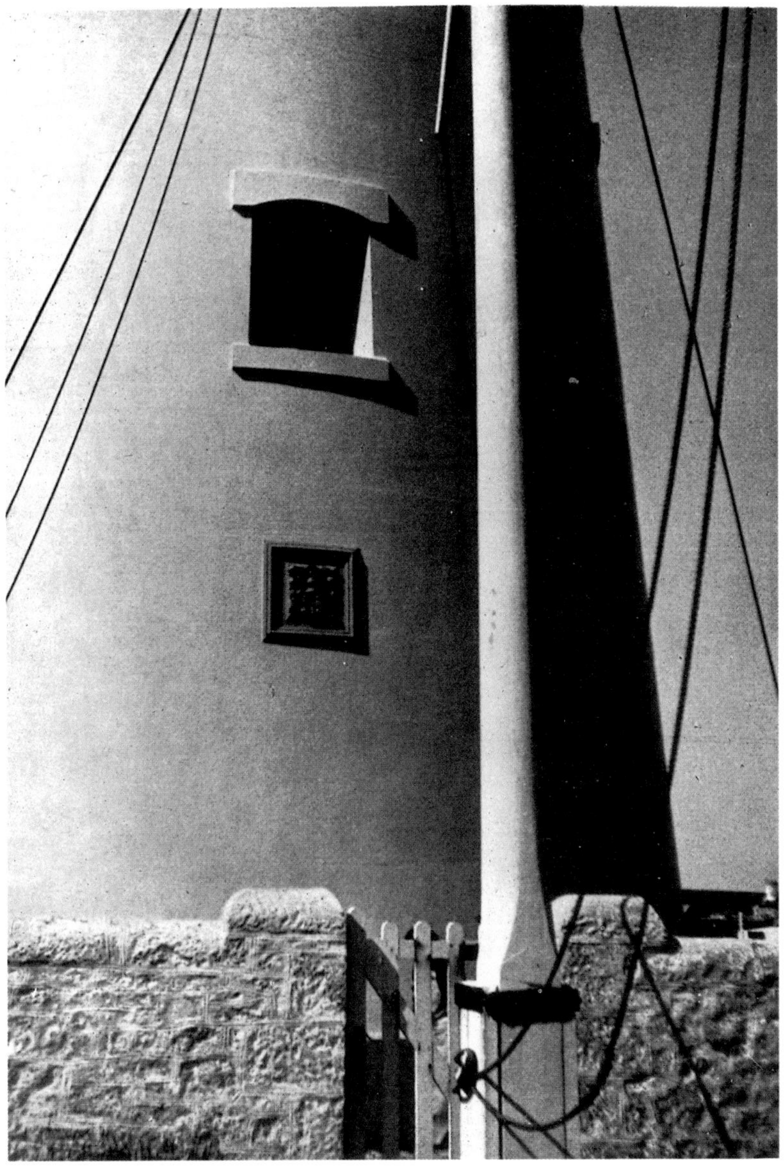

Ralph Steiner (1899–1986) was an American photographer who played a wide variety of photographic roles without ultimately bringing them together into what could be seen as a single career. He photographed the new work of the architect William Lescaze in a manner that not only expressed its excitement but showed as well how it should be used. In a bird's-eye view of the terrace of Lescaze's own house (1934) on East 48th Street in New York, the architect is shown stretched out on cushions demonstrating a form of noon-hour relaxation though dressed in a three-piece suit (129). The canted frame of the terrace walls, one corner almost touching the top edge of the picture, served effectively to isolate the terrace from its nonmodern neighbors, which could only have distracted from this view of what the world would look like when rebuilt in the new style.

Earlier Steiner had taken pictures of details of everyday objects—vernacular houses, signs, typewriter keys, cars—a selection of which was reproduced in *Fortune* magazine in 1930 with a text that (lest we forget that America had its eye cocked constantly on England in these years and much later too) compared the American landscape with the English. The text said: "Essentially the English scene is sad and the American scene is happy. It is smelly, but it is also exuberant and vigorous to strew the country with things worn out and left over." Note that this American debris, part architecture and part landscape, has served ever since as a principal subject of American photography. Steiner later became a movie cameraman and producer. It was a characteristic of the thirties to see so much as yet undone that any one photographer could with success play several unrelated roles.

F. S. Lincoln (1894–1976) was more of a specialist, and his skill and craftsmanship made him the dominant New York photographer of new architecture in the thirties. In the late twenties he had worked in association with Peter Nyholm, taking articulate, heady pictures for Art Deco architects. On his own in the thirties, Lincoln's special contribution was the synthesis of his version of the abstract, decorative style of the previous decade with a thirties commitment to the austere—if not downright meagre—products of the International Style in America. As Lincoln photographed it, the facade of an exhibition house by Frederich Kiesler was shown head on, but the interiors were taken with full experiential emphasis. The floor covering was sponge rubber, and the substance of this material was made memorable by a close-up of the floor with the toe of a man's leather shoe resting on it, a picture reproduced, like most of the others of this structure, full page in a 1934 issue of *Architec-*

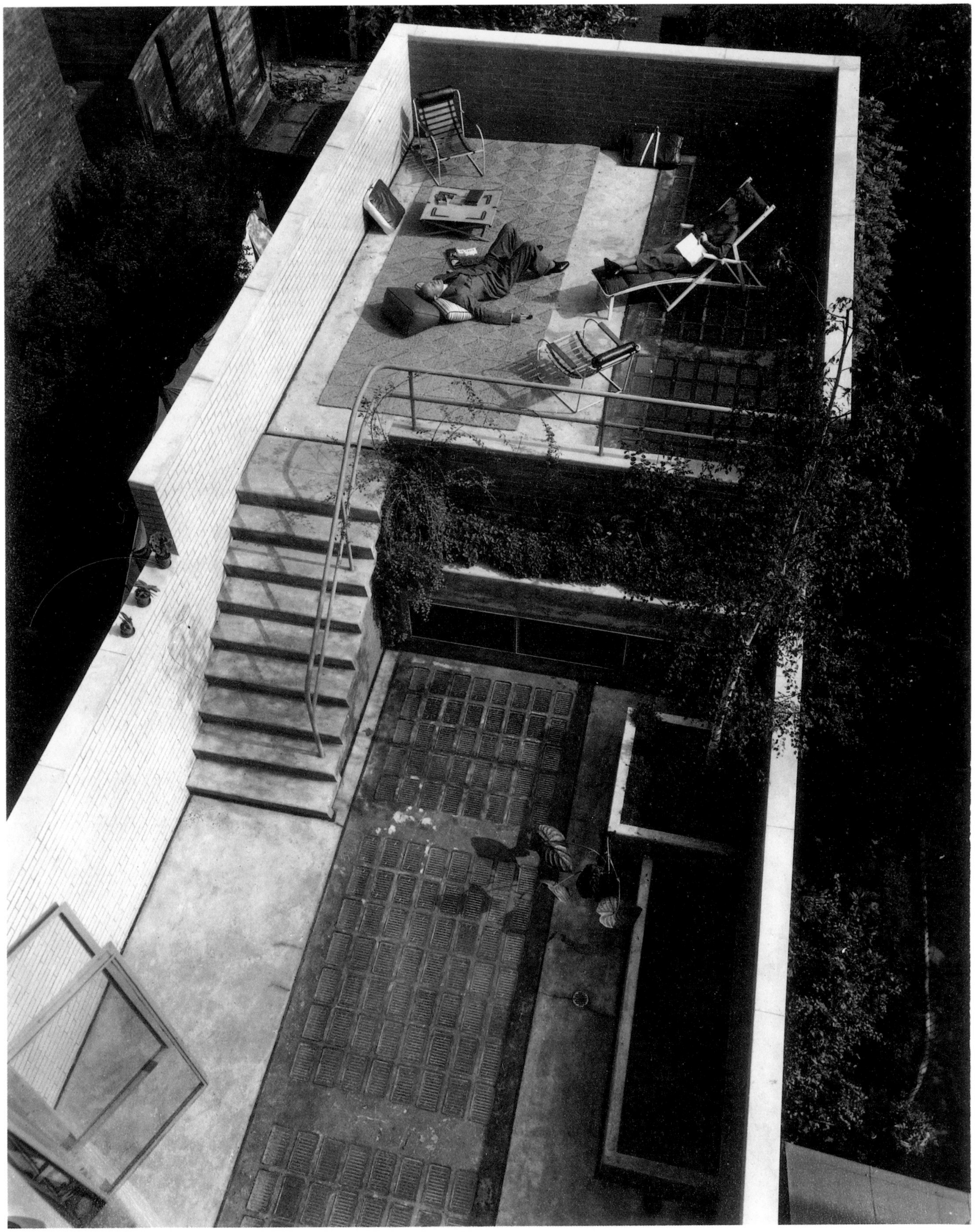

129 *Ralph Steiner*

New York, Lescaze house, 1934. William Lescaze Collection, George Arents Research Library for Special Collections at Syracuse University.

tural Record (130). In a view down an adjacent double staircase, edges and corners and rows of lighting fixtures are kept in careful and purposeful relationship to the borders of the picture while two models, a man and a woman, stand poised heading up those sponge-rubber-covered stairs (131). (Whether significantly or not, like most posed figures in architectural photographs, the woman faces the camera while the man keeps his back to it.) The same experiential quality verges on the manic in pictures Lincoln took for a manufacturer of demountable partitions in which groups of men, in waistcoats, attempt to pull the product over. In a picture of a prefab aluminum bathroom of 1936 the sink edge, toilet seat, and upper bath corners, by their relationship to the edges of the picture, lend a vigor it would otherwise lack (132). And of course the presence of the room's designer, Buckminster Fuller, demonstrating the function of the tub makes the bathroom seem a reality, not a mere mock-up.

Lincoln did photograph some older architecture, most notably buildings of Colonial Williamsburg and Charleston, South Carolina, and Mont-Saint-Michel in France, but for older structures his enthusiastic style often seemed less appropriate. In taking a chapel in the Wren building at Williamsburg, where one would have expected a more distanced view, he brought candlesticks and an open bible immediately in front of his camera. For a picture of the Council Chamber in the capitol he logically kept the axis of his camera parallel to that of the oval room in order to avoid deepening it askew with his short lens, but he also brought this lens close to the head chair at the table and almost as low as the eyes of a sitter in order to thrust the viewer into the experience of the room (133). In the Williamsburg pictures such maneuvers serve to remind us that the subjects are often twentieth-century constructs and not the old building they appear. But on other buildings his approach can seem obtrusive.

The work of Ken Hedrich (1908–1972), the founder of the Chicago firm of Hedrich-Blessing, who began photographing at about the same time as Lincoln, is less emotional and more intellectualizing, relying on juxtapositions rather than on tipped perspectives; indeed, the collaborative form of this firm would inevitably lead it to a more muted style of work. Hedrich's pictures show buildings at some distance and are often remarkable for the inclusion of part of an automobile in one near corner. One appeared in his picture of the Dodge Half-Ton Truck Plant (1938) and another in a picture of Mies van der Rohe's Metallurgy Building at IIT (1943) (119, 134). In the latter the distant, posed figure of a man is also characteristic of Ken Hedrich's pictures. The fenders and figures do more than provide a foreground and scale to his pictures. The fenders suggest functionalism and modernity (as the automobiles that were often pointedly parked in photographs of Le Corbusier's buildings were intended to). The figures invest an industrial style of architecture with humanity; cumulatively, because they clearly had been posed, these figures retain an air of significance that unposed figures always lack.

Ben Schnall (b. 1906) applied the two approaches, the factual and the experiential, to a single building exterior when he photographed George Howe's house, Fortune Rock, at Mount Desert in 1939. One view, from the water's edge, did much that a sectional drawing of the house would have done to explain its cantilevered construction, while the other showed the house in the context of the view that it enjoyed (135, 136). Although the choice of the two camera positions was clearly determined in large part by what was possible—it would have been difficult to take pictures from the water with an eight-by-ten view camera—the two pictures interact as two expressive extremes for describing the house. The experiential view offers the oblique surfaces of the sea and the house to draw us into the scene; the tree on the left confirms the photographer's approval of the house (just as the presence in a picture of a telephone pole would suggest his emotional distance from a structure). In the other a man, looking out to sea, testifies to the fact that there is a view to be had in that direction. The deadwood at the water's edge is a romantic note that is more likely to appear in British photographs of new buildings than in American pictures, where it tends to confirm the dilapidation of a building.

Yet other examples can be given of the thirties' practice of including something outside the building that would shape the viewer's attitude toward it—like the statue of Henri IV that dominates the place Dauphine in Paris, though it stands outside it on the pont Neuf. One could, for instance, include an automobile or a major building visible through a window such as the two buildings by Shreve, Lamb & Harmon—500 Fifth Avenue and the Empire State Building—visible through a window that lend importance to an interior by Morris Lapidus taken by Samuel H. Gottscho (1875–1971) (137).

Ezra Stoller (b. 1915), who had started photographing in the late thirties, by the forties was using two approaches to buildings, one the head-on perspective of his widely reproduced picture of 1940 of the Chamberlain house by Gropius and Breuer, the other a manner of taking pictures of interiors particularly suited to those with the new, wall-size sheets of glass. In a 1941 photo-

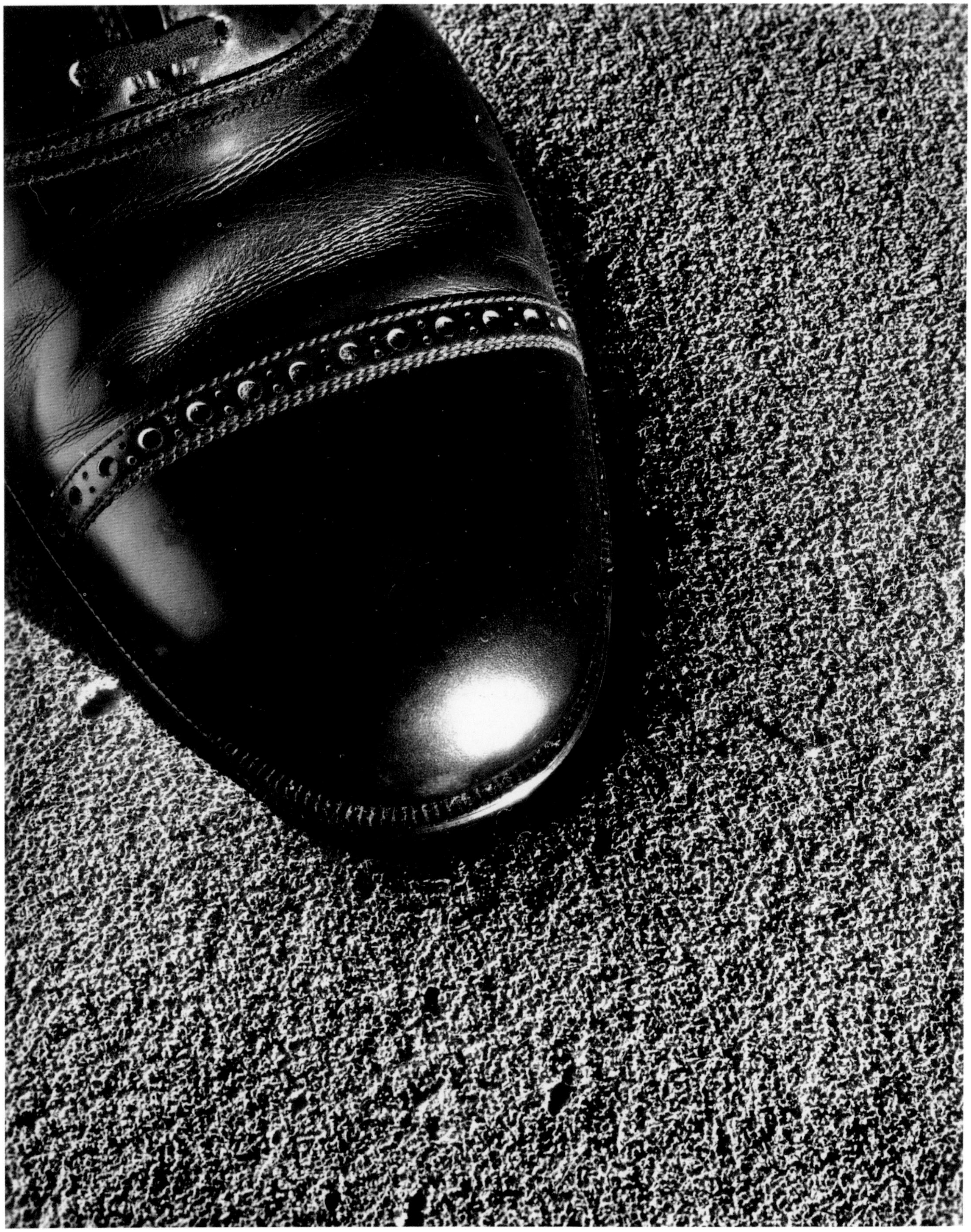

130 *F. S. Lincoln*

New York, Space House floor covering, 1934.

Fred L. Pattee Library, Pennsylvania State University Libraries.

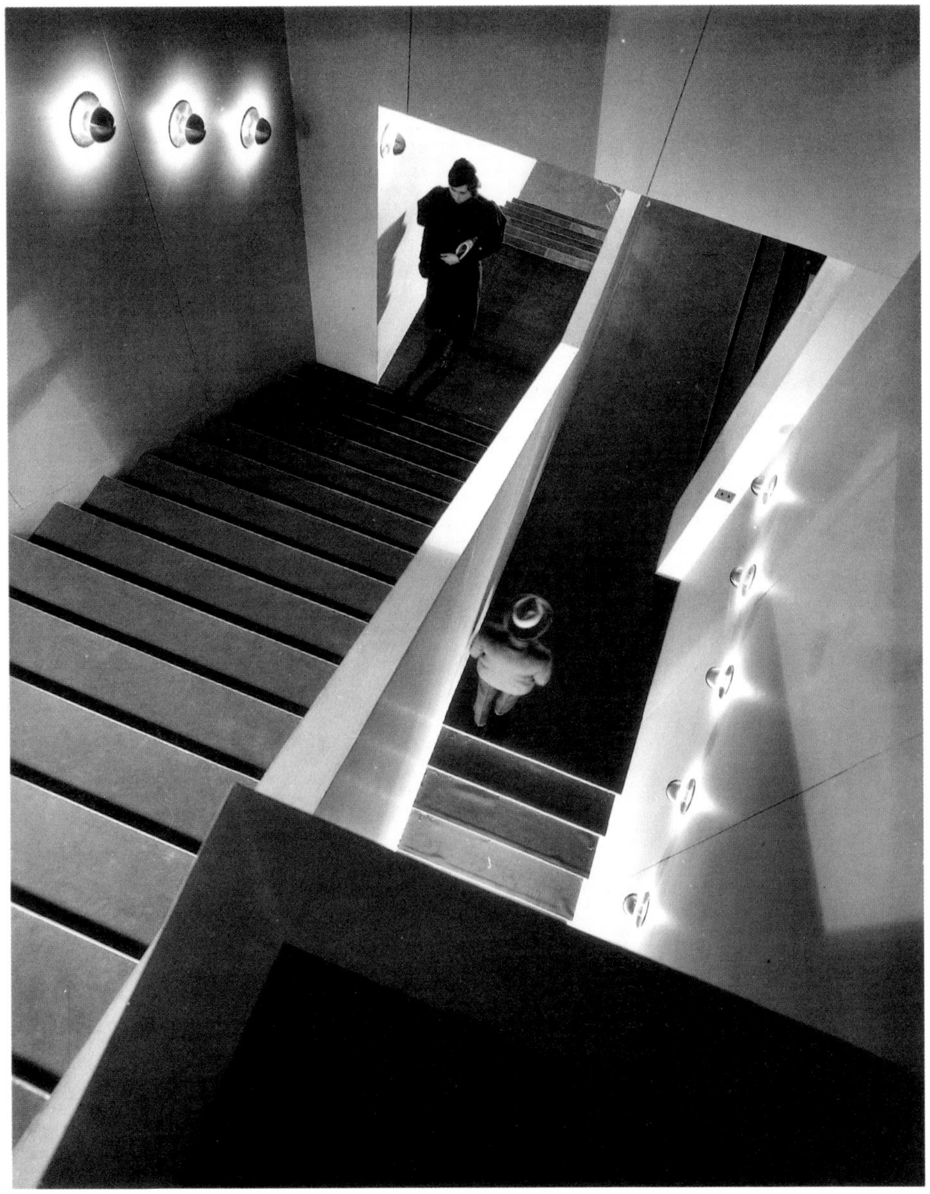

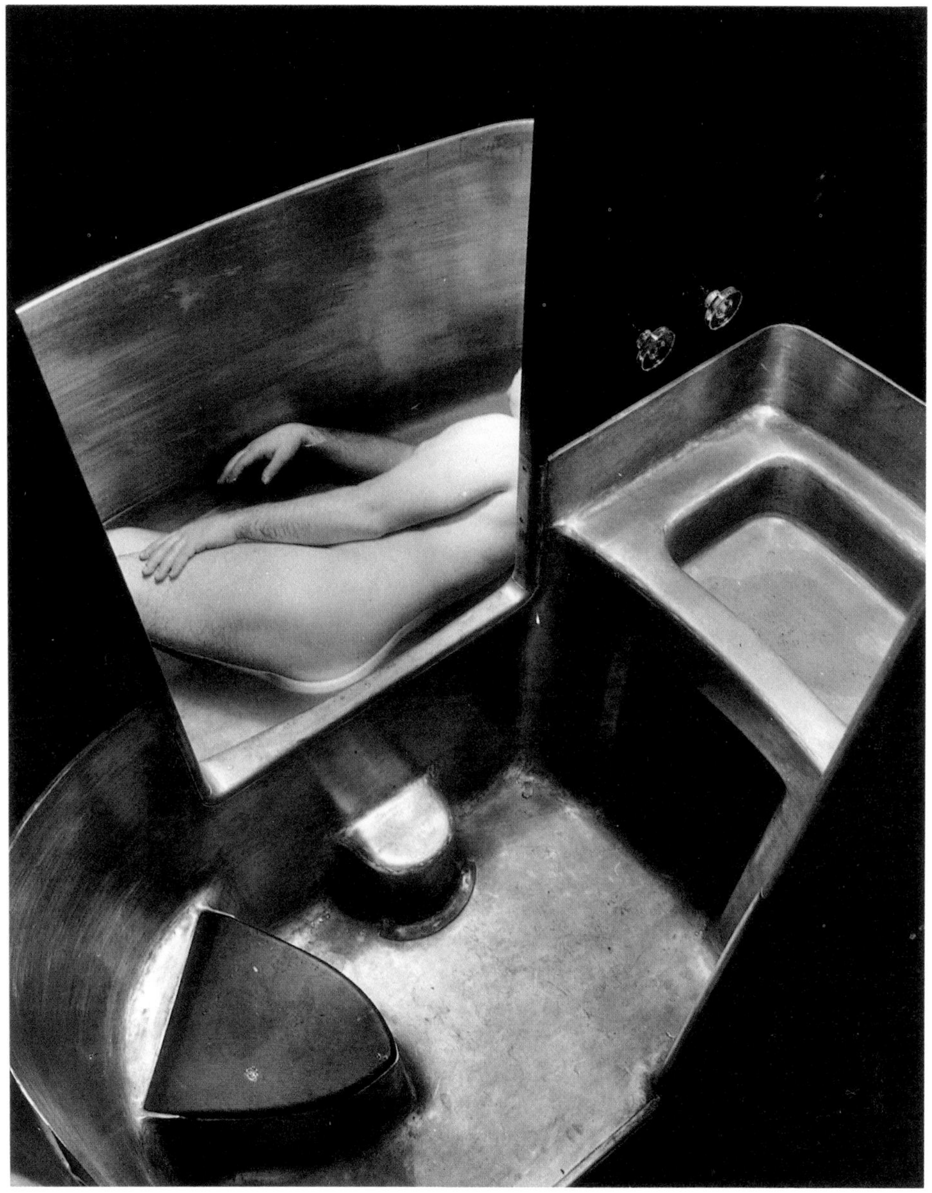

131 *F. S. Lincoln*

New York, exhibition hall staircase adjoining Space House, 1934.
Fred L. Pattee Library, Pennsylvania State University Libraries.

132 *F. S. Lincoln*

"Five by Five," Phelps-Dodge integrated bathroom, 1936.
Fred L. Pattee Library, Pennsylvania State University Libraries.

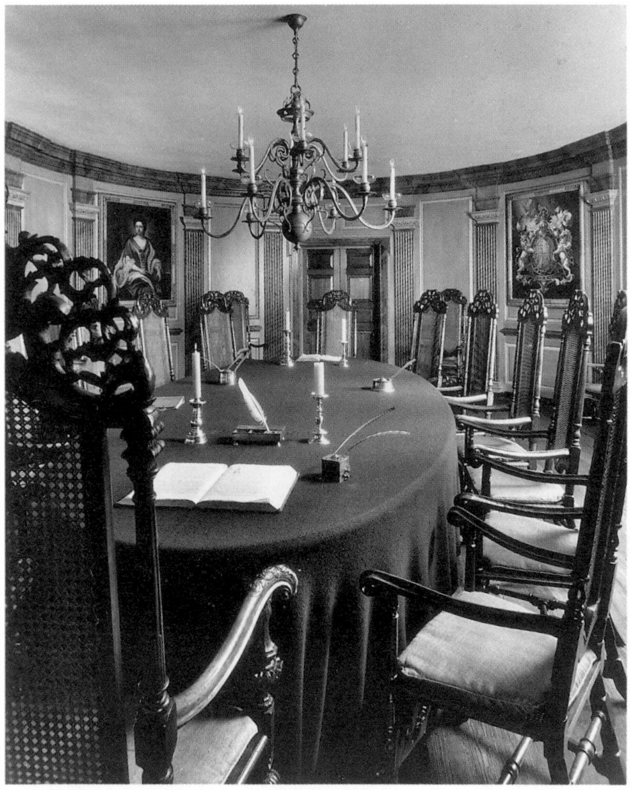

133 *F. S. Lincoln*

Colonial Williamsburg, Council Chamber, 1935.
Fred L. Pattee Library, Pennsylvania State University Libraries.

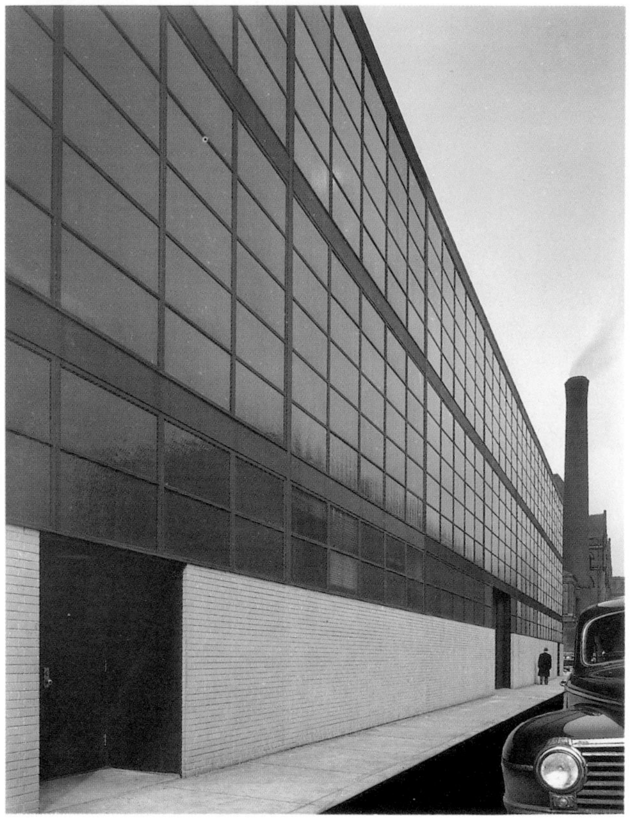

134 *Ken Hedrich*

Chicago, Illinois Institute of Technology, Metallurgy Building, 1943.
Courtesy Hedrich-Blessing.

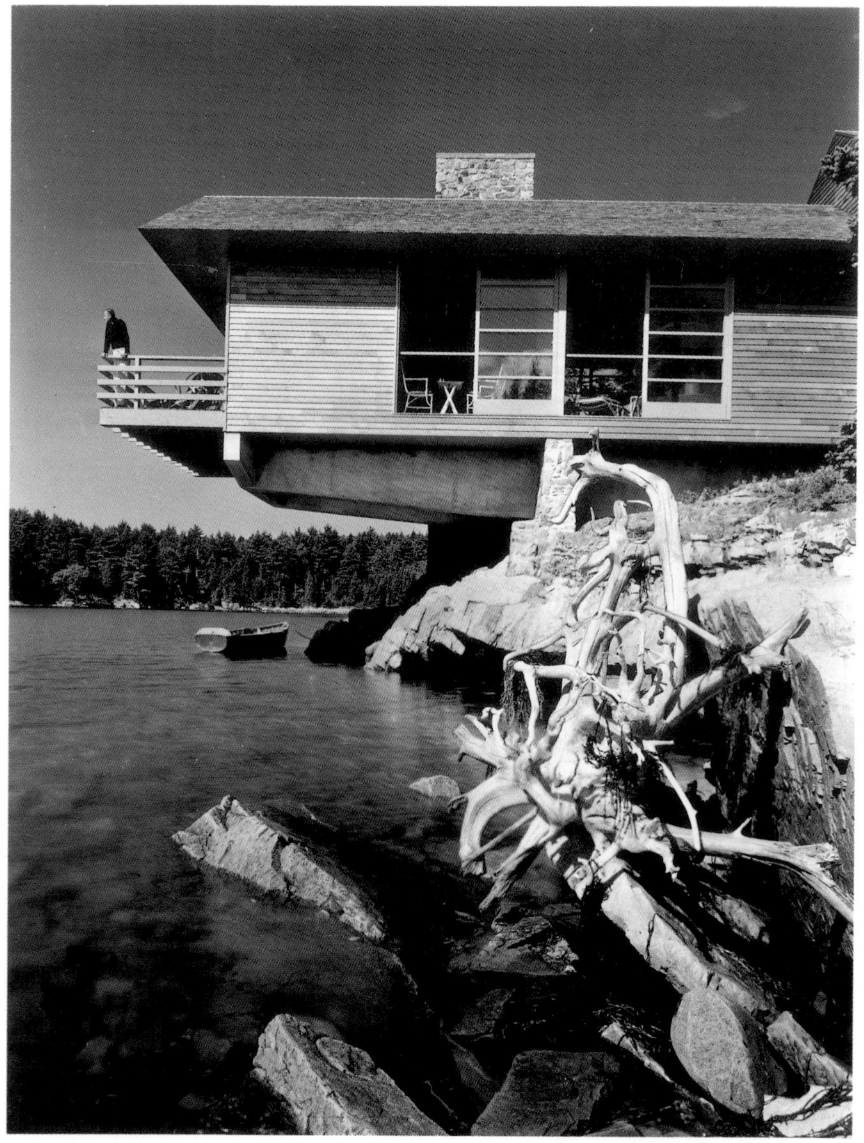

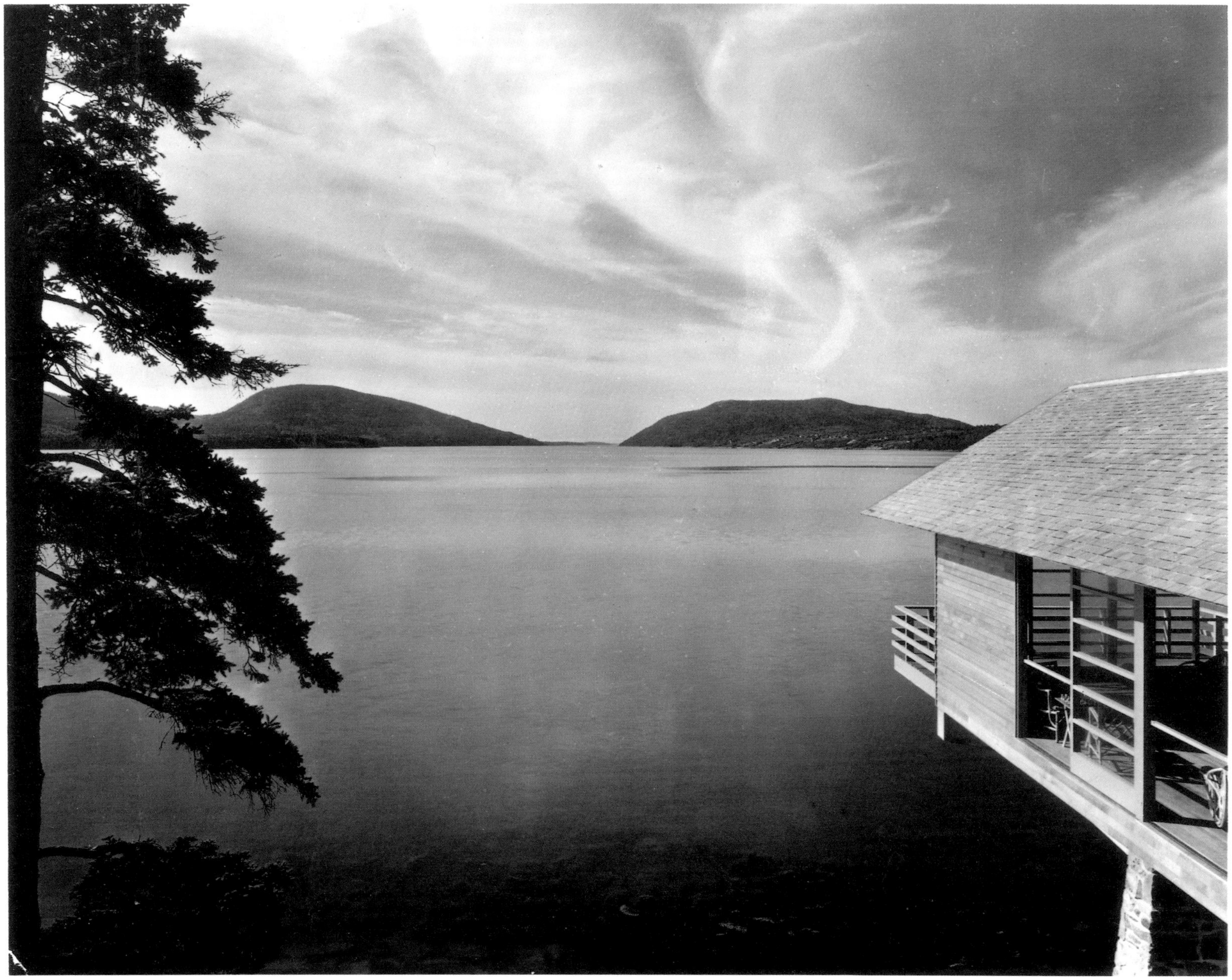

135 *Ben Schnall*
Mount Desert, "Fortune Rock,"
ca. 1939.
Museum of Modern Art, New York.

136 *Ben Schnall*
Mount Desert, "Fortune Rock,"
ca. 1939.
Museum of Modern Art, New York.

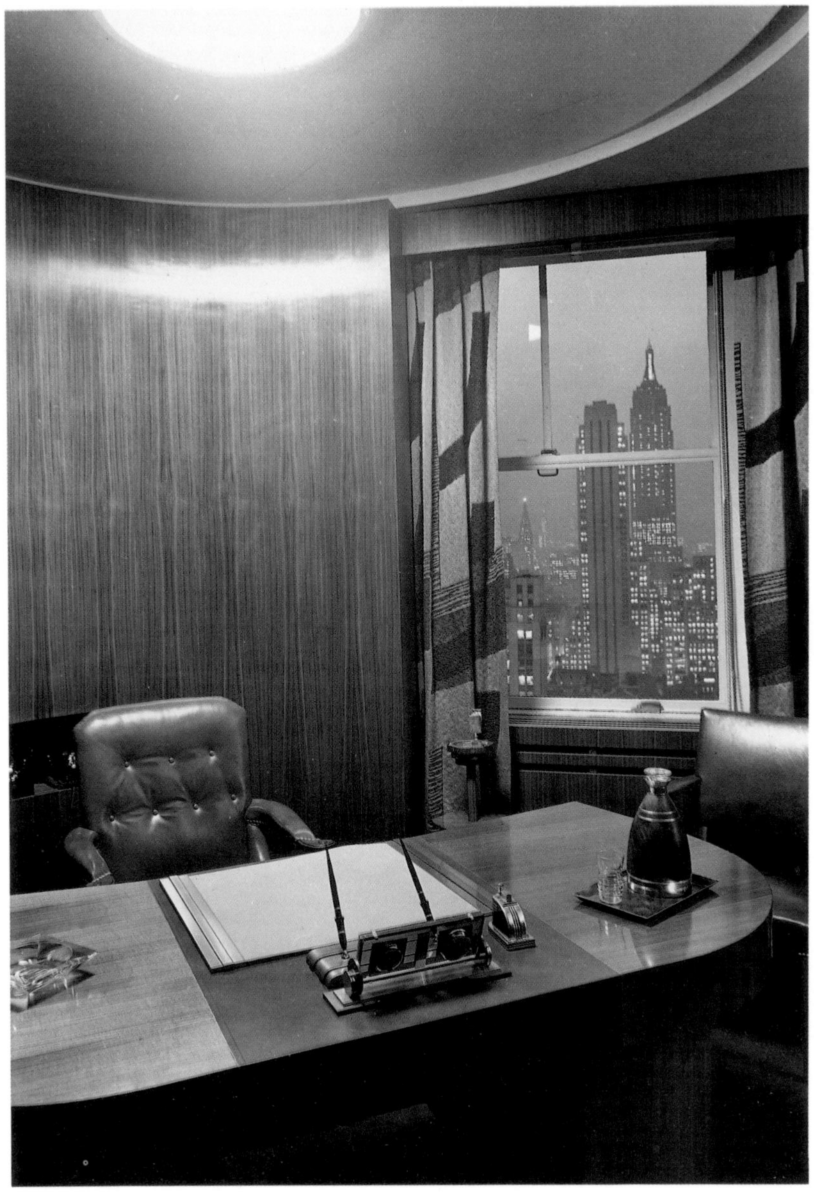

137 *SAMUEL H. GOTTSCHO*

New York, office for Bulova Watch Company, 1939.
Collections of the Library of Congress.

graph of Philip Johnson's house in Cambridge, Massachusetts, taken at a time when the winter sun reached deep into the interior, the season brought the brightness of the room into balance with the yard outside (a device that had been occasionally used in the previous decade with less glassy interiors by British photographers encouraged by England's almost arctic summer light) (138). The device also suggests the continuity of indoor and outdoor space, and turns the carpet into one of those textured surfaces that reach toward the camera in experiential pictures.

While these photographers were gradually developing their skills on the modest American examples of the International Style, other American photographers took a different route. These photographers, though they too had shed much of the artistic self-consciousness and disinterestedness of the twenties, were committed less to the new architecture than to making a portrait of the contemporary world, perhaps inspired by Civil War photographers of sixty years before or Atget whose posthumous book of ninety-six pictures was published in 1930.

Their new approach is apparent in the work of two photographers who returned to New York from Paris in the late 1920s, Berenice Abbott (b. 1898) and Walker Evans. Abbott had had a career as a portrait photographer in Paris in the twenties and had returned to New York to pursue it. But having no success, she turned to photographing the city, following the example, if not the style, of Atget, whom she had met shortly before his death and a body of whose work she had salvaged. Eventually, from 1935 to 1938, she received generous Federal support for a project "Changing New York," including funding for a driver, two laboratory technicians and two researchers.

The eight-by-ten camera with which Abbott worked gave her pictures a professional quality. Her manner of using the camera, however, was casual and impatient, her choice of light and command of technique often perfunctory. Her pictures often showed an old building apposed to a new one. In one she juxtaposed W. Wheeler Smith's Church of St. Nicholas (ca. 1869; since destroyed) to the Time & Life Building (then in construction), the RCA and Goelet buildings, and a smaller, earlier structure on Fifth Avenue by William Van Alen (139). The perspective looks up, but not so much for the sake of adding dynamics to the scene as to include the top of the RCA slab. Much of the bottom of the church is in shadow, however, and her rendering of the buildings might well have benefited by a wait until the sun had moved to the left, which would have removed the base of the church from shadow and in-

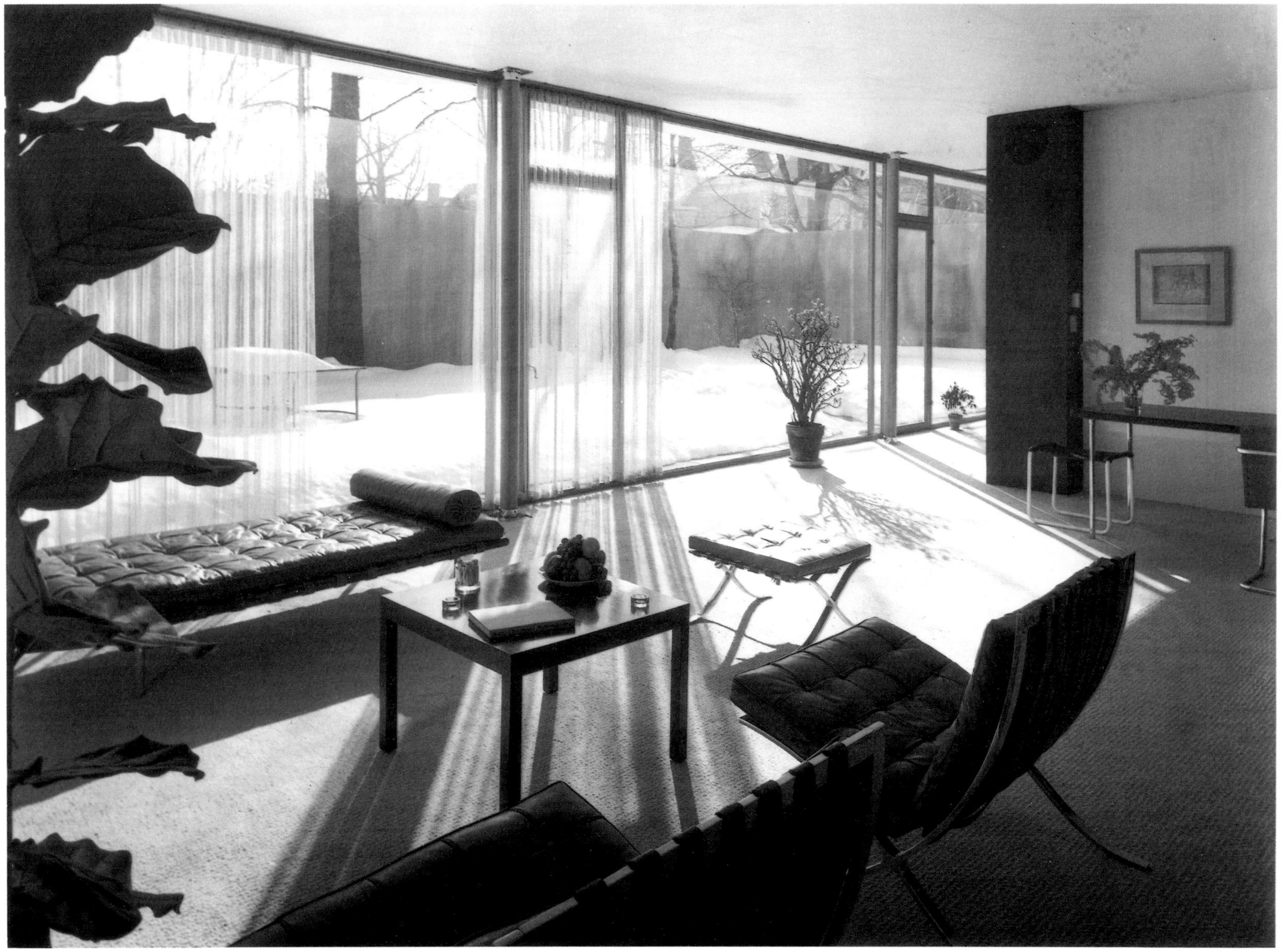

138 *Ezra Stoller*

Cambridge, Johnson house, 1944.
Courtesy the photographer.

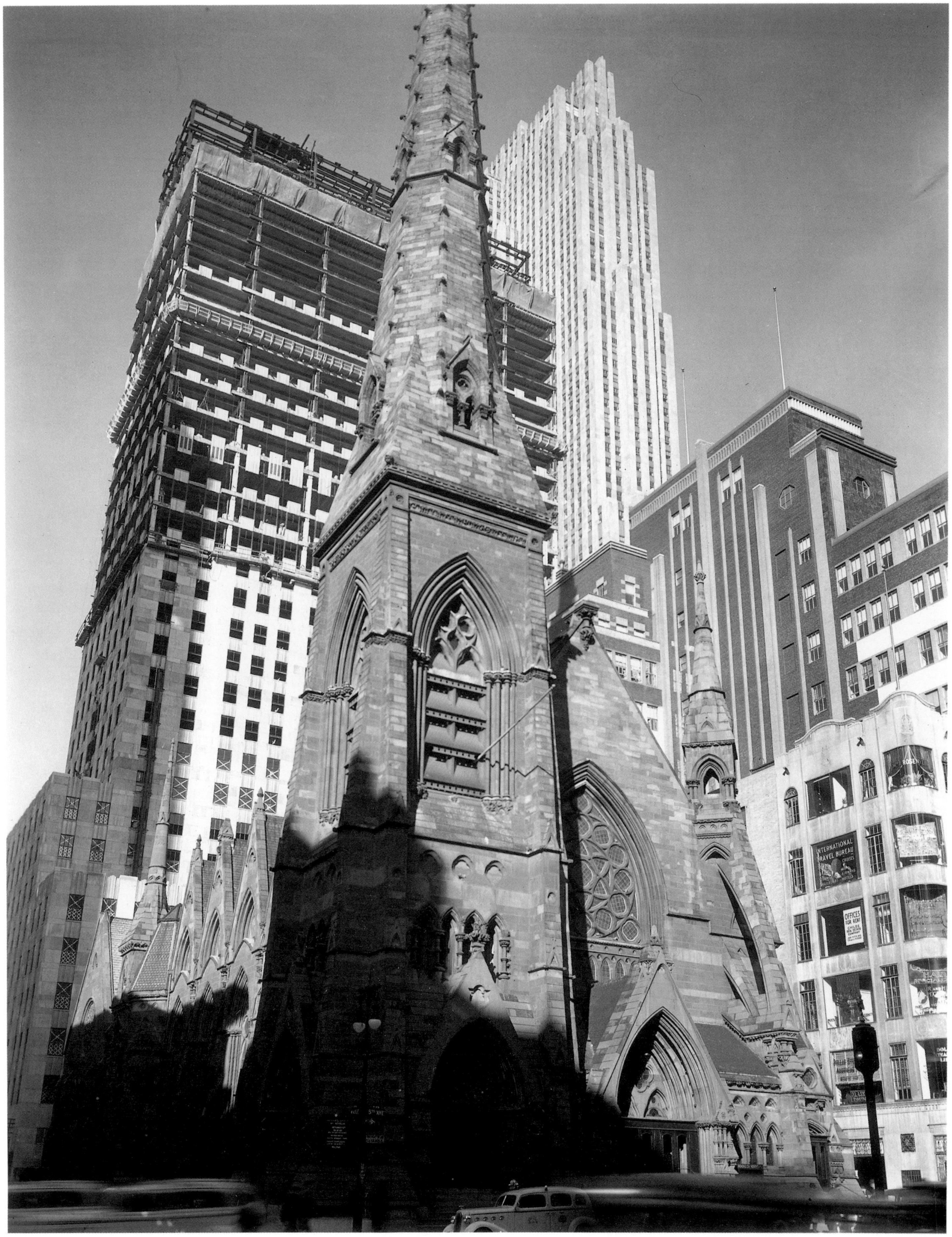

139 *Berenice Abbott*

New York, Collegiate Church of St. Nicholas, 1936.
Parasol Press, Ltd., New York.

creased the plasticity of all of the buildings. Yet the shadow contributes to the ambiguity of her picture, which reverses the ingredients of Dell and Wainwright's picture of the Daily Express Building with the Wren spire, since the older building takes pride of place over the newer Rockefeller Center. It was apparently such combinations that interested Abbott since she often did not include all of an old or a new structure. Her photographs nevertheless did provide the first view of a broad spectrum of New York City's architecture free of the points of view of the booster, the rich man, or the real estate agent (which were available in, respectively, *King's Views*, the photographs of the Byron studio, and the photographs of the firm of Wurts Brothers). Ultimately the remarkable thing about her photography was that its subject was a city at all—a subject characteristically shunned by other American photographers who, after the 1920s at any rate, preferred to take pictures of small towns, roads, and landscapes marred by man.

At the end of 1938 Abbott was demoted from project supervisor to staff photographer, resigned her government job, abandoned her project of photographing New York, and turned to scientific photography.

Walker Evans (1903–1975) had started out in the late twenties making pictures with small rollfilm cameras and often in worm's- or bird's-eye perspective of urban subjects—street vistas and building details—that were probably intended to show a way of seeing the city but that were clearly not intended to concentrate a viewer's attention on specific subjects. In 1930 the *Architectural Record* reproduced a set of these, enlarged for the occasion so that they looked gross and fuzzy on the magazine page. Shortly thereafter Evans turned to a different style with a bigger camera, a style that had parallels to those of the 1880s and before, his subjects free standing and seen head-on but now with a fresh awareness of juxtapositions. His approach suggested that choosing the part of a picture to use after it was taken was as important an act for Evans as taking it in the first place. In one example a house and car were taken from two head-on camera positions to produce two negatives, the second of which was made from nearer the building and so was more tightly framed (118). Two differently cropped prints were made from the first negative, one of which was used in Evans's book *American Photographs*. The process was one of photographing from varying distances or of later editing parts of a picture away. (It is worth noting that the perspective least distorted by such a procedure is a head-on one.) An (uncropped) photograph made in Georgia in 1936 of two houses with a row of billboards in front of them incorporates the same head-on perspective of the house and car photograph (140). Here too there are similarities between the advertisements and the buildings (as there were between car and house): the oval eyelike openings in the second-story porches resonate with the eyes on the posters, Carole Lombard's black eye in particular. In other respects there is tension between the houses and signs. The precise positioning of the smoke stack and of the support for trolley wires make it clear that the photograph is anything but a casual observation. In a picture taken in 1935 in West Virginia the telephone pole in the foreground upstages the town behind it (as Le Corbusier's *objets type* did the Villa Savoye or Berenice Abbott's Church of St. Nicholas did Rockefeller Center) and, like the tree in Ben Schnall's picture or the car in Ken Hedrich's, provides a key to how the subject of the picture is to be accepted: in this instance the pole serves to distance the photographer (and the viewer) from the town depicted (141). In Walker Evans's works we read meanings into these juxtapositions of buildings to cars, signs, or telephone poles.

Working for various clients, most significantly Lincoln Kirstein, Time Inc., and the Resettlement (later Farm Security) Administration, Evans assembled a body of work that included unfashionable and vernacular architecture, signs, sculpture, the land worked by man, and people in public places. In 1938 a selection of these pictures taken in derelict parts of older eastern U.S. cities as well as Cuba was exhibited in the Museum of Modern Art. The catalog for this exhibition, *American Photographs*, which was organized with a basic division between uncaptioned pictures of people and of architecture, provided an influential model for later books of photographs. It presented a visual summary that achieved unity by its consistency of style and by an undercurrent of similarity between Evans's pictures—of, say, a heroic battlefield monument, a sleeping derelict, or a landscape of wrecked cars—and Civil War pictures by Alexander Gardner and Timothy O'Sullivan. Despite the fragmentary view of America these photographs presented, the mixture of people, landscape, and architecture give an illusion of completeness.

The question of the proper form for a book of photographs was raised repeatedly through the 1940s. *American Photographs* had had no text and gave only the town and the year in which each picture had been taken in a list at the end of each of the two parts of the book. Its suggestion on how to structure a book was the most extreme, because it banished any explanatory text, but also the most old fashioned, for it presented the textless pictures as plates, one to each recto.

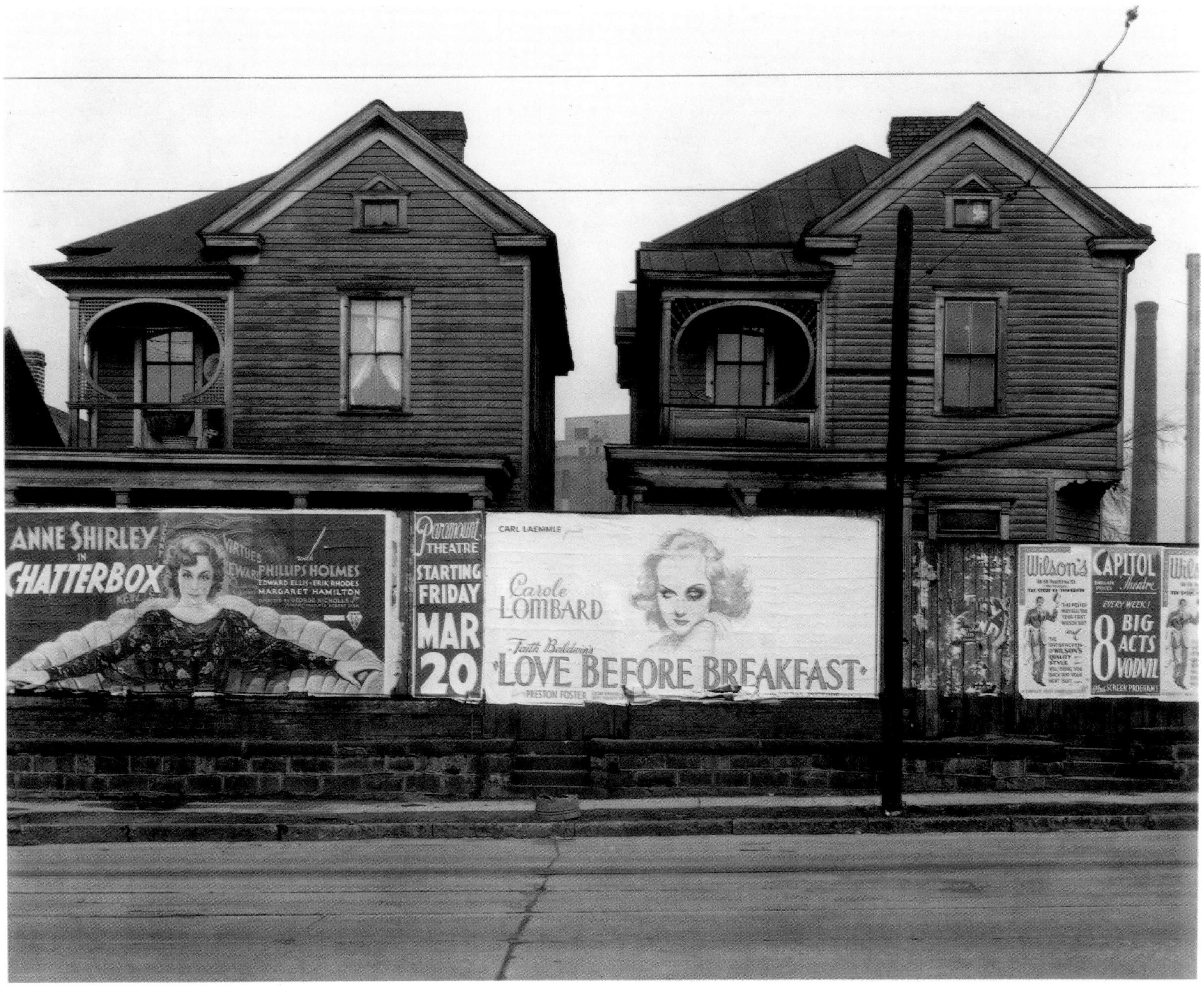
ANNE SHIRLEY
IN
CHATTERBOX
PHILLIPS HOLMES
EDWARD ELLIS-ERIK RHODES
MARGARET HAMILTON
Paramount THEATRE
STARTING FRIDAY
MAR 20
CARL LAEMMLE
Carole LOMBARD
Faith Baldwin's
LOVE BEFORE BREAKFAST
PRESTON FOSTER
Wilson's
CAPITOL Theatre
EVERY WEEK!
8 BIG ACTS VODVIL
SCREEN PROGRAM

140 *WALKER EVANS*

Atlanta, billboards and frame houses, 1936.
Collections of the Library of Congress.

141 *WALKER EVANS*

Morgantown, West Virginia, 1935.
Collections of the Library of Congress.

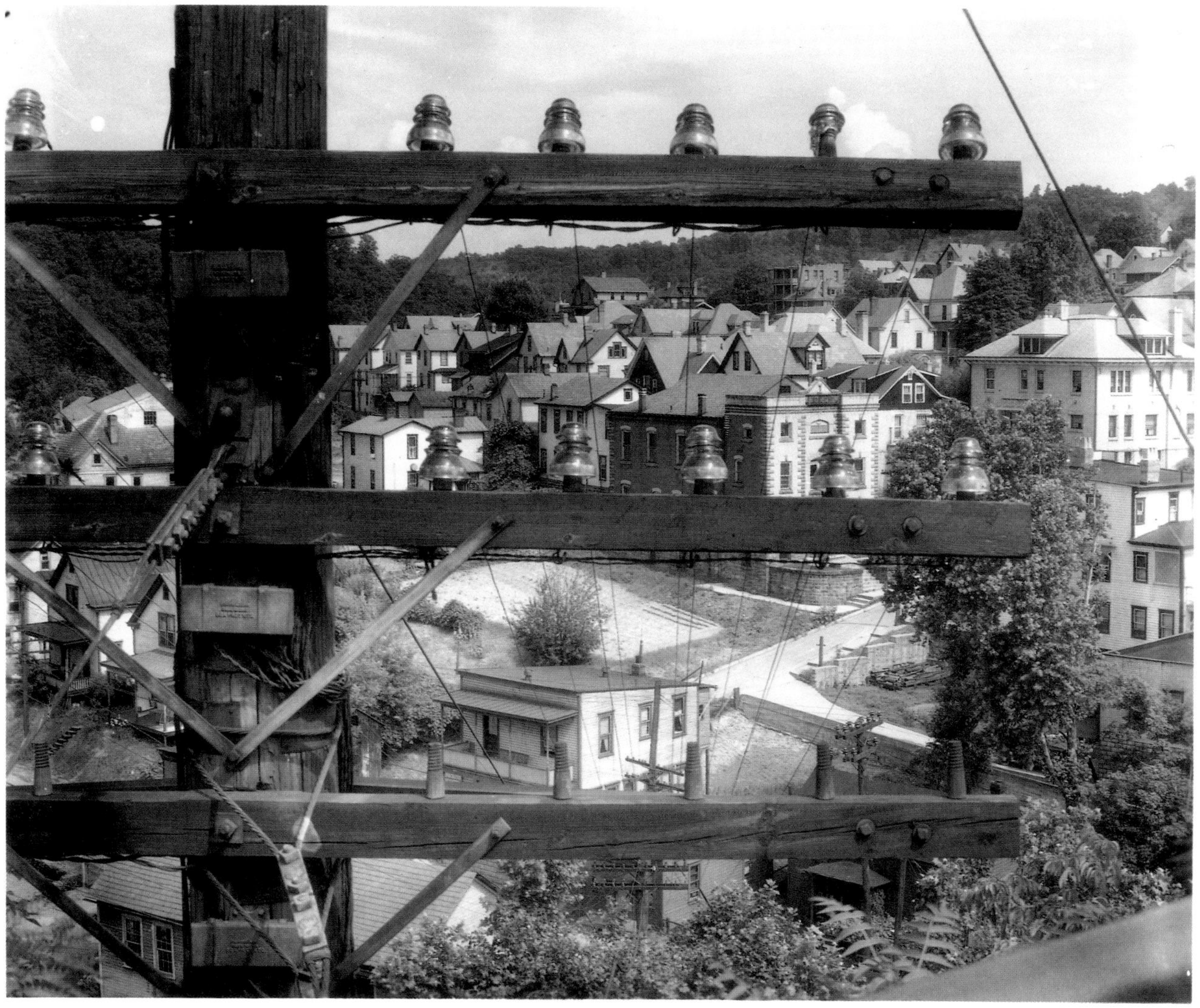

Wright Morris's (b. 1910) portrait of America, his book, *The Inhabitants*, was less of a visual construct than Evans's, for its essential juxtapositions were between his pictures and the short texts he had written to accompany them, which were by no means descriptions of what appeared in the pictures but stood separate and equal. The photographs themselves might contain internal juxtapositions, but their message was less that of America at a particular time of strife than was Evans's. They attempted to give a more timeless picture, however transient the objects depicted. In a picture taken in New Mexico in the forties there are both striking similarities and contrasts between a palm tree and an industrial building with smokestack, and it is this witty juxtaposition, whether appreciated by the inhabitants of Lordsburg or not, that is the point of the picture (142). The combination within a book of separate but equal texts and pictures is always an uneasy one. Here it was effective primarily as an illustration of Morris's ambivalence between photography and the writing to which he subsequently turned.

World War II stopped many photographers from working, some mainly because they could no longer obtain photographic supplies but others because the armed services in which they found themselves did not make use of their skills. When picture taking resumed after the war, energies were at first directed to summing up places or regions, as had been done in the thirties.

Paul Strand (1890–1976), thirteen years older than Walker Evans and eight years older than Berenice Abbott, had begun to photograph as early as 1911, when he adopted the fragmentary style of the period. In the late twenties he had taken pictures in New England of plants and trees, and in the midforties he and historian Nancy Newhall joined forces to produce *Time in New England* (published in 1950) for which he took additional photographs of buildings or fragments of buildings along with some portraits of people and landscapes. A Strand picture of 1945 from this book shows how he constricted architectural subjects within the picture's edges, telling very little about their settings (143). The presence of a tree trunk in the foreground, which he has carefully situated between the central window, and the side windows provides a rationale for the vertical format, which isolates the building. Where Evans's and Abbott's photographs were inclusive, though far from casual about what they included, Strand's tended to show just the building or its parts. In his New England there were villages but no towns, certainly no cities. There were farms, churches, and seacoasts but nothing modern. These pictures were juxtaposed to Newhall's selected quotations from the literature of the region going back as far as the seventeenth century. The result is a New England too timeless for us to find convincing.

In the late forties and early fifties Clarence John Laughlin (1905–1985) turned to documenting a rural South that in some ways overlapped Evans's except that it too like Strand's was timeless and without contradictions. Earlier he had brought out a book, *Ghosts Along the Mississippi* (1946) of his clumsily printed photographs that often featured ghostly figures created by double exposure. But by the early fifties the ghosts had departed from his work, and his approach to printing was more straightforward. In a picture taken in Lafourche Parish, Louisiana, in 1951 a ravaged tree is as carefully placed in front of two ruinous houses as was the tree in Strand's picture and serves as a device to reinforce the derelict condition of the buildings, intentionally impeding our view of one of them in the manner of Walker Evans's telephone pole in Morgantown (144).

Thus, starting with Erich Mendelsohn's *Amerika*, a series of books had explored the ways in which America could be described in photographs. The series had started with a cross section of modern cities but had turned from urban subjects to rural ones, from overviews of several sites to portraits of single ones, and from subjects locked in a particular time to ones that the photographer hoped were timeless.

The question of the proper form for such a book, however, soon became moot, for architecture as a subject for photography became in the fifties a specialized genre engaged primarily in filling the needs of the architectural profession.

In the early forties G. E. Kidder Smith (b. 1913) had taken photographs for Philip Goodwin's Museum of Modern Art exhibition and book, *Brazil Builds* (1943), which presented both historical and modern buildings, and Smith's version of the 1930s style was equally effective for both the old buildings and the new. From 1946 to 1955 he wrote and photographed, under grants from the American-Scandinavian and the John Simon Guggenheim Foundations, for three books using as a model his book with Goodwin. Two, *Sweden Builds* and *Switzerland Builds*, were published in 1950 and the third, *Italy Builds*, in 1955. Each of these books consisted, as *Brazil Builds* had, of two sets of pictures and essays, one on those historical, urban, and vernacular works that seemed relevant to a committed modernist, the other on modern buildings, the pictures serving as illustrations to the texts, which analyzed the strengths of the older traditions and the accomplishments of the new. It was

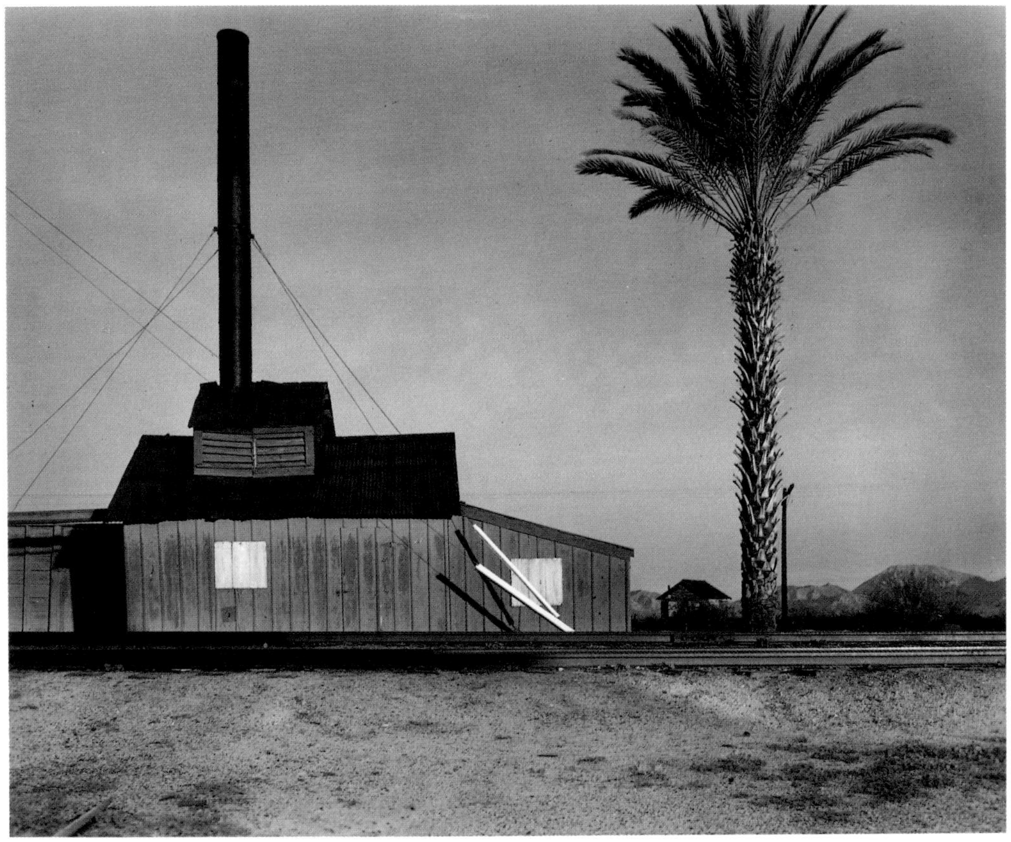

142 *Wright Morris*

Vicinity of Lordsburg, New Mexico, powerhouse and palm tree, 1940. Courtesy Witkin Gallery.

143 *Paul Strand*

Maine, "Palladian window," 1945. Copyright © 1950, 1980 the Paul Strand Foundation.

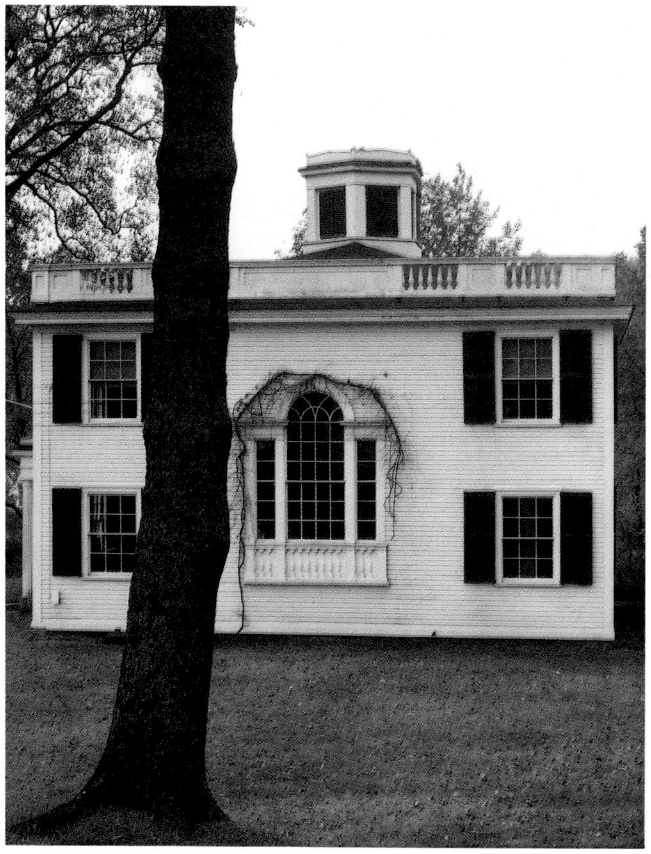

144 *Clarence John Laughlin*
Lafourche Parish, vicinity of Raceland, 1951.
Collections of the Library of Congress.

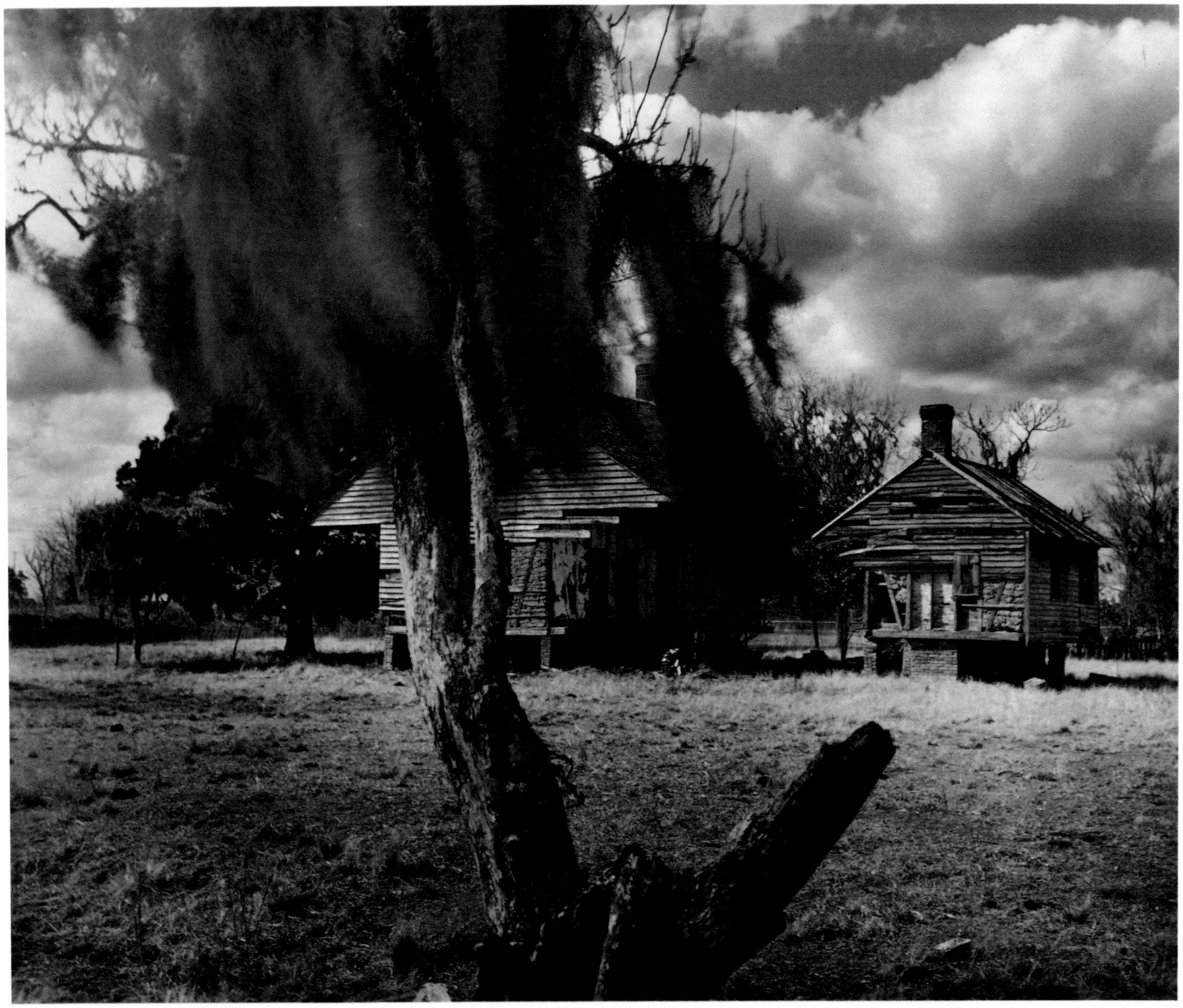

clear from Smith's pictures that he worked quickly. The pictures were direct, precise, and uncontrived, and most were exterior views that were especially successful in giving a sense of urban space. A picture from the third book looks directly along the facade of the cathedral at Orvieto in such a way that the sculptures on the front, in shadow in the morning light, are seen as silhouettes against the sky (145). We can see how Smith, with that basic idea in mind, went about taking his picture. We know from other pictures in the set that appeared in the book that he set his camera up just in front of some trees on the south side of the piazza that would otherwise have encroached on the upper part of the sky and church. Though the space of the piazza is essentially horizontal (and so would be appropriately shown in a horizontal format), using a vertical format set up a tension between the space and the building (represented by its southwest pier). That decided, he had only to drop the horizon to the bottom of the picture (by the use of what photographers call a "rising front") and point the camera just enough to the left to emphasize the space of the piazza (rather than the mass of the building) and to include the opening of the Via del Duomo with its clock tower, and the picture was made.

Smith's photographic equipment was that of the photojournalist of the day, not the more cumbersome camera of a professional architectural photographer, and his smaller cameras and faster lenses helped him to include people in many of his pictures. In a second picture from *Italy Builds*, one of Giovanni Greppi's Sacrarium at Redipuglia, in which an oblique plane leads from the camera into the distance to create an experiential picture, the presence of people sets the appropriately solemn, reflective tone for the subject (146). This is one of those rare photographs in which unposed figures carry the full weight of the meaning. Smith was in fact both a trained designer and skillful cameraman, and he became the quintessential architect-photographer of the postwar years.

In England after the war the quality of rebuilding was modest, but the *Architectural Review*, which had been the principal magazine to espouse modern architecture in the thirties, quickly became the dominant journal in the English-speaking world in the late forties and fifties. And it resumed its interest in the character and strengths of the vernacular world. In the December 1949 issue one of the magazine's editors made the proposal that something be done about what he described as "the brick-a-brackish mid-twentieth century world of barbed wire, pig-wire, steel-wire, wire-mesh, telephone wire, electric cables on crazy fir standards, through which as through a cage darkly we are permitted to get an eyeful of lone villas, poultry farms, Radar stations, motor-car graveyards, Homes for Incurables—all clipt around with plantations of larch and fields of surprised looking wheat. It is not only the decay of rurality," he went on, "it is the waste, in the towns and outside them, the clutter, the vast areas of No-Man's-Land. We foul our nest." Of course this was the very subject matter that American photographers relished in their own country and that had been central to much progressive American photography for a generation, if not far longer. The *Review*'s editor proposed that to the two solutions in which functionalism had split, that is, the "rational or classic or crystalline . . . (figurehead Corbusier) and the romantic or . . . organic . . . (figurehead Frank Lloyd Wright)," there be added a radical one "nourishing itself . . . upon the embodied, the differentiated, the phenominal world. . . ." He suggested that neglected virtues of vernacular design in cities, towns, and the countryside be documented in the magazine as a series of "cases" to be called "Townscape."

Through the succeeding years "Townscape" appeared periodically. A special issue of the magazine in December 1950 called "Man-Made America" was devoted to the subject of townscape analysis in northeastern United States. A summary of European examples, *Townscape*, was published in 1959 and *The Italian Townscape* in 1963. For the most part the photographs reproduced in these publications, which were taken by different photographers, were described by a word or phrase that was amplified in a short paragraph. The words might be "thisness, intricacy, bluntness and vigour, entanglement, metaphor, noticeable absence, building as sculpture, geometry, scale."

Most "Townscape" pictures were taken with the dominant camera of the late forties and early fifties, the twin-lens Rolleiflex, held at waist level, from which vantage point there was an inevitable emphasis on street pavements, steps, bollards, and other street furniture. A picture by Eric de Maré (b. 1910) of the Albert Docks in the 1950s may have been taken with slightly larger equipment and from an even lower vantage point but demonstrates the experiential emphasis on nearby surfaces in these pictures and the prominent role of bollards, whose presence in many American cities to separate pedestrian from vehicular traffic, testifies to the influence of the "Townscape" pictures on the United States (147). Another de Maré photograph from the fifties, of Montpellier Walk, Cheltenham, England, shows that even where it was not a pavement that the camera emphasized and the bollards were distant, the experiential device of bringing part of the subject close to the camera to draw the viewer into the picture was customary (148). Nothing is distanced. If the

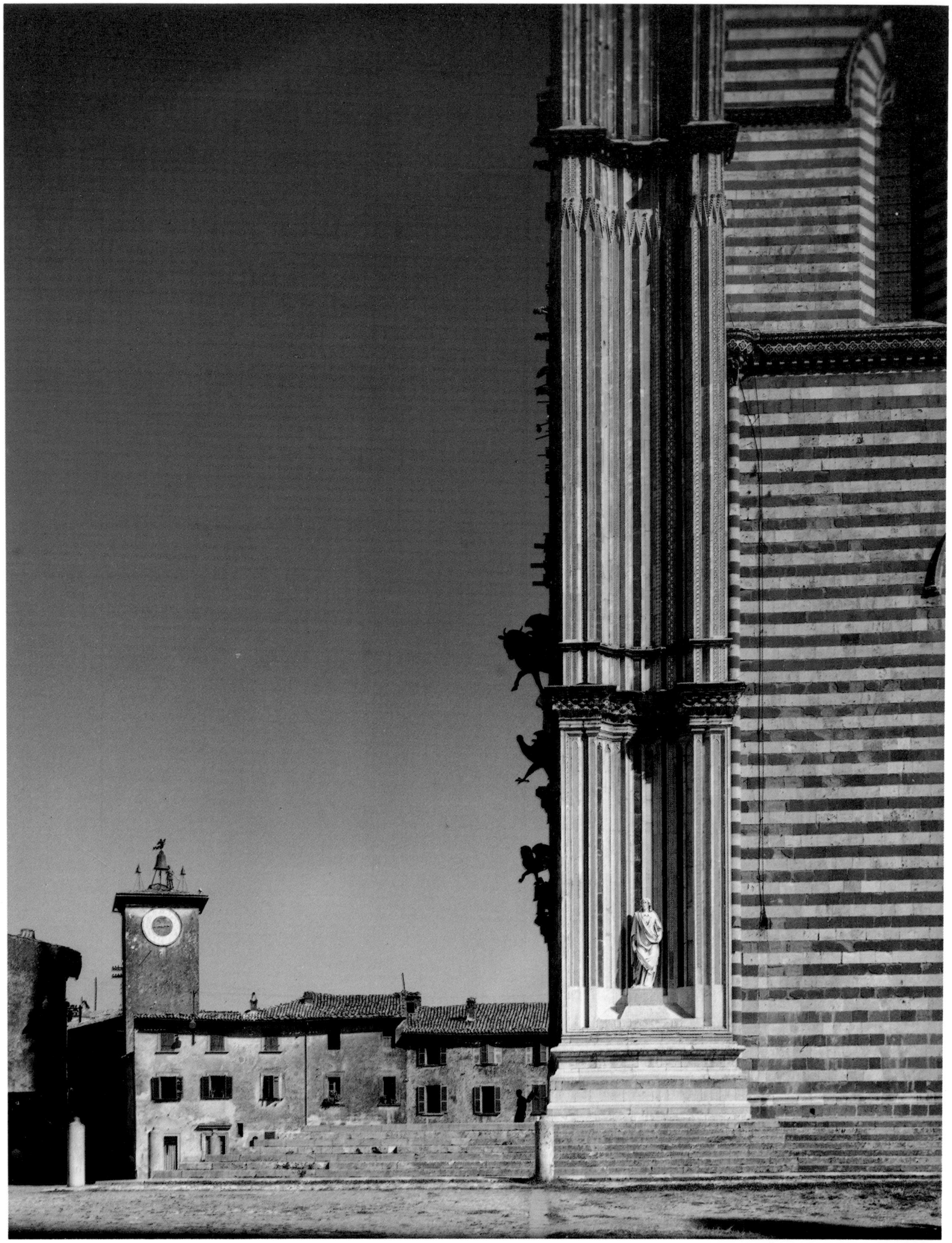

145 *G. E. Kidder Smith*

Orvieto, Duomo and piazza, ca. 1954.
Courtesy the photographer.

146 *G. E. Kidder Smith*

Redipuglia, Sacrarium, ca. 1954.
Courtesy the photographer.

147 *Eric de Maré*

Liverpool, Albert Docks, 1957.
Courtesy Architectural Press, London.

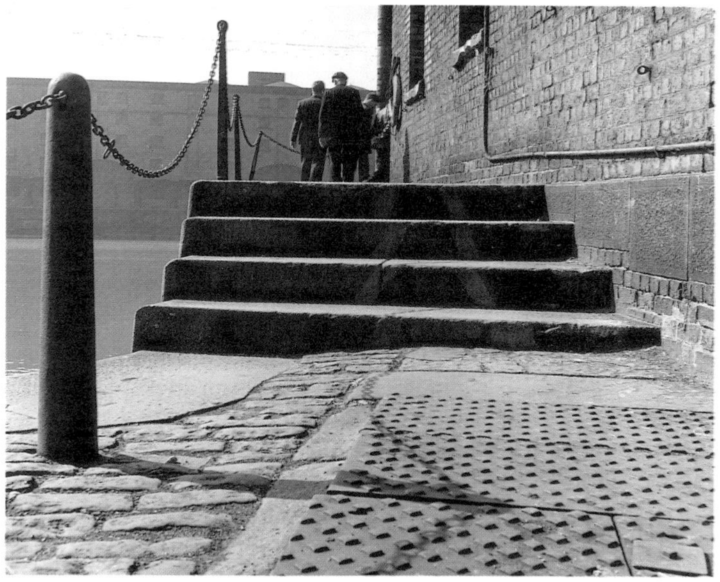

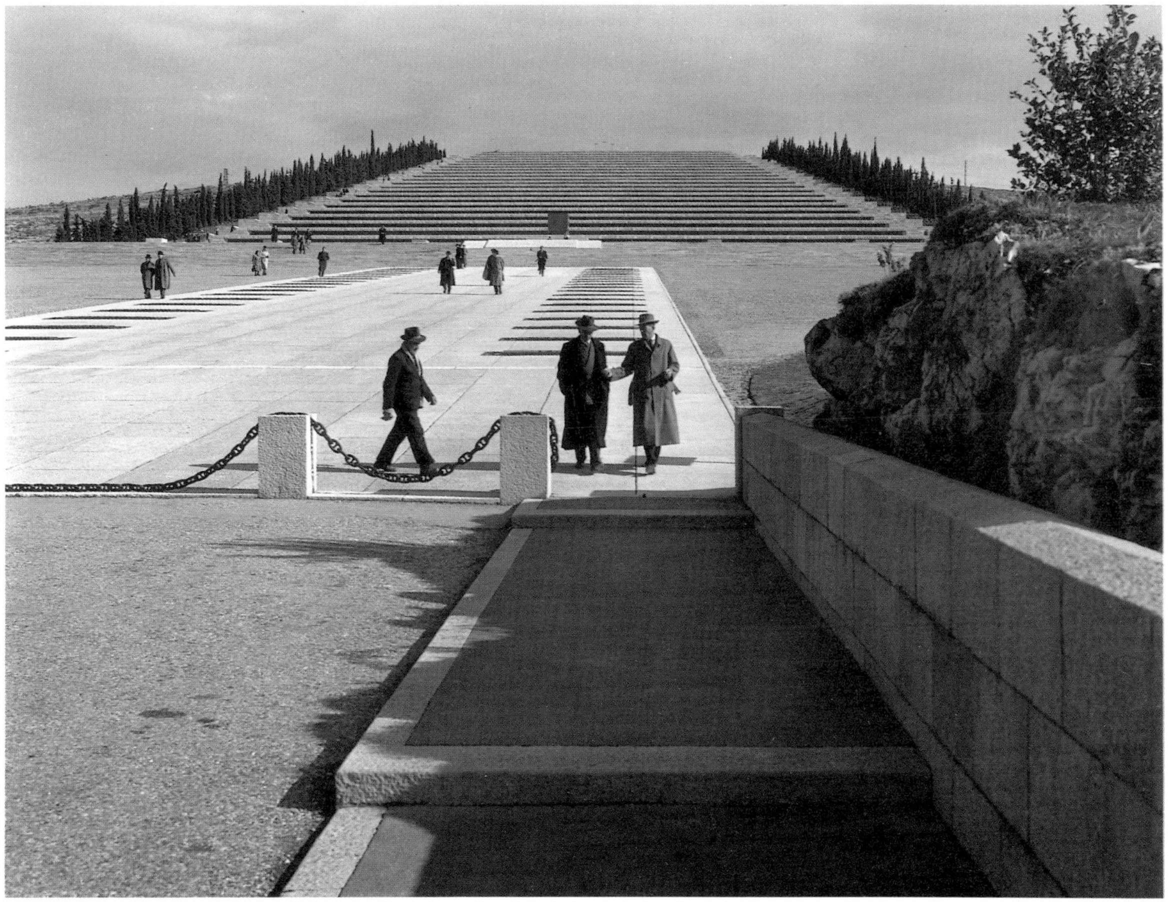

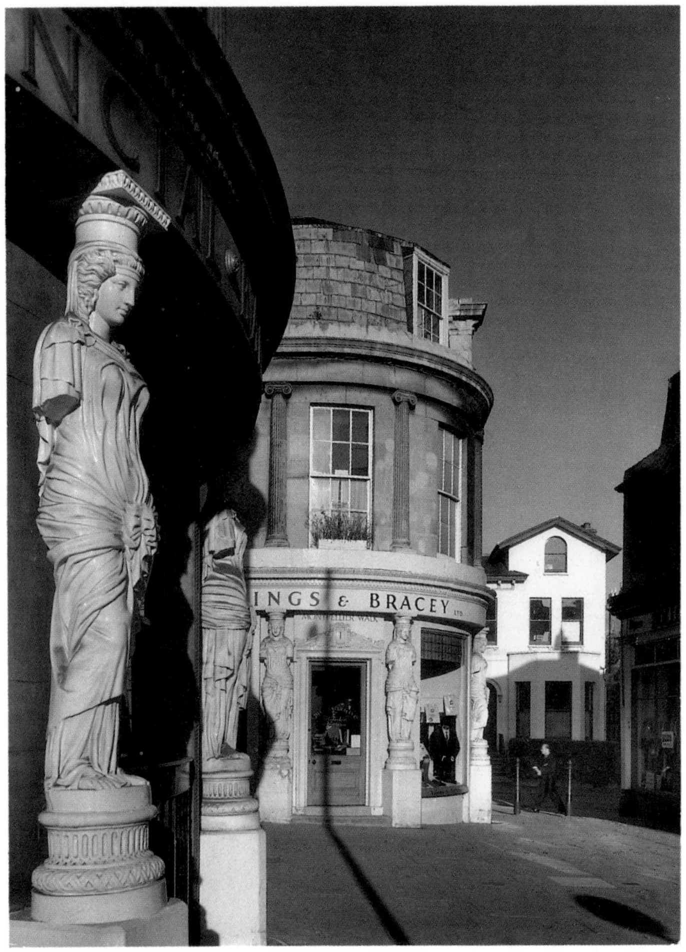

148 *ERIC DE MARÉ*
Cheltenham, Montpellier Walk, 1950s.
Courtesy Architectural Press, London.

influence of "Townscape" on design is apparent on our streets, its influence on journalism is apparent in "Portfolios" in *Fortune* and "Galleries" in another Time Inc. magazine, *Architectural Forum*.

Walker Evans, who had been photographing for *Fortune* since the war, began in the late forties to do Portfolios (accompanied by his own texts), the majority of which were, broadly speaking, on architectural subjects. He also did galleries for *Architectural Forum*. These were independent photo essays laid out by the photographer and also with his texts, and on subjects that might or might not be relevant to the other articles in an issue. His accomplishment in assembling them was to absorb the lesson of the "Townscape" pictures' purposefulness and immediacy and to transform the ethical, didactic, and collaborative model of the original into a personal and aesthetic one.

The change in Evans's work can be seen in the comparison of a picture of a colonnade taken in 1946 for a portfolio, "Chicago: A Camera Exploration of the Huge, Energetic Urban Sprawl of the Midlands" (February 1947) with a column detail from "Imperial Washington" (February 1952) (149, 150). The Chicago picture juxtaposes a giant sign of a sort that was an early interest of Evans's to a semicircular classical colonnade. The top of the sign repeats the colonnade's curved form, and Evans must have been aware of both the similarities between the structures' forms and the contrast between their manners of expression as he took the picture. He committed himself to neither structure. Six years later (post-"Townscape"), however, when he took the column base for his Chicago portfolio, his picture was single-minded. His subject filled the frame and all but burst out of it. His point was the direct experience of the column and no longer an equivocation between two objects that were similar yet different. Again in a picture of a lifeboat that illustrated the effect "of paint on paint over paint" from an *Architectural Forum* gallery "Ship Shapes and Shadows" (October 1958) Evans continued in this new manner, filling the full square format of his Rolleiflex, his lens close enough to his subject for its surface to be nearby, oblique, and immediate (151).

If for Evans the change was one from equivocation to a new directness, for "Townscape" it was a change from an ethical purpose to an aesthetic one, a shift that architecture has shared with photography, for modern architecture tended to lose its ethical and political baggage in the Atlantic crossing. In photography we may even be able to posit some Grimm's law for change: there is a shift from the ethic to the aesthetic and allied ones from hostile to posi-

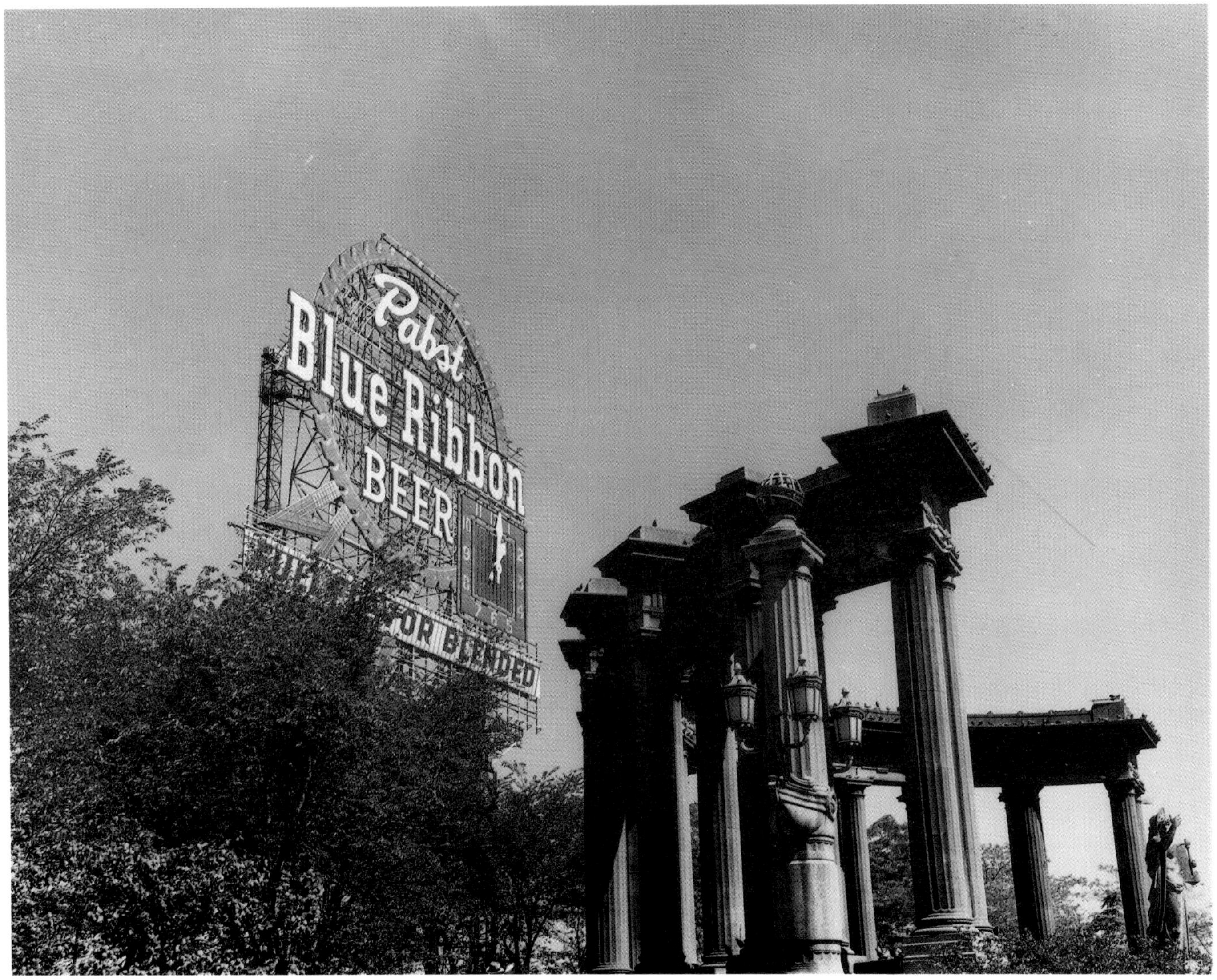

149 *Walker Evans*

Chicago, 1946.
The Estate of Walker Evans.

150 *Walker Evans*

Washington, Supreme Court Building.
From *Fortune* (1952).

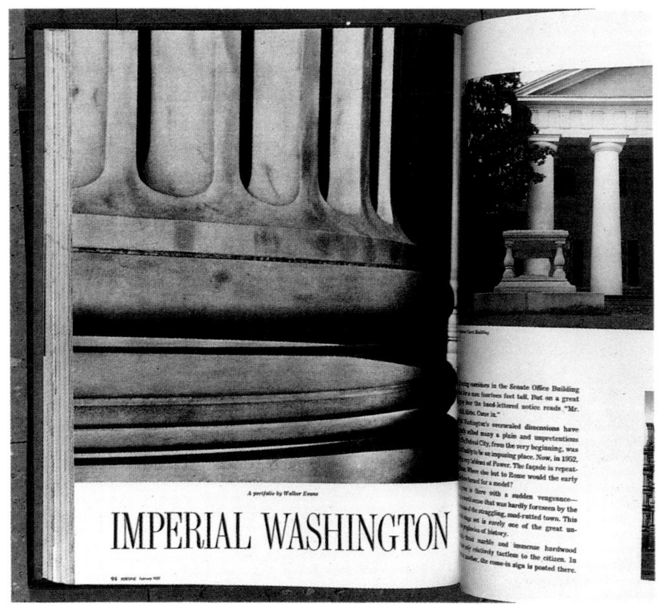

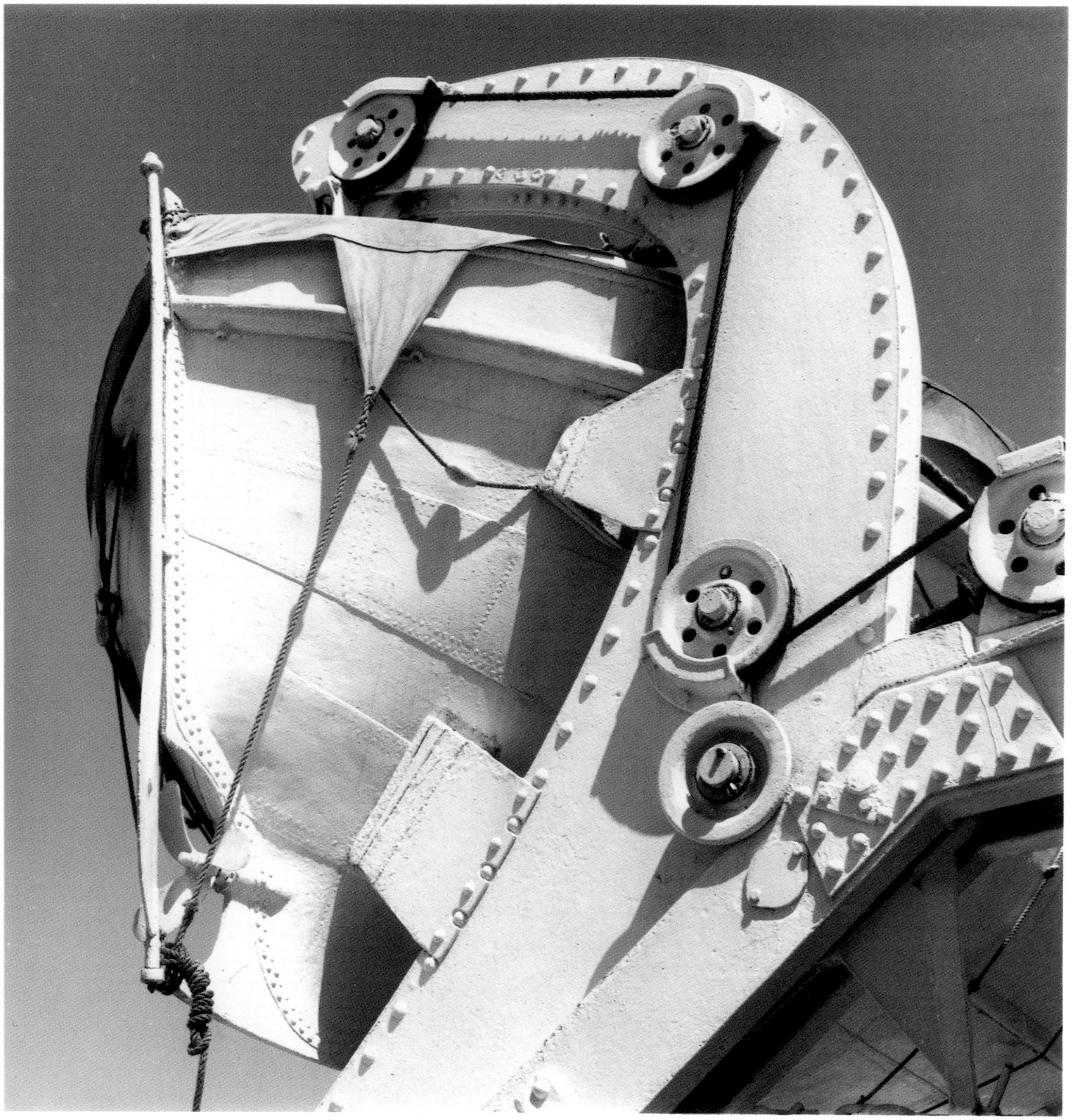

151 *Walker Evans*

"Boat-and-davit on the *Liberté* portside," 1958.

The Estate of Walker Evans.

tive, from equivocal to direct, and perhaps from emphasis on the qualities of light to the formal qualities of subject matter.

With the resumption of construction in the United States after World War II and the enthusiastic adoption of the International Style, there arose a need for a kind of architectural photography that would, rather than dramatize the minimal accomplishment of the thirties, handle articulately the increasing number of significant new buildings. Since U.S. photographers rarely worked on the staffs of magazines, but were free lances with an eye on both the architects and the journals, they had not only to find ways of handling larger volumes of work but had to learn to serve two masters (besides themselves)—architects, who wanted confirmation that they had realized their intentions, and journals, which wanted pictures suited to their page layouts.

One person takes a picture, so unlike architecture or moviemaking, photography does not lend itself to team work. There has nevertheless been a temptation to reach for a larger volume of work by organizing a firm with partners. The firm of Hedrich-Blessing had always had several members, some from the Hedrich family. After World War II it turned from the individual style of Ken Hedrich's pictures of the thirties to a more anonymous one—or perhaps simply from a thirties to a postwar style. An architect-client could choose to work with the photographer he found most congenial and receive pictures that were not radically different from those one of the other photographers would have taken. A common laboratory staff ensured that service and craftsmanship would be consistent in all of the firm's work. In the fifties Hedrich-Blessing became the hero firm of photographers who saw their own job as that of doing craftsmanlike, self-effacing work. A telling act of the firm was the assembling of a collection of what they called "signature prints," large, especially well-printed pictures that were autographed, not by the photographers, but by the architects whose buildings were shown in them. They were kept by the firm, who in so doing presented themselves as humble fans of the architects.

On the East Coast F. S. Lincoln's career did not survive the war in any significant way. Until the recent era of photographers' galleries, when a photographer's career slowed down, a large file of negatives became a burden. New commissions no longer came in, only occasional, unprofitable orders for reprints. And one of Lincoln's last plans was to have some of his more picturesque work drawn by an artist for a series of greeting cards that he would have had printed.

In the postwar years Ezra Stoller quickly became the exemplary professional architectural photographer. He consistently punctuated his sets of pictures with photographs in the two extreme perspectives, the experiential and the factual, and he added a third, problematic one to the pair. His iconic pictures of the Chamberlain and Johnson houses, taken in the early forties and each demonstrating one of the two perspectives, have been familiar since the publication of the Museum of Modern Art's *Built in USA* in 1945. And in taking Paul Rudolph's Cocoon house at Sarasota, Florida, in 1951 he made a pair of photographs that encompassed the expressive range of the two perspectives. One shows the building head on and with ample space above and below it and on the water side of the house to show the building's locale (152). We are distanced from the house and shown very much what a sectional drawing to explain its structure would have. The second picture is of a part of the house seen from close-up that extends over the water (153).It not only offers us an assortment of surfaces—of louvres, wooden flooring, mattress, and glass table—but cushions to rest on, sandals to wear, a book to read, and fruit to eat (some of it already peeled for us). One picture offers us the facts of the house, and the other the sensation of its comfort and use.

Stoller, as many photographers do, acknowledged the imperatives of magazine layout. When a print was ordered from him in these years, he would ask whether the purchaser wanted it cropped according to his (the photographer's) judgment or full frame so that it could be cropped as needed for a layout. Since both vertical and horizontal pictures are needed for a varied magazine layout, both types are taken even if they do not come naturally from the forms of a building. However, vertical pictures especially appeal to a photographer because they can be full page and lend themselves for use on magazine covers. In the nineteenth century when magazine plates were customarily vertical, photographers did not hesitate to make vertical photographs, though such pictures could go completely against the character of their subjects. In more recent years many a photographer has used the presence of a tree as the excuse to make a vertical photograph of a building that was primarily horizontal in nature.

Not only were the tree branches that made up the top of such a picture perfunctorily included, since the proper subject of the picture was the building at its bottom, but they were harder, for technical reasons that obtained particularly in the fifties and before, for the photographer to see in his ground glass at the back of his view camera. Stoller took his share of such trees, but he also

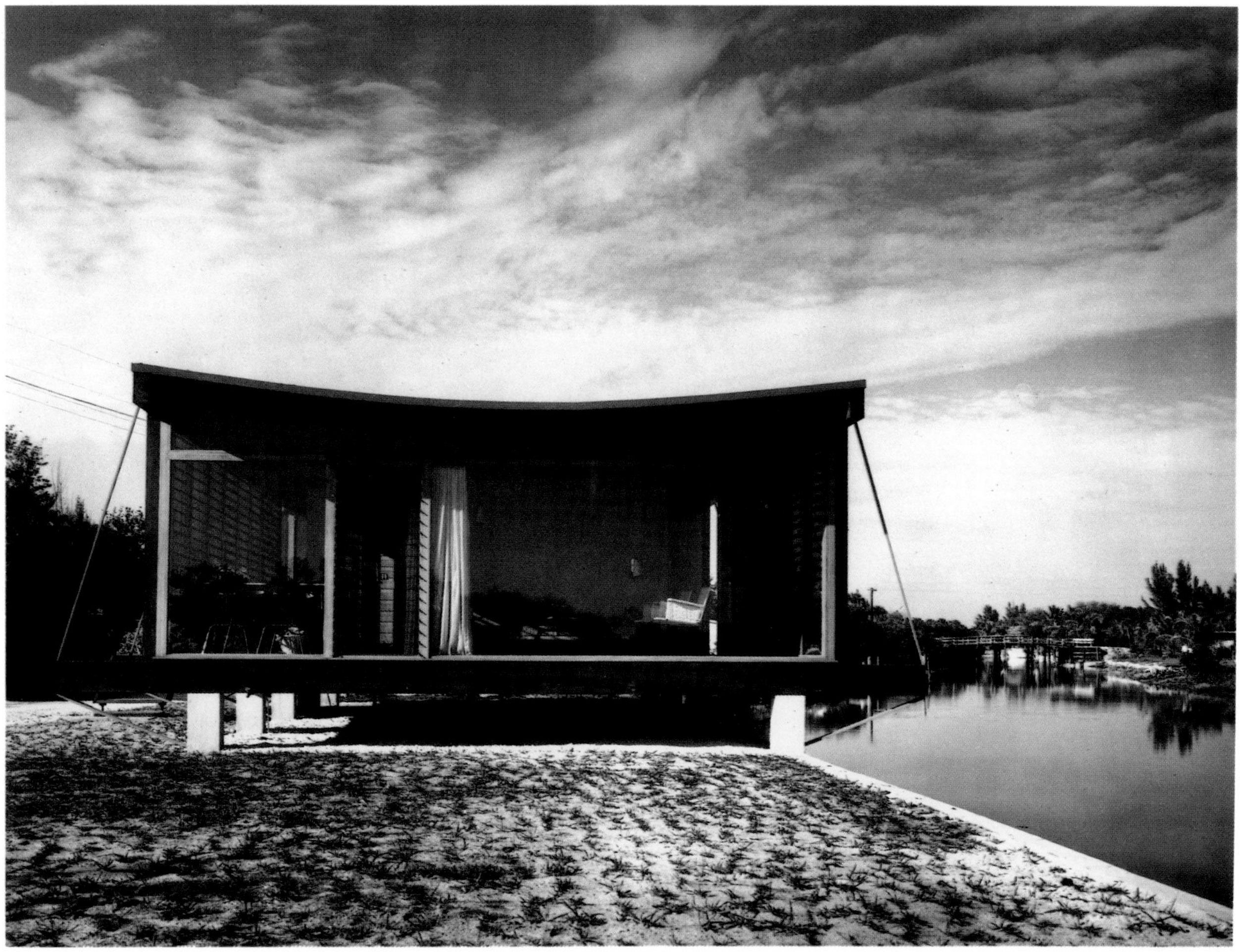

152 *Ezra Stoller*

Sarasota, Cocoon house, 1951.
Courtesy the photographer.

153 *Ezra Stoller*

Sarasota, Cocoon house, 1951.
Courtesy the photographer.

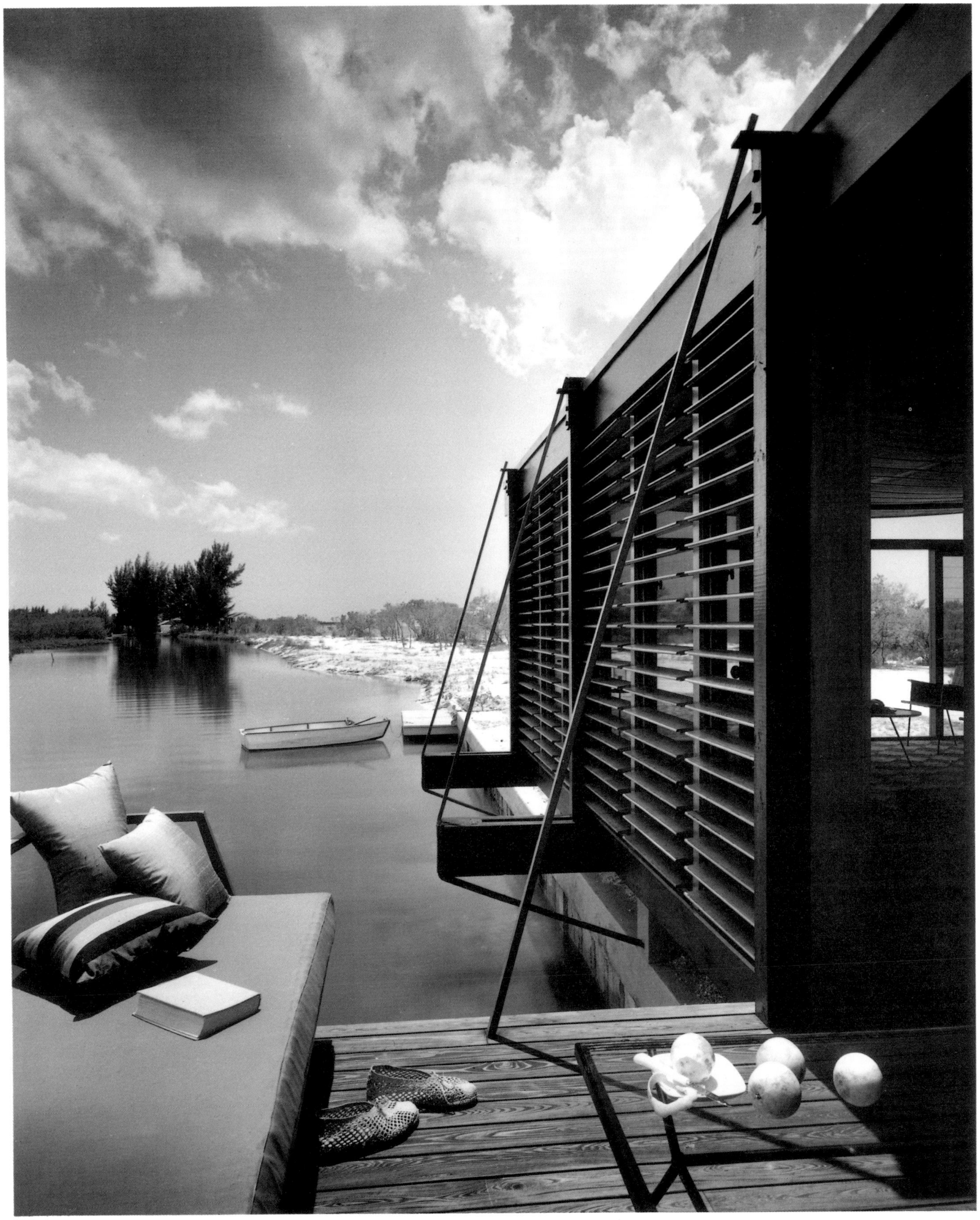

took a kind of picture in which a column or a pier seemed to justify a vertical picture, while a core of sharp detail remained directly across from the camera at the level of the horizon. He took such pictures of Skidmore, Owings & Merrill's Kitt Peak Observatory (1962) and of Eero Saarinen's TWA Terminal (1962) and Dulles Airport (1964). A picture of Dulles Airport exemplifies this sort of organic, monumental, and (despite the fact that the subject was a structural element) irrational picture (154). Precisely because such pictures were often, on balance, dictated more by the need to come up with a vertical format than from the inherent character of their subject, they can easily become tiresome. Lest we think that Dulles itself led inevitably to the vertical picture, a picture by Norman McGrath (b. 1931) demonstrates that there is at least one alternative and quite different way of approaching the same subject (155).

Stoller, like other photographers of the fifties, juxtaposed sculpture and industrially designed objects, as well as plants and trees, to buildings, but rarely human figures; his interior lighting was characterized by the clarity with which he separated, by shadow or light, the edges of elements in his pictures; his craftsmanship was solid if not dazzling. The parts that made up his style were not unique to him, however. Among those who took similar pictures was Alexandre Georges (b. 1916) who specialized in interiors. Nevertheless, Stoller brought together a coherent style that seemed for a time capable of solving any problem that modern architecture, at least, could present.

Nor were other photographers necessarily clones of Stoller. George Cserna (b. 1919) could make an elegant juxtaposition such as seen in his picture of Philip Johnson's Asia House (1959) and an adjacent brownstone, a picture we would not have gotten from Stoller (156). And people could more easily appear in the photographs of Julius Shulman (b. 1910), an energetic worker in Southern California, who from the thirties on has been responsible for taking much of the progressive domestic architecture in that area. The familiar picture of Richard Neutra's Kaufmann house (1947) at Palm Springs is a dusk shot in which the architect's wife Dione appears beside the pool on the left (157). In a photograph of Irving Gill's Dodge house (1916), taken for the writer Esther McCoy in 1954, diners and a waiter appear in the far doorway thanks to the building's being used at the time as a school for domestic servants (158).

In the Bay Area Morley Baer (b. 1916) took pictures that relied less on pyrotechnics or even on an assertive personal style than on his considerable technical craftsmanship and a willingness to place buildings in their contexts and to bend to the needs of particular buildings. The effortlessness with which

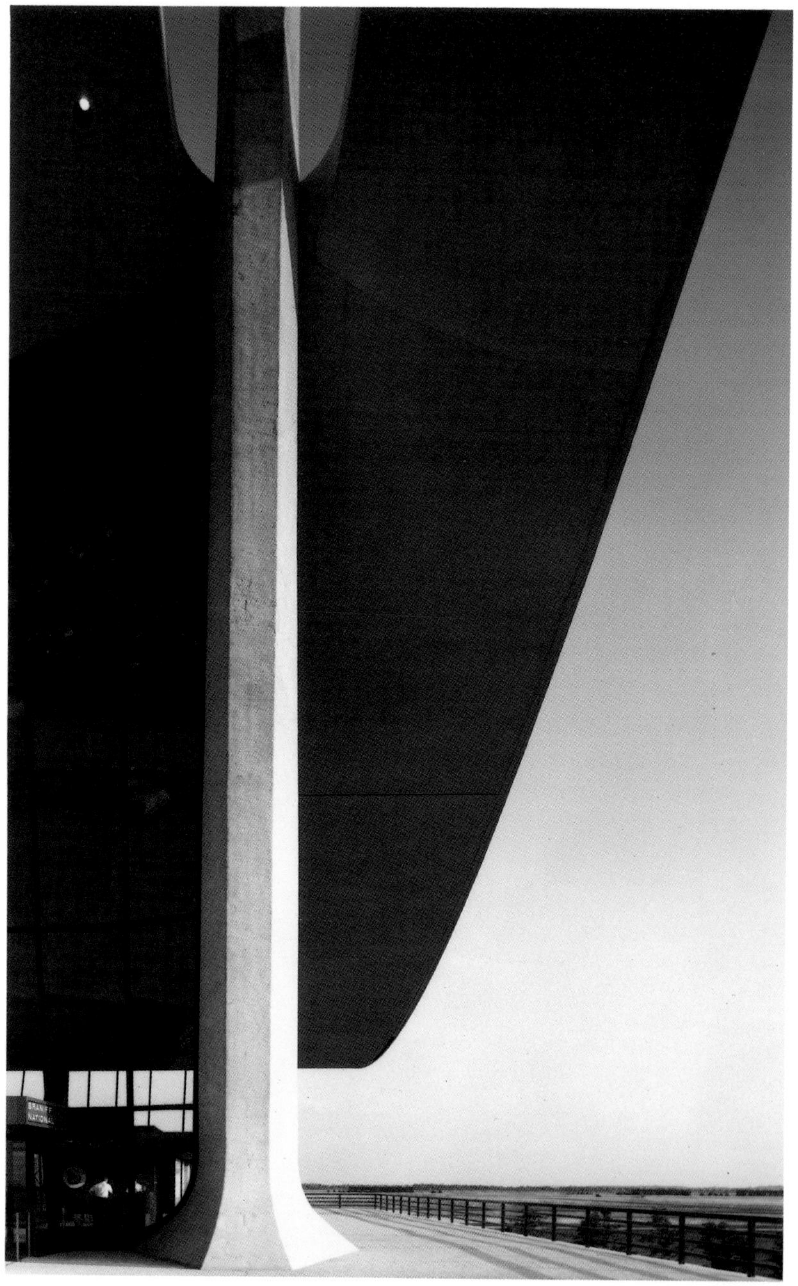

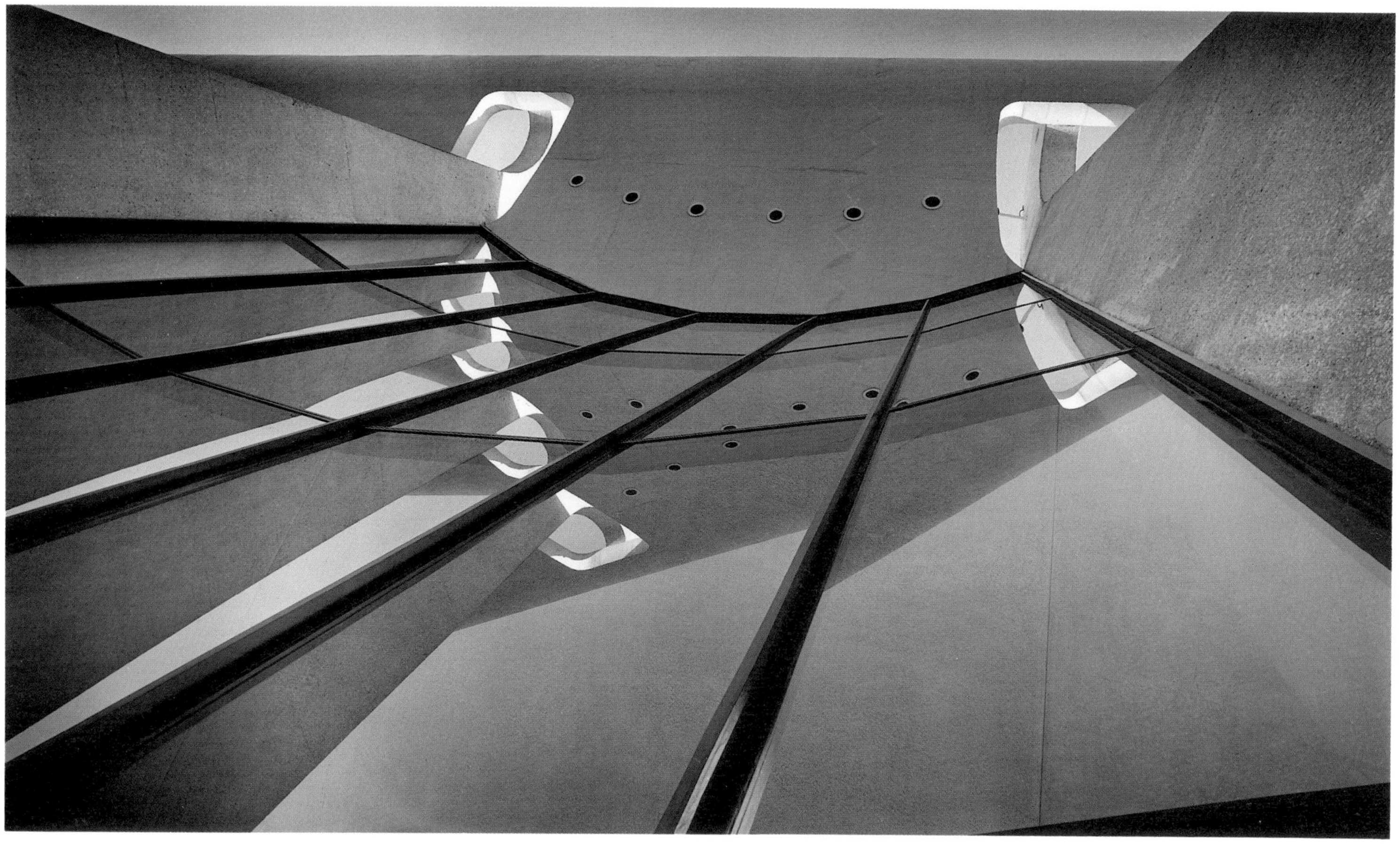

154 *Ezra Stoller*

Chantilly, Dulles Airport, 1964.
Courtesy the photographer.

155 *Norman McGrath*

Chantilly, Dulles Airport, ca. 1969.
Courtesy the photographer.

156 *George Cserna*

New York, Asia House, 1959.
Courtesy the photographer.

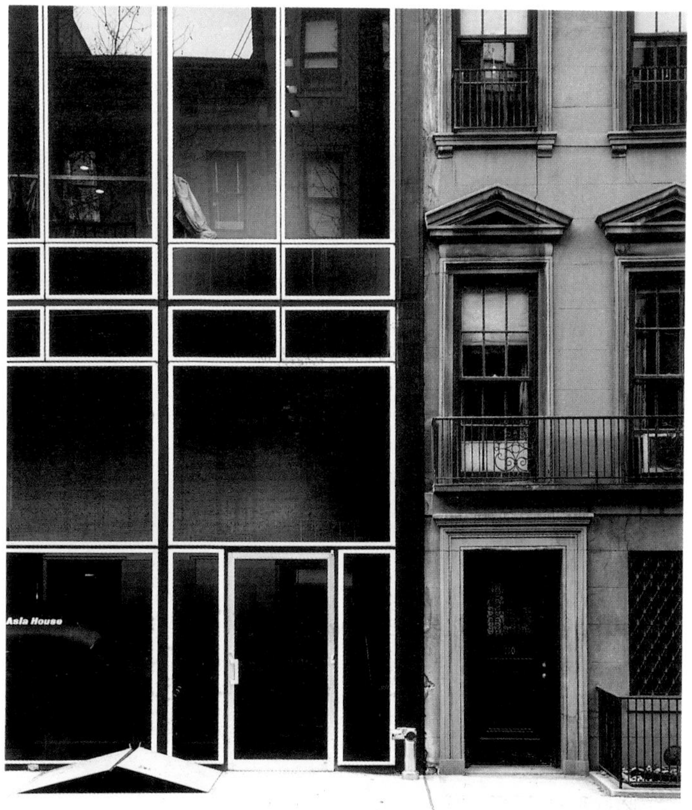

157 *Julius Shulman*

Palm Springs, Kaufmann house, 1947.
Courtesy the photographer.

158 *Julius Shulman*

Los Angeles, Dodge house, 1954.
Courtesy the photographer.

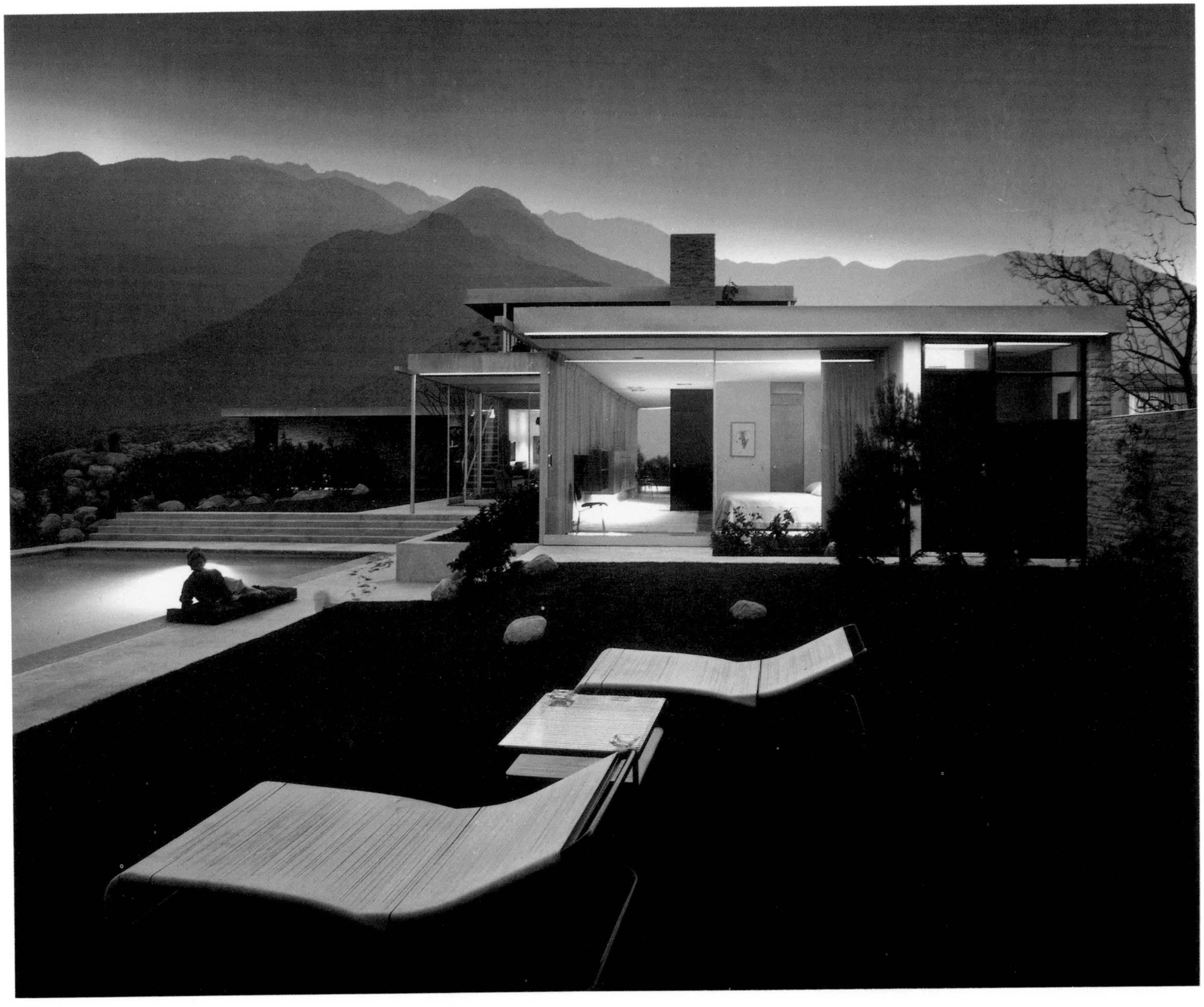

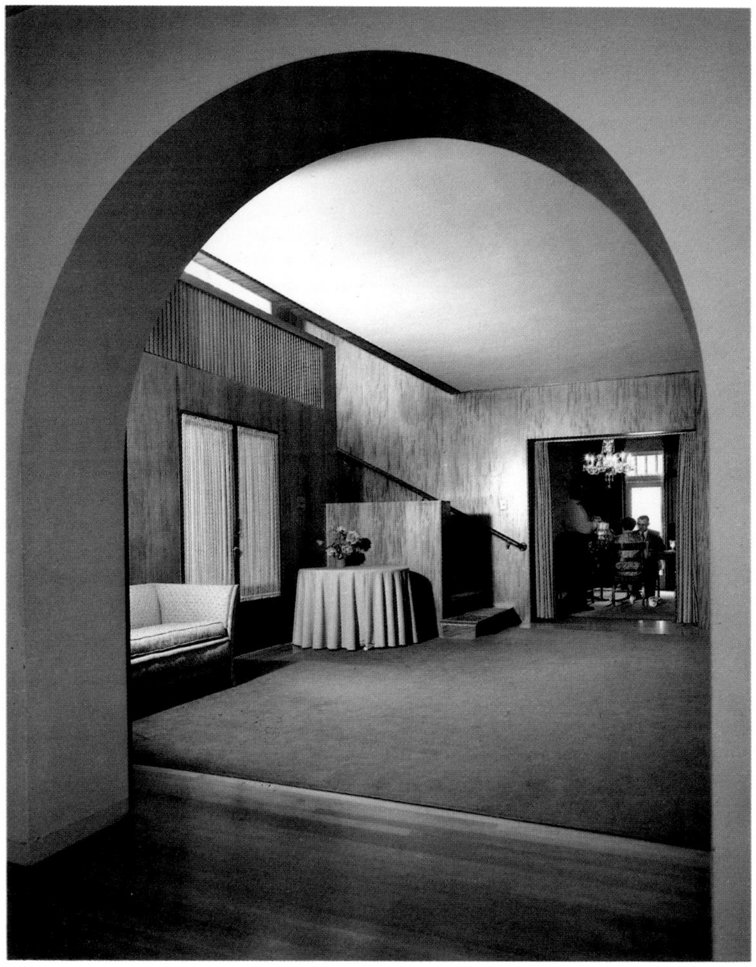

his head-on view of Charles Moore's apartment (1966) at Sea Ranch, California, seems to have been taken, an interior carefully arranged by the architect like virtually all interiors when they are to be photographed, belies the care and craftsmanship with which it was actually made—care that is apparent for instance in the way the edges of planes that define the space are lit so as to stand in relief against the surfaces behind them (159). His earlier view of Skidmore, Owings & Merrill's Crown Zellerbach Building (1959) not only accepts but exploits the urban context of the building in the form of the San Francisco Bay Bridge and Foster's English Muffins to an extent that an East Coast photographer, trained to isolate modern buildings from their older contexts, would probably have been loath to do (160).

Since the publication of Sigfried Giedion's *Space, Time and Architecture* (1941), certain examples of historic architecture had been considered significant as antecedents of modern architecture. These were buildings, or types of buildings—cast-iron architecture for instance—that could be regarded in isolation and favorably. The works of Louis Sullivan were so regarded, and when John Szarkowski (b. 1925), working under a grant from the John Simon Guggenheim Foundation in 1954, photographed this architect's work for a book, *The Idea of Louis Sullivan* (1956), he did so in much the spirit in which other photographers were taking the work of contemporary architects. His was not a disinterested study. He accepted the contemporary view of Sullivan as a tragic figure and was clearly sympathetic toward the man. True, Szarkowski was more likely than many photographers taking new buildings at that time to place one of his subjects in its context and to show part of a building, not all of it, and he was more accepting of the light under which he happened to find a building, but then Sullivan's materials may photograph better under an overcast sky than does, say, reinforced concrete. In his use of juxtapositions Szarkowski worked very much in the spirit of the photographer of new buildings. His juxtapositions either told one, like Ken Hedrich's cars, in what spirit one was to take the Sullivan building or they were presented as ironic contrasts to it. A detail of the Getty Tomb (1890) entrance gate included a prominent dead leaf; a detail of the Auditorium Building (1890) in Chicago the skeleton of a dead bird (which had a resemblance to Sullivan's ornament); and a photograph of the Wainwright Building (1891) in Saint Louis, in juxtaposition to it, the mausoleum top of Charles Treft's Civil Courts Building (1930) (161). In the book quotations adjacent to the whole photograph and to a detail of it showing

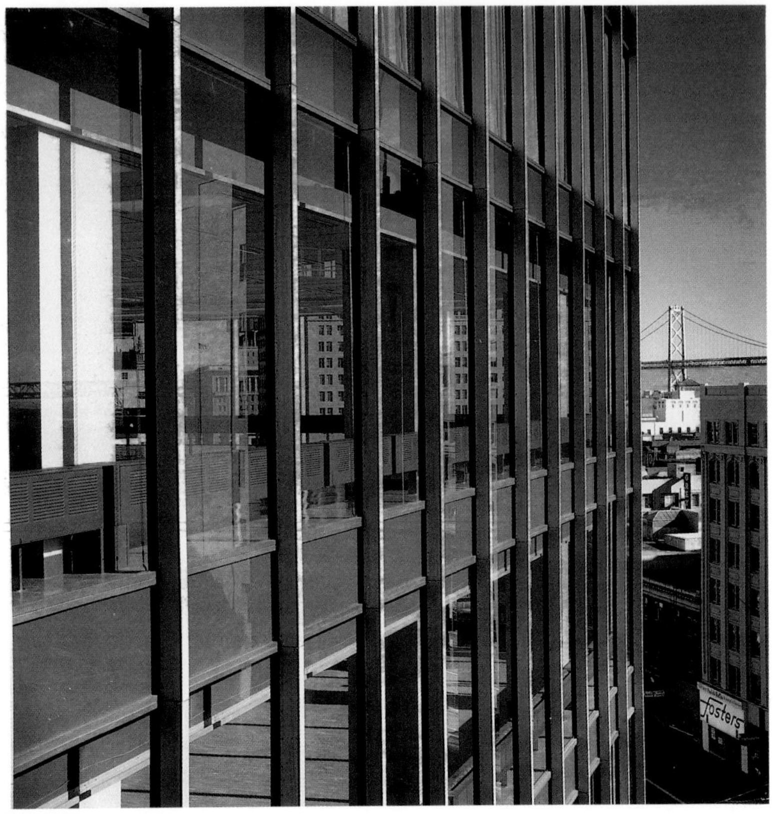

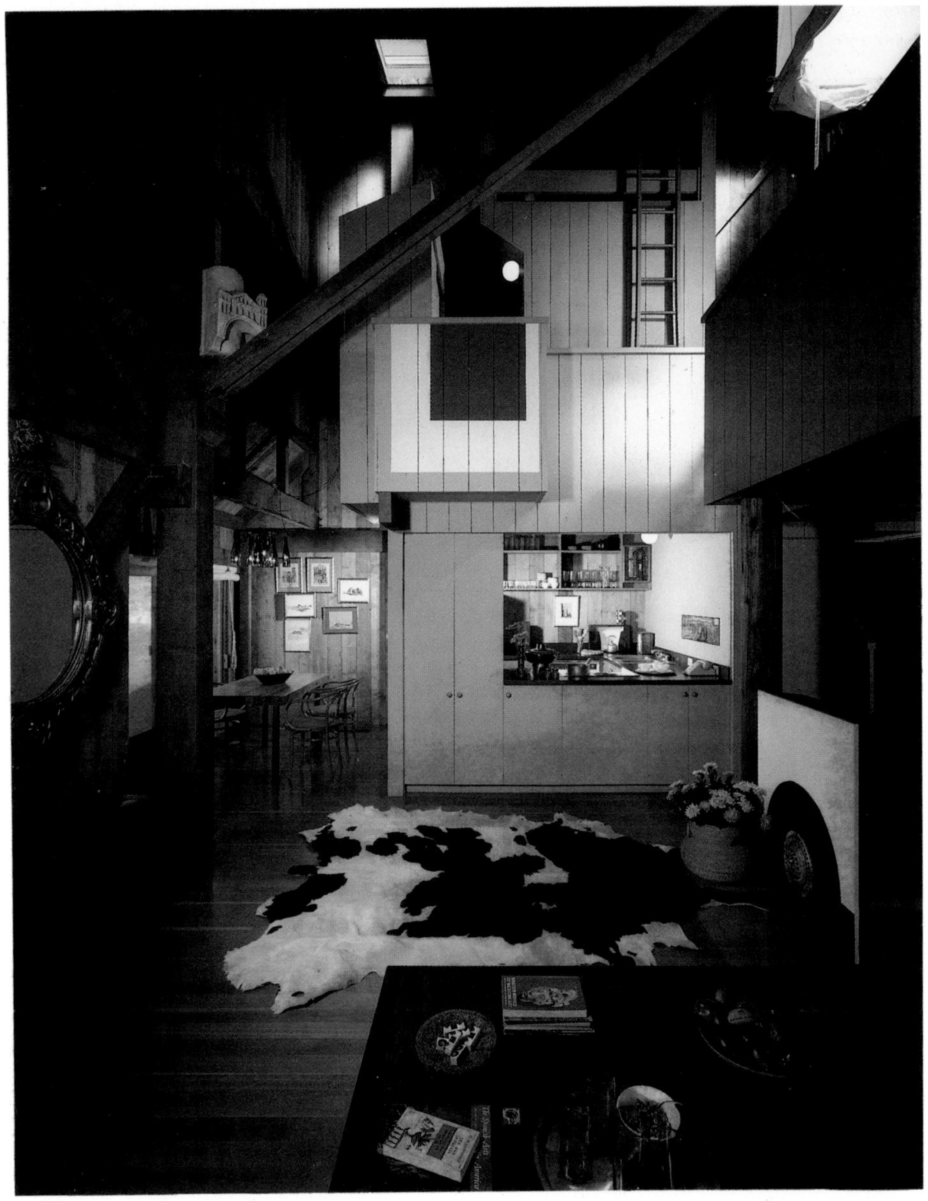

159 *Morley Baer*
Sea Ranch, Moore apartment, 1965.
Courtesy the photographer.

160 *Morley Baer*
San Francisco, Crown Zellerbach Building, 1960.
Courtesy the photographer.

161 *John Szarkowski*
St. Louis, Wainwright Building, ca. 1954.
Courtesy the photographer.

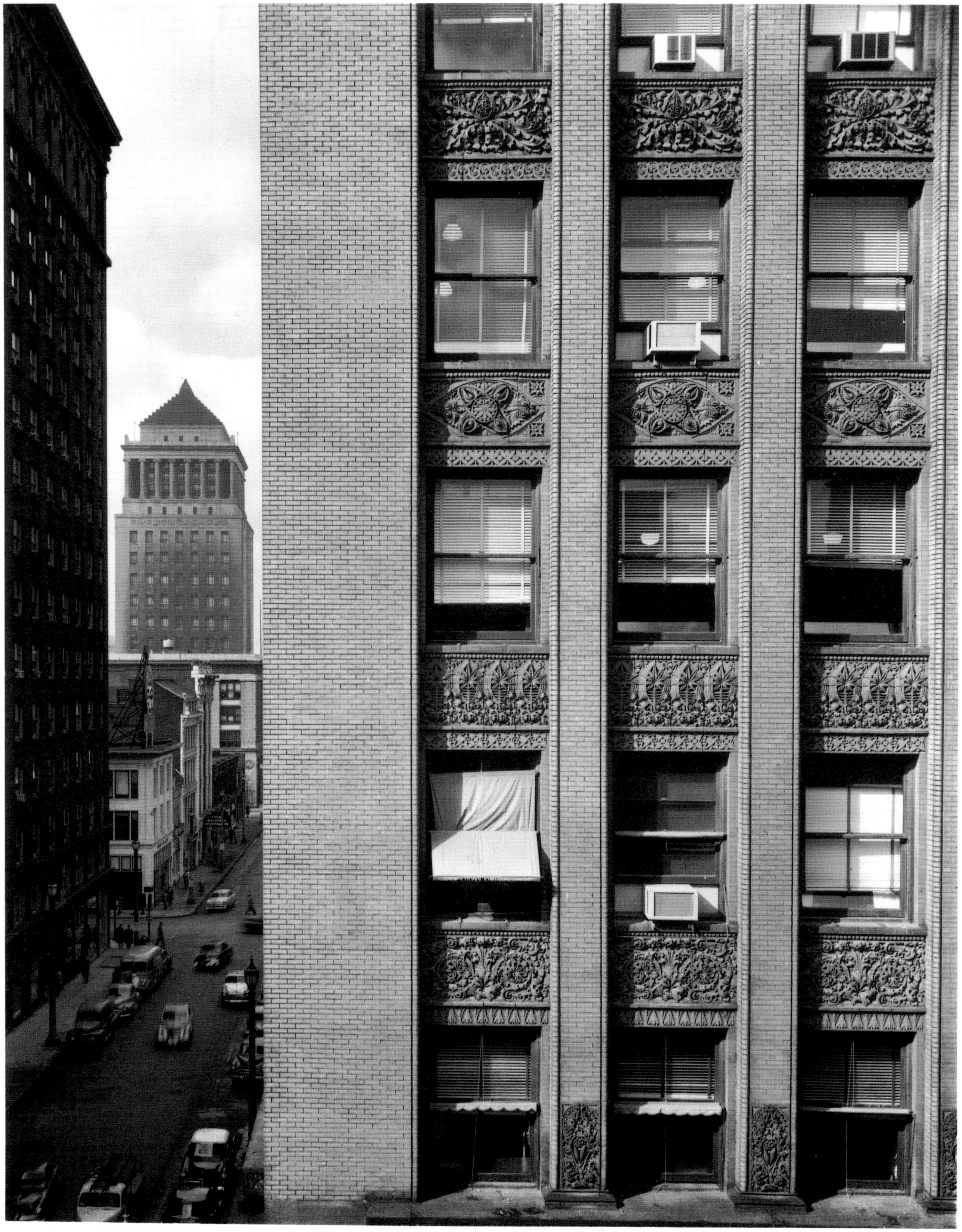

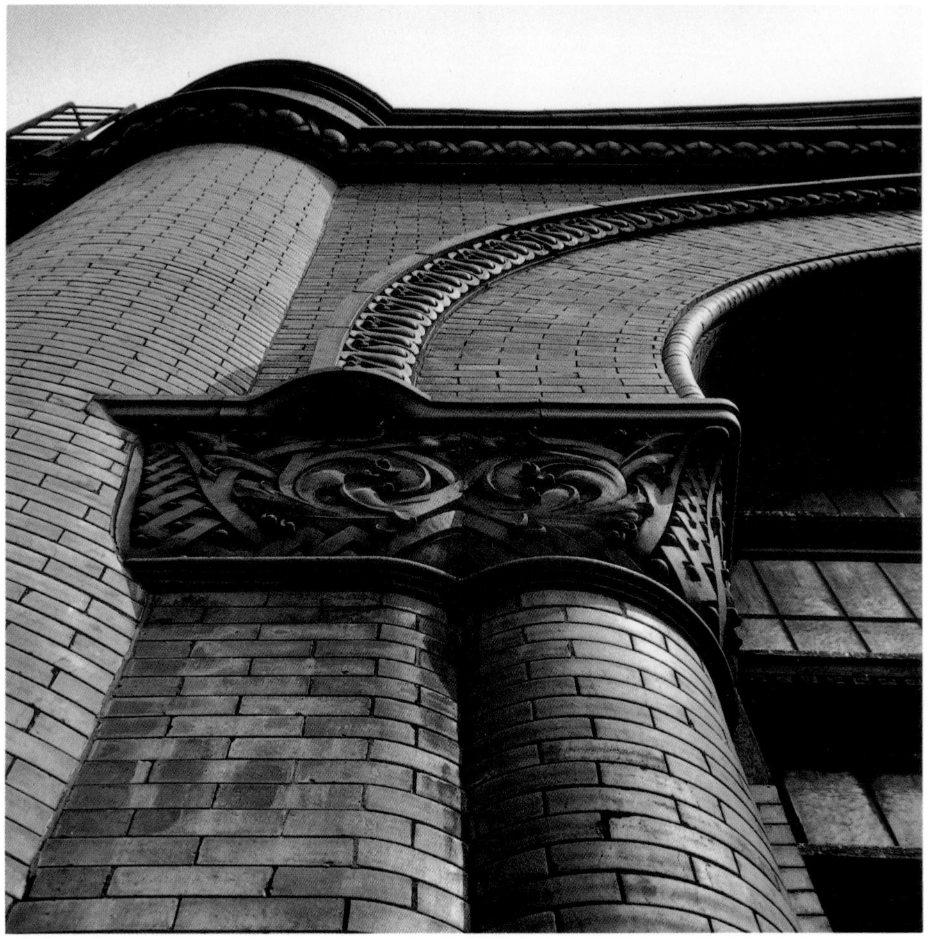

the Courts building left no doubt that one was to see the Sullivan building as good and the Treft one as bad.

Sullivan, though his tragedy came eventually to seem caused less by classicizing easterners than by his break with Adler and his alcoholism, was an irresistible subject to several photographers. In 1953 students of Aaron Siskind (b. 1903) at the Illinois Institute of Technology photographed every building in the Chicago area that could conceivably be by Sullivan. Among Siskind's students was Richard Nickel (1928–1972), whose thesis (1957) on Adler and Sullivan launched a lifelong devotion to recording the work of Sullivan and his contemporaries. Indeed, he lost his life in a collapse within the Chicago Stock Exchange Building during its demolition. The photograph reproduced here taken high up on Burnham & Root's Board of Trade Building (1888) in Kansas City was one of a set Nickel made for *Architectural Forum* before the building's demolition in 1967 (162). Its oblique perspective emphasizes the substance of the building's brick and terra cotta but says nothing about its organization. A lack of emotional distance from subject matter was a common characteristic of all categories of architectural photography in the fifties and early sixties.

Experiential views of older architecture served a special need of architectural magazines. Its richer imagery and substance could provide relief from the bland surfaces of the modern buildings which was these magazines' primary purpose to publish. In many issues of the *Forum* in the fifties and sixties Giedion's selection of historically relevant structures was either examined in greater detail by photographers or slowly expanded on. The historical world "out there" seemed full of riches that could be rediscovered and gradually introduced into the body of work that was considered relevant, and pictures that the *Forum* used to provide this relief were often oblique, experiential ones. If its editors presented the facts of an older style it might seem they were advocating a return to it, but to give its texture was acceptable. George Cserna (b. 1919) did *Forum* galleries on Henry Hardenbergh's Dakota apartment house and on Jefferson's buildings at the University of Virginia, from which a photograph of an immense, leaf-strewn lawn is memorable. Clemens Kalischer (b. 1921) took a set of pictures of the surfaces of brickwork, stone, and copper flashing on Boston's Beacon Hill. One, of the worn granite setts and cobblestones that pave the driveway of Charles Bulfinch's second Harrison Gray Otis house (1802), is, like Nickel's Kansas City photograph, an exemplary experiential picture (163).

162 *Richard Nickel*
Kansas City, Board of Trade Building, 1967.
Richard Nickel Committee.

163 *Clemens Kalischer*
Boston, second Harrison Gray Otis house, driveway, 1961.
Courtesy the photographer.

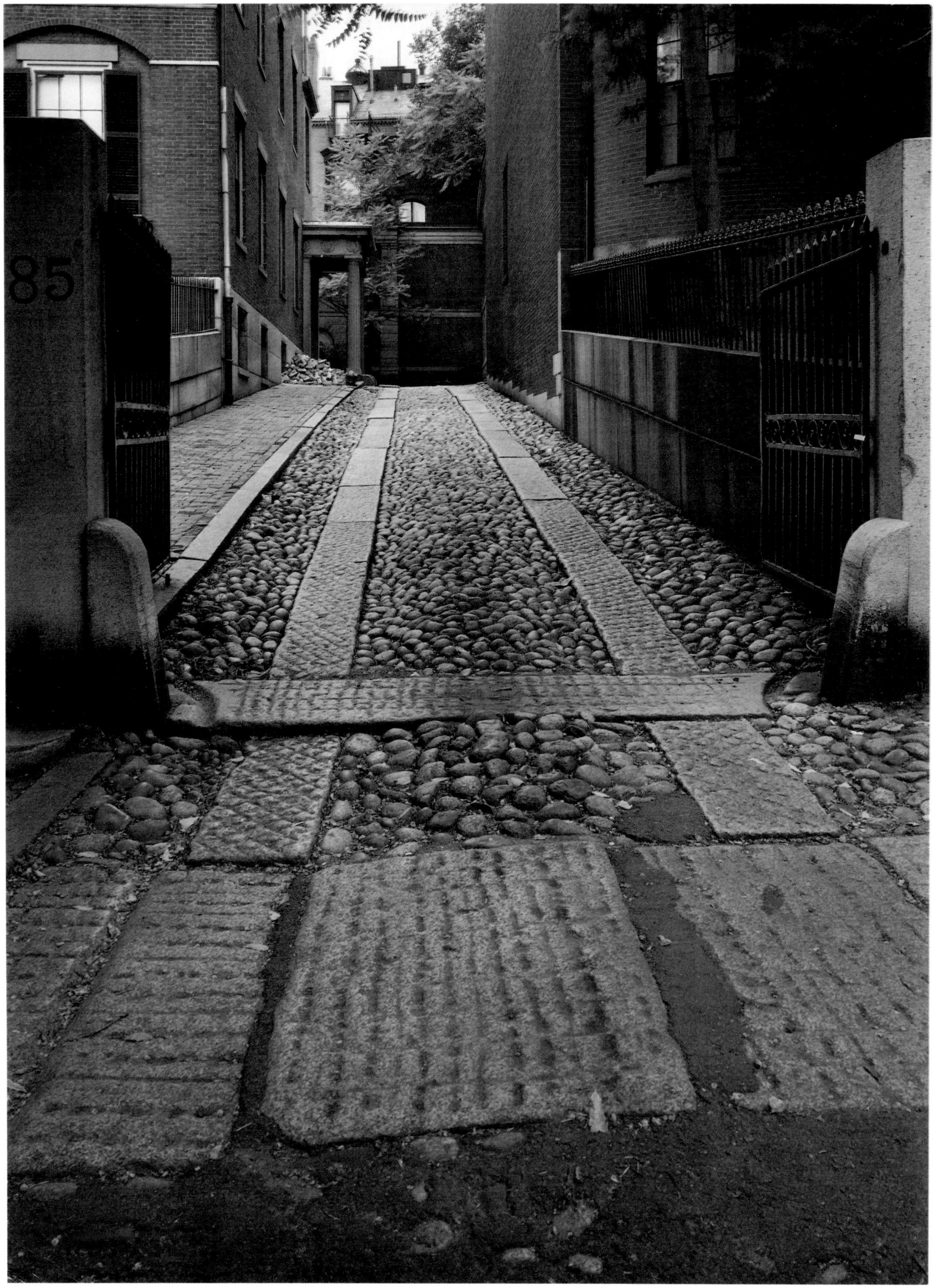
85

164 *Norman McGrath*

New York, Pennsylvania Station, 1964. Courtesy the photographer.

165 *Cervin Robinson*

New York, Municipal, Tribune, and American Tract Society buildings from Times Building, 1966.

The needs of the *Forum* were not the only impetus behind the taking of historic buildings. Norman McGrath, just as he turned from engineering to photography, took pictures of McKim, Mead & White's Pennsylvania Station (1910) under demolition in 1964. One of these, a view looking across at a Corinthian capital and entablature, shows standing in the remains of the mostly demolished cornice, from which a pair of modillions hang, the figure of a man who appears to be unconcernedly reloading his camera (164). The metal frame of the cornice that McGrath chose to photograph reveals the true nature of this massive and apparently solid classical structure, and the man by his unconcern sets in relief the feeling of outrage that the building's destruction caused.

Two years later it was just possible to show older buildings, not one by one, but juxtaposed unhistorically, and to show new buildings in the context of the older buildings in which they had been built. In that year for a *Forum* gallery I photographed the tops of some dozen older New York skyscrapers, including sets of from two to four buildings in each picture. To have taken them singly, one to a picture, would have implied that each was a good and historically significant (and relevant) structure. Taking them in sets made them interact with each other, none better or worse than the others, each vying for attention, each setting off the others. The picture that convinced the editors to go ahead with my project was one of McKim, Mead & White's Municipal Building (1908), Richard Morris Hunt's Tribune Building (1875), and R. H. Robertson's American Tract Society Building (1896) seen from George B. Post's Times Building (1889) (165). In another picture not part of the gallery, I showed I. M. Pei's pair of apartment towers in New York's Greenwich Village rising out of a sea of older Village buildings, whereas before that it would have been obligatory to show them as isolated structures.

Architectural magazines were not the only outlets for photographs of older architecture. Evelyn Hofer made a set of pictures of Florence in the German tradition of the picture book of a town and its cathedral for Mary McCarthy's *The Stones of Florence* (1957) and subsequently combined that tradition with another German one, familiar through the portraits taken by August Sander, of the collection of portrait types—"Member of Congress," "Cartoonist," "Civil servant," "Trash man," "Chauffeurs"—in a series of books on which Hofer collaborated with the writers V. S. Pritchett, James Morris, and William Walton on the subjects of London (1962), Spain (1964), New York City (1965), Washington, D.C. (1966), and Dublin (1967). Her pictures in *The Stones of*

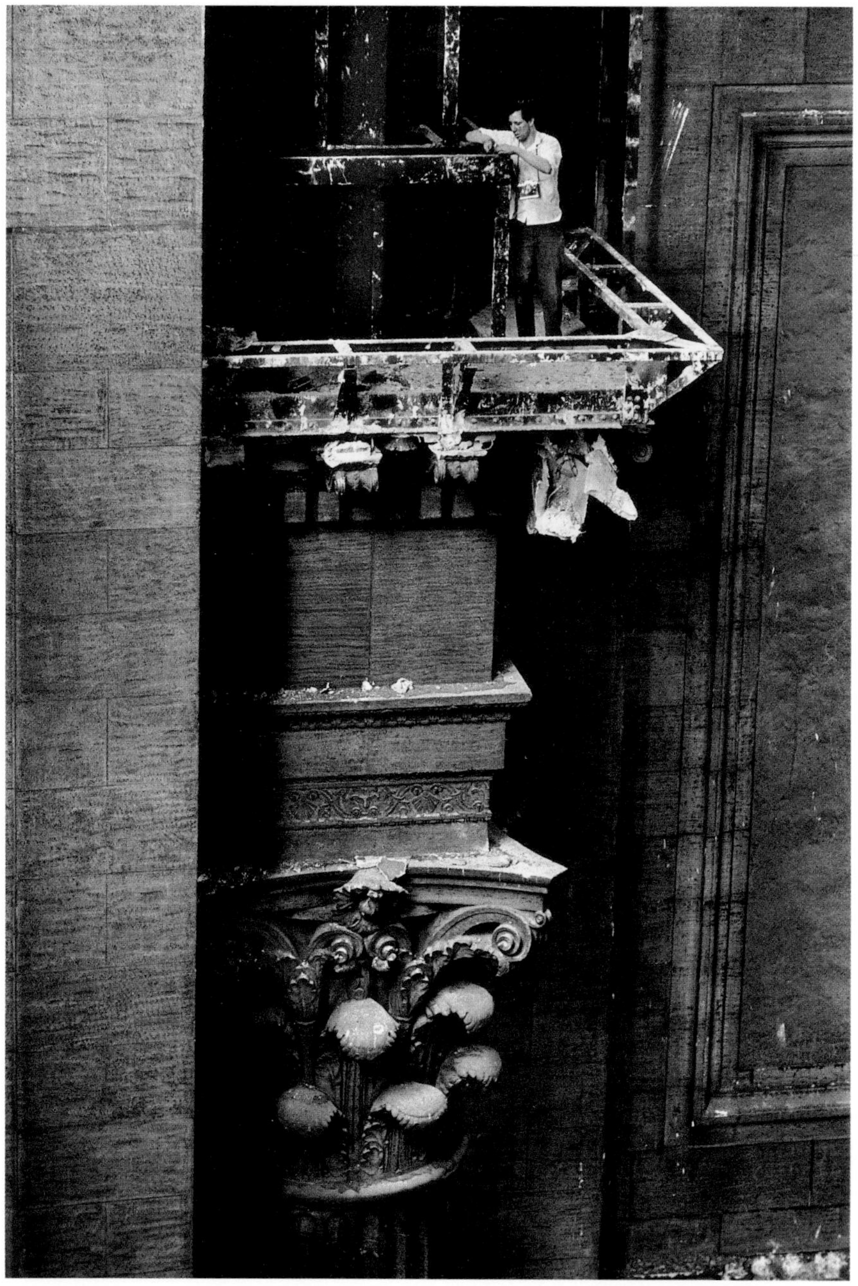

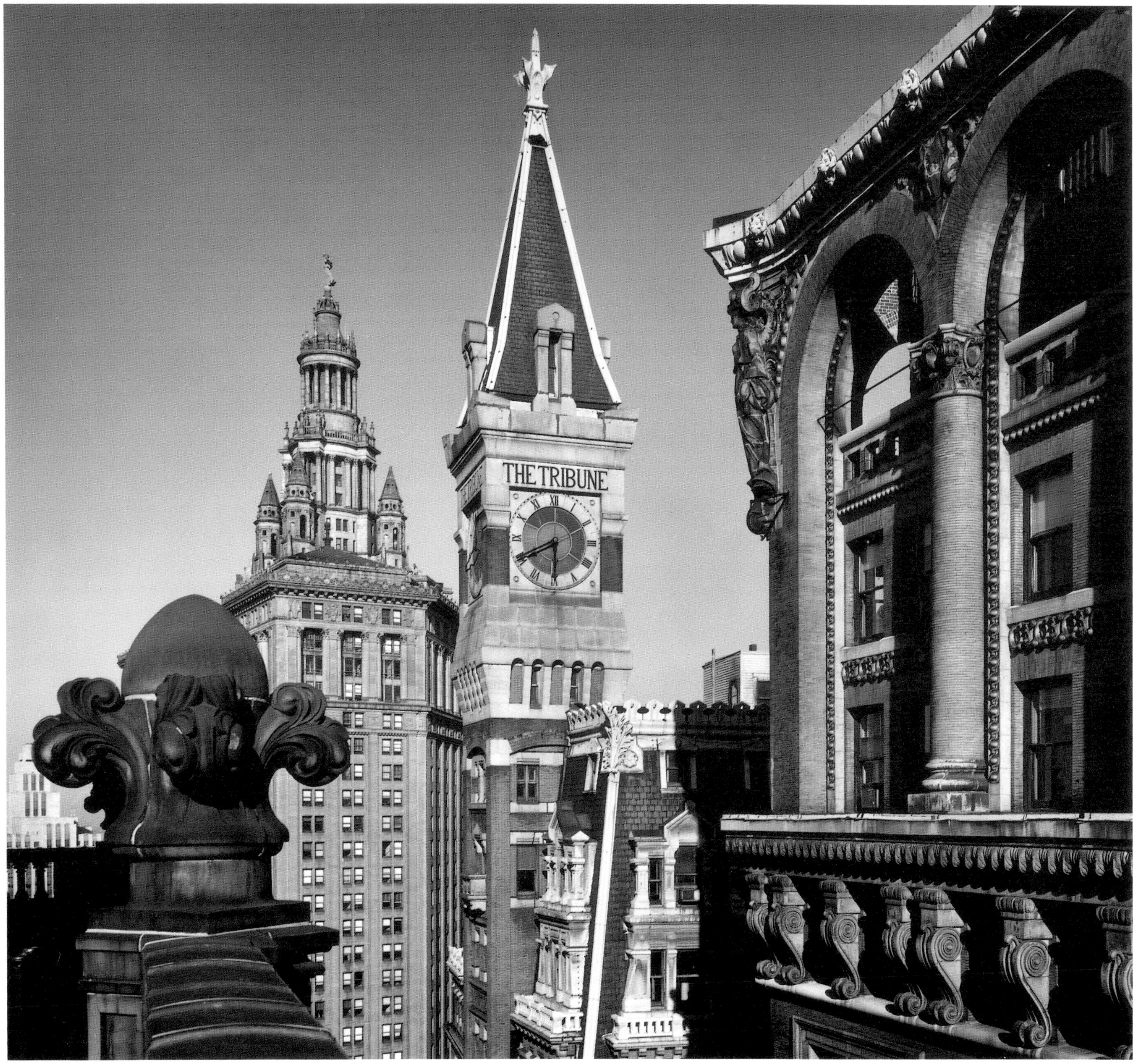
THE TRIBUNE

Florence, which make up something over half the photographs in the book, are mostly architectural. Some are head-on views of facades that fill the picture and therefore show nothing of the surrounding city or countryside, such as her view of Alberti's Palazzo Rucellai (1451) (166). Others are oblique and permit a glimpse of a building's environment, such as her picture of buttresses outside the central apse of the Duomo with the hills of the Tuscan countryside in the distance (167). For some photographers the parts of pictures near their edges are of great importance (and you cannot crop these pictures without diminishing them); for others what is near the edges is less important, and their photographs lend themselves especially to bleed layouts (or to being cropped by art directors). Hofer has come increasingly to be one of the second group, and the manner in which her books have been printed—in gravure and bled—is especially appropriate for them. In her later books, all of them with many portraits as well as buildings, the architectural subjects, like the portraits, have more and more tended to have a central core of interest around which radiates less essential subject matter. Or they have been of receding symmetrical spaces, rather than surfaces.

The skies Hofer worked under in these books varied; sometimes she used bright sunlight, sometimes diffuse light from overcast skies (as in the two pictures shown here). Part of learning to photograph is finding out what light is articulate and can be counted on, and most architectural photographers have confined themselves to clear skies and sunlight. It is a pleasure to be given the illusion, as one often is in Hofer's pictures, that any sky that is characteristic of the setting can be included in a photograph.

Hofer's synthesis of the two traditions of architectural photographs and portraits aimed to create a plausible accounting of a place, just as Walker Evans's and Paul Strand's did. Few posed portraits look as though they can have been as much a pleasure to sit for as hers do. Her books are insiders' views, unacerbic and intelligent, of largely unchanging older cities—or so she leads us to believe—inhabited by attractive and benign people. They therefore go against an American tradition that says a portrait should represent something like a conflict between photographer and sitter. Her construct is probably most plausible in her *Dublin, A Portrait* (1967), done with V. S. Pritchett.

In the late 1940s and early 1950s, just as modern architecture was being almost universally accepted, there had been a feeling in the air that photography might do more than it did, that it was distorting what was being done by telling only part of the truth and should in general tell the bad news as well as the good. The belief was that photographs did not show buildings in their real contexts or with people in them, that they cast buildings in too good a light. W. Eugene Smith (1918–1978) was responding to this feeling when in 1956 on quitting *Life* magazine he equipped himself with a view camera (which he quickly abandoned for his more familiar 35mm cameras) and undertook to photograph a selection (the AIA's) of recent American architecture for an exhibition and book, *100 Years of American Architecture* by Frederick Gutheim published in 1957 on the occasion of the centennial of the American Institute of Architects. Smith intentionally took these pictures from other points of view than that customary in photographs of new buildings, that is, the architect's. He took some housing from the perspective of neighborhood children; Hellmuth, Yamasaki & Leinweber's terminal at Lambert–St. Louis Airport (1956) from the perspective of an air crew; and Skidmore, Owings & Merrill's Connecticut General Insurance Company building (1957), not from that of a user of the building, but of a hunter walking across neighboring winter fields (168). We see what Smith is trying to do—that is, to show the building as it "really" looked rather than as it was intended to look. It is, however, all too easy for a photographer to overwhelm a building with the environment in which he means to show it, and in his picture we can neither see the detailing of the Connecticut General building nor understand its organization. The landscape upstages and diminishes it to no useful effect, and the picture is at best well-meaning.

Smith did not pursue architectural photography after this one experience, and no other photojournalist—at last none with comparable credentials—undertook in those years to solve architectural photography's problems.

There was, however, still another way in which buildings were photographed. In his book *The Roots of Japanese Architecture* (1962) Yukio Futagawa (b. 1932) organized architecture into ten categories of building materials, structural elements, and spaces. In illustrating these—where a western photographer would have accentuated the differences between even similar buildings—Futagawa where possible took corresponding parts of the some sixty major buildings that were included, in the same way—views of the verandas of different buildings, for instance, or views *from* verandas were by and large each taken in the same way. His pictures, while emphasizing the elements of a building and often isolating them as well, are in the familiar perspectives: the facade of the Gokuru-bo priests' quarters at Gango-ji, Nara Prefecture, is shown head on (and isolated from roof and ground) (169). The picture of the

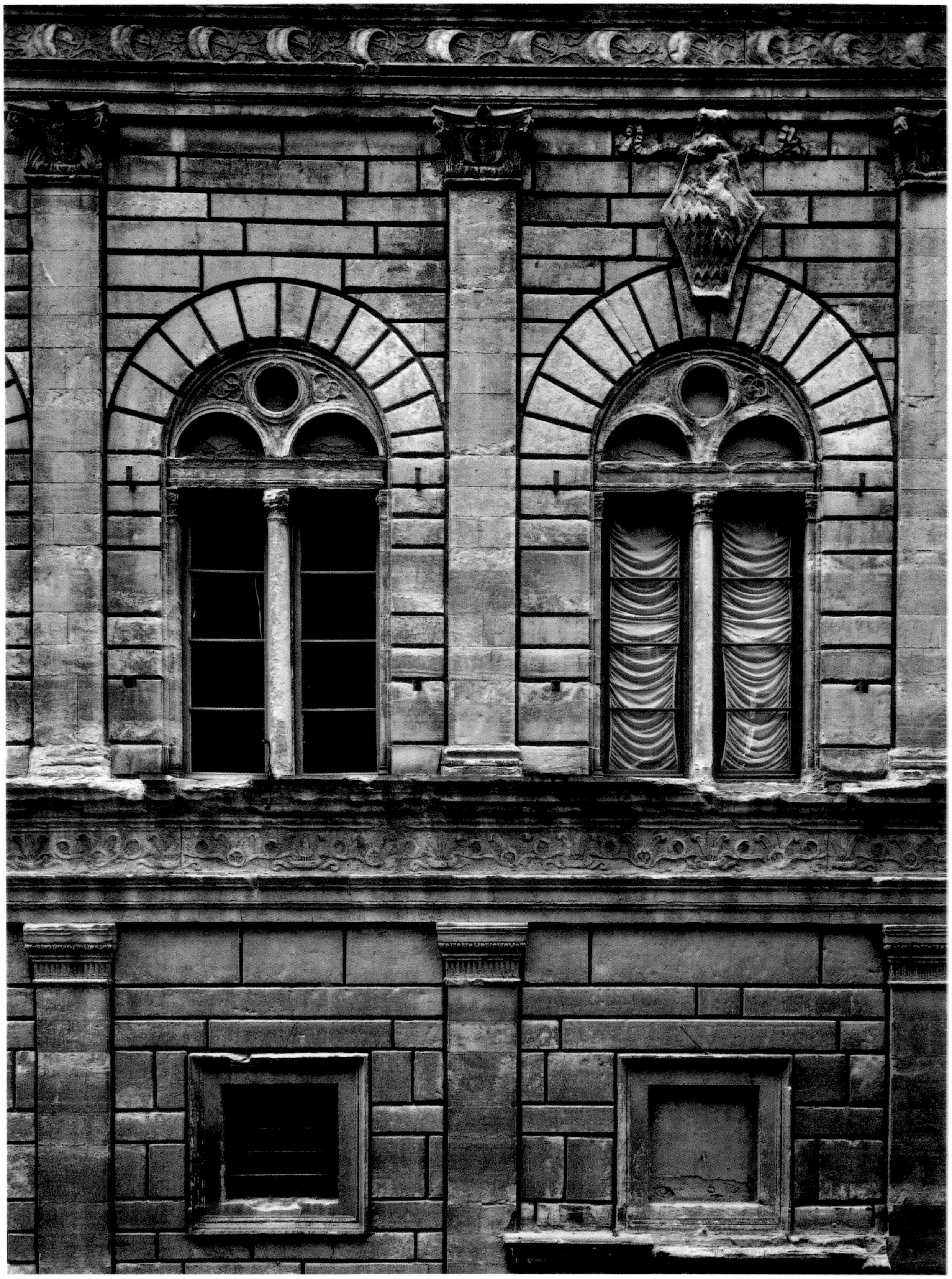

166 *Evelyn Hofer*

Florence, Palazzo Rucellai, ca. 1958.
Courtesy the photographer.

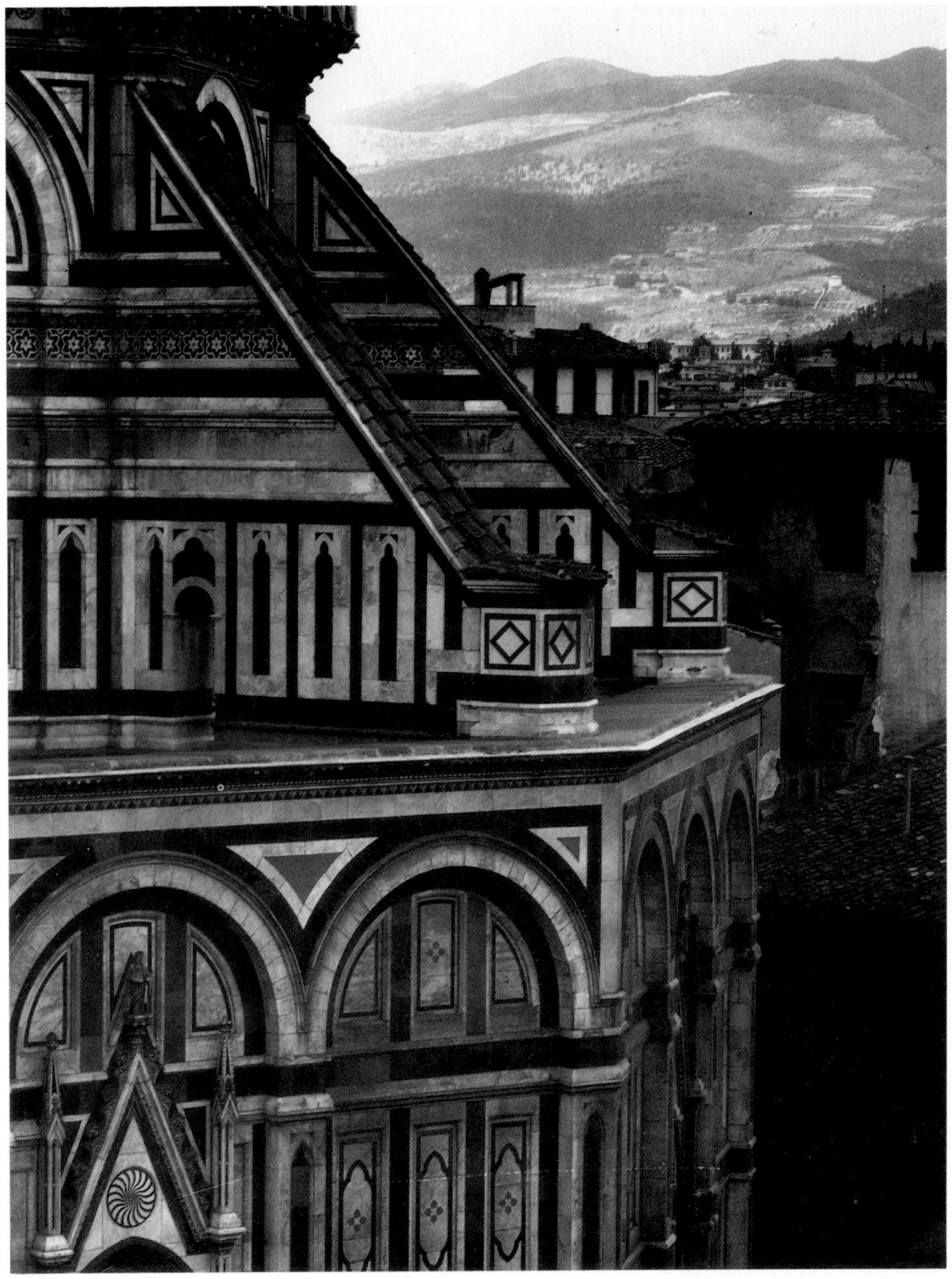

167 *Evelyn Hofer*

Florence, Duomo, ca. 1958.
Courtesy the photographer.

168 *W. Eugene Smith*

Bloomfield, Connecticut General building, 1956.
American Institute of Architects Archives.

169 *Yukio Futagawa*

Nara Prefecture, Gango-ji, ca. 1961.
Courtesy the photographer.

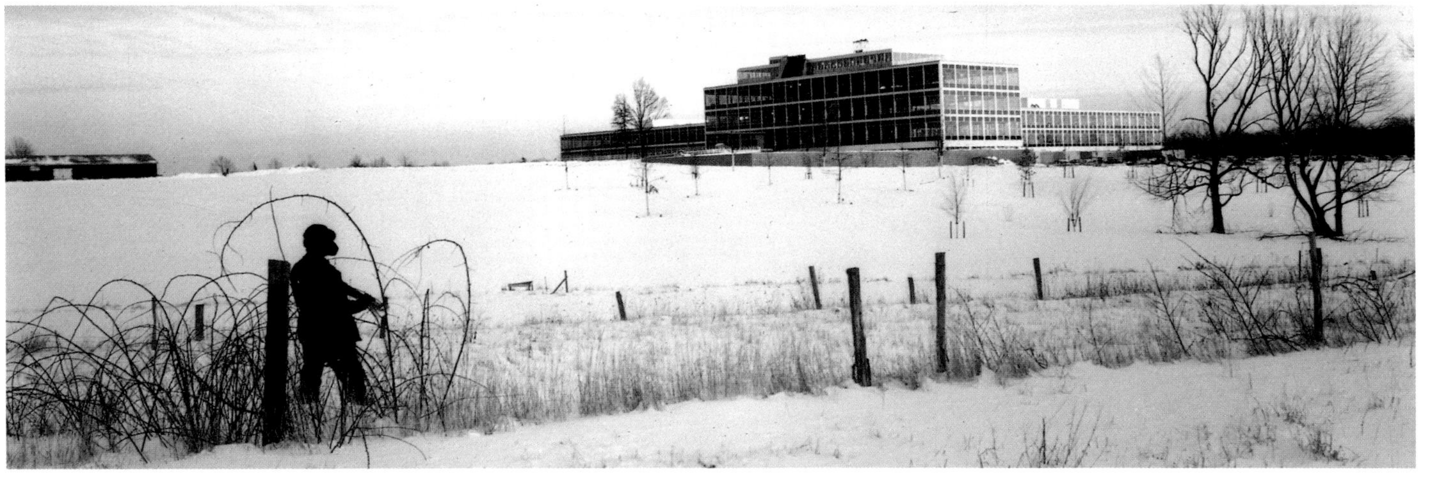

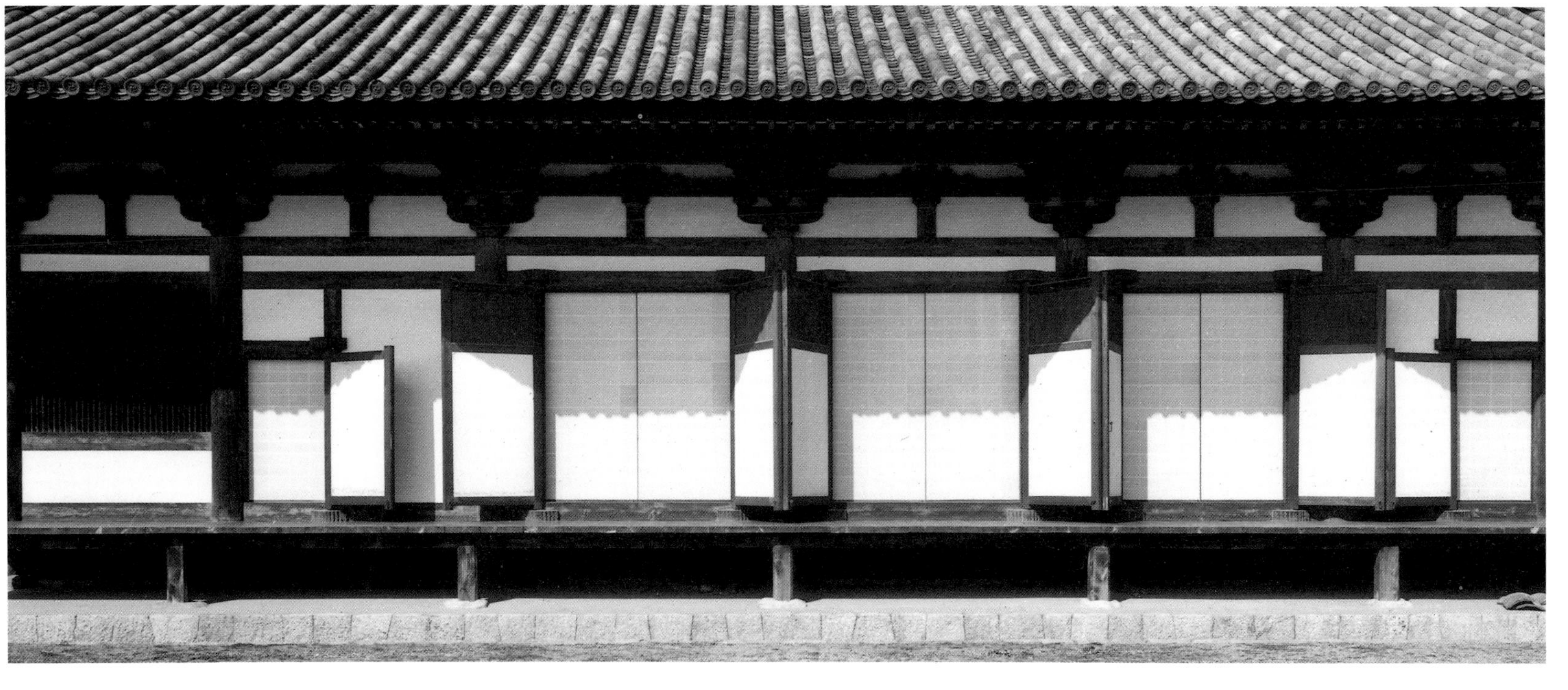

temple stairway at Jingo-ji at Kyoto, which gives barely a hint of what it leads to, is a characteristic experiential view (170).

The methodology apparent in *The Roots of Japanese Architecture*—its breakdown of the architecture into essential elements, its manner of approaching each of these in a set way, and its tendency to ignore both the human presence and the descriptive powers of the harsh raking sunlight that western photographers favor—goes a long way to explain Futagawa's subsequently prolific output in the 1970s in his Global Architecture book series, which examined major examples of modern architecture and its forerunners. A comparison is instructive of Bill Hedrich's (b. 1912) iconic photograph of Frank Lloyd Wright's Fallingwater made in 1937 with one by Futagawa in his volume *Frank Lloyd Wright, Kaufmann House, "Fallingwater," Bear Run, Pennsylvania, 1936,* edited and photographed by Yukio Futagawa, with a text by Paul Rudolph (1970) (171, 172). Hedrich shows us the relationship of the house and its terraces to each other and to the rocks and water below under strong sunlight that clearly defines each element. Underneath the terraces he shows the slabs that support them. The house is explained. Futagawa begins his book with a view from almost the same camera position but one that abstracts as elements the concrete terraces, the trees above them, and the rocks and water below. To show them he has used diffuse light from an overcast sky, which changes little with time of day or orientation, rather than Hedrich's harsh sunlight that must be used at the moment it shines from the right direction. Futagawa has ignored the visitors to the building whose blurred figures appear on the terrace in the color photograph that appears in the book (just as he had ignored the occasional small figures that found their way into the pictures of his *Roots* and which play no role in them). Futagawa's manner of photographing is a sort of shorthand expedited by his not having to wait for people to play useful roles in his pictures or for demanding sunlight to shine from the right direction. His methodology, instead of offering an alternative and more truthful way of photographing architecture, merely facilitates his prolific output.

A need for photographs that would tell the bad news about architecture was clearly implicit in the *Review*'s editorial announcing "Townscape's" casebook, and in 1955 the magazine launched "Outrage" (and followed it up with "Counterattack"). Ian Nairn (1930–1983) took a trip from the south of Britain to the north photographing the "out there" that the earlier editorial had summed up as nest fouling. Nairn took his pictures under the often unflattering light he found himself in, not "Townscape's" holiday sunshine. One shows a Booth's gin advertisement on a billboard "with coy drystone walls and blushing shrubs in front" (173). Beside the billboard we see part of a brick house with a car parked in its drive and the tip of a bicycle wheel. Many of the "Outrage" photographs were reproduced on uncoated paper in heavily inked letterpress with a coarse screen to emphasize the rudeness of the indictment. Nairn, twenty years later, followed his old route, rephotographed his subjects and determined that there had not been a change for the better.

American eyes in these years were still cocked on what was being done in England, and in May 1961 *Horizon* magazine illustrated an article in which Peter Blake, editor of *Architectural Forum* criticized America's trashing of its landscape, with photographs that seemed to undercut Blake's argument, for the skill that had gone into pictures of situations that were clearly undesirable and the handsomeness of the reproduction made them interesting pictorially, and that made them seem almost all right. Hunt out the ugly and you will develop a taste for it, at which point it becomes picturesque. When Blake put together his subsequent book, *God's Own Junkyard* (1964), he made sure that the presentation had a down-to-earth factual manner that would not convert an ugly object into an art object. Indeed, now some of the pictures were by Blake himself. Though a critical photograph may (without a caption) be mistaken for an inept one, a clumsy picture can be the most convincingly critical, for how could it lie?

The most successfully critical photograph of all must have been one taken two years earlier by Lee Balterman at the dynamiting of one of Hellmuth, Yamasaki, and Leinweber's buildings at Pruitt-Igoe, St. Louis, Missouri, in 1962, a picture that seems to have proved almost as effective an argument against large housing developments as were the pictures taken in 1937 of the burning of the dirigible Hindenburg at Lakehurst, an effective argument against airships. The photograph, which demonstrated an American belief that architecture can be responsible for social problems (the obverse of the belief that it can solve them) and that, if buildings become slums, they should be punished for it, betrayed an American taste for the sublime. If its subject was too expensive and dangerous to become an art form, in subsequent years the companies that specialized in demolition recorded their work not only for their own records but to fill a wide demand for both stock motion picture footage and for still photographs of these events (174).

In the midfifties architectural photography seemed to provide a supple and varied language for showing new buildings, vernacular and historical build-

170 *YUKIO FUTAGAWA*

Kyoto, Jingo-ji, ca. 1961.
Courtesy the photographer.

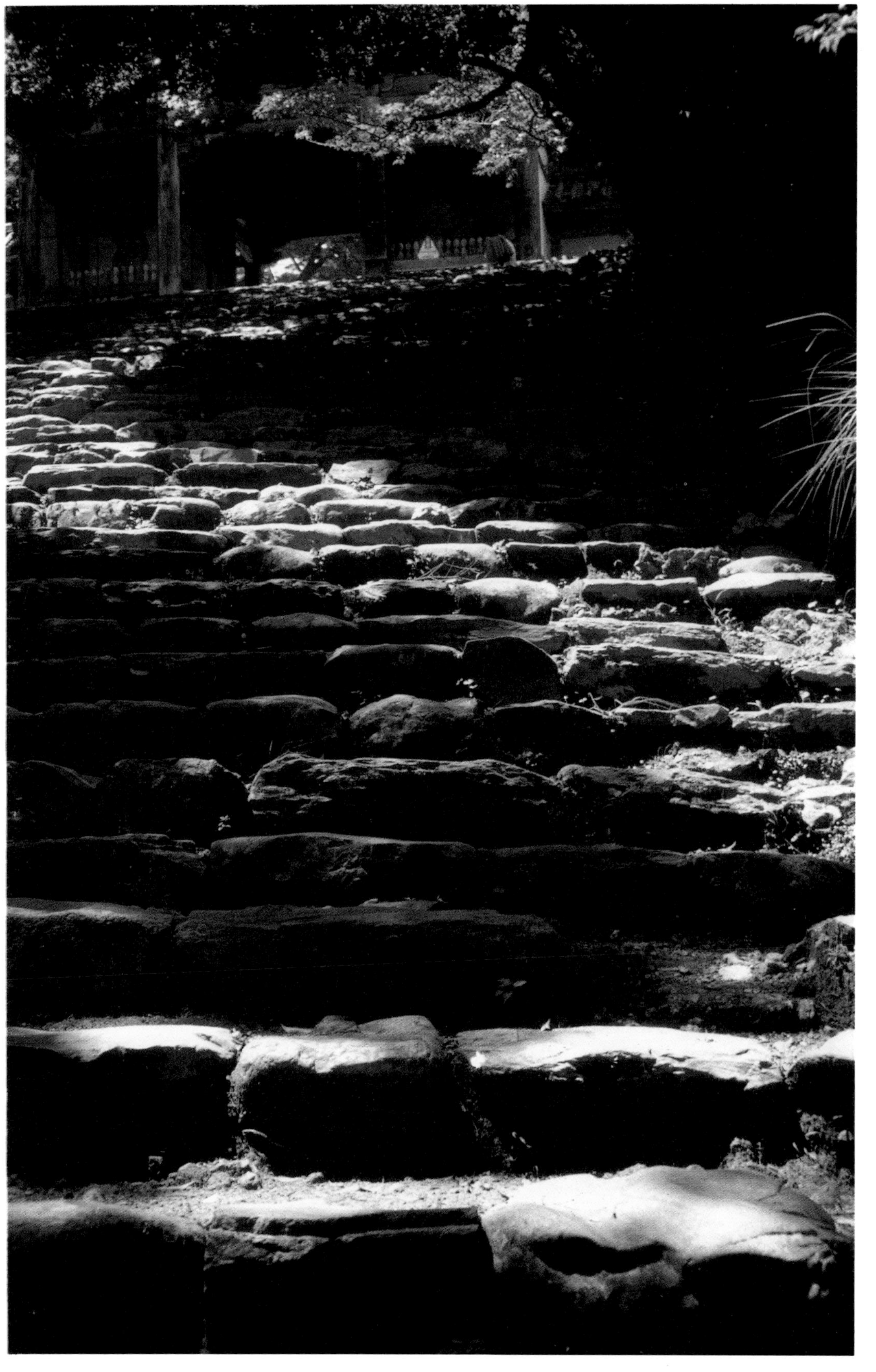

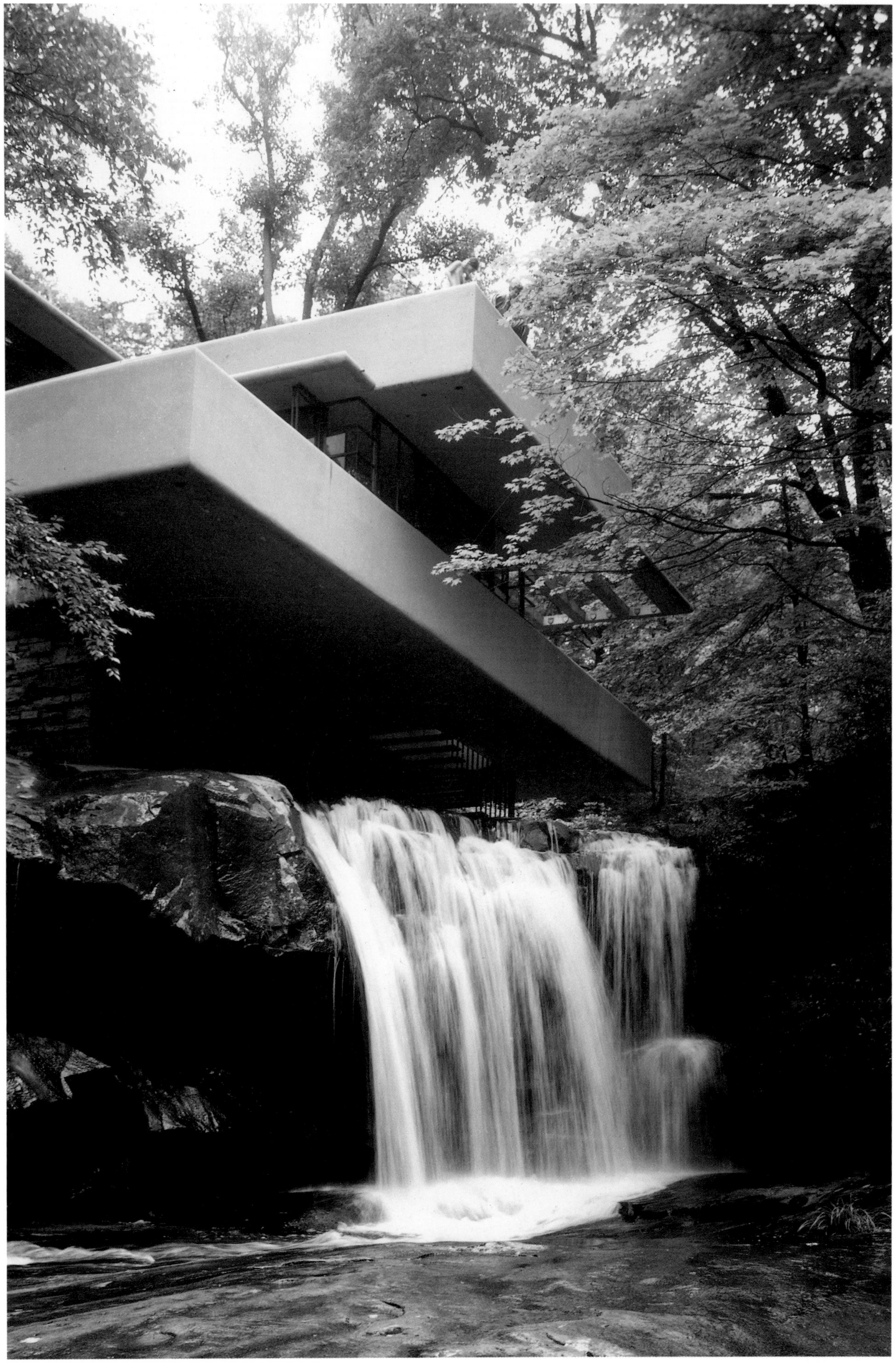

171 *Yukio Futagawa*

Bear Run, Fallingwater, ca. 1969.
Courtesy the photographer.

172 *Bill Hedrich*

Bear Run, Fallingwater, 1937.
Courtesy Hedrich-Blessing.

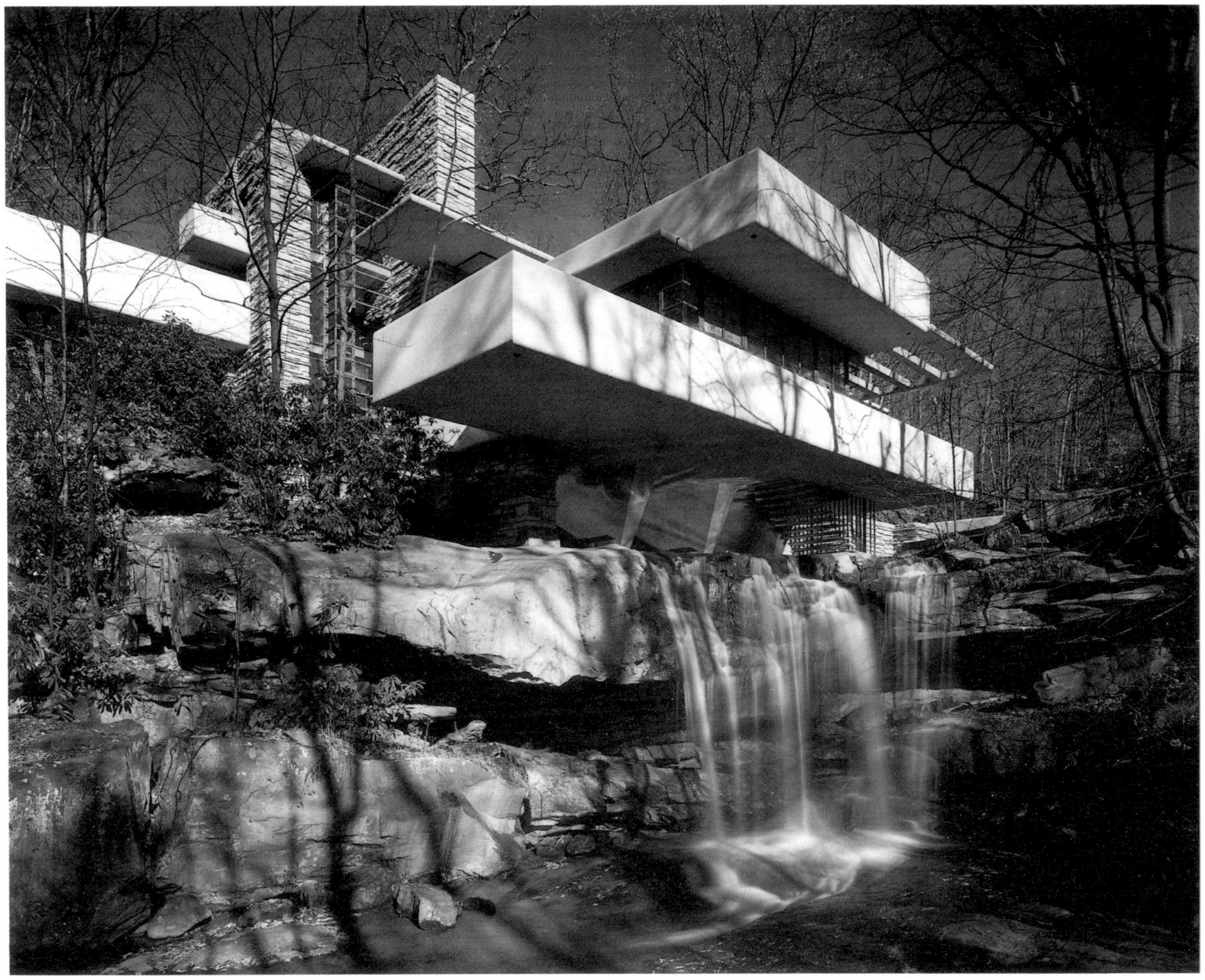

173 *Ian Nairn*

Northwich, billboards, 1956.
Courtesy Architectural Press, London.

174 Oklahoma City, destruction of Biltmore Hotel, 1977.
Controlled Demolition, Inc.

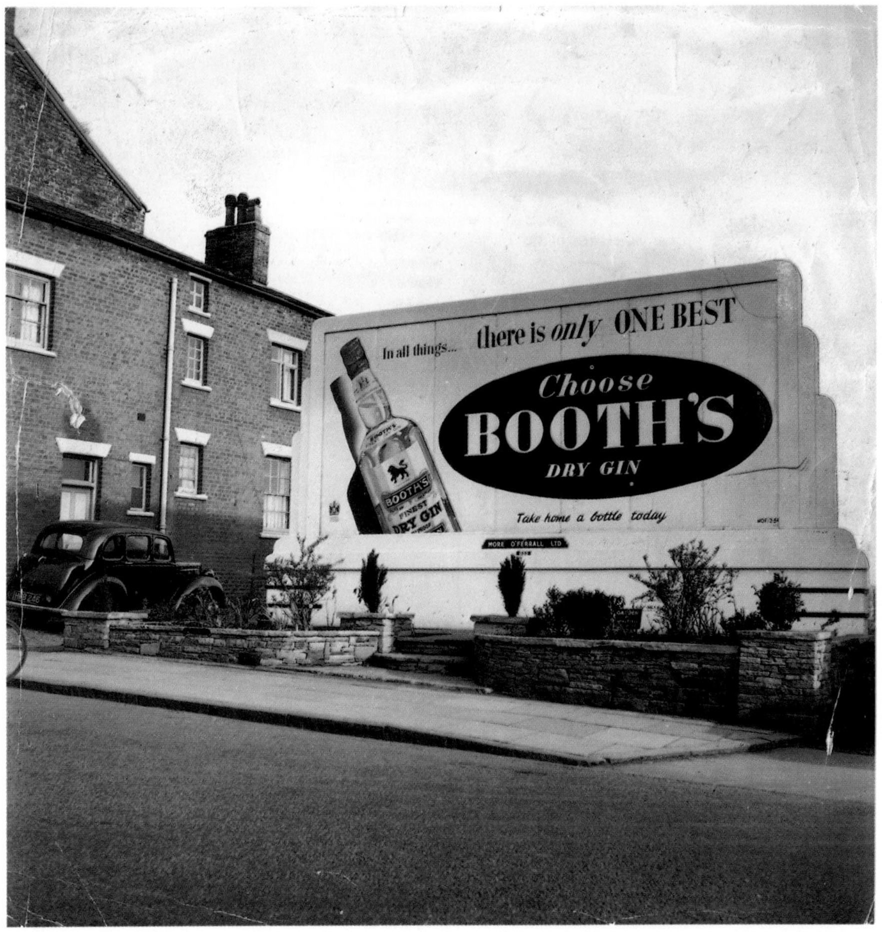

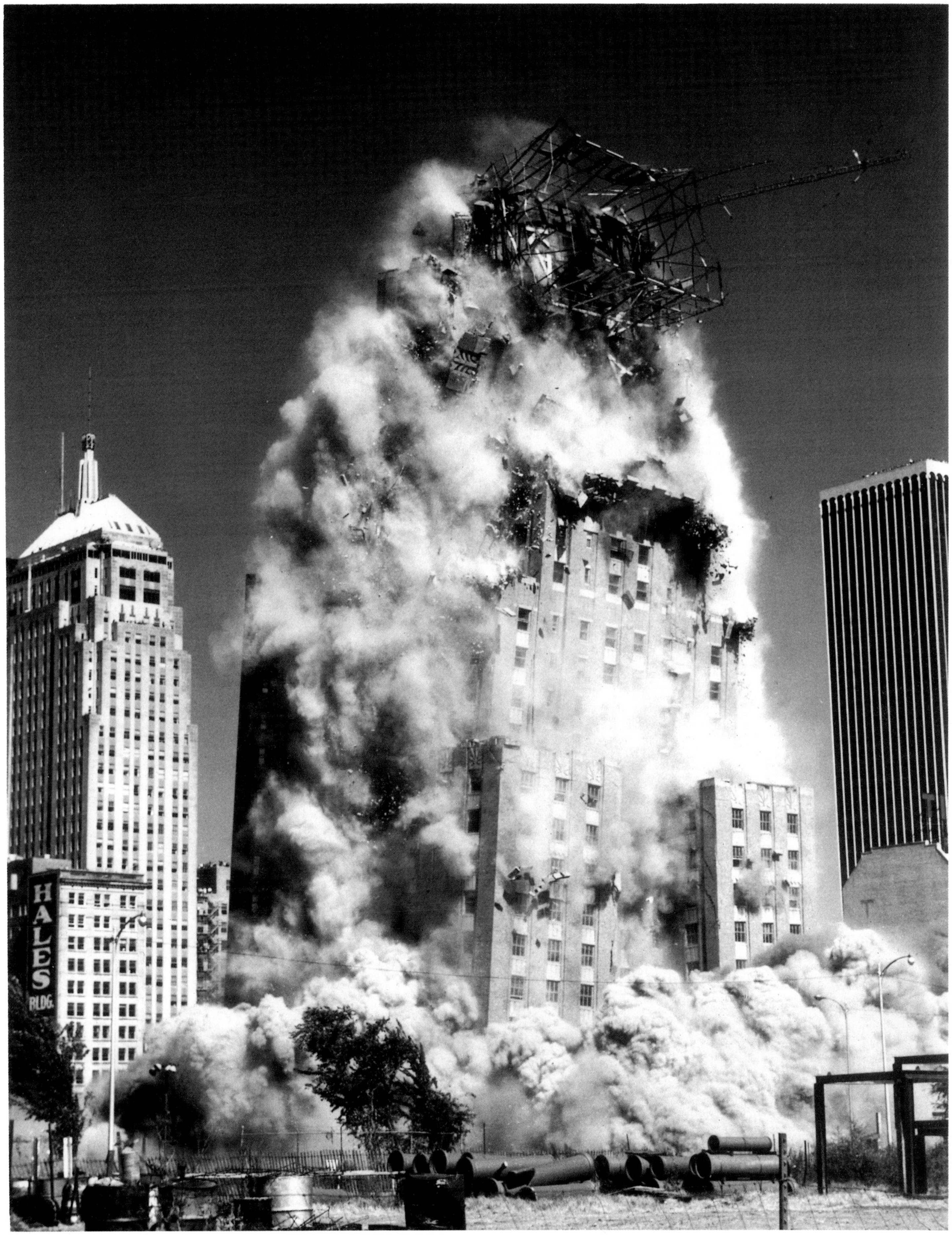
HALES
BLDG.

175 *Eric de Maré*

Windsor, Frogmore, Royal Dairy, 1969.
Courtesy Architectural Press, London.

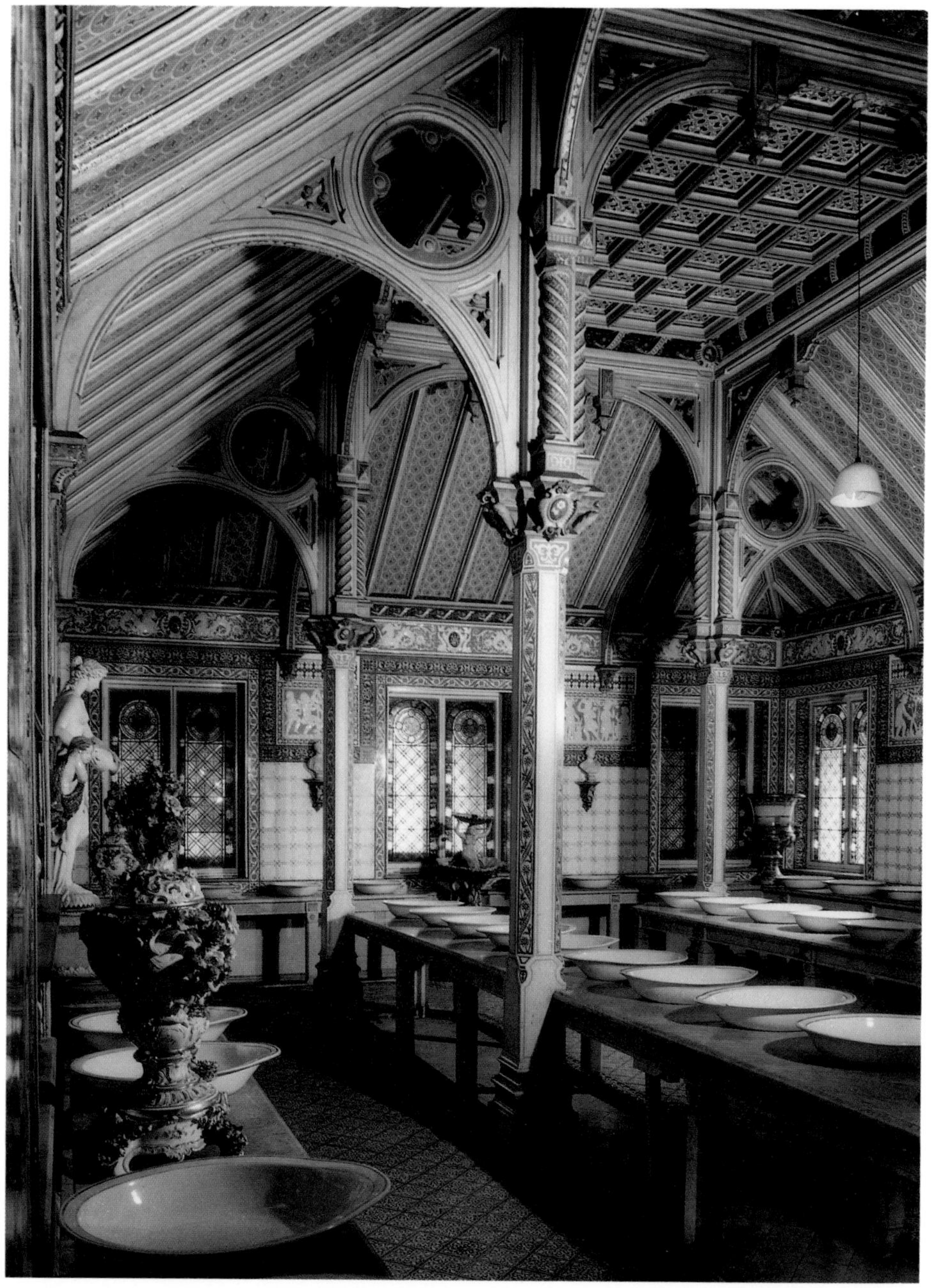

ings, and even bad buildings. By the end of the sixties it had come to seem that new architecture was being photographed only as well as one could expect, since skilled partisans of the architects were hired to take it, and that hostile photographs must inevitably come to justify their subjects—you couldn't keep Blake's "Junkyard" from becoming Venturi's "Almost All Right." Simultaneously vernacular and historical buildings escaped their compartmentalization and were becoming ever more numerous, rich, and varied.

Adjustments could still be made to the system, however. In 1969 and 1970 the *Architectural Review* decided to apply the skills of the photojournalist to architecture in a series of eight special issues called "Manplan," an attempt "to prepare for the . . . last third of the twentieth century . . . by reviewing the state of the nation in [the] areas of . . . architecture and planning." How different the imagery of "Manplan" was from that of the usual *Review* of apparent in the comparison of a picture by Tim Street-Porter (b. 1939) (a vertical version of which was used in the magazine) with one by Eric de Maré that was published in a non-"Manplan" issue in 1969. Both show interiors used for food processing. De Maré's is of the creamery of the royal dairy at Frogmore, Windsor, and Street-Porter's of an air tent housing the butchery department of a cannery (175, 176). Both bring significant objects close to the camera, the nearest separating basin in one picture, the ribs of a butchered animal in the other. De Maré, however, has used a bigger camera and has lit his interior to show its ceramic decorations and painting ceiling. Street-Porter has used a wide-angle lens as much to put the bones on the viewer's lap as to show the form of the tent. He has used the tool of the photojournalist of the time, a 35mm camera, and has included the black edges of the frame in his print because not to do so would have been euphemistic—it would have suggested that he had toyed with and improved on the picture he originally took (in a way that would have seemed wholly reasonable or even necessary to a Walker Evans or Ezra Stoller). The butchers appear to be doing precisely what they would have been doing had the photographer not turned up, though it is quite possible that the two who are talking in the middle distance were asked by the photographer to stand there and that he also asked the nearby butcher to resume a task he had already finished. It is this photograph's manner to say that this is the way the air tent is actually used, this is what it is like in it, whereas it is the manner of the de Maré to show us under the photographer's artificial lights some architectural facts about the creamery. But in fact the distinctions between the two are not really so clear.

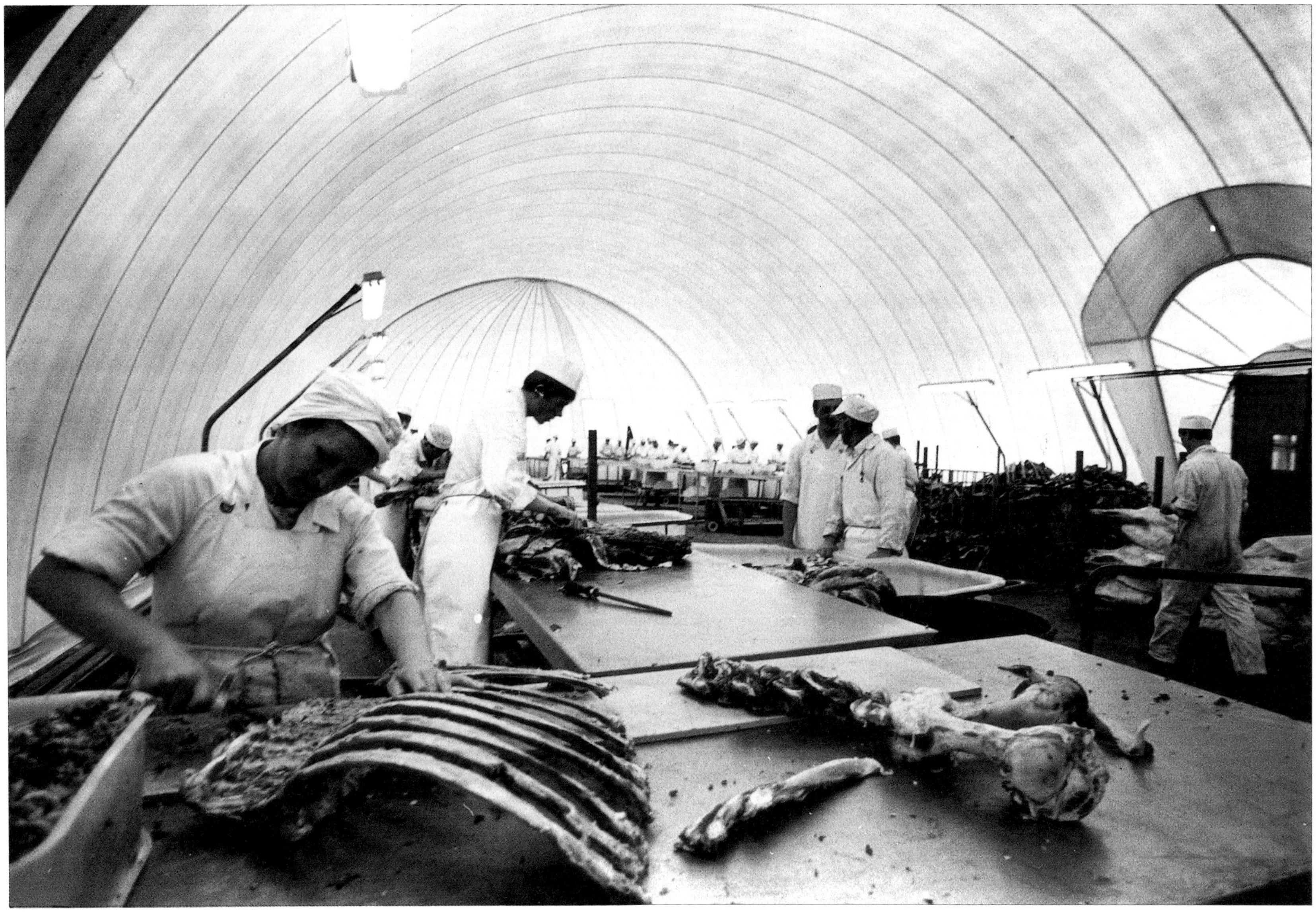

176 *Tim Street-Porter*

Irvine New Town, Eglinton Park, butchery department, 1969. Courtesy Architectural Press, London.

177 *Patrick Ward*

Bedfordshire, Woburn Abbey, ca. 1970.
Courtesy Architectural Press, London.

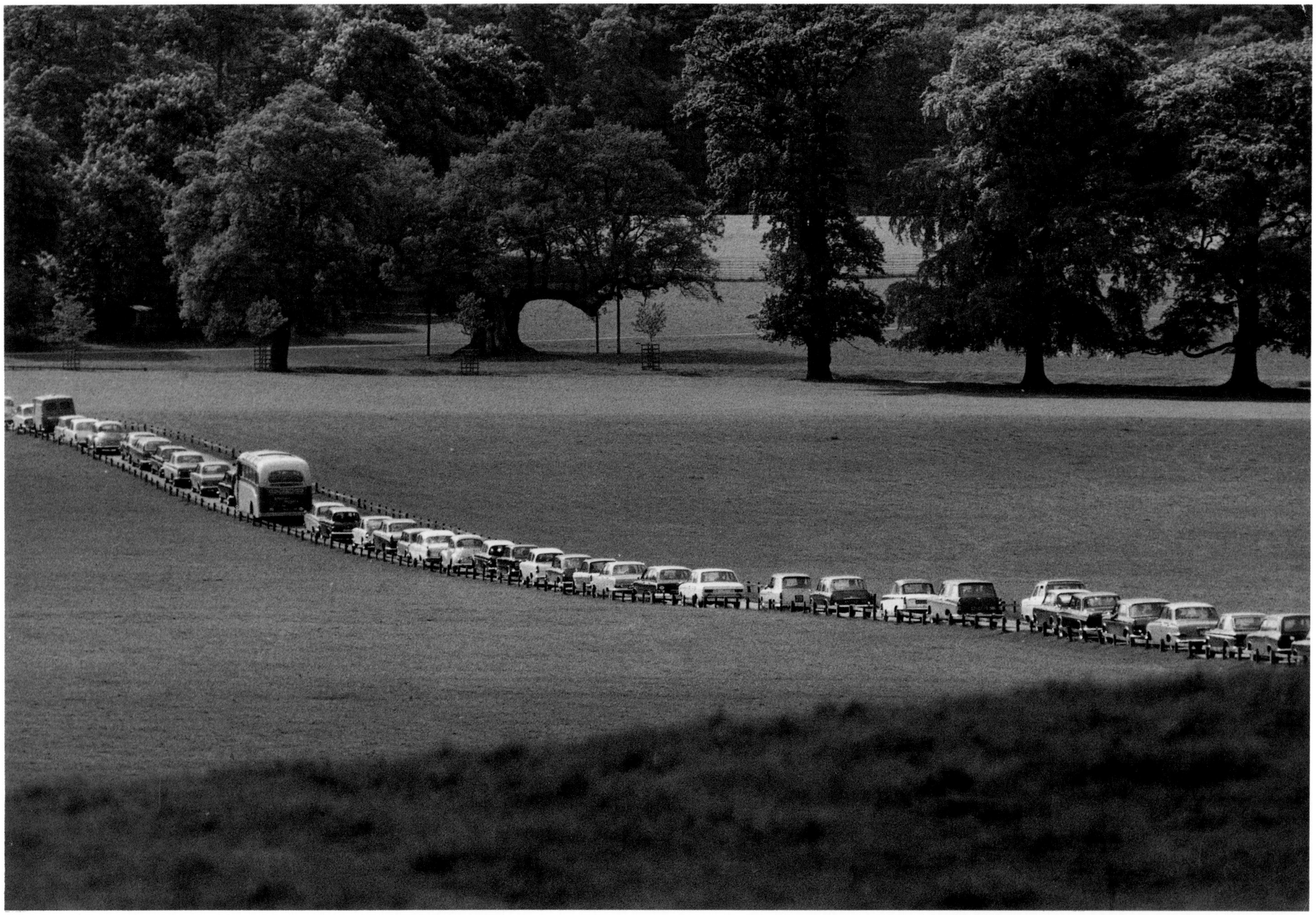

The "Manplan" guest photographers brought with them a consistent manner of using short (wide-angle) lenses to thrust the inhabitants of their congested world toward the viewer and long (telephoto) lenses to show the congestion of buildings and traffic. In a remarkable picture by Patrick Ward, one of a set made to illustrate "one month of British frustration," the automobile—no longer a symbol of functionalism and modernity, now the principal ingredient of photographs of urban congestion—is shown lined up waiting to enter the grounds of Woburn Abbey, to whose parkland they are juxtaposed but whose trees still retain their lyrical meaning in architectural imagery (177).

Part IV

1970 to the Present

Left to their own devices photographers and editors would have finished the seventies much as they had begun them and gone into the eighties fine tuning a language of photojournalism that had reached maturity in the 1960s. But two influences made this impossible. One was the return of artist-photographers to architecture as a subject and the sudden market for their pictures in galleries and museums. The other, and in the long run more significant, was a successful pressure on magazines by advertisers, their pressure supported by improvements in reproduction technology, to use more color pictures on editorial pages. Not only to advertisers but to architects and photographers as well, color was to prove seductive.

Black-and-white pictures were still the center of attention in the first half of the seventies. In Britain the example of "Manplan" led to a more crowded look (America by this time no longer had an eye cocked on England). In pictures spaces looked smaller and more cluttered, and people, looking unposed, often appeared in them. An interior space would be arranged to look much as it would have appeared in use, like the photograph by Richard Einzig (1932–1980) of the studio at Camden Town (1974) designed by Georgie Wolton which suggests its occupant has just stepped away from his desk (178). The display of objects in the foreground, especially the glasses, harks back to Claude Gravot's view of the Villa Savoye, and the sunlight entering the room is exploited (as Ezra Stoller had in photographing Philip Johnson's house) to bring the brightness of the room into balance with the exterior view of neighboring London buildings. Despite its descent from "Manplan" pictures made with hand-held cameras, this is anything but a casual shot, as the top of the sliding window and the container for pencils tell us by the way they almost touch the top, left, and bottom edges of the picture or as the space between the raised window edge and the building across the street also tell us. Not that Einzig always showed small and cluttered spaces. In the case of an exterior view of Howell, Killick, Partridge & Amis's College of Estate Management at the University of Reading (1973) he attempted a different effect, using a gnarled tree in the foreground to highlight the picturesque setting (without using it as an excuse for a vertical picture) (179).

In America photographers adapted their perspectives to suit the needs of changing architecture, each photographer doing so in his own manner. When Morley Baer took Willis Polk's Polk-Williams house (1892) for the book *Bay Area Houses* (1976), one of his pictures was of the living room seen from the gallery (180). Baer turned his camera down to make an untipped bird's-eye view that serves a clear descriptive purpose without in any way evoking the heady excitement of a twenties or thirties picture. Ezra Stoller was presented with a somewhat similar situation, an area of the living room open to view from the upper floors, in Richard Meier's Douglas house (1973). But Stoller looked directly down two floors from just inside the entrance to produce a head-on view of the floor below (181). Stoller's tendency to turn to wholly (rather than almost) head-on views is characteristic and one of the pleasures to be had from his pictures, just as it is characteristic of Baer, and one of his virtues, to bend only to the individual needs of a setting.

Those who photographed "for themselves" never entirely abandoned architecture as a subject (provided it seemed redeemingly ancient). Paul Strand included it in a series of books that brought *Time in New England*'s idyllic view to other parts of the world. Among the products of younger photographers is a view, taken in 1967, by Paul Caponigro (b. 1932) that juxtaposes a vine-covered tree trunk to one of the sarsens of the prehistoric Avebury Stone Circle in Wiltshire, England (182). The impassivity of the stone, the contortions of the ivy set close to the camera, and the pastoral element of cattle grazing in the distance give the picture a special emotional tension. Like Norman McGrath's picture of Penn Station where the subject is the untimely destruction of a mammoth cornice of a bygone era (whether that era is of Imperial Rome or of the more recent Empire State), the combination of a structure and its circumstances has lead the photographer to produce an elegiac picture.

Working in Germany since the late 1950s and later to some extent in Britain, Bernd (b. 1931) and Hilla Becher (b. 1934), whose interest was industrial archaeology, had taken late nineteenth-century and early twentieth-century watertowers, colliery winding gear, and wooden cooling towers. A selection of these appeared in the *Architectural Review* in 1967 and 1968. They also photographed lime kilns, blast furnaces, gas holders, silos, warehouses, and half-timbered houses. All of these they took under generally overcast skies or in the hazy sunlight of midcontinental industrial zones and from as many as eight viewpoints, each set including a head-on view of the facade and one view toward each corner. Their stylistic approach remained so consistent that their pictures of half-timbered houses taken in the late fifties are indistinguishable from the ones taken in the midseventies, when a book of their pictures of *Framework Houses of the Siegen Industrial Region* (1977) was in preparation. A head-on picture taken in 1972 of a house from Büschergrund (built in 1800) shows the characteristic look of the pictures (183). The Bechers's concern with

178 *Richard Einzig*

Camden Town, studio, 1974.
Courtesy Richard Bryant.

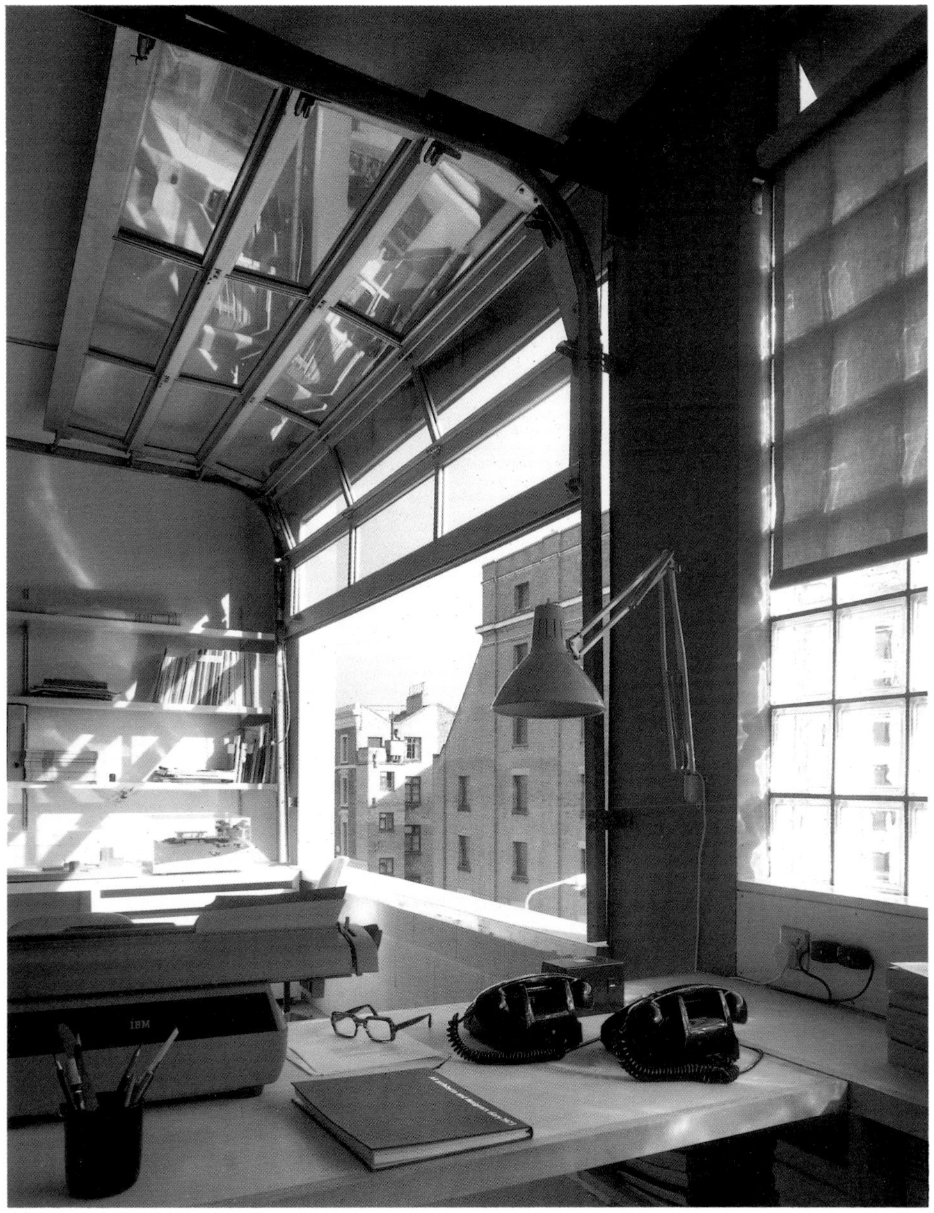

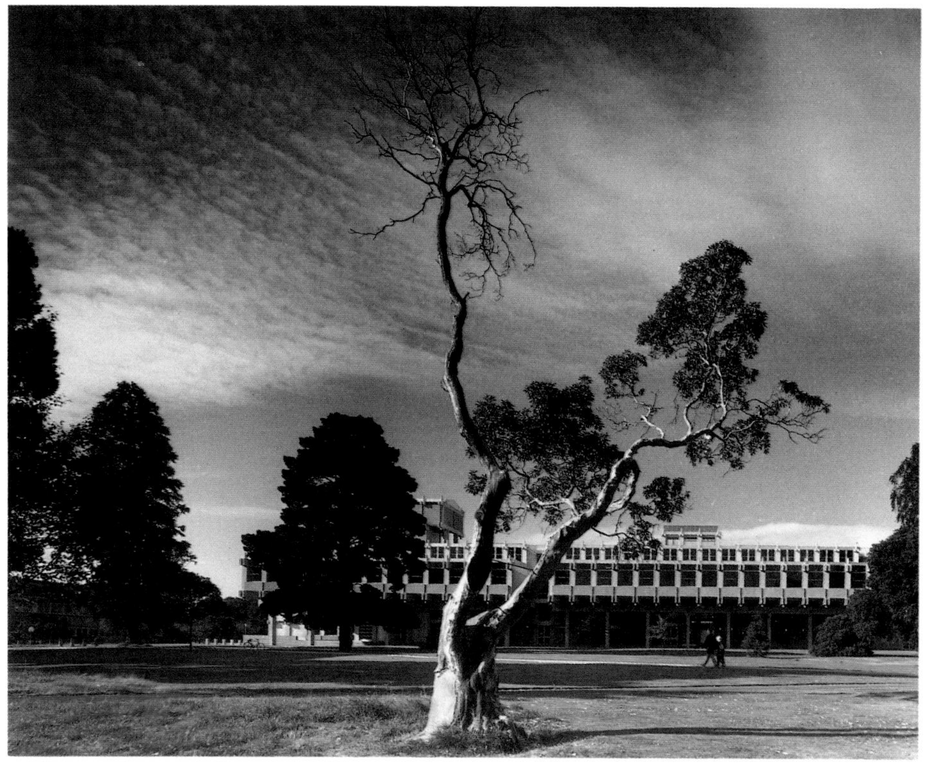

179 *Richard Einzig*

University of Reading, 1973.
Courtesy Richard Bryant.

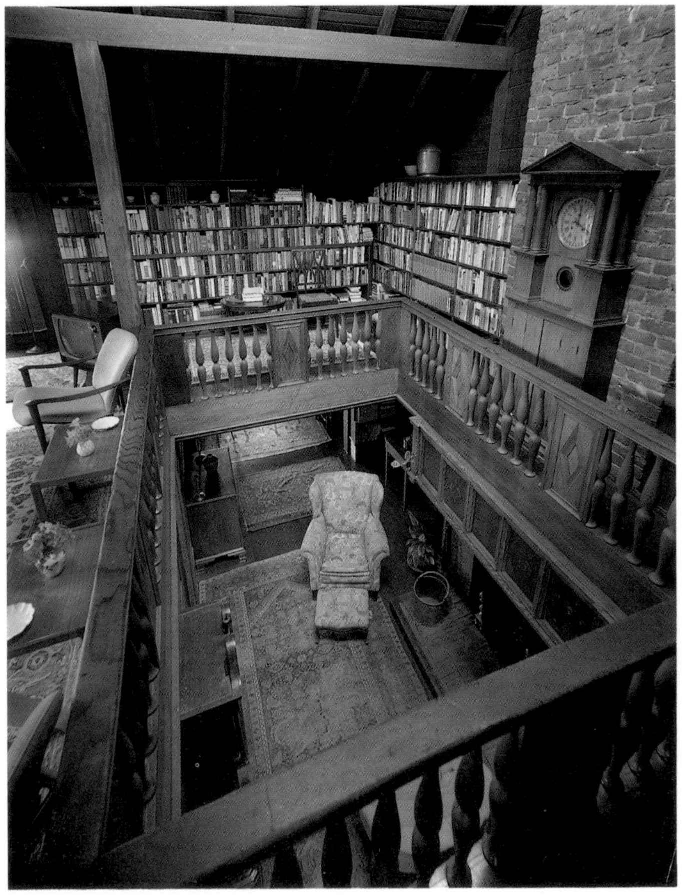

180 *Morley Baer*

San Francisco, Polk-Williams house, 1975.
Courtesy the photographer.

181 *Ezra Stoller*

Harbor Springs, Michigan, Douglas house, 1974.
Courtesy the photographer.

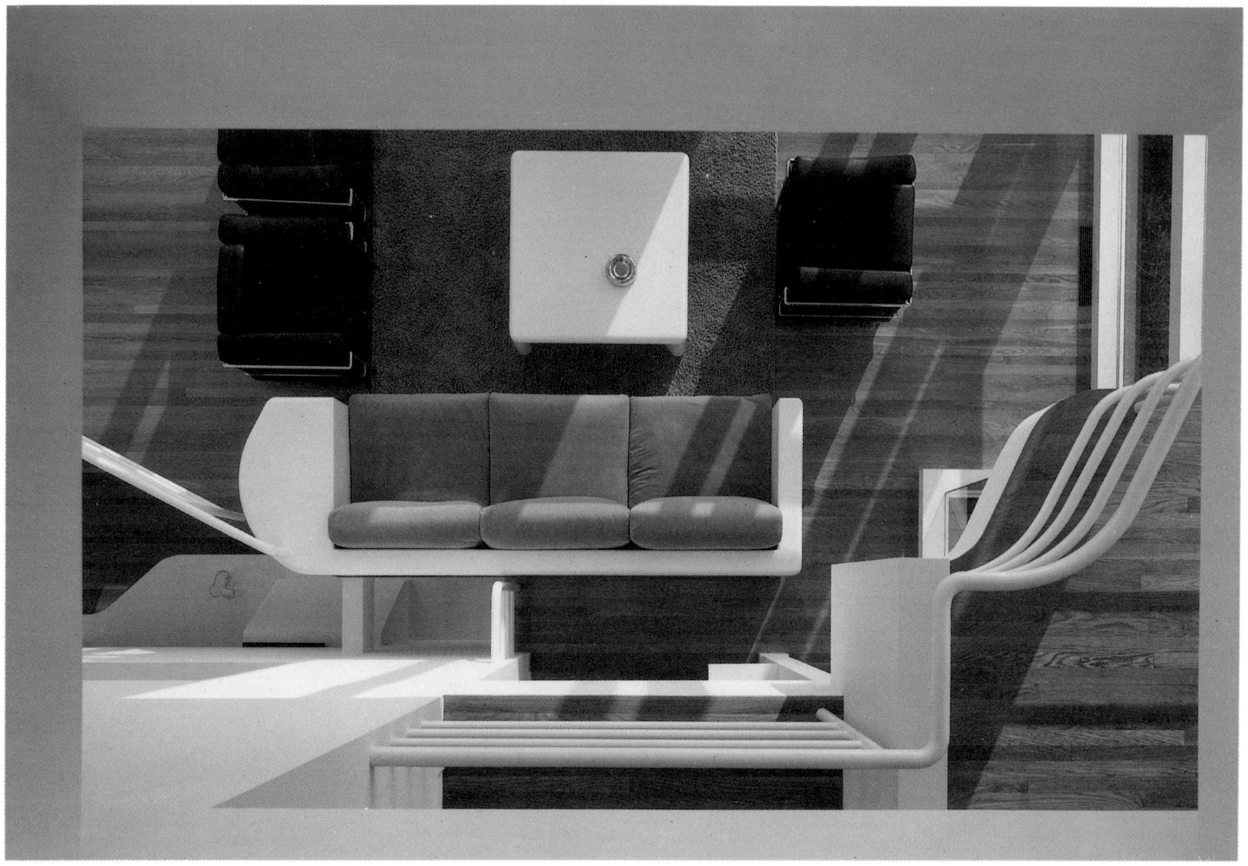

perspective may well remind us of the techniques of the Königliche Preussische Messbildanstalt. Their interest in industrial forms also is in a German tradition for many of the same structures had appeared in Werner Lindner and Georg Steinmetz's *Die Ingenieurbauen in ihrer guten Gestaltung* (1923). The pictures the Bechers show in this book are interesting both singly and in groups, where the effect of comparable facades of different houses can be mesmerizing. Such sets of pictures had an appeal in the seventies to both collectors of conceptual art and younger American photographers. The latter may have misinterpreted the Bechers's work as being quite as banal as that of Edward Ruscha (b. 1937) whose sets of pictures, such as his *Thirty-four Parking Lots in Los Angeles* (1967), also influenced young American photographers.

The subject of new buildings was not so wholeheartedly embraced by photographers of the seventies as that of older architecture. New buildings could be shown only if kept at arm's length. Lewis Baltz (b. 1945) took pictures in an industrial park at Santa Ana in 1974, in one of which scrawny trees are juxtaposed to a head-on view of a one-story office building (184). The trees have apparently been planted to close off access to a short path leading to a central door. Trees and building suggest parallels such as Walker Evans's billboards and rowhouses. By carefully identifying his banal subjects by orientation, company and division names, and street address, Baltz underlines his own disinterested stance toward it.

Pictures by Lewis Baltz and Bernd and Hilla Becher were included in an exhibition at the International Museum of Photography at George Eastman House in 1975 called "New Topographics: Photographs of a Man-Altered Landscape." In the catalog to the show William Jenkins, quoting Frank Gohlke, another photographer in the show, summarized the philosophy of the photographers included as maintaining a sense of neutrality in the way the edges of the picture function—that is, they approached their subject matter with "an essentially *passive* frame." Another participant quoted in the catalog, Joe Deal, offered some further insights:

> By being at a greater distance from my subject matter it became difficult to significantly alter the angle of view or organization of the image by a step or two in any direction; . . . the point of view and distance from the subject allowed an acceptance by the lens of a greater amount of contextual information without allowing too great a dominance of one object over another.

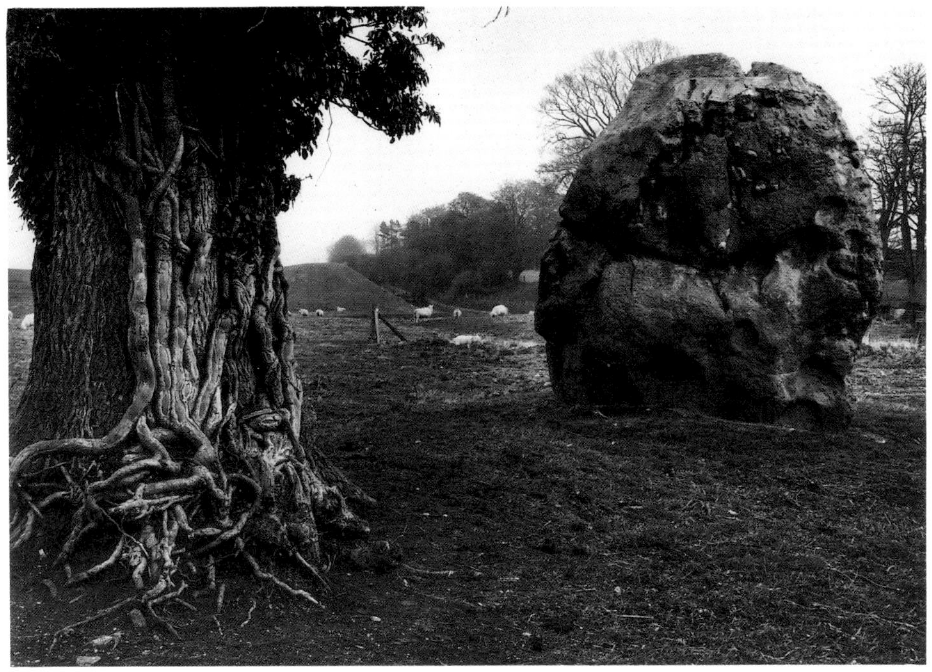

182 *PAUL CAPONIGRO*

Wiltshire, Avebury Stone, 1967.
Museum of Modern Art, New York.

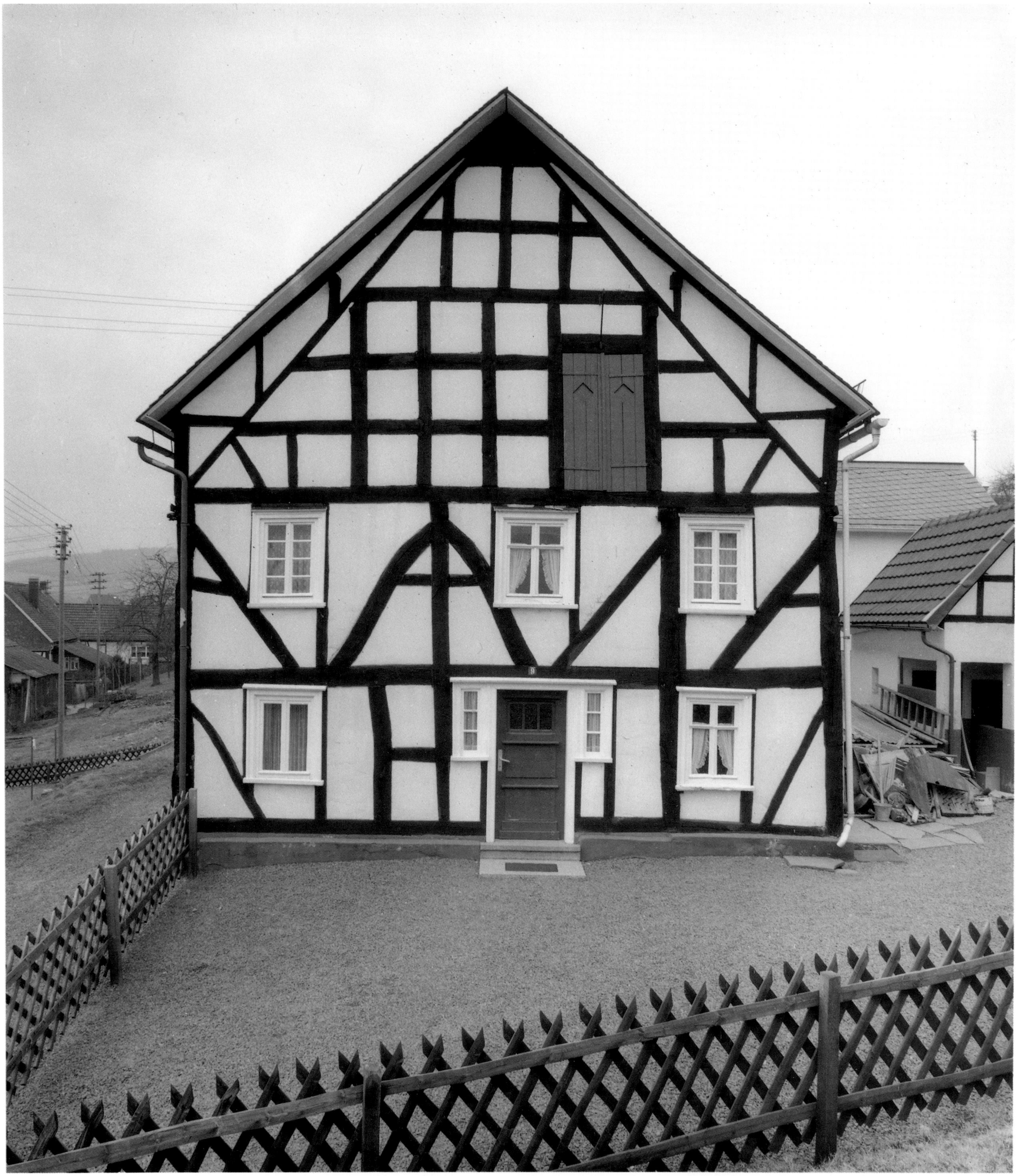

183 *Bernd and Hilla Becher*

Büschergrund, Büscherstrasse 9, 1972.
Courtesy the photographers.

184 *Lewis Baltz*

Santa Ana, east wall, Business Systems Division, Pertec, 1881 Langley, 1974.
Courtesy Castelli Graphics, New York.

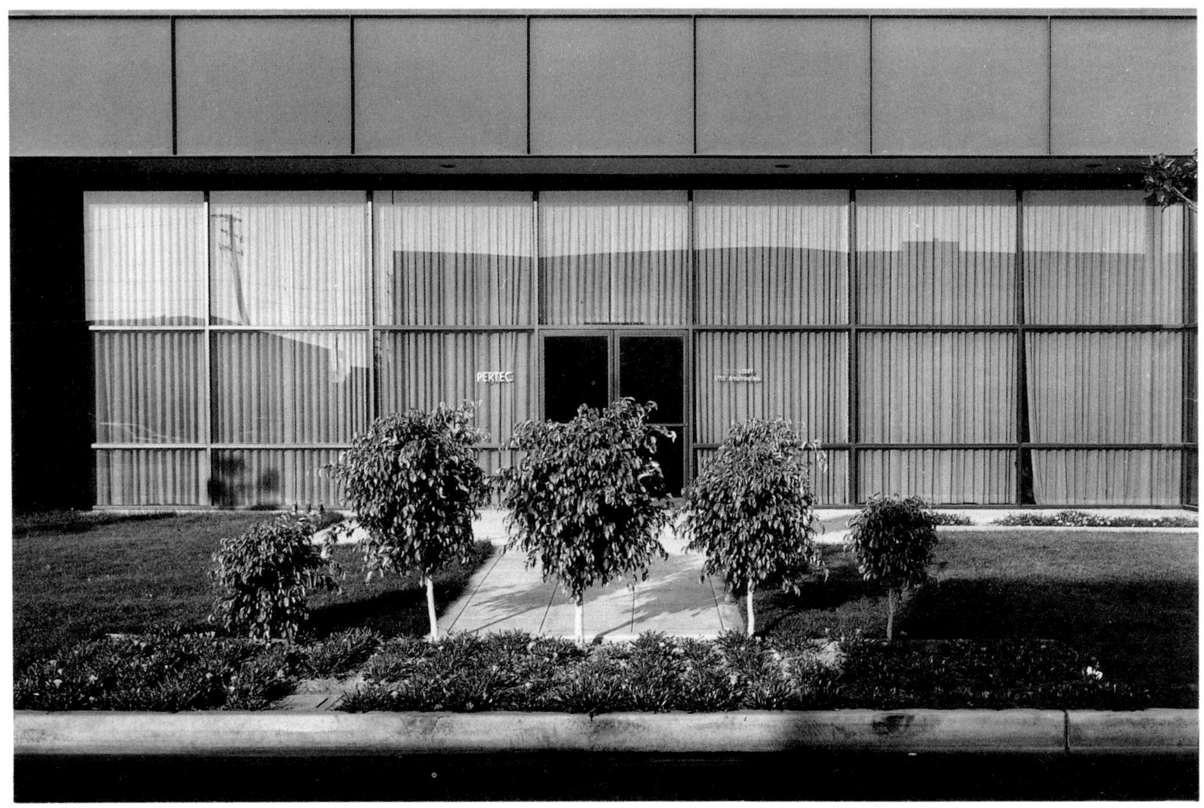

Four of the photographers who exhibited in New Topographics were among twenty-four hired by Joseph E. Seagram and Sons, Inc., to take pictures of American courthouses for the occasion of the U.S. Bicentennial. Some of these buildings were major works of architecture, many clearly deserved recording, a few were crushingly uninteresting, that is, desirably banal. Although courthouses were the subject of the undertaking, even—or perhaps especially—where buildings were of considerable interest, many of the photographers were shy of them, as though it could be dangerous to be interested in one's subject or to present it as of direct interest. They characteristically introduced an intentionally uneasy and unbalanced relationship between building, environment, and light—an imbalance that often made exterior views seem cluttered (like contemporary British interiors but more distractingly so). This approach was, however, productive in a picture by Nicholas Nixon (b. 1947) taken from the high vantage point of one of the new skyscrapers that were transforming downtown Boston (185). It looks from above what used to be Scollay Square toward the Back Bay, though the nominal subject is George A. Clough's mansarded courthouse (1894) at center. The picture includes far more. It shows old Boston cluttered with new buildings and relationships between parts of the city that usually remain unreconciled in the minds of Bostonians—given Boston's streetplan—and gives much the same sort of pleasure provided by nineteenth-century and earlier bird's-eye views of towns and cities.

This wary approach to major architecture could also produce pictures whose subjects had been badly and offhandedly lit or whose subjects were almost completely obscured. Frank Golhke's (b. 1942) picture of the City-County Municipal Building (1906), Hennepin County, Minneapolis, shows it from side to side and from bottom to top (almost) without either explaining the building's overall form or its detailed substance (186). The light on the building at the moment he chose to take it does evoke a time of day and year but fails to light the building articulately. Again the nominal subject of a picture by William Clift (b. 1944) is Henry Singleton, Robert S. Mitchell, and William Rumbold's Old St. Louis County Courthouse (1845, 1863) which we see obscurely reflected in the glass curtain wall of Hellmuth, Obata & Kassabaum's Equitable Building (1971) (187). The balance between subject and ambiance in this photograph has tipped to the point where the subject is allowed only barely to appear, and the environment is there not to tell us the photographer was moved by his subject (not to say critical of it or a partisan of it) but for its own banal sake. In many of the Seagram pictures we sense a laudable intention (whether achievable or not) of showing buildings as they look in the litter of their contexts, but here Clift demonstrates inadvertently that a picture that aims to be disinterested can seem self-absorbed instead.

Another photographer involved in the Seagram project was Stephen Shore (b. 1947). Shore also photographed for Venturi & Rauch, Steven Izenour, and Denise Scott-Brown's exhibition "Signs of Life: Symbols of the American City" at the Renwick Gallery of the National Collection of Fine Arts (1976). A picture of a bungalow juxtaposed to Cesar Pelli's Pacific Design Center (1975), reproduced in the catalog, shows imbalance used to elegant effect. Shore gave a banal, vernacular building pride of place over a big new building that one would have expected to be the primary object of interest. Neither is given short shrift, and because the camera lens was a normal one (rather than a telephoto lens that could juxtapose two things that were in actuality far apart) the apposition, like one of Atget's, is clearly valid.

These younger photographers were also interested in ways that sets of pictures might be tied together structurally. In 1980 in an exhibition and book, *St. Louis and the Arch*, Joel Meyerowitz (b. 1938) demonstrated that it was possible to organize a topographic book at least in part on distant views of one dominating structure, the pictures forming something very loosely like a panoramic series with camera pointing toward the axis of rotation. (He had already demonstrated two years before in photographing for the exhibition "American Images: New York by Twenty Contemporary Photographers," sponsored by the American Telephone and Telegraph Company, that such an organization used exclusively could seem lazily conceived.) In 1982 to 1983 Jim Dow (b. 1942), another photographer who had taken part in the Seagram county courthouse project, took American and National League baseball fields in the form of rudimentary but precise panoramic sets, three pictures to a field, on eight-by-ten color negative film.

Many of the photographers who worked on these exhibitions used precisely the sort of large camera that earlier architectural photographers had stopped using after the 1950s because there no longer seemed an advantage to its size. The younger photographers used these big cameras—and announced that they used them—partly to be able to say they used nothing new and special, partly to be seen to use something very special indeed, the sort of camera that Walker Evans and Eugène Atget (not to say virtually every other architectural or commercial photographer up into the 1950s) had used. Many—Shore, Dow, and

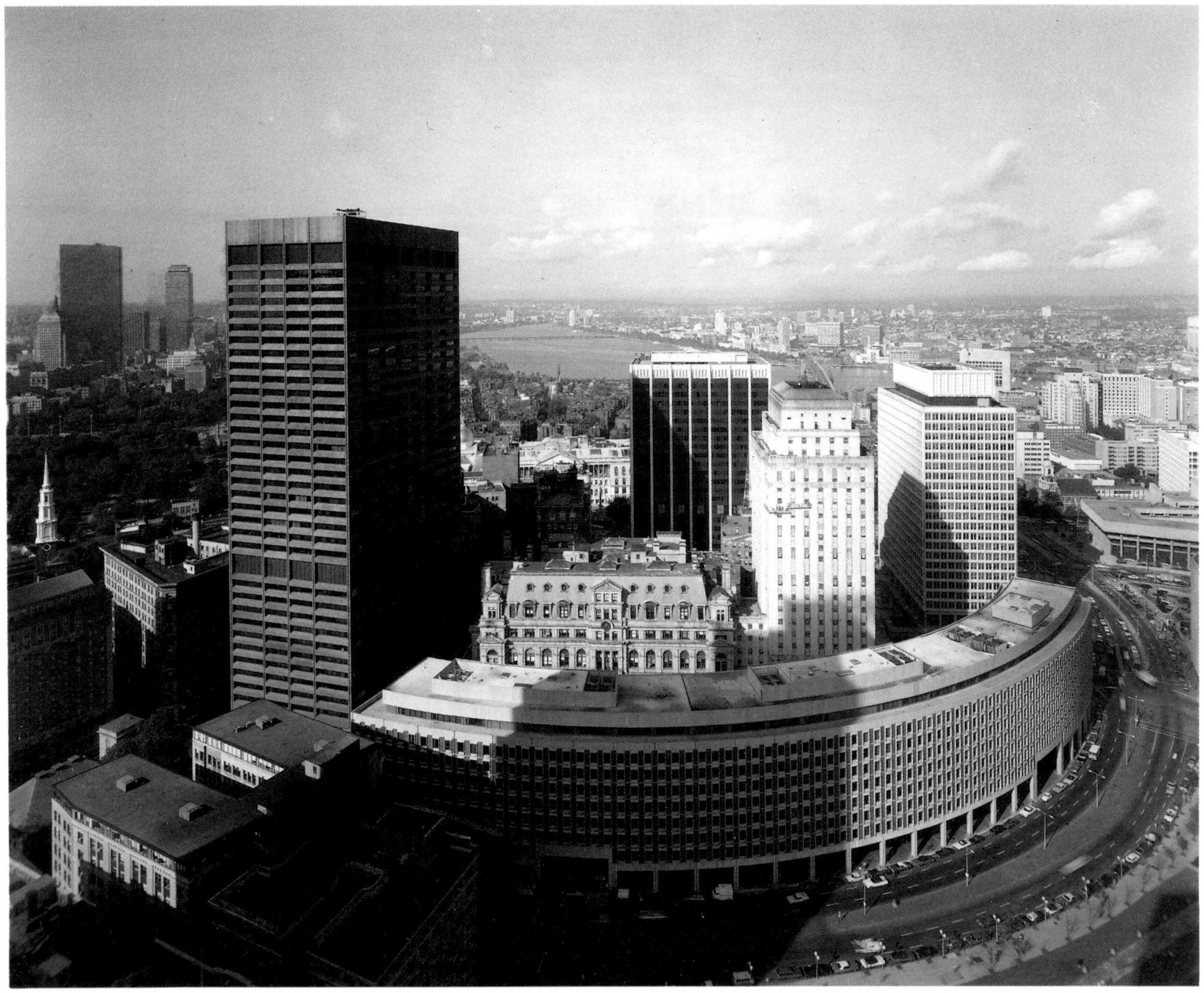

185 *Nicholas Nixon*

Boston, Suffolk County Courthouse, 1975.
Seagram County Court House Archives, Library of Congress.

186 *Frank Gohlke*

Minneapolis, City-County Municipal Building, Hennepin County, 1975.
Seagram County Court House Archives, Library of Congress.

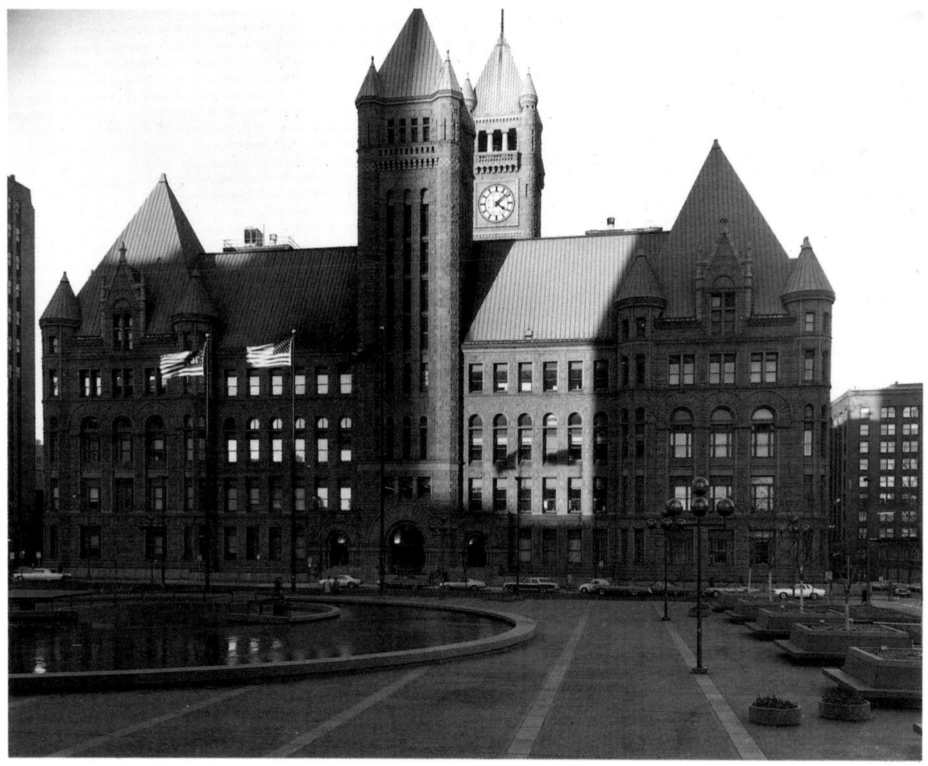

187 *William Clift*

St. Louis, Old St. Louis County Courthouse reflected in the Equitable Building, ca. 1975–1976.
Seagram County Court House Archives, Library of Congress.

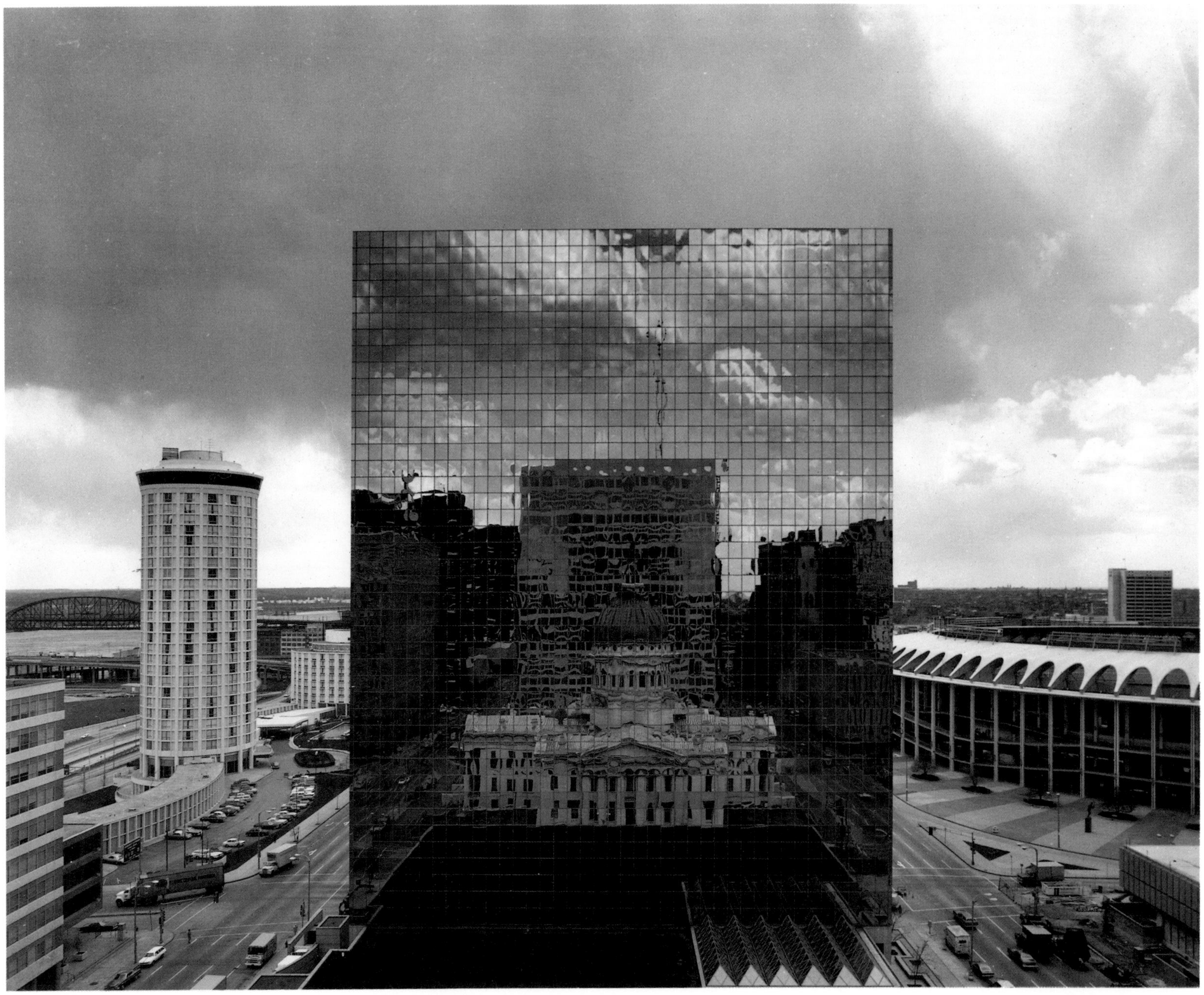

Meyerowitz among them—used modern color negative film with these cameras, and they paid a high price in practicality in the process. Meyerowitz has written that his exposures might often be between four and ten minutes long (partly to increase depth of field with his large camera, partly to make up for the limitations of his older lens).

Technical development is clearly present in photography, but technical progress is harder to argue for. A director of the Eastman Kodak Research Laboratories, L. Jack Thomas, has been quoted as saying that "film speeds have been doubling about every ten years," yet photographers in the first decade of this century were able to freeze the motion of pedestrians that a modern architectural photographer would not expect to be able to stop. And most productive photographers have always seemed wisely content to stick to equipment and techniques that were current when they began their careers.

At the beginning of the 1970s, thanks to the use of smaller cameras and faster black-and-white films, magazine photographers were able to include unposed people in virtually any architectural photograph; at the end of the seventies they were using color film that had a fraction of the speed of black-and-white film, and they were "bracketing" exposures. If they repeated a picture on four sheets of film at four different lens openings to make sure they ended up with one correct exposure, the chance that the picture with the best arrangement of pedestrians and vehicles in it would also be the best exposed was only one out of four.

For each picture they took they might typically expose a set of films that would allow them to provide a transparency to a journal and black-and-white and color prints and color slides to the architect. Add delays caused by the passing of clouds across the sun and by the surges of pedestrian and vehicular traffic caused by stoplights, and at that point a picture was likely to take longer to make than a daguerreotype or calotype had taken in the first days of photography. Thus color formed a trap.

Photographers fell into still another trap, for part of their new skill with color film lay in the reconciling, by the use of multiple exposures, of different kinds of light (fluorescent, incandescent, and daylight), that were less compatible on their films than they were to the eye. Their energies applied to this complex procedure could at best only result in pictures that looked unremarkable.

The use of color pictures became virtually universal, in part because the technology of color reproduction improved while printers lowered the quality of their black-and-white reproductions and in part because color was a seductive medium that advertisers encouraged journals to use on their editorial pages. In the late seventies and early eighties its use seems to have been most successful, not where the materials of a building were either brightly or subtly colored but where color film could distinguish between special qualities of light.

In a picture by Balthazar Korab (b. 1926) of Caudill Rowlett Scott's Indiana Bell Telephone Company Switching Center (1978) at Columbus, Indiana, the special quality of the color original, here seen in black-and-white, is the difference between the light coming directly from the blue sky behind the building and that reflected in the glass curtain wall (188). The careful placement of the reflected church works effectively in both the color version and the black-and-white. In a head-on picture of Cesar Pelli's Winter Garden (1977) at the Rainbow Center at Niagara Falls Norman McGrath accepted (perforce) in the color version very errant rendering of the pavement and bollard illumination in the foreground as compared to that in the building itself (189). It is a bright greenish blue, and this makes the picture a more informative statement than if the light were more accurately shown.

In the same years, partly because of hard times, architects turned increasingly to designing interiors, and taking pictures of them became an attractive specialty to photographers. One of the more skillful of these specialists was Jaime Ardiles-Arce (b. 1939) who, with his lights shining up through plant leaves and with lens characteristically thrust next to chairs (or pillows) and plants, could leave his own mark on even an interior as modest as that of the Michael Schaible apartment (190). With his lights, plants, and pillows he was able to create spaces that one was convinced may never have existed.

But the most effective role for color pictures seems to have been in showing ephemeral light. A black-and-white picture of the John Hancock Building in Boston by Harry Cobb of I. M. Pei's & Partners was among a set that Steve Rosenthal (b. 1940) made for the *AIA Journal*, most of them in color, on days when a late sun shone past clouds (191). It shows the building from the vicinity of the Massachusetts Turnpike at an instant when the afternoon sun, shining under heavy overcast, has just started to reflect off the building's south facade.

But the evocative sense of ephemeral light that color photographs can give does not survive translation into black and white. As reproduced in this book, pictures can only illustrate other qualities that in their transience are compara-

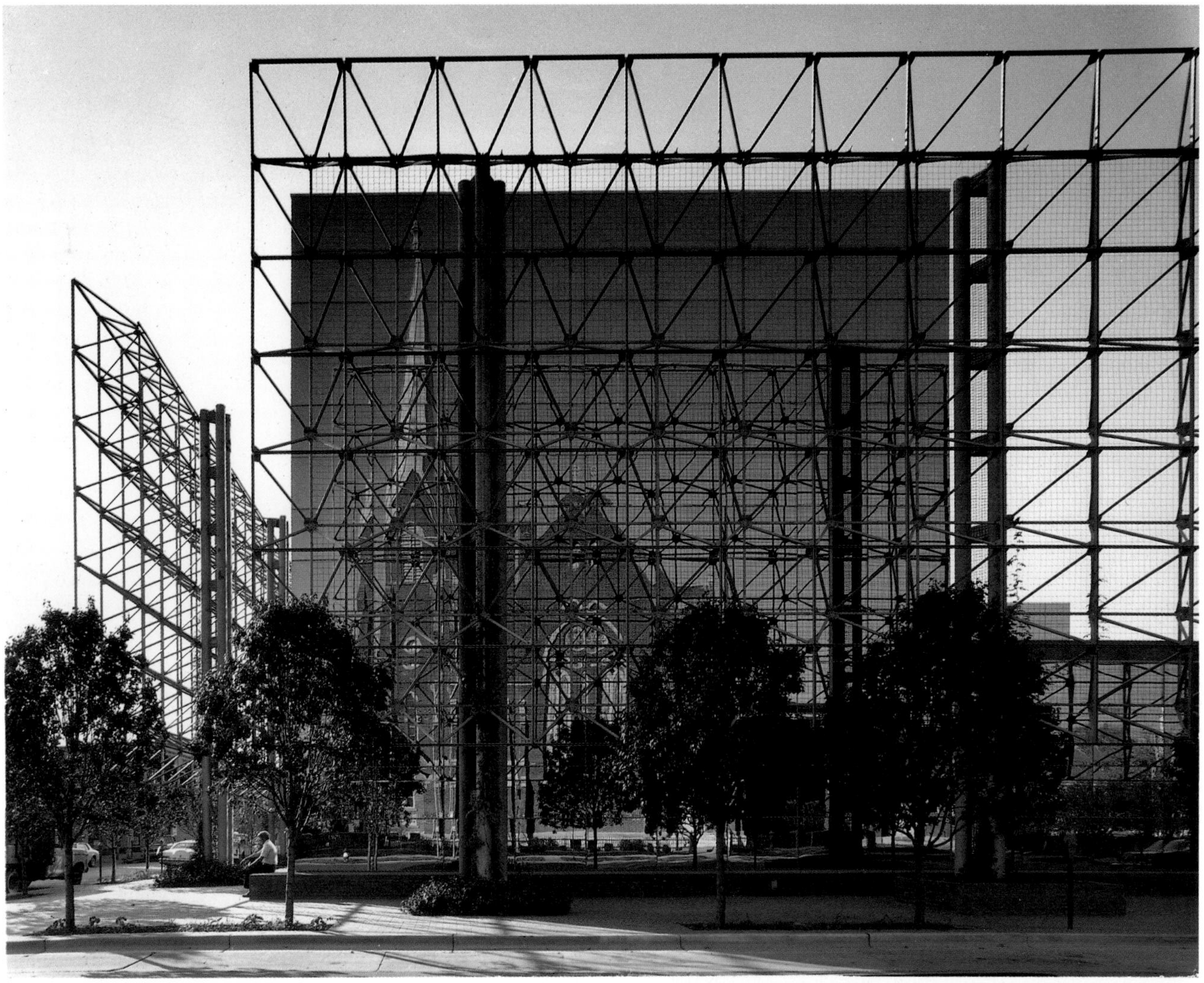

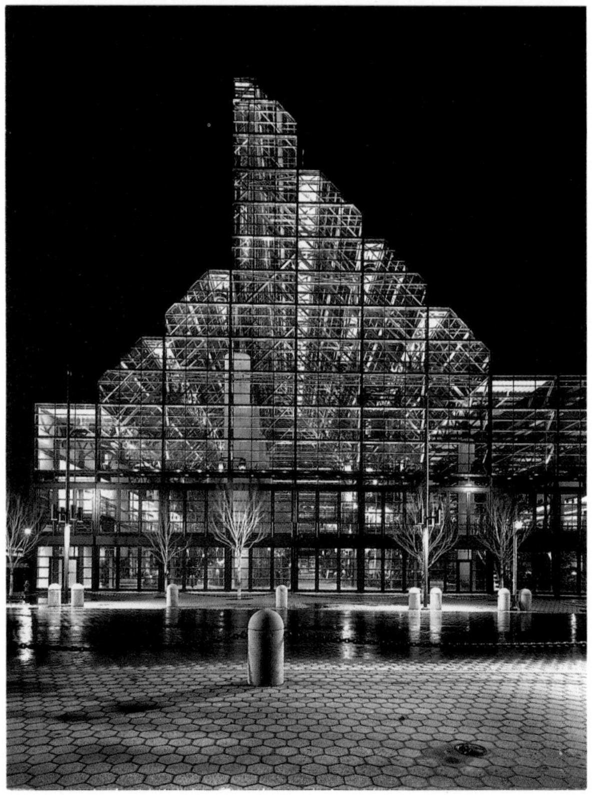

188 *Balthazar Korab*

Columbus, Indiana Bell Telephone Company Switching Center, ca. 1979.
Courtesy the photographer.

189 *Norman McGrath*

Niagara Falls, Rainbow Center Winter Garden, ca. 1978.
Courtesy the photographer.

190 *Jaime Ardiles-Arce*

New York, Michael Schaible apartment, 1979.
Courtesy the photographer.

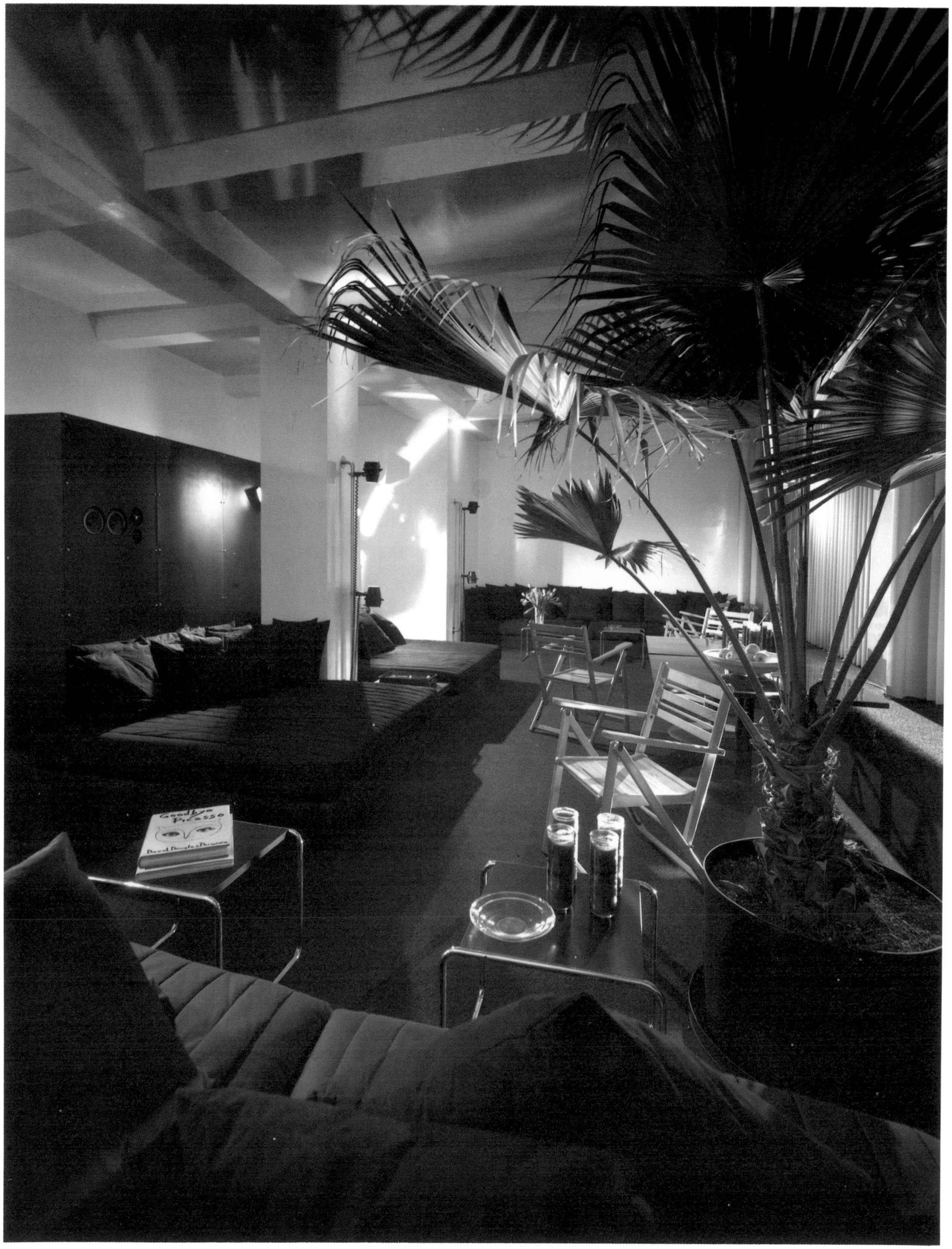
Goodbye Picasso

191 *STEVE ROSENTHAL*

Boston, John Hancock Building, 1980.
Courtesy the photographer.

192 *RICHARD BRYANT*

Camden Town, television studios, 1983.
Courtesy the photographer.

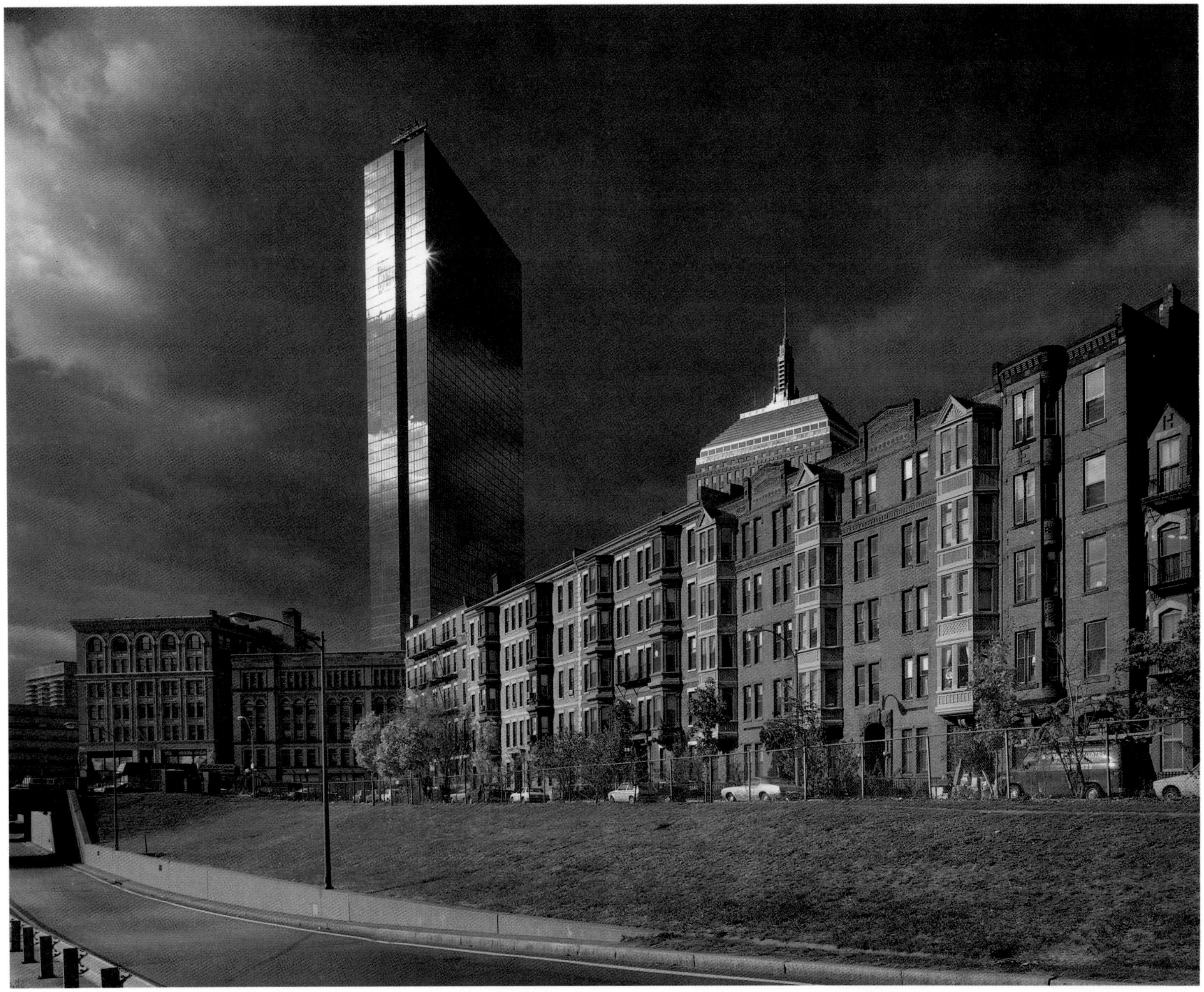

ble to that of light in color pictures. Though the emphemeral dusk (or dawn) light in Richard Bryant's (b. 1947) color picture of Terry Farrell's TV-am Building (1983) in Camden Town, London, is not apparent in the reproduction here, the trace of what seems to be a bouncing bicycle light on the sidewalk of Hawley Crescent gives something of the same feeling in black and white (192). And in a picture by Timothy Hursley (b. 1955) the placement of the tree trunks with respect to the windows of Philip Johnson's studio (1980) are as precise as that of the tree in Paul Strand's photograph with respect to the Palladian window (193). But the ephemeral instant of the exposure is evoked by the passage of a bus behind the building.

Thus a medium that had seemed through the sixties to provide an increasingly articulate language for describing the built world appears in the eighties to have gone back to its point of departure—to describing qualities of light more than architecture. A historian can predict with confidence that before long there will arrive a time when this new way of using color photography will come to be a cliché. Though he cannot predict what will follow, he can point out that at least twice before in almost a century and a half of photography a generation has placed a primary emphasis on qualities of light. It happened not only in the decades before the First World War, it happened in the earliest days of photography, at the time of the early calotypes. Just as the later of these two periods was followed by a "new objectivity," the earlier was followed by one of the great ages of visual discovery. It is certainly likely that before long photographs will again take a fresh, hard, objective look at architecture.

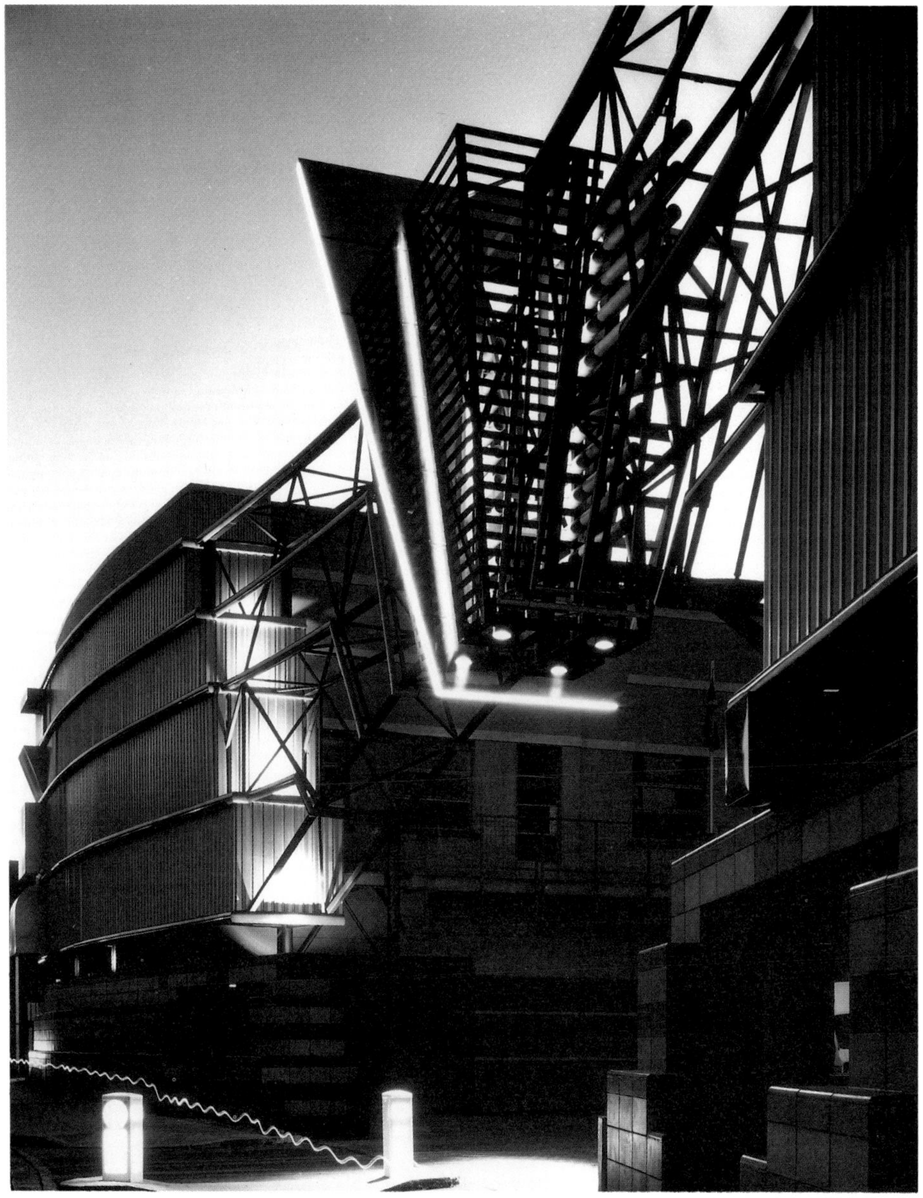

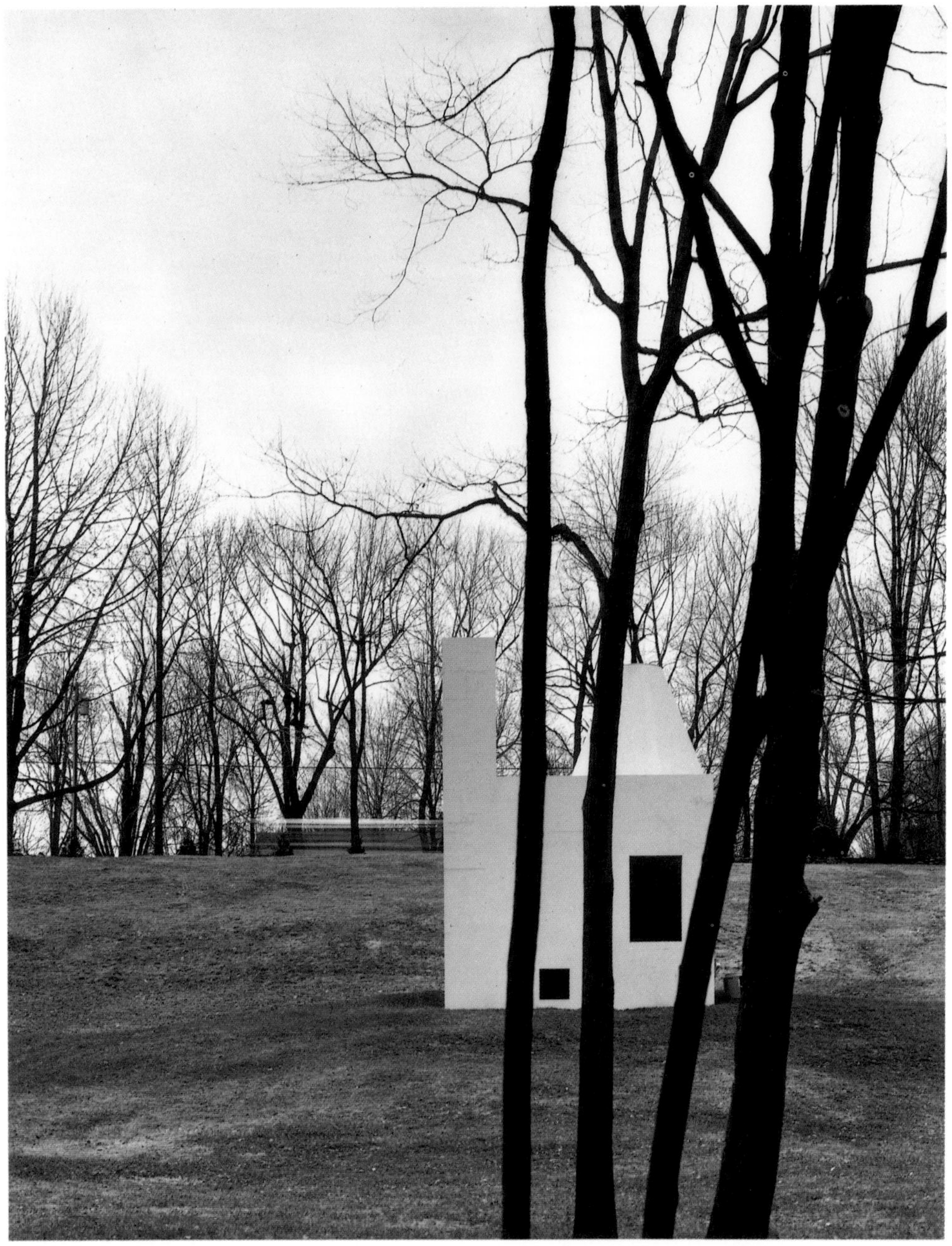

193 *Timothy Hursley*

Greenwich, Johnson studio, 1980.
Courtesy the photographer.

Biographical List of Photographers

In *The Shape of Time* George Kubler wrote that, "most artists' lives are uninteresting . . . Cellini, who was not an interesting artist, led an exciting life, which kept him from the difficult business of art." Photographers are no exception to this statement. Although little is known of the lives of most photographers, there is little that is remarkable about those lives that are fully documented. There is no corporate ladder or chain of command for a photographer to climb. Typically his pictures appear with increasing frequency in the professional magazines until a time comes when their frequency falls off. Few photographers write a word about their work or their lives, and their eventual death generally goes unmarked by an obituary in the city where they worked. Until very recent times, when a market for gallery sales developed, they had every reason to lie low once their productive years had passed; all that could follow was a losing business in reprint orders, and it too would eventually fall off. In the 1970s one prominent photographer of the late thirties to the fifties, upon moving from a house to an apartment during his retirement, threw out all his negatives.

The information that follows is therefore designed less to give shape to the listed photographers' lives than to suggest where more of their pictures can be found and to indicate sources of further data. The letters *PA&I* indicate that the photographer is included in a standard reference work, Turner Browne and Elaine Partnow, *The Macmillan Biographical Encyclopedia of Photographic Artists and Innovators* (1983). If photographers were active before 1880, their usual techniques are specified.

Abbott, Berenice. b. Springfield, Ohio, July 17, 1898. *PA&I*, 4. Ohio State University. Active 1926 to 1950s in Paris and New York. Publications: *Changing New York*, 1939; *A Guide to Better Photography*, 1941. Taught: New School for Social Research, 1935–1958.

Alinari, Leopoldo. (Florence 1832–1865) *PA&I*, 12. Wet collodion glass plate.

Annan, Thomas. (1829–1887; Glasgow slums, 1868–1887) *PA&I*, 18. Wet collodion glass plate.

Archer, Frederick Scott. (Hertfordshire, 1813–1857) *PA&I*, 20. Invented wet collodion process.

Ardiles-Arce, Jaime R. b. La Paz, Bolivia, 1939. Columbia University BArch 1968. Active 1974 to present.

Arnold, Charles Dudley. (Canada, 1844–Buffalo, 1927). Active, based in Buffalo and New York 1880s through 1910s. Photographer of World's Columbian Exposition, Chicago, 1893, and Pan-American Exposition, Buffalo, 1901.

Atget, Jean-Eugène-Auguste. (1857, Libourne, France–1927, Paris) *PA&I*, 23. National Conservatory of Music and Drama, 1879–1881. Active 1888–1927 in Picardy and Paris.

Baer, Morley. b. Toledo, Ohio, 1916. *PA&I*, 29. University of Michigan, BA 1936, MA 1937 (English literature and theater). Active 1946 to present, based in San Francisco. Member: American Society of Magazine Photographers; Friends of Photography, Carmel. Publications: *Here Today*, 1968; *Adobes in the Sun*, 1972; *Bay Area Houses*, 1976; *Painted Ladies*, 1978; *Room and Time Enough*, 1979. Awards: AIA Gold Medal for Architectural Photography, 1965; Midcareer Fellowship, American Academy in Rome, 1980. Taught: San Francisco Institute of Art, ca. 1962–1965. Address: P.O. Box 2228, Monterey, California 93940.

Baldus, Edouard-Denis. (1820–1882) *PA&I*, 31. Calotype and wet collodion glass plate.

Balterman, Lee. American, active 1960s to present.

Baltz, Lewis. b. Newport Beach, California, September 12, 1945. *PA&I*, 32. San Francisco Art Institute, BFA 1969; Claremont Graduate School, MFA 1971. Active 1967 to present. Member: Society of Photographic Educators, 1975–1976. Publications: *The New Industrial Parks near Irvine, California*, 1974; *New Topographics*, International Museum of Photography at George Eastman House catalog, 1975; *Court House* (Pare), 1978. Awards: National Endowment for the Arts Photographer's Fellowship, 1973; John Simon Guggenheim Fellow, 1976; U.S.–U.K. Exchange Fellowship, 1980. Taught: Pomona College, Claremont, California, 1970–1972; California Institute of the Arts, Valencia, Fall 1972. Address: P.O. Box 366, Sausalito, California 94965.

Barnard, George N. (1819–1920) *PA&I*, 35. Wet collodion glass plate.

Bayard, Hippolyte. (Breteuil-sur-Noye, 1807–1887) *PA&I*, 38. Processes of own invention.

Beato, Felice A. (Venice ?–1903) *PA&I*, 41. Wet collodion glass plate.

Becher, Bernhard (Bernd) and Hilla. *PA&I*, 42. Bernd: b. Westphalia, 1931. Staatliche Kunstakademie, Stuttgart, 1953; Staatliche Kunstakademie, Düsseldorf, 1957. Has collaborated with Hilla since 1959. Hilla: b. Potsdam, 1934. Düsseldorf Staatliche Kunstakademie, 1957–1961. Publications: *Anonyme Skulpturen: Eine Typologie technischer Bauten*, 1970; *Die Architektur der Förder- und Wassertürme*, 1971; *Fachwerkhäuser des Siegener Industriegebieten*, 1977. Address: am Muhlenkamp 16, 4000 Düsseldorf-Wittlaer.

Bedford, Francis. (1816–1894) *PA&I*, 38. Wet and dry collodion glass plate.

Bisson, Auguste-Rosalie. (Paris, 1826–1900) *PA&I*, 57. Daguerrotype, wet collodion glass plate.

Bisson, Louis-Auguste. (Paris, 1826–1900) *PA&I*, 58. Daguerreotype, wet collodion glass plate.

Blanquart-Evrard, Louis-Désirée. (Lyons, 1802–1872) *PA&I*, 60. Waxed calotype, invented albumen paper process.

Blossfeldt, Karl. (1865, Schiele, Germany–1932, Berlin) *PA&I*, 62. Professor in the United States Schools of Free and Applied Art, Berlin. Publications: *Urformen der Kunst*, 1925; *Wundergarten der Natur*, 1932.

Boissonas, Frederich. (1858–1947) Swiss. Active 1900s to 1920s.

Bonfils, Félix. (1831–1885) *PA&I*, 66. Active in Beirut ca. 1867ff. Wet collodion glass plate.

Bool, A. and J., Henry and T. J. Dixon. (?–?). In 1867 they were commissioned by the Society for Preserving the Relics of Old London to photograph historic buildings in London that were threatened by the modernization of the city or were in ruinous condition. By 1886, 124 photographs had been published as carbon prints in a series of albums. By 1879 the Bools had dropped out of the project, and the Dixons, father and son, continued it to the end. (Source: Pare, Richard. *Photography and Architecture, 1839–1939*. Montreal: Canadian Center for Architecture, 1982 [The MIT Press, 1985]; Bush, Graham, *Old London*. London: Academy Editions, 1975.)

Bourke-White, Margaret. (1904, New York City–1971, Stamford, Connecticut) *PA&I*, 69. Clarence White School of Photography; Cornell, 1927. Active 1927 through forties based in Cleveland and New York City.

Braun, Adolphe. (Alsace, 1811–1877) *PA&I*, 75. Daguerreotype, wet collodion glass plate.

Bryant, Richard. b. Wolverhampton, England, September 8, 1947. Rencomb College; Kingston School of Architecture, DArch. Active 1973 to present, based in London. Address: 4 St. Winifred's Road, Teddington, Middlesex TW11 9JR.

Büxenstein, Georg. Active, based in Berlin, 1890s, 1900s.

Caponigro, Paul, b. Boston, Massachusetts, December 7, 1932. *PA&I*, 99. Boston University, 1950–51, 1955–56, 1958–59. Active ca. 1958 to present. Awards: Guggenheim Fellowship, 1966, 1975; National Endowment for the Arts Photographer's Fellowships, 1971, 1975. Taught: Yale, 1970–1971; New York University, 1967–1970; Boston University, 1960–1961. Address: Route 3, Box 960, Santa Fe, New Mexico 87501.

Chevojon Freres. Active, France, 1880s to present (as firm).

Clifford, Charles (London, 1819/20–Spain, 1863). English, came to Spain in 1852 and was listed as Queen Victoria's official photographer and, after 1858, the photographer of Spain's Queen Isabel II. He worked in both calotype and wet collodion glass plate processes, photographing architecture, construction and works of art. (Source: Fontanella, Lee: *Photography in Spain in the Nineteenth Century*. Dallas and San Francisco: Delahunty and Fraenkel Galleries, catalog, 1983.)

Clift, William Brooks III. b. Boston, Massachusetts, January 5, 1944. *PA&I*, 113. Active 1963 to present, based in Boston and Sante Fe. Publications: *Old Boston City Hall*, a portfolio of 108 prints, 1971; *Beacon Hill, A Walking Tour* (Alex McIntyre), 1975; *Court House* (Pare), 1978; *American Images*, edited by Renato Danese, 15 photographs by each of 20 photographers. Awards: National Endowment for the Arts Photographer's Fellowship, 1972, 1979; Guggenheim Fellowship, 1974, 1980. Address: 618 Onate Place, Santa Fe, New Mexico 87501.

Cserna, George. b. Budapest, Hungary, March 14, 1919. Studied law at college. Active 1959 to present, based in New York City. Member: American Society of Magazine Photographers. Taught: School of the Visual Arts, New School, City University of New York. Address: 80 Second Avenue, New York 10003.

Cundall, Joseph. (?–?). Active late 1840s through 1860s. An English photographer-publisher, he was principal of the publishing firm, Cundall, Downes and Co. He was a charter member of the Calotype Club, founded in London in 1847. In 1862 the firm published *Wells, Architectural Details of the Cathedral and Close* and *Sculpture of the West Front of Wells Cathedral*, the first presumably and the latter definitely under the aegis of the Architectural Photography Association. Cundall, Downes had also published *English Flower Gardens* in 1861.

Daguerre, Jacques-Louis-Mandé. (Cormeuilles, 1787–1851) *PA&I*, 133. Invented daguerreotype.

Delamotte, Phillip Henry. (1821–1889) *PA&I*, 144. Calotype.

Dell, M. Oliver (?–1959). With H. L. Wainwright, official photographer for *Architectural Review* in 1930s and forties.

De Maré, Eric.b. Enfield, Middlesex, England, September 10, 1910. St. Paul's School, London; Architectural Association School, London. Editor, *Architects' Journal*, London, 1942–1946. Active 1947 to present, based in London. Member: Royal Institute of British Architects, Architectural Association, The Art Workers' Guild. Publications: *The Canals of England*, 1950; *Time on the Thames*, 1952; *The Bridges of Britain*, 1954; *Photography*, 1957; *The Functional Tradition*, 1958; *London*, 1961; *Photography and Architecture*, 1961; *Saint Francis of Assisi*, 1962; *Cambridge*, 1964; *Oxford*, 1965; *City of Westminster*, 1968; *Architectural Photography*, 1975; *The Houses of Parliament*, 1975. Address: The Old House Studio, Mill Lane, Henley-on-Thames, OXON. RG9 4HB, England.

DuCamp, Maxime. (Paris, 1822–1894) *PA&I*, 160. Calotype.

Einzig, Richard. (London, 1932–London, 1980). Cambridge University. London County Council Architect's Department. Active 1960s and 1970s.

Evans, Frederick Henry. (London, 1853–London, 1943) *PA&I*, 182. Active 1890s through 1930s. Member: The Linked Ring, Royal Photographic Society, London Salon Club. Award: Honorary Fellow, Royal Photographic Society, 1928.

Evans, Walker. (St. Louis, 1903–New Haven, 1975) *PA&I*, 182. Williams College. Active 1928 to 1970s, based in New York City and Old Lyme, Connecticut. Worked for Farm Security Administration, 1935–1938; Time, Inc., 1943–1965. Publications: *The Crime of Cuba* (Beals), 1933; *American Photographs*, 1938; *Let Us Now Praise Famous Men* (with Agee), 1941; *The Mangrove Coast* (Bickel), 1942. Awards: Guggenheim Fellowships, 1940, 1941, 1959. Taught: School of Art and Architecture, Yale University, 1965–1975.

Fenton, Roger. (Heywood, 1819–1869) *PA&I*, 191. Calotype, wet collodion glass plate.

Fischer, Sigurd, b. Denmark. Active in 1920s and 1930s, based in New York City.

Frith, Francis. (Chesterfield, 1822–1898) *PA&I*, 212. Calotype, wet collodion glass plate.

Fuermann, Clarence Albert. (1883, Waterloo, Wisconsin–1983). Active ca. 1905 to ca. 1933, based in Chicago. Photographer for brother Henry's firm.

Futagawa, Yukio. b. Osaka, Japan, November 4, 1932. Graduated Waseda University, Tokyo, 1956. Active 1959 to present. Publications: 1962, *Nihon no Minka* (The Essential Japanese House), Bijutsu Shuppan-sha, *Nihon Kenchiku no Ne* (The Roots of Japanese Architecture), Bijutsu Shuppan-sha; 1963, *Nihon no Katachi* (Forms in Japan), Bijutsu Shuppan-sha, *The Roots of Japanese Architecture* (trans. Harper & Row), *Architecture Japonaise*, Office du Livre; 1964, *Okinawa no Mingei* (Folk Crafts of Okinawa), Bijutsu Shuppan-sha; 1966, *Forms in Japan*, East-West Center Press; 1967, *Forms in Japan*, Suddeutscher Verlag, *Sukiya—The Elegant Japanese House*, Weatherhill; 1968, *Contemporary Architects Series*, 15 vols., Bijutsu Shuppan-sha; 1970, *Contemporary Architects Series*, Simon & Schuster, Thames & Hudson; 1971 *Gendai no Sukiya* (The Classic Tradition in Japanese Architecture), Tanko-sha; 1972, *The Elegant Japanese House*, Weatherhill, *The Classic Tradition in Japanese Architecture*, Weatherhill.

Main publications by A.D.A. EDITA Tokyo Co., Ltd. photographed and edited by Yukio Futagawa: 1970 Global Architecture Series, 64 vols. as of March 1984; 1971–1975 Global Interior Series, 10 vols.; 1973–1975, Villages and Town Series, 10 vols.; 1975, *Houses by MLTW/Moore* Lyndon, Turnbull and Whitaker, Kevin Roche/John Dinkeloo and Associates, Vol. 1, 1962–75; 1976–, GA Houses Series 15 vols. as of January 1984; 1977, *Charles Gwathmey & Robert Siegel Residential Works 1966–77; 1978, Wooden Houses in Europe*; 1980 *Traditional Japanese Houses*.

Georges, Alexander. b. New York City, May 22, 1916. Manhattan School of Music; worked with Ansel Adams and Clarence White, Jr. Active 1947 to present. Staff photographer for *Interiors*, 1952–1972, *Interior Design*, 1972–1978. Award: AIA Medal for Architectural Photography, 1971. Address: Call Hollow Road, Pomona, New York 10970.

Gohlke, Frank William. b. Wichita Falls, Texas, April 3, 1942. *PA&I*, 234. University of Texas, Austin, BA 1964 (English); Yale University, MA 1966 (English). Active late 1960s to present. Awards: Guggenheim Fellowship, 1975; National Endowment for the Arts Photographer's Fellowship, 1978; Bush Foundation Artist's Fellowship, 1979–1980. Taught: Blake Schools, 1973–1975; visiting artist, Colorado College, Colorado Springs, 1977 to present.

Gottscho, Samuel Herman. (1875–1971). Active 1925 to 1950s?

Gravot, Claude. French, active 1920s and thirties.

Hedrich, Ken. (1908–1972). Active from 1929, based in Chicago.

Hedrich, William C. b. Chicago, June 21, 1912. University of Illinois, Institute of Design (photography, sculpture, interior design). Assistant to brother Ken. Active 1931 to present, based in Chicago, for Hedrich-Blessing. Member: Professional Photographers of America, Architectural Photographers' Association, American Society of Interior Designers (Associate); American Institute of Architects (Associate). Address: Hedrich-Blessing, 11 West Illinois, Chicago, Illinois 60610.

Henneberg, Hugo. (Vienna, 1863–Vienna, 1918). Studied physics, chemistry, astronomy, and mathematics in Jena and Vienna. Active 1890s to ca. 1904. Member: The Linked Ring, Wiener Photo-Club.

Hill, David Octavius. (Perth, 1802–1870) *PA&I*, 277, and Robert Adamson. (1821–1848) *PA&I*, 8. Calotype.

Hillers, John K. (Germany, 1843–United States, 1925) *PA&I*, 278. Wet and dry collodion glass plate.

Hofer, Evelyn, b. Marburg, Germany. *PA&I*, 282. Studied in Zurich and Basel. Active 1953 to present, based in New York City. Publications: *The Stones of Florence* (McCarthy), 1959; *London Perceived* (Pritchett), 1962; *The Presence of Spain* (Morris); *New York Proclaimed* (Pritchett), 1965; *The Evidence of Washington* (Walton), 1966; *Dublin: A Portrait* (Pritchett), 1967.

Hursley, Timothy. b. Bloomfield, Michigan, July 19, 1955. Assistant to Balthazar Korab. Active 1979 to present. Address: The Arkansas Office, 115 East Capitol, Little Rock, Arkansas 72201.

Jeanneret, Charles Edouard (Le Corbusier). (1887–1965). Architect.

Johnston, Frances Benjamin. (Grafton, West Virginia, 1864–New Orleans, Louisiana, 1952) *PA&I*, 310. Academie Julien, Paris, 1883–1885; Art Students League of Washington, D.C. Active 1890s through 1930s. Member: New York Camera Club; American Institute of Architects (Honorary, 1945).

Kalischer, Clemens. b. Hoyren, Bavaria, March 30, 1921. *PA&I*, 317. Cooper Union; New School for Social Research. Active 1948 to present, based in New York City and Stockbridge, Massachusetts. Taught: Berkshire Community College, Williams College. Address: Image Photos, Main Street, Stockbridge, Massachusetts 01262.

Kamman, Jan. (Schiedam, Holland, 1898–Woudrichem, Holland, 1983) Active 1920s and thirties, based in Schiedam.

"Mein Chef-Architekt Karweik." So identified by Erich Mendelsohn in his book *Amerika*.

Korab, Balthazar. b. Budapest, Hungary, February 16, 1926. Polytechnicum, Budapest; École des Beaux-Arts, Paris, 1954. Active 1957 to present, based in Birmingham, Michigan. Member: Michigan Society of Architects (Honorary), 1975. Award: AIA Medal for Architectural Photography, 1964. Address: 5051 Beach Road, Troy, Michigan 48098.

Köster, Arthur, German. Active 1920s and 1930s.

Latham, Charles. English. Active 1900s. Publications: *Formal Gardens in England and Scotland*, 1902; *The Gardens of Italy*, 1905; *In English Homes*, 1904–1909 (3 vols.).

Laughlin, Clarence John. (Lake Charles, Louisiana, 1905–1985) *PA&I*, 357. Active 1934 through sixties based in New Orleans. Publications: *New Orleans and Its Living Past*, 1941; *Ghosts Along the Mississippi*, 1948.

Laurent, Juan. (?–?). Active Paris, mid-1850s; Spain, 1857 (?)–1892(?). Began as a daguerreotypist in Paris in the mid-1850s and moved to Spain around 1857, where he set up the Madrid firm which bore his name. Working in the wet and dry plate collodion processes, he amassed an enormous photographic archive, much of which was printed on a paper of his own invention. Some 20,000 of his negatives survive, in more or less printable condition. (Source: Fontanella, Lee. *Photography in Spain in the Nineteenth Century*. Dallas and San Francisco: Delahunty and Fraenkel Galleries, catalog 1983.)

Le Gray, Gustave. (1820–Cairo, 1882 [?]) *PA&I*, 362. Calotype, invented waxed calotype process.

Le Secq, Henri. (Paris, 1818–Paris, 1882) *PA&I*, 365–366. Used calotype and waxed calotype.

Lincoln, Fay Sturtevant. (Keene, New Hampshire, 1894–Centre Hall, Pennsylvania, 1975). MIT, 1922 (biology, no degree). Valuation clerk for a firm of engineers in New York, 1925. Active 1929 to 1965, based in New York City, for the first few years in partnership with Peter Andreas Nyholm (b. Denmark).

Lönberg-Holm. Architect in Detroit, 1920s.

MacPherson, Robert. (1811–1872) *PA&I*, 385. Wet collodion glass plate.

Marville, Charles. (1816–ca. 1880) *PA&I*, 397. Calotype, wet collodion glass plate.

McGrath, Norman R. C. b. London, England, June 10, 1931. Schools in U.K. and Ireland; Trinity College, Dublin, MA and BAI (engineering). Assistant to Hans Namuth; studied under Alexey Brodovitch. Active 1964 to present. Member: American Society of Magazine Photographers, Society of Designers of Ireland. Publication: *Children Spaces* (with Molly McGrath), 1978. Award: AIA Institute Honor Award, 1985. Taught: Cooper Union, 1974. Address: 164 West 79th Street, New York 10024.

Mendelsohn, Erich. (1887–1953). Architect.

Méstral, O. (?–?). A French calotypist who used the waxed paper process of Gustave Le Gray. Possibly a pupil of Le Gray, he had developed a reputation as a portraitist by 1851. He worked closely with Le Gray on their respective Heliographic Missions in 1851, Mestral's responsibility being southwest France. He occasionally exhibited in the fifties but nothing further is known of his career. (Source: Direction des Musees de France. *La Mission Héliographique*. Paris: Musées de France, 1980.)

Meyerowitz, Joel. b. New York City, 1938. *PA&I*, 414. Ohio State University, Columbus, BFA 1959. Active ca. 1965 to present, based in New York City. Publications: *Cape Light*, 1978; *St. Louis & The Arch*, 1980. Awards: Guggenheim Fellowships, 1970, 1978; New York State Council on the Arts CAPS Grant, 1976; National Endowment for the Arts Photographer's Fellowship, 1978. Taught: Cooper Union, adjunct professor of photography, 1971 to present, Mellon lecturer in photography, 1977; Princeton University, associate professor of photography, 1977.

Moholy, Lucia. b. Austria, 1900. *PA&I*, 425. University studies in philosophy, philology, art history. Active 1920s and thirties. Member: Royal Photographic Society (Fellow), European Society for the History of Photography, Deutscher Werkbund, Schweizerischer Werkbund. Collections: L. Fritz Gruber, Cologne; Wallraf Richartz Museum, Cologne, Neue Sammlung, Munich. Address: Rotfluhstrasse 10, 8702 Zollikon, Switzerland

Morris, Wright. b. Central City, Nebraska, January 6, 1910. *PA&I*, 430. Pomona College, Claremont, California, 1930–1933. Active 1935 to ca. 1954. Publications: *The Inhabitants*, 1946; *The Home Place*, 1948. Awards: Guggenheim Fellowships, 1942, 1946.

Nairn, Ian Douglas. (Surrey, England 1930–1983).

Naya, Carlo. (Venice, ?–1873) *PA&I*, 447. Wet collodion glass plate.

Negre, Charles. (Grasse, 1820–1897) *PA&I*, 447. Calotype.

Nickel, Richard. (1928–1972). Active from early 1960s until his death, based in Chicago.

Nixon, Nicholas. b. Detroit, Michigan, 1947. University of Michigan, BA 1969 (American literature); University of New Mexico, MFA, 1975. Active 1975 to present, based in Cambridge, Massachusetts. Awards: National Endowment for the Arts Photographer's Fellowship, 1976; Guggenheim Fellowship, 1977. Taught: Massachusetts College of Art.

Normand, Alfred-Nicholas. (1822–1909). Went to Rome as a Prix de Rome in Architecture in 1846, and between 1847 and 1851 made calotypes of monuments of classical antiquity in Rome, southern Italy and Athens. He claimed to have helped Maxime Du Camp print some of his Egyptian photographs. Normand returned to France to become a leading architect; especially known for his Maison Pompéienne for Prince Napoleon, finished in 1860. In the 1880s he produced an extensive photographic documentation of European architecture, while maintaining a successful career as an architect. (Source: Jammes, André, and Eugenia Parry Janis. *The Art of the French Calotype*. Princeton: Princeton University Press, 1983.)

Piper, John Egerton Christmas. b. December 13, 1903. Artist.

Plumbe, John, Jr. (Wales, 1809–Dubuque, Iowa 1857) *PA&I*, 485. Daguerreotype.

Ponti, Carlo. (Venice, ?) *PA&I*, 487. Active 1858–1875. Wet collodion glass plate.

Renger-Patzsch, Albert. (1897, Wurzburg–1966, Wamel Dorf nr. Essen) *PA&I*, 504. College at Sonderhausen; Kreuzschule, Dresden; Technical College, Dresden (chemistry). From ca. 1920, director photography department, Folkwang Publishing House, Hagen. Publications: *Das Chorgestuhl von Kappenberg*, 1925; *Die Halligen*, 1927; *Die Welt ist Schön*, 1928; *Lübeck*, 1928; Hamburg: Photographische Aufnahmen, 1930; *Eisen und Stahl*, 1931.

Robertson, James. (?–?) *PA&I*, 513. Active 1852–1865. Wet collodion glass plate.

Robinson, Cervin. b. Boston, Massachusetts, May 18, 1928. *PA&I*, 513. Harvard, AB 1950. Active 1957 to present, based in New York City. Publications: *The Architecture of Frank Furness* (O'Gorman), 1973; *Skyscraper Style: Art Deco New York* (Bletter, coauthor), 1975; *Cervin Robinson: Photographs, 1958–1983*, The Farish Gallery, Rice University and the Wellesley College Museum exhibition catalog, 1983. Awards: Guggenheim Fellowship, 1971, AIA Honor Award, 1986. Taught: Columbia University Summer School, 1977 to present. Address: 251 West 92nd Street, New York 10025.

Römmler & Jonas. Active 1880s and 1890s, based in Dresden, Germany.

Rosenthal, Steve. b. Hartford, Connecticut, September 26, 1940. Yale, BA 1962 (magna cum laude), Harvard, MA 1962. Active 1971 to present, based in Boston area. Member: American Society of Magazine Photographers. Taught: Harvard Graduate School of Design Continuing Education Seminars, 1975 to present; Boston Architectural Center, ca. 1970. Address: 59 Maple St., Auburndale, Massachusetts 02166.

Salzmann, Auguste. (Alsace, 1824–1872/5) *PA&I*, 530. Calotype, wet collodion glass plate.

Samhaber, Constantin. German, active 1890s.

Sander, August. (1876, Herdorf-am-der-Steig–1964, Cologne) *PA&I*, 533. Dresden Academy of Art. Active 1892 to 1930s, based in Cologne.

Schmölz, Hugo. (1879, Sonthofen–1938). Active 1924–1938. Member: Vereinigung Kölner Fachphotographen. Publication: Karl-Hugo Schmölz and Rolf Sachse, *Hugo Schmölz: Fotografierte Architektur 1924–1937*, 1982.

Schnall, Ben. b. New York City, August 15, 1906. Rabinovich Workshop of Art Photography, Cooper Union; New York School of Photography. Active 1931–1973, based in New York. Member: American Society of Magazine Photographers, Architectural Photographers Association of America. Address: 2750 N.E. 183rd Street, North Miami Beach, Florida 33160.

Sheeler, Charles. (1883, Philadelphia–1965, Dobbs Ferry) *PA&I*, 554. School of Industrial Art, Philadelphia, 1900–1903; Pennsylvania Academy of the Fine Arts, 1903–1906. Active 1912 through 1930s.

Shore, Stephen b. New York City, October 8, 1947. *PA&I*, 558. National Endowment for the Arts Photographer's Fellowship, 1974; Guggenheim Fellowship, 1975.

Shulman, Julius, b. Brooklyn, New York, October 10, 1910. University of California, Los Angeles and Berkeley. Active, based in Los Angeles 1936 to present. Member: American Society of Magazine Photographers, Professional Photographers of America, Honorary AIA. Publications: *Photographing Architecture and Interiors*, 1962; *Photographing Architectural Design*, 1977. Taught: University of California, Los Angeles. Address: 7875 Woodrow Wilson Drive, Los Angeles, California 90046.

Smith, George Everard Kidder. b. Birmingham, Alabama, October 1, 1913. *PA&I*, 566. Princeton University, BA 1935 and School of Architecture, MFA 1938. Active 1939 to present. Fellow of the American Institute of Architects. Publications: *Brazil Builds* (photographs only), 1943; *Switzerland Builds*, 1950; *Sweden Builds*, 1950; *Italy Builds*, 1955; *The New Architecture of Europe*, 1961; *The New Churches of Europe*, 1964; *A Pictorial History of Architecture in America*, 1976; *The Architecture of the United States*, 1981. Article: "Photography for the Architect," *RIBA Journal*, September 1965. Awards: Guggenheim Fellowship, 1946; American-Scandinavian Foundation Fellowship, 1946; President's Fellowship from Brown University, 1949; Fulbright Research Fellowships, 1950 and 1965; Samuel H. Kress Foundation Grant, 1967; Graham Foundation for Advanced Studies in the Arts, 1967 and 1974; AIA Gold Medal for Architectural Photography, 1963; National Endowment for the Arts 1967 and 1974; Ford Foundation grants, 1970 and 1975.

Smith, W. Eugene. (1918, Wichita, Kansas–1978, Tucson) *PA&I*, 568. University of Notre Dame, 1936–1937. Active 1937 to 1978.

Steichen, Edward Jean. (1879, Luxembourg–1973, West Redding, Connecticut) *PA&I*, 580. Studio in New York City, 1923–1938; U.S. Navy, 1942–1946; Director, Department of Photography, Museum of Modern Art, 1947–1962.

Steiner, Ralph (1899–1986, Thetford Hill, Vermont). *PA&I*, 582. Dartmouth College, AB 1921; Clarence White School of Photography, 1921–1922. Active 1923 into 1930s as still photographer (later a motion picture cameraman and producer). Exhibition: "Film und Foto," Stuttgart, 1929. Photography critic for *PM* in the forties. Publication: *A Point of View*, 1978. Address: Thetford Hill, Vermont.

Stieglitz, Alfred. (1864, Hoboken, New Jersey–1946, New York City) *PA&I*, 589. City College of New York, 1879–1881; Realgymnasium, Karlsruhe, 1881; Technische Hochschule and University of Berlin, 1882–1890. Active 1887 through 1930s. Member: Society of Amateur Photographers, 1891–1896.

Stillman, William James. (1828–1901, Surrey, England). American born and educated, from 1848–1855 he studied painting in London. In 1849 he met John Ruskin, who was a major influence on him. Apppointed U.S. Consul on Crete in 1865, he was forced to leave in 1868 and went to Athens where he photographed the Acropolis. He published the photographs as *The Acropolis of Athens Illustrated Picturesquely and Architecturally in Photography* (London, F. S. Ellis), 1870. Stillman later came into contact with the family of Dante Gabriel Rossetti and the Pre-Raphaelite circle. (Source: Pare, Richard. *Photography and Architecture, 1839–1939*. Montreal: Canadian Center for Architecture, 1982 [The MIT Press, 1985].)

Stoller, Ezra. b. Chicago, 1915. New York University, School of Architecture, associate design degree. Active 1939 to present based in New York. Exhibition: Max Protetch Gallery, 1981. Publications: Richard Pratt, *Treasury of Early American Houses* (2 vols.); Howard Barnstone, *The Galveston*

That Was (with Henri Cartier-Bresson). Article: "Photography and the Language of Architecture," *Perspecta 8*. Awards: American Institute of Architects Gold Medal for Architectural Photography, 1961. Address: Esto Photographics, Inc., 222 Valley Place, Mamaroneck, New York 10543.

Strand, Paul. (1890, New York City–1976, Orgeval nr. Paris) *PA&I*, 593. Ethical Culture High School. Active 1912–1976. Publications: *Time in New England*, 1950; *La France de Profil*, 1952; *Un Paese*, 1954; *Tir a' Mhurain: Outer Hebrides*, 1962; *Living Egypt*, 1969; *Ghana: An African Portrait*, 1976.

Street-Porter, Tim. b. Kennet, Suffolk, England, November 6, 1939. Regent Street Polytechnic, School of Architecture. Active 1967 to present, based in London and Los Angeles. Member: Associated Federation of Advertising and Editorial Photographers, London. Publications: *Interiors*, Monibus Press/Flash Books, 1980; *Musical Houses*, Running Press, 1980. Address: 749 North Hudson Avenue, Los Angeles, California 90038.

Szarkowski, John Thaddeus. b. Ashland, Wisconsin, December 18, 1925. *PA&I*, 604. University of Wisconsin, Madison, BS 1948. Active 1948 to 1962. Director, Photography Department of Museum of Modern Art, 1962 to present. Publications: *The Idea of Louis Sullivan*, 1956; *The Face of Minnesota*, 1958. Guggenheim Fellowships 1954 and 1961. Taught: Albright Art School of University of Buffalo, 1951–1953; Graduate School of the Arts, New York University, 1966; Department of Art History and Archaeology, Columbia University, 1981.

Talbot, William Henry Fox (Melbury, Dorset, 1800–1877) *PA&I*, 607. Invented calotype.

Thompson, Charles Thurston. (1816–1868). A British photographer, he began as a wood-engraver, following in the footsteps of his father, John Thompson. He started to work in photography in the late 1840s and in 1851 took up Archer's wet collodion process. In 1856 he was recruited by Henry Cole, first director of what would eventually become the Victoria and Albert Museum to establish a photographic service in the museum, the first such service known. Under the sponsorship of the Department of Science and Art he began the photographic training of Sappers from the Royal Engineers. With R. J. Bingham, he photographed the Paris Exhibition of 1855. On returning to England he photographed the Raphael and Holbein drawings in both the Royal Collection and that of Oxford University. In 1858 he photographed the Raphael Tapestry Cartoons, then at Hampton Court Palace. Photographs by Thompson and his Sappers were sold to the public through the museum. (Source: Physick, John. *Photography and the South Kensington Museum*. London: The Victoria and Albert Museum, 1975.)

Ward, Patrick.

Yerbury, Francis Rowland. (1885–London, 1970) *PA&I*, 681. Secretary of Architectural Association, London, 1911–1937; Director, The Building Centre, 1932–1961. Publications: *Georgian Details of Domestic Architecture*, 1926; *Modern European Buildings*, 1928; *Small Modern English Houses*, 1929; *Eighteenth Century Bath*, 1930; *Modern Dutch Buildings*, 1931; and books in collaboration with other authors.

Selected Bibliography

The following works provided significant assistance in the preparation of this essay.

Abbott, Berenice. *Changing New York.* New York: Dutton, 1939.

D. Appleton & Co. *Artistic houses: being a series of interior views of a number of the most beautiful and celebrated houses in the United States, with a description of the art treasures contained therein.* New York: D. Appleton, 1883–84.

Atget, Photographe de Paris. Paris: Henri Jonquières, 1930.

Baier, Lesley K. *Walker Evans at* Fortune: 1945–1965. Wellesley: Wellesley College Museum, catalog, 1977.

Baltz, Lewis. *The New Industrial Parks near Irvine, California.* New York: Castelli Graphics, 1974.

Barnard, George. *Photographic Views of Sherman's Campaign,* preface by Beaumont Newhall. New York: Dover, 1977.

Bartram, Michael. *The Pre-Raphaelite Camera.* Boston: Little, Brown, New York Graphic Society, 1985.

Becher, Bernhard, and Hilla. *Anonyme Skulpturen: Eine Typologie technischer Bauten.* Düsseldorf: Art-Press-Verlag, 1970.

Becher, Bernhard and Hilla. *Die Architektur der Förder- und Wassertürme.* Munich: Prestel-Verlag, 1971.

Becher, Bernhard and Hilla. *Framework Houses of the Siegen Industrial Region.* Munich: Schirmer/Mosel, 1977.

Bibliothèque Historique de la Ville de Paris. *Charles Marville, photographe de Paris de 1851 à 1879.* Paris: Bibliothèque Historique de la Ville de Paris, catalog, 1980.

Blake, Peter. *God's Own Junkyard: The Planned Deterioration of America's Landscape.* New York: Holt, Rinehart and Winston, 1964.

Blake, Peter. "Ugly America." *Horizon* 5 (May 1961), 4–19.

Blossfeldt, Karl. *Urformen der Kunst: Photographische Pflanzenbilder.* Berlin: Wasmuth, 1929.

Borcoman, James. *Charles Nègre, 1820–1880.* Ottowa: National Gallery of Canada, catalog, 1976.

Buckland, Gail. *Reality Recorded: Early Documentary Photography.* Greenwich: New York Graphic Society, 1977.

Bush, Graham. *Old London* London: Academy Editions, 1975.

Caponigro, Paul. *Landscape.* New York: McGraw-Hill, 1975.

Close, Leslie Rose, ed. *Portrait of an Era in Landscape Architecture: The Photographs of Mattie Edwards Hewitt.* Bronx: Wave Hill, catalog, 1983.

Collignon, Maxime, ed. and comp. "Photographies de Frédéric Boissonas et W. A. Mansell & Co." *Le Parthénon: l'histoire, l'architecture et la sculpture.* Paris: C. Eggimann, c.1913.

Cullen, Gorden. *Townscape.* London: Architectural Press, 1961.

Danese, Renato. ed. *American Images: New Work by Twenty Contemporary Photogaphers.* Museum of Fine Arts, Houston. Washington: Casini Press, catalog, 1979.

De Maré, Eric. *Photography and Architecture.* London: Architectural Press, 1961.

De Wolfe, Ivor. *The Italian Townscape.* London: Architectural Press, 1963.

Direction des Musées de Fance. *La Mission Héliographique, photographies de 1851.* Paris: Musées de France, catalog, 1980.

Drexler, Arthur, ed. *The Architecture of the Ecole des Beaux-Arts.* New York: Museum of Modern Arts, 1977.

Drexler, Arthur, ed. and comp. *Ezra Stoller: Photographs of Architecture, 1939–1980.* New York: Max Protetch Gallery, catalog, 1980.

Eastman Kodak Company. *Kodak Studio Light.* Centennial Issue, 1980.

Eder, Josef Maria. *History of Photography*, trans. by Edward Epstean. New York: Dover 1978.

Edwards, Ernest. *The Heliotype Process.* Boston: J. R. Osgood, 1876.

Evans, Frederick H. "Pictorial Pointers for Architectural Photographers." *The Practical Photographer* I, 8 (1904), 47–50.

Evans, Walker. *Walker Evans at Work: 745 Photographs Together with Documents Selected from Letters, Memoranda, Interviews, Notes,* ed. by Jerry L. Thompson. New York: Harper and Row, 1982.

Evans, Walker. *Walker Evans: Photographs for the Farm Security Administration, 1935–1938,* New York: Da Capo, 1975.

Evans, Walker. *American Photographs.* New York: Museum of Modern Art, 1938.

Fitch, James Marston. "Single Point Perspective—Learning about Las Vegas." *Architectural Forum* 140:1 (1974), 92–93.

Fontanella, Lee. *La Historia de la Fotografia en Espana desde sus origines hasta 1900.* Madrid: Ediciones El Viso, 1981.

Fontanella, Lee. *Photography in Spain in the Nineteenth Century.* Dallas and San Francisco: Delahunty Gallery, Fraenkel Gallery, catalog, 1983.

Futagawa, Yukio, ed. *Frank Lloyd Wright, Kaufmann House, "Fallingwater," Bear Run, Pennsylvania, 1936,* photo. by Yukio Futagawa. A.D.A Edita, 1970.

Futagawa, Yukio. *The Roots of Japanese Architecture.* New York: Harper and Row, 1963.

Galassi, Peter. *Before Photography: Painting and the Invention of Photography.* New York: Museum of Modern Art, catalog, 1981.

Garrigan, Kristin Ottesen. *Ruskin on Architecture, His Thought and Influence.* Madison: University of Wisconsin Press, 1973.

Gernsheim, Helmut. *Focus on Architecture and Sculpture.* London: The Fountain Press, 1949.

Gernsheim, Helmut and Alison. *The History of Photography from the Camera Obscura to the Beginning of the Modern Era.* London: Thames and Hudson, 1969.

Gernsheim, Helmut. *The Origins of Photography.* New York: Thames and Hudson, 1982.

Goodwin, Philip L. *Brazil Builds: Architecture New and Old, 1652–1942,* photo. by G. E. Kidder Smith. New York: Museum of Modern Art, 1943.

Grad, Bonnie, and Timothy A. Riggs. *Visions of City and Country.* Worcester: Worcester Art Museum, catalog, 1982.

Gresleri, Giuliano. *Le Corbusier, Viaggio in Oriente: Gli inediti di Charles Edouard Jeanneret, fotografo e scrittore.* Venice and Paris: Marsilio Editori and Fondation Le Corbusier, 1984.

Gutheim, Frederick. *One Hundred Years of Architecture in America, 1857–1957.* Centennial publication of the American Institute of Architects. New York: Reinhold, 1957.

Hannavy, John. *Roger Fenton of Crimble Hall.* Boston: David R. Godine, 1976.

Harris, John, Jill Lever, and Margaret Richardson. *Great Drawings from the Collection of the RIBA.* New York: The Drawing Center, catalog, 1983.

Heilbrun, Françoise, and Phillipe Néagu. *Charles Nègre.* Paris: Editions des Musées Nationaux, 1980.

Hillers, John K. "Photographed all the Best Scenery." *Jack Hillers' Diary of the Powell Expeditions, 1871–1875,* ed. by Don Fowler. Salt Lake City: University of Utah Press, 1972.

Jachna, Joseph, and M. W. Newman, eds. and comps. *Architectural Photographs by Richard Nickel.* Chicago: Falcon Press, catalog, 1973.

Jammes, André, and Eugenia Parry Janis. *The Art of the French Calotype.* Princeton: Princeton University Press, 1983.

Jammes, André. *Die Kalotypie in Frankreich.* Essen: Folkwang Museum, catalog, 1965.

Jammes, Isabelle. *Blanquart-Evrard et les origines de l'édition photographique française.* Geneva: Librairie Droz, 1981.

Jenkins, William, ed. and comp. *New Topographics: Photographs of a Man-Altered Landscape.* Rochester: International Museum of Photography at George Eastman House, catalog, 1975.

Jussim, Estelle. *Visual Communication and the Graphic Arts.* New York: Bowker, 1974.

Latham, Charles. *In English Homes: The Internal Character, Furniture and Adornments of Some of the Most Notable Houses of England Historically Depicted from Photographs Specially Taken by.* Vols. 2 and 3. London: Country Life, 1904–1909.

Latham, Charles. *The Gardens of Italy: Being a Series of Illustrations from Photographs Taken by Charles Latham of the Most Famous Examples of these Gardens, with Descriptive Text by Evelyn March Phillipps.* London: Country Life/G. Newnes, 1905.

Laughlin, Clarence John. *Clarence John Laughlin: The Personal Eye.* Millerton: Philadelphia Museum of Art and Aperture, catalog, 1973.

Leominster Illustrated, 2nd ed. Gardner, Mass.: Lithotype Printing Co., 188–?

Lindner, Werner, and Steinmetz, Georg. *Die Ingenieurbauten in ihrer guten Gestaltung.* Berlin: Wasmuth, ca. 1923.

Lloyd, Valerie. *Photogaphy, the First Eighty Years.* London: P.& D. Colnaghi, catalog, 1976.

Mantz, Werner. *Werner Mantz: Architekturphotographie in Köln, 1926–1932.* Cologne: Museum Ludwig, 1982.

McCarthy, Mary. *The Stones of Florence,* photo. by Evelyn Hofer and others. New York: Harcourt Brace, 1959.

Metropolitan Museum of Art. *After Daguerre: Masterworks of French Photography (1848–1900) from the Bibliothèque Nationale.* New York: Metropolitan Museum of Art and Paris: Berger-Levraut, catalog, 1980.

Mendelsohn, Erich. *Amerika: Bilderbuch eines Architekten.* Berlin: R. Mosse, 1926.

Mendelsohn, Erich. *Amerika: Bilderbuch eines Architekten.* Berlin: R. Mosse, 1928.

Meydenbauer, Albrecht. *Handbuch der Messbildkunst in Anwendung auf Baudenkmäler- und Reise-Aufnahmen.* Halle: W. Knapp, 1912.

Meyerowitz, Joel. *Cape Light.* Boston: Museum of Fine Arts/New York Graphic Society, 1978.

Meyerowitz, Joel. *St. Louis & The Arch.* Boston: New York Graphic Society in association with The St. Louis Art Museum, 1980.

Middleton, Robin, ed. *The Beaux Arts and Nineteenth-Century French Architecture.* Cambridge: The MIT Press, 1982.

Mock, Elizabeth, ed. *Built in USA: 1932–1944.* New York: Museum of Modern Art, 1945.

Moholy-Nagy, Laszlo. *Von Material zu Architektur.* Munich: Albert Langen Verlag, 1929.

Morris, Wright. *The Inhabitants.* New York: Scribner, 1946.

Mozley, Anita Venturi. *Photography, Past into Present.* Seattle: University of Washington Press, catalog, 1976.

Naef, Weston J. *The Collection of Alfred Stieglitz: Fifty Pioneers of Modern Photography.* New York: Viking, 1978.

Naidenov, N. A. *Moscow: Views of Some Urban Localities, Churches, Remarkable Buildings and Other Structures.* 3 vols. Moscow: E. N. Kushnerov, 1884, 1888, 1891.

Nairn, Ian. *Outrage.* London: Architectural Press, 1955.

Néagu, Phillipe, and Françoise Heilbrun. "Baldus—paysages, architecure." *Photographies* 1 (1983), 57–77.

Newhall, Beaumont. *The History of Photography from 1839 to the Present.* Rev. ed. New York: Museum of Modern Art, 1982.

Newhall, Beaumont. *Photography: A Short Critical History.* New York: Museum of Modern Art, catalog, 1937.

O'Gorman, James F., ed. *Cervin Robinson: Photographs, 1958–1983.* Wellesley: Wellesley College Museum, catalog, 1983.

O'Gorman, James F. "On Vacation with H. H. Richardson, Ten Letters from Europe, 1882." *Archives of American Art Journal* 1 (1979), 2–14.

Pare, Richard, ed. *Court House: A Photographic Document.* New York: Horizon Press, 1978.

Pare, Richard. *Photography and Architecture, 1839–1939.* Montreal: Canadian Center for Architecture, 1982; Cambridge: The MIT Press, 1985.

Peters, Ursula. *Stilgeschichte der Fotografie in Deutschland 1839–1900.* Cologne: Dumont Buchverlag, 1979.

Pevsner, Nikolaus. *Some Architectural Writers of the Ninteenth Century.* Oxford: Oxford University Press, 1972.

Philadelphia Museum of Art. *The Second Empire, 1852–1879: Art in France under Napoleon III.* Philadelphia: Philadelphia Museum of Art, catalog, 1978.

Physick, John. *Photography and the South Kensington Museum.* London: Victoria and Albert Museum, 1975.

Pritchett, V. S. *Dublin: A Portrait,* photo. by Evelyn Hofer. New York: Harper and Row, 1967.

Richardson, Henry Hobson. *The Ames Memorial Building[s], North Easton, Mass.* Boston: Ticknor, 1886.

Robinson, Cervin. "County Courthouse Project: Group Work, Assigned Work." *Photograph* 1:4 (1977), 10–13.

Ruskin, John. *The Works of John Ruskin*, eds. E. T. Cook and Alexander Wedderburn. New York: Longmans, Green; London: George Allen, 39 vols., 1903–1912.

Schmölz, Karl Hugo, and Rolf Sachse. *Hugo Schmölz: Fotografierte Architektur 1924–1937.* Munich: Mahnert-Lueg, 1982.

Sheldon, George William, ed. *Artistic Country-Seats: Types of Recent American Villa and Cottage Architecture; with Instances of Country Clubhouses.* New York: D. Appleton, 1886–87.

Smith, G. E. Kidder. *Italy Builds: Its Modern Architecture and Native Inheritance.* New York: Reinhold, 1955.

Smith, G. E. Kidder. "Photography for the Architect." *RIBA Journal* 72 (1965), 457–464.

Sobieszek, Robert A., ed. *The Architectural Photography of Hedrich-Blessing.* New York: Holt, Rinehart and Winston, 1984.

Sobieszek, Robert A. *Hedrich-Blessing: Architectural Photography, 1930–1981.* Rochester: International Museum of Photography at George Eastman House, catalog, 1981.

Stoller, Ezra. "Photography and the Language of Architecture." *Perspecta* 8, n.d.

Strand, Paul, and Nancy Newhall. *Time in New England.* New York: Oxford University Press, 1950.

Szarkowski, John. *The Idea of Louis Sullivan.* Minneapolis: University of Minnesota Press, 1956.

Szarkowski, John. "Photographing Architecture." *Art in America* 47 (1959), 84–89.

Szarkowski, John, and Maria Morris Hambourg. *The Work of Atget.* 4 vols. New York: Museum of Modern Art, 1981–1985.

Thomas, D. B. *The Science Museum Photography Collection.* London: The Science Museum, 1969.

Thorvaldsen Museum. *Rome in Early Photographs: The Age of Pius IX.* Copenhagen: Thorvaldsen Museum, catalog, 1977.

Venturi & Rauch. *Signs of Life: Symbols in the American City.* Washington, D.C.: Aperture, Inc. and Renwick Gallery of the National Collection of Fine Arts, Smithsonian Institution, catalog, 1976.

Vitry, Paul. *Hôtels et maisons de la renaissance française.* 3 vols. Paris: Lévy, n.d.

Welling, William. *Photography in America, the Formative Years, 1839–1900.* New York: Thomas Y. Crowell, 1978.

Wilton-Ely, John. "The Rise of the Professional Architect in England." In *The Architect,* ed. by Spiro Kostof. New York: Oxford University Press, 1977.

Witkin, Lee D., and Barbara London. *The Photograph Collector's Guide.* New York: Oxford University Press, 1977.

Woodbridge, Sally, ed. *Bay Area Houses,* photo. by Morley Baer, Roger Sturtevant, and others. New York: Oxford University Press, 1976.

Woods, Mary N. *"The American Architect and Building News,* 1867–1907." Ph.D. dissertation. Columbia University, 1982.

Index

Page numbers for photographs are in italics